THE

EXPANSION

OF

MANAGEMENT

KNOWLEDGE

THE

EXPANSION | Carriers,

OF | Flows,

MANAGEMENT | and

KNOWLEDGE | Sources

Edited by
**Kerstin Sahlin-Andersson
and Lars Engwall**

STANFORD BUSINESS BOOKS
An Imprint of Stanford University Press

Stanford University Press
Stanford, California

Printed in the United States of America
on acid-free, archival-quality paper.

Library of Congress Cataloging-in-Publication Data
   The expansion of management knowledge : carriers, flows, and sources /
Kerstin Sahlin-Andersson and Lars Engwall (eds.).
      p.   cm.
   Includes bibliographical references and index.
      ISBN 0-8047-4197-2 (cloth : alk. paper)—
ISBN 0-8047-4199-9 (pbk. : alk. paper)
      1. Management.   2. Management— Research.   3. Business education.
4. Business consultants.   5. Knowledge management.   I. Sahlin-Andersson,
Kerstin.   II. Engwall, Lars.
HD31 .E873 2002
658.4'038— dc21   2002004729

Original Printing 2002

Last figure below indicates year of this printing:
11   10   09   08   07   06   05   04   03   02

Typeset by BookMatters in 10/13.5 Sabon

Contents

Figures

Tables

The Authors

KERSTIN SAHLIN-ANDERSSON is professor of management at Uppsala University, Sweden. She has published books and articles about the global spreading of organizational models and standards, organizational changes in the public sector, and the organizing of large projects. Her most recent research has included the coordination of a research program on transnational regulation and state transformation.

LARS ENGWALL has been professor of management at Uppsala University, Sweden, since 1981. He has published several books and some hundred articles in the management area. He is an elected member of a number of learned societies and is former second vice president of the Royal Swedish Academy of Sciences. His most recent research has included the coordination of the research program Creation of European Management Practice (CEMP), supported by the European Commission.

JOHN MEYER is professor of sociology (emeritus) at Stanford University. He has studied, with neoinstitutional ideas, the impact of wider environments on organizational structure and in particular examines the effects of institutional models in world society on the evolution of national states and other organizations.

BERIT ERNST received her Ph.D. in business administration at the University of Mannheim. Her main research interests are perceptions and judgment in the context of management consulting.

ALFRED KIESER is professor of organizational behavior at the University of Mannheim Business School. He received his Ph.D. and habilitation in business administration from the University of Cologne. He has published in *Administrative Science Quarterly*, *Organization Science*, *Organization Studies*, and other scientific journals. His research interests concentrate on organization theory, consulting and management fashions, decision making in organizations, and the history of organizations.

MARTIN RUEF is assistant professor of strategic management and sociology at Stanford University, California. His current research examines institutional change, organizational culture, and the role of entrepreneurs and business professionals in proliferating new forms of organizational arrangements.

THOMAS ARMBRÜSTER is a lecturer in organizational behavior at the University of Mannheim, Germany. He received a Ph.D. at the London School of Economics. His research interests are management consulting and critical-liberal approaches to management and organization theory.

MATTHIAS KIPPING is associate professor at the Universitat Pompeu Fabra in Barcelona and also holds a part-time position at the University of Reading. He has published extensively on the evolution of different carriers of management knowledge, namely business education and management consultancy. He recently edited, with Lars Engwall, *Management Consulting: The Emergence and Dynamics of a Knowledge Industry* (Oxford, 2002). A monograph on the consultancy business is forthcoming at Oxford University Press.

KJELL ARNE RØVIK is professor of political science at the University of Tromsø, Norway. His research and publications focus on organizational learning and the creation, diffusion, and implementation of popular management ideas.

PETER WALGENBACH is professor of Organization Theory and Management in the Faculty of Law, Economics, and Social Sciences at the University of Erfurt, Germany. He received his Ph.D. and Habilitation at the University of Mannheim, Germany. He was a visiting scholar at Stanford University, California, in 1997.

NIKOLAUS BECK works as an assistant lecturer at the Chair of Organization at the University of Erfurt. He received his Ph.D. in business administration at the University of Mannheim. His research interests include organizational change, organizational rules, and sociology of the family.

NICK TIRATSOO is visiting research fellow at the Business History Unit, the London School of Economics. He is co-editor (with Duncan Tanner and Pat Thane) of the centenary volume *Labour's First Century* (Cambridge University Press, 2000).

XIAOWEI LUO is an assistant professor in the Department of Business Administration at University of Illinois at Urbana-Champaign. She recently received her Ph.D. from the Department of Sociology, Stanford University. Her dissertation examines the rise of personal development training in organizations and the driving forces behind it. She is interested in the historical changes in organizations and the diffusion and innovation of organizational practices in the cross-national context.

HALDOR BYRKJEFLOT is project director and research fellow at the Stein Rokkan Center for Social Studies at the University of Bergen. In 1999 he defended his doctoral thesis, "Modernization and Management." He has published articles on the Nordic model and historical-comparative studies on education systems, management, and employment systems. One of his last projects was a cross-national study of management education within the European Union–funded project Creation of European Management Practices (CEMP).

EVA WALLERSTEDT is associate professor at the Department of Business Studies at Uppsala University. Her research encompasses the development of business administration and organizational foundations and closures in a regulated environment in addition to the development of the auditing field in Sweden.

Preface

The idea of writing this book came as we were planning a seminar on "Carriers of Management Knowledge" in September 1999 at SCANCOR (Scandinavian Consortium for Organizational Research) at Stanford University, California. The call for papers emphasized this concept: Management ideas do not flow automatically but are actively shaped and transformed as they are being transferred and circulated by educational institutions, consultancies, the media, and other carriers of management knowledge. The focus of the seminar was thus to analyze how such carriers are organized, how they act and interact, and how they shape and reshape circulated knowledge.

This volume is based on a selection of the papers presented at the workshop. Its three main parts deal with carriers, flows, and sources of management knowledge, respectively. The chapters are based on extensive empirical studies, carried out in several parts of the world. Together they combine and cross-fertilize insights from various theoretical traditions. In this way we seek to add "flesh and blood" to general institutional explanations to the flow of ideas. The analyses provide explanations as to why management has expanded so dramatically during the past few decades; they also demonstrate how and why the character of management knowledge changes over time and across situations.

In the follow-up to the workshop we have worked intensively with the authors to clarify our analyses and fulfill our aim to create a coherent book. We would like to thank the authors for their cooperation and hard work when revising their papers into chapters, their patience, and to some extent also for their persistence in maintaining their own ideas and their own style of reasoning. The experience has taught us worthwhile lessons about various perspectives on how management knowledge is perceived and carried.

Apart from the authors, several other persons have contributed valuable ideas, substantial work, and encouraging words. Among them, we first would like to thank the participants in the SCANCOR workshop who made the seminar discussions interesting and enlightening. The workshop spurred our desire to dig deeper and find some order in the diverse thoughts around the expansion of management knowledge and its carriers.

Woody Powell, the director of SCANCOR, has provided us with invaluable support and encouragement both in the arrangements of the workshop and during the work with this volume. He has given us excellent ideas and comments on the structure and main arguments of the book. In addition, we have had the pleasure of discussing our ideas on several occasions with Jim March. His brilliant intellectual comments have been inspiring, as ever.

We would also like to express our thanks for constructive comments, critiques, and productive ideas to one anonymous reviewer and to our colleagues at the Department of Business Studies at Uppsala University, SCORE (Stockholm Center for Organizational Research), the CEMP project (Creation of European Management Practice), and the TREO project (Transnational Regulations and the Transformation of States).

The arrangement of a workshop and the editing of a volume demanded much expertise. Barbara Beuche at SCANCOR helped with the practical arrangement of the workshop. Svante Nieminen at the Department of Business Studies assisted us with the bibliography. A whole group of people in Uppsala, Stockholm, and at SCANCOR have been welcome colleagues as they helped with numerous practical details along the way.

We owe special thanks to SCANCOR for their support in financing the workshop. We are also very grateful to the European Commission, SCORE, the Swedish Research Council, and the Swedish Research Council for Working Life for their financial support of our research.

Finally, we would like to express our thanks for excellent editorial work and support from Bill Hicks, Kate Wahl, Judith Hibbard, and their colleagues at Stanford University Press and to Suzanne Copenhagen for inspiring copyediting.

Kerstin Sahlin-Andersson
Lars Engwall
Uppsala, October 2002

THE

EXPANSION

OF

MANAGEMENT

KNOWLEDGE

I Introduction

1   Carriers, Flows, and Sources of Management Knowledge

Kerstin Sahlin-Andersson and Lars Engwall,
Uppsala University, Sweden

Introduction

The Expansion of Management Knowledge

The 1980s and 1990s have witnessed a dramatic expansion and rapid flow of management knowledge across continents and societal sectors. As part of this development, a wide range of providers and promoters of management knowledge have appeared and grown. Management education programs are prospering throughout the world (Engwall and Gunnarsson 1994; Engwall and Zamagni 1998; Sahlin-Andersson and Hedmo 2000; Locke 1984, 1989, 1996; Thrift 1997). Management consulting and business advisory firms have been formed and expanded, and their models have been applied to many new areas of operations (Kipping and Engwall 2002; McKenna 1995; Strange 1996). Management publications of various kinds—including the scientific, popular, and business press—have proliferated, as have research and writing about management (Abrahamson 1996; Alvarez *et al.* 1999; Furusten 1999; Røvik 1996; Thrift 1999). More generally, management "gurus" and management researchers have played an important role in disclosing, coining, and circulating management concepts and recipes (Clark and Greatbatch 2001; Czarniawska-Joerges 1990; Czarniawska 1997). We have also seen the appearance of a number of companies that have established whole departments, such as "knowledge centers" and "future centers," devoted to management knowledge development in general or to developing specific management ideas and techniques (Crainer and Dearlove 1998: 53; Engwall 1999: 65–67; Prusak 1997).

New techniques for better management are frequently introduced and widely spread around the world (Abrahamson 1991; Lindvall 1998; Collins 2000), some of them specifically labeled with acronyms that quickly become recognized parts of management vocabulary. These waves have included total quality management (TQM), business process reengineering (BPR), management by objectives (MBO), supply chain management (SPC), new public management (NPM), project management, integrated management control, intercultural management, knowledge management, and others. Some of these techniques have spread at a rapid rate until interest in them has faded; others have become more rooted in organizations, developing into well-known aspects of the expanded body of management knowledge. The spread of such techniques suggests that we have witnessed not only an expansion of management knowledge but also an increase in its formalization and a change in its packaging (Røvik 1998; Sahlin-Andersson 2000; Strang and Meyer 1994).

Parallel to the wide proliferation of these popular models, management has become a dominant model in various contexts. Not only business corporations but all kinds of organizations and operations around the world are said to be in need of better management. Meanwhile, those assessing them tend to pay increasing attention to how these entities are managed and how they might be managed differently. New users of management models have appeared in societal sectors that were ruled previously by other types of logic, such as professional or bureaucratic logic (Bentsen *et al.* 1999; Scott *et al.* 2000). With the widespread introduction of new public management reforms (Hood 1991, 1995; Olson *et al.* 1998), for example, public services have increasingly been looked upon as groups of organizations in need of management (Brunsson and Sahlin-Andersson 2000). Recently, calls for more and better management have often been heard in international organizations, such as the European Union and the United Nations.

Another trend often observed and reported is that organizations are becoming increasingly similar, at least in how they are presented and accounted for. As a result of coercive, normative, and mimetic pressures (DiMaggio and Powell 1983), organizations tend to be structured in line with sets of rationalized myths (Meyer and Rowan 1977). They develop according to the logic of appropriateness (March and Olsen 1995). By adopting specific management techniques such as total quality management (Abrahamson 1996; Westphal *et al.* 1997), human resource management (Dobbin and Sutton 1998), business process reengineering (Hammer and Champy 1993), and accounting models (Olson *et al.* 1998), they attempt to appear modern and to maintain their legitimacy. The tendency for organizations to become more similar to one another has been connected to the pressure to become more management-oriented (Baron *et al.* 1986; Czarniawska and Sevón 1996; DiMaggio and Powell 1983, 1991; Engwall 1999; Pollitt 1990; Scott *et al.* 2000; Strang and Meyer 1994)—and these are all dynamics that reflect an expansion of the idea of management.

The Nature of Management Knowledge

With the expansion of management knowledge it has become widespread custom to take the concept of management for granted in all kinds of situations and places. However, despite or perhaps because of this expansion, it is not quite clear what management knowledge is. If we go to dictionary entries, *The Concise Oxford Dictionary* (7th edition, 1982) defines *management* as "administration of business concerns or public undertakings; persons engaged in this," whereas *Merriam-Webster's Dictionary* provides the entry: "the act or art of managing: the conducting or supervising of something (as a business)." Used in a narrow sense, both definitions could be considered to refer strictly to administration and supervision of personnel. However, this usage of *management* would be inconsistent with later developments in research and practice. Management problems tend to be seen as including not only internal organizational issues but also, more generally, the management of an organization and its environmental links. This broader view of management is applied in the many scholarly journals dedicated to the science of management (*Academy of Management Journal, Academy of Management Review, Journal of Management Studies,* and *Scandinavian Journal of Management,* to mention a few). The dictionary definitions quoted further point out that management is a matter of both administration and control—to manage organizations is not just a matter of administering the present but also of actively changing and leading the organization into the future.

Management is thus a concept without a narrowly specified content and meaning. It is not associated with any particular types of activity, but rather with where, how, and by whom activities are carried out. In other words, management knowledge only exists in and through the processes of circulation. Certain activities, models, and ideas become known as aspects of management knowledge when they are being collected, processed, distributed, and used in a management context—by *carriers* who see themselves and are perceived as being concerned with management.

With the expansion of management knowledge, an increased number of models, problems, and organizational procedures have been seen to be of concern for management consultants, management journalists, management researchers, and more generally those who are actually managing. As these carriers concerned with management pick up and circulate certain pieces of knowledge, they contextualize, frame, and package this knowledge as management knowledge. However, what is circulated as management knowledge today has in many cases developed out of earlier, often less general and more sector-specific, knowledge. Issues of personnel training, quality, and the skills of top executives, for example, have been matters of concern to business organizations for a long time. However, issues such as these have developed over time from an understanding that they were mainly a matter of technical skills to which sector-specific knowledge would apply. Instead, they have become understood as more general management issues to which may be applied the ideas and recipes provided by management consultants, management education programs, management publications, and other carriers of management knowledge. Hence, what one can witness is a dual dynamic of the expansion of management knowledge: management knowledge has spread more widely while more models and activities have come to be seen as management knowledge.

The Purpose of This Book

In this book, we seek to direct attention—more clearly than has been the case in most writings dealing with the homogenization of organizations and the expansion of management—particularly to those who are professing, providing, and circulating management knowledge, as well as the nature of the ideas that are widely held. With such a focus we seek to further understanding of the dynamic aspects of these developments. We acknowledge the importance of taking into account actors, space, localities, and time in order to understand how ideas and knowledge flow, aspects too often underexplored in neoinstitutional writings (Czarniawska and Joerges 1996; DiMaggio 1988; Westphal *et al.* 1997). Historical and broad contextual studies combined with close-up studies of the development of certain carriers and management ideas show how and why management knowledge expands; through these studies we also gain a better understanding of the nature of management knowledge.

The purpose of this book is thus to portray how management knowledge has diffused so extensively and rapidly and to provide explanations for this expansion. The book analyzes the flow and expansion of management knowledge as an active process by focusing on how the carriers of such knowledge act and interact and how they shape, reshape, and co-construct the knowledge circulated.

The book comprises nine chapters that describe and provide explanations of the expansion of management knowledge in diverse areas of activity, two introductory chapters, and one concluding chapter. Overall, the book analyzes the expansion of management knowledge as a self-sustaining and self-enforcing system in which carriers of this knowledge play a salient role.

Earlier analyses of the expansion of management knowledge have followed the development of specific users of this knowledge through studies of individual companies or specific fields. Examples are studies of (1) the increased use of management consulting (for example, O'Shea and Madigan 1997; Ramsay 1996), (2) the widespread use of management techniques (for example, Abrahamson and Fairchild 1999; Collins 2000; Lindvall 1998; Røvik 1998; Thrift 1997; Westphal *et al.* 1997), and (3) the more general turn to management in various areas (for example, Scott *et al.* 2000), a trend that has been termed *managerialism* (for example, Considine and Painter 1997; Pollitt 1990). This research has added to our understanding not only of the role of management in various types of organizations but also of why and how certain management ideas have traveled so widely in the organizational landscape. Despite this, explanations that point to expanded demands seem insufficient as a response to the question: Why has such a dramatic expansion and rapid flow of management knowledge emerged? Explanations of this expansion do not lie solely in the adopting organizations but require a closer look at those professing, circulating, and shaping this knowledge and the institutional settings under which the users and carriers of management knowledge operate. In addition, we need to analyze what is spreading and how that expansion occurs. Even though the flow and expansion of management knowledge is embedded in more general institutional developments, these processes do not develop and flow automatically; rather, management knowledge is actively shaped, transferred, and transformed (Czar-niawska and Sevón 1996).

We intend, therefore, within this book to provide a more thorough understanding of how and why management knowledge expands, why it expands in certain directions and places rather than in others, and why certain aspects are developed at the expense of others. The central chapters combine broad contextual and historical studies with close investigations of the activities of individual carriers and activities that make up the flow of specific management ideas. An institutional argument runs through the book. The carriers are considered carriers not only of management knowledge but also of societal institutions. Hence the activities of these carriers must be understood as grounded in, and adding to, institutional developments in society.

In this chapter we present three features of the expansion of management knowledge. First, we deal with the *carriers of management knowledge*, that is, actors who play significant roles in the framing, packaging, and circulating of management ideas. Three kinds of carriers of management knowledge have been found to be particularly significant for the flow and expansion of management knowledge: business schools, management consultants, and business media. Recent research has also pointed out the need to consider the interaction among the kinds of carriers (for example, Engwall 1999).

However, since earlier research has shown that ideas do not remain unchanged as they are being distributed, we turn in the second section of this chapter to *the flow of management knowledge*, that is, how and to what extent ideas are translated and transformed on their way from one context to another. In this way, we demonstrate the variations that management ideas may exhibit in practice due to different kinds of transformations.

Analyses of the flow of ideas point to the important activities that facilitate and drive the expansion and flow of management knowledge. However, to understand the dual dynamic of the expansion of management knowledge (management knowledge has spread more widely while more models and activities have come to be seen as management knowledge) it is insufficient to examine the present activities of carriers. Therefore, we will also analyze the roots of today's management knowledge. In order to understand the expansion and distribution of modern management ideas, we focus in the third section of this chapter on *the sources of management knowledge*. An important feature of management knowledge is that it draws on many diverse sources, which in turn provide the basis for its applicability to the many areas from which this knowledge has grown.

These three features of the expansion of management knowledge constitute the basis for the structure of the book, as will be further demonstrated at the end of this introductory chapter, where we give a brief overview of the remaining chapters.

Carriers of Management Knowledge

As one tracks the providers of management knowledge, it is possible to detect two interrelated developments that have added to its expansion. First, organizations devoted to producing and promoting management knowledge have increased in number and size. Second, these carriers have developed new and extended types of management knowledge, and they have circulated this knowledge more widely over time. Earlier research has focused mainly on how and why these carriers have developed but has focused to a more limited extent on the role of these carriers in the expansion of management knowledge. We will demonstrate this claim in a brief summary of earlier research that follows. However, before elaborating, it is necessary to look more closely at the carrier concept itself.

The Carrier Concept

We have chosen to term those who circulate management knowledge as *carriers*. For some, this concept may have a somewhat passive association: someone or something carrying a package, a passenger, or even a disease. The way the concept has been used in theoretical writings, however—especially in the field of institutional theory—has been to convey a mix of passivity and activity, of supporting, transporting, and transforming. Jepperson (1991) used the carrier concept to point to the importance of activities to institutional development. Institutions do not just exist independently but are enacted in a host of supporting and reproducing practices. Even though such activities reproduce and transform institutions, in highly institutionalized situations and settings these activities are embedded in institutions or they constitute enactments of institutions. Thus, one should distinguish such activities from actions: "If one participates conventionally in a highly institutionalized social pattern, one does not take action, that is, intervene in a sequence, make a statement" (Jepperson 1991: 148). Hence, both the reproduction and the alteration of institutions involve activity: this ongoing activity is directed and limited by institutions while the activity reproduces as well as alters institutions (Scott 1995; see also Giddens 1979, 1984).

In their analysis of modernization, Berger and associates (1973), highly influenced by Max Weber, focused mainly on what they termed the "primary carriers" of modernization: technological production and the bureaucratically organized state. However, the authors identified a multiplicity of "secondary carriers" related to these fundaments of modern society that serve as transmitting agencies for the knowledge and ideology derived from the primary carriers. Inspired by how Alvarez (1998: 38) translated the concept in order to analyze "the diffusion and consumption of business knowledge," we are mainly concerned here with these secondary carriers and especially with those that "can attain considerable autonomy as agents in themselves" (Berger *et al.* 1973: 9). In other words, when analyzing those who circulate management knowledge as carriers, we want to view them as both mediators of specific ideas and those whose activities are supported by, as well as supporting, reproducing, and transforming the more fundamental institutions in modern society.

If we were to view the carriers only as passive mediators, there would be little point in paying attention to them. Sometimes it appears that diffusion perspectives—where the diffusion of ideas is perceived to take place through more or less automatic processes and the main explanation for the success of an idea is its original strength—have turned the attention of scholars away from the carriers. Attention has, rather, been directed toward settings where it is assumed that the action is taking place: in local business where new practices may be found and management ideas are received. This identity of a carrier has often been one that a carrier will pursue and perceive for itself; that is, the identity of one who reports on what is going on in different places but is itself neither an activating entity nor a reporter with influence. For example, researchers, media, expert committees, and international organizations are presumed to report on actions and events occurring elsewhere but without taking action and pursuing any interest themselves (for example, Barnett and Finnemore 1999; Finnemore 1996; Sahlin-Andersson 2000).

John Meyer (1994, 1996) has used the term "others" to capture the specific features of such organizations and their activities, thereby distinguishing them from actors who are assumed to pursue their own interests and policies and are held responsible for their actions. Even though "others" may present themselves as neutral mediators, these organizations engage in activities that are crucial for the flow and development of ideas. Such organizations not only mediate ideas, they influence and shape the activities that take place under their auspices, as they "discuss, interpret, advise, suggest, codify, and sometimes pronounce and legislate [and] develop, promulgate, and certify some ideas as proper reforms, and ignore or stigmatize other ideas" (Meyer 1996: 244). Moreover, like all organizations, they are institutionally embedded. Hence, to explain why management knowledge has expanded so rapidly and extensively and to determine how it is collected, processed, and distributed by the carriers, we also need to analyze in more detail how, and under which conditions, the carrying organizations develop, act, and interact.

The Expansion of Significant Carriers

A basic prerequisite for the expansion of management knowledge has been the development of large multiproduct enterprises. As shown by Alfred Chandler (1990), such enterprises started to appear in the late nineteenth century and developed considerably in the first decades of the twentieth century. These companies by themselves came to constitute carriers of management knowledge. They developed and applied new organizational forms. In this way, they provided examples for other firms in how to manage large enterprises. However, parallel to this expansion of large multidivisional companies there also occurred a development of other types of carriers of management knowledge: the business school, management consultancies, and media companies. Significant foundations for these organizations appear to have been laid in the 1880s.

In terms of *business schools*, the foundation, in 1881, of the Wharton School in the United States and l'École des Hautes Études Commerciales in Europe is considered the starting point for the later rapid expansion of management education (Engwall 1992; Engwall and Gunnarsson 1994; Engwall and Zamagni 1998; Locke 1984, 1989, 1996). With the development of the large corporation and with growing markets for goods and services, management education has become a booming business. Thus, at the beginning of the twenty-first century, management education constitutes a dominant part of many systems of higher education throughout the world.

It has taken the form of regular academic programs at undergraduate, graduate, and doctoral levels as well as more practitioner-oriented, often tailor-made, programs for post-experience studies and executive training. In the past decade there has been an increasing internationalization of these programs through student and faculty exchange, alliances, and foreign admissions. Management education has expanded particularly strongly in the United States, where business schools constitute significant and profitable units of many prestigious universities (Crainer and Dearlove 1998). However, it has also expanded in most other parts of the world. Management education programs, such as MBA programs and executive education programs, have expanded at an increasing rate during the last century, and the world-wide expansion of such educational programs has often been depicted as an expression and driving mechanism for the expansion of management knowledge. Business schools have become key institutions for the selection of top managers and the dissemination of managerial concepts (Crainer and Dearlove 1998; Thrift 1999).

In fashion similar to the growth of business school and management education programs, a number of large *management consultancies* have emerged during the past century. Again, their development can partly be seen as a response to the evolution of the large modern enterprise, but driving forces have also emerged among the various consultancies and other carriers mentioned here that have expanded the supply of management knowledge. In the large consultancies, two, basically different, origins can be found: one from engineering, another from accounting. Arthur D. Little, which was founded as a chemical research laboratory in 1886, is an example of the first group, whereas Accenture (formerly Andersen Consulting), an offspring of the accounting firm of Arthur Andersen, belongs to the second (Kipping and Armbrüster 1999: 33). The development of the consultancy field during the twentieth century has been such that the world market presently is dominated by a small number of Anglo-American consultancies such as Accenture, Boston Consulting Group, PricewaterhouseCoopers, Deloitte & Touche, Ernst & Young, McKinsey, and KPMG (see, for example, Kipping and Armbrüster 1999; O'Shea and Madigan, 1997). Their dominance has inspired several authors to challenge their activities (see, for example, Ashford 1998; O'Shea and Madigan 1997; Pinault 2000).

It has even been questioned whether consultancies really transfer any knowledge. In particular, it has been pointed out that managers hire consultants in response to the pressure to appear modern and in an attempt to reduce uncertainty. However, there is also evidence that managers use consultants to resolve upcoming problems that they have neither the capacity nor the knowledge to handle (Engwall and Eriksson 1999). In this way, the use of consulting has been institutionalized through industry norms, state regulation, and wishes for economies of scale. It can also be maintained that the use of consultants is characterized by herd behavior; that is, that the use of consultants by dominant actors in an industry will lead others to follow suit (Engwall 1999: section 6.3). It can be expected that all these circumstances will lead to an expansion of consultancy services.

Media companies that today are significant carriers of business and economic news were also founded in the 1880s, such as the British *Financial Times* (founded in 1888) and the U.S. *Wall Street Journal* (founded in 1889). Of course, it is true that business press partly developed much earlier as a result of the interest of business people in the communication of information important to them, such as prices, freights, and the supply of goods in significant trading ports (Hadenius and Weibull 1972: 73). However, with the growth of industrialism, this interest increased even further, until nowadays most dailies carry business pages. In addition, special business newspapers following the tradition of the *Financial Times* and the *Wall Street Journal* now exist in many countries. Larger media groups, which are also active in other types of dissemination, commonly publish these titles. One of the most important is the Pearson Group, which in addition to its publishing of business newspapers, such as the *Financial Times*, *Les Echos*, and *Expansión*, is also a significant publisher in higher education, with imprints such as Addison-Wesley, Longman, Allyn & Bacon, Penguin, and Prentice-Hall [www.pearson.com]. In this way, the group plays a very strong role in the dissemination of management knowledge, not only to the business community but also to academia and consultants. Similar groups are the targets for an increasing body of business periodicals such as the *Harvard Business Review* and its various European editions. In addition to management journals and magazines, popular books are important for carriers of management knowledge (see for example, Deal and Kennedy 1982; Hamel and Prahalad 1994; Kanter 1983, 1989; Peters and Waterman 1982). These widely circulated management books have a strong opportunity to influence business behavior. First, through their visibility alone, they will attract the attention of many managers. Second, as more and more managers take their messages on board, their advice will also be communicated through the actions of their companies.

The Interaction Among Carriers

Over time, there has been an intensive interaction among the carriers of management knowledge discussed in this section: business schools, consultancies, media companies, and practice in companies at large (see Figure 1.1). Business schools interact with practice through (1) empirical studies, (2) teaching by practitioners, and (3) the dissemination of graduates to employment. They interact with consultancies through (1) the consulting activities of professors, (2) the flow of graduates into consulting, and (3) collaborative projects with consultancies. In relation to the media, business schools (1) provide texts and other material for dissemination and (2) use texts and other material in education and research.

In a similar way, consulting interacts with practice through (1) the advice given to companies, (2) the learning of practices in their cooperation with companies, and (3) the supply of candidates for executive positions. With media companies, consultants tend to interact by (1) publishing texts about their business ideas and (2) using material from the media industry.

Media companies, finally, have a close interaction with practice through their reporting of business news. In this way they play a significant role in the formation of worldviews on business conditions, best practice, leadership, and so forth. Inversely, practitioners, and particularly CEOs, increasingly tend to use the media to create an impression of their companies. Their relationships with academia and consulting have already been mentioned.

The interaction between the four types of carrier of management knowledge has led to a gradual blurring of borders. At present it is not only a question of the exchange of information and individuals but also of very close cooperation of carriers of one type performing activities that were previously exclusively the domain of another type of carrier. Thus, in accordance with Figure 1.2, we can see a mixture of activities and ties among the carriers. This means that management education nowadays is an activity in which academic institutions experience stiff competition from corporate universities, consultancy training programs, and new media ventures (Crainer and Dearlove 1998; Grayden 2000). Similarly, consultants are subject to com-

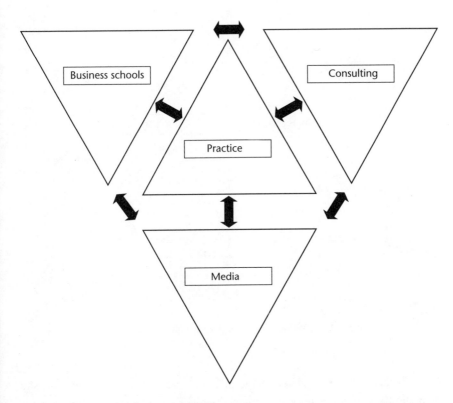

FIGURE **1.1** Interaction of managerial fields

petition from business schools and media companies, whereas the latter have to face mass communication activities of business schools and consultancies. However, it is not only a question of competition, that is, of one carrier taking up the activities for which other carriers previously had a competitive advantage, it is also to a considerable extent a matter of close collaboration. Thus, corporate universities often work as small units that buy services from established academic institutions, and they do so in long-term relationships. Similarly, we have recently seen examples of close relationships between academic institutions and media companies (see, for example, Crainer and Dearlove 1998: 8) and between academic institutions and consultancies (Kipping and Amorim 1999).

The blurring of borders between the four types of carrier of management knowledge that we have described could be better understood if we

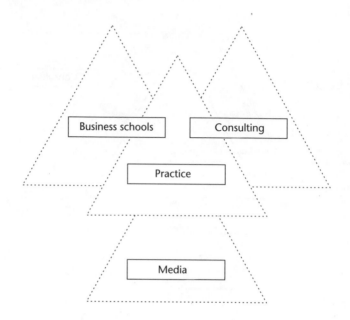

FIGURE 1.2   The blurring of the borders of managerial fields

look closer at the technology of the different carriers. In short, we can say that the fundamental mechanism by which the carriers create management knowledge is by the collection, processing, and distribution of different kinds of information (Table 1.1). These three activities can be characterized by (1) their degree of quality control, (2) interaction with the receiver, and (3) the size of their audience. Traditionally the collection activity, that is, the gathering of data and compiling of information, of business schools is characterized by a high degree of control and rigor. Consultants, however, have been subject to far less control and can be less stringent in their claims. Through their professional rules, media companies can be characterized as an intermediate case. As far as the processing of information is concerned, consulting necessitates, as pointed out above, a high level of direct interaction with clients, whereas the media represents the other extreme, with academic institutions coming in between. Finally, in terms of distribution, the media relies upon mass distribution to large audiences, whereas consultants, even though they may have the same message for all, conduct their work on a client-by-client basis. Business schools normally communicate with groups of students.

TABLE 1.1   A Comparison of Three Carriers of Management Knowledge

Activity	Key Variable	Academia	Consultants	Media
Collection	Control	High	Low	Medium
Processing	Interaction	Medium	High	Low
Distribution	Audience size	Medium	Low	High

As the borders between the various types of carrier become blurred, we can also see changes in the patterns just described. Consultants are being pushed to become more rigorous in their data collection, whereas business schools are being pressed to become more relevant for business practice. In the same way, *interaction* has become a key word for all the carriers. Business schools are expected to become interactive in developing curricula and teaching material. However, what is most significant, of course, is the development of the available media through the widespread availability of information technology, which has made interactive teaching possible. This has also facilitated tailor-made solutions for media in the distribution phase, and has increased the audience sizes for academic institutions. And finally, consultants have been given the opportunity to standardize and commodify their products (Suddaby and Greenwood 2002). Thus, all in all, the tendency seems to be toward an increasing similarity between the various carriers of management knowledge.

With the blurred boundaries, it is impossible to make a clear distinction between those creating, those mediating, and those using ideas. Even though we can point to differences among carriers in terms of how their activities are structured and shaped (Table 1.1), with the blurred borders these differences become less pronounced. Carriers translate, elaborate, and codify ideas as they transfer them, so such a transfer involves aspects of creation and use as well. Those described as creators of ideas are often found to build on and recycle old ideas, and thus to a great extent their creation is a matter of mediation and use. And users may find that they have become known as examples or role models for others to follow, a reputation that turns them into mediators and creators as well as users of management knowledge.

Carriers are often interrelated in more or less complicated ways: they collaborate, compete, and parallel each other, and one carrier can be a creator, mediator, and user of management knowledge all at the same time. In fact, it can be argued that the character of the interaction among carriers partly holding supplementary roles, partly competing, and partly developing in symbiosis explains the dramatic expansion of management knowledge and management advice services. However, these interactions also explain how management knowledge has become formalized, commodified, and standardized.

Competition between the providers of management knowledge drives the expansion of management knowledge—as they compete, these organizations are encouraged to develop new ideas and enter new areas where they can promote and profess their ideas or sell their services. Competition among carriers may also drive conformity (Abrahamson and Fairchild 1999; Westphal *et al.* 1997). In this way, management knowledge also tends to be universalized so that it is possible to distribute it widely with reasonable cost and effort. In other words, the nature of interactions among carriers also explains what shape management knowledge takes—how it has become formalized, standardized, and universalized.

In terms of the significance of the carriers of management knowledge we have mentioned, it appears that consultancies and advisory firms have become a particular class of secondary carriers through their *direct* contact with practice, whereas the contacts of business schools and media companies are more indirect. Such a view is in contrast to the traditional idea, not least pursued among university scholars, that knowledge is created in universities and then spread to and implemented in practice. Business schools and universities, however, do not seem to play this orchestrating role. They tend to be followers rather than leaders (Barley *et al.* 1988; Strange 1996), reporters and analysts rather than trendsetters. Similarly the output of media companies is primarily reporting and analyzing and thereby influencing in an indirect way. Consultancy and business advisory firms have, however, through their direct contacts with acting managers come to orchestrate the field of management more generally. Another factor behind the increasingly leading role that consultancies now seem to play in the field follows from their efforts to package ideas in a way that makes disseminating them to larger publics possible. Accordingly, the chapters about carriers that follow focus mainly on these orchestrating consultants and business advisors, but they also analyze the important close interaction between consultants and other carriers of management knowledge.

Flows of Management Knowledge

The reason for paying attention to the providers and promoters of knowledge in a work dedicated to the expansion of management knowledge is that we do not perceive this expansion to flow automatically. The carriers actively shape, promote, and transfer such knowledge. The expansion of carriers means that carriers have added to the expansion of management knowledge. However, as we follow the flow and forms of management knowledge, we also find that the flow of management knowledge gives impetus to new and expanded carriers, as well as users of such knowledge and interactions between them. Hence, to better understand the expansion of management knowledge and the shape management knowledge has taken with this expansion, we need to analyze in more detail how such knowledge is circulated, under what conditions it is circulated, and how the knowledge is formed and transformed as it is circulated. As a foundation for such an analysis, we elaborate, based on earlier research, on the routes along which management knowledge is circulated, the institutional conditions facilitating the extended flow of management knowledge, and the processes of knowledge formation and transformation as knowledge is circulated.

Knowledge Circulation

A brief look at widely disseminated management knowledge shows that it consists to a large extent of well-packaged and labeled techniques or models that seem to travel easily between settings and spheres (Czarniawska and Joerges 1996). Widespread management ideas claim almost universal applicability. This means that similar quality assurance models can be applied to a car factory, a hospital, or a government agency, regardless of where these organizations are located. Widely disseminated management ideas are also formed in very general terms. They point to the importance of leaders and leadership, or they display a general emphasis on quality, financial management (see, for example, Olson et al. 1998), and strategic forms of organizing (Considine and Painter 1997). The ideas themselves, however, take on different shapes. Although many such management ideas are quite nonspecific, typically distributed in the form of anecdotes or analytical models, others are more formalized and standardized. One example of the latter is the quality standard ISO 9000, which has become extremely popular, especially in Europe (Mendel 2001; Walgenbach 2000).

Apparently, some ideas have flowed more rapidly and extensively than others and they have flowed better in some settings than in others. In addition, as management knowledge has expanded and replaced other areas of expertise, some ideas have expanded more than others. With the concepts of diffusion and the discourse around best practice these differences have been thought to follow from differences in the nature of the ideas under investigation. Such discourses may give the impression that ideas have a stable content, at least a core, that remains the same as the ideas diffuse; this view has led researchers and practitioners in search of best practices to seek out "the original" source of the idea. The perspective is an instrumental one—good and powerful ideas are assumed to spread more widely than less effective ones. This reasoning may lead to a call for more historical studies to satisfy the need to go back to search for the original source.

Once we start analyzing and comparing ideas, however, it is difficult to distinguish any intrinsic success criteria for ideas that will "make it." Hence, it is often pointless—if not downright impossible—to find an origin (Bourdieu 1977). So it appears to be not so much a case of ideas flowing widely because they are powerful, but rather, of ideas becoming powerful as they flow. For example, some ideas seem to become popular, not primarily because of their properties but because of who transports and supports them and how they are packaged, formulated, and timed (Czarniawska and Joerges 1996; Røvik 1998). Ideas become legitimate, popular, and even taken for granted as being effective and indispensable as a result of having been adopted by some actors in the field (Tolbert and Zucker 1983; Westphal *et al.* 1997). In this way, managerial fads and fashions evolve, some ideas becoming popular for a time then disappearing again or becoming institutionalized (Abrahamson 1991, 1996; Collins 2000). Again, historical and contextual studies are called for, but not solely with the aim of looking for the original source of diffused ideas; close studies of the circulation of management ideas do, in fact, show why some turn out to be so attractive and powerful.

The metaphor of travel has been used to describe the circulation of ideas to emphasize that management ideas do not flow automatically, but follow certain often highly structured and well-worn routes (Czarniawska and Sevón 1996). Furthermore, the transfer of ideas is an active process: there are means of transportation that carry the ideas from one place to another. The travel metaphor is helpful in the sense that it directs our attention to travel routes and means of travel. Connections between actors in the field may explain the likely routes through which ideas travel and the rate and speed of diffusion (Rogers 1983). The formation of networks and other contacts thus enables ideas to flow. With intensified interactions among carriers, channels have opened for the transfer of ideas.

Just as the term *circulate* indicates, the processes involve not only the transport, flow, or movement through established channels—like blood circulating through the arteries and veins of the body—but also the distribution, spreading, transmission, or broadcasting of messages to wider groups. When knowledge is circulated, it is either passed on from one place to another and from one user to the next, or it is broadcast from one source to a set of possible users (March 1999: 137). When tracing the circulation of one particularly popular set of management ideas—New Public Management, for example—it has been found that these ideas were passed on from one country to another (Boston *et al.* 1996; Hood 1995; Sahlin-Andersson 2001). This was especially true in the countries that first adopted the ideas and started to reform their public services along these lines, that is, Anglo-Saxon countries that already had elaborated contacts with each other. As these management ideas started to spread, however, they were observed and labeled by international organizations such as the Organization for Economic Cooperation and Development (OECD 1995) and researchers (for example, Hood 1991, 1995). Given this development, the ideas became well known and packaged, and this format made it possible for OECD, among others, to circulate the ideas to wider audiences (Sahlin-Andersson 2001). The flow of knowledge therefore cannot solely be explained by interaction but must also take into account more general institutional developments.

Institutional Change and the Expansion of Management Knowledge

Cognitive, normative, and regulative changes have accompanied and paved the way for the expansion of management knowledge (Scott 1995; Scott *et al.* 2000). This expansion has followed from changed patterns of identification. Organizations tend to identify with and imitate those considered to be similar to them in one way or another (Sahlin-Andersson 1996; Sevón 1996), and organizations that are perceived as similar tend to be subject to the same widespread ideas (DiMaggio and Powell 1983). When organizations that were previously perceived to be different in character come to be viewed as being similar, they become receptive to similar ideas and this receptivity in turn enables knowledge to flow (Strang and Meyer 1994). When schools, hospitals, business firms, state departments, international associations, and churches have been analyzed and theorized as organizations, similarities among these units have been pointed out. They have been defined as being part of one category—organizations—and this means that they all have become subject to management ideas aimed at improving them (Brunsson and Sahlin-Andersson 2000). In general, many management ideas that flow extensively are closely associated with modern institutions of science, rationality, and the modern actor (Meyer *et al.* 1987; Meyer 1994; Meyer and Jepperson 2000).

Thus, the expansion of management knowledge is partly explained by the rise of new institutions, but the expansion also follows from the decline of previously dominant institutions. The development of the health care field from professional dominance to managed care followed the decline of old governance structures, institutional logic, and actors as well as the rise of new ones (Scott *et al.* 2000). With the decline—or the retreat—of the state, space has opened up for the establishment and dominance of more management-oriented settings, such as the dominance of big transnational accountancy firms, and for new transnational governing and ruling structures in society at large (Strange 1996). The examples indicate that an analysis of the expansion of management knowledge calls for analysis and explanations of how new institutions emerge, as well as how earlier practices, regulations, ideas, carriers, and institutions have declined. Furthermore, the explanations for the decline of the old are not necessarily the same as the explanations for the evolution of the new.

In general, the expansion of management knowledge follows and may be explained by general institutional changes in society, but it is also true that the flow of certain models and ideas may open up and drive institutional change. Many ideas take on "a life of their own," and new interests, relations, meanings, and actors evolve as the ideas are circulated (Marcusen 2000). Many consultants, executive education programs, management publications, management research units, expert committees, international organizations, and standardization bodies have evolved, as well as relationships among them formed in the wake of widespread and expanded management ideas. In other words, not only do management ideas follow certain routes, but also new routes are endogenously shaped as ideas flow (March 1999). This reciprocal relation among general institutional development, the expansion of management ideas, and carriers of ideas indicates that the widespread circulation of management knowledge is a central part of modern social development. Transformations and expansions of management knowledge not only follow institutional changes but also drive institutional change. Hence, to further explore the dynamics of this development, we need to explore how certain ideas have been formed, transferred, and transformed.

Knowledge Transformation

The content and shape of ideas explain their expansion. This should not be understood as a claim that ideas have stable and intrinsic features but rather that ideas are shaped, framed, reshaped, and reframed as they flow and partly as a result of how they flow. Ideas gain power as they flow, and as a result of becoming powerful they continue to flow. Some ideas are stated in global and expanded ways, a characteristic that makes it more likely that they will flow extensively, whereas other ideas tend to be quite time- and space-specific and therefore do not spread as much. And ideas tend to be framed in global and expanded ways as a result of their having flowed extensively. This again directs our attention to how ideas are shaped and reshaped as they are circulated.

The reasoning presented here suggests that the travel metaphor, which was referred to previously, should not be overstated. Ideas are not goods. They are not stable entities with a fixed content; rather, they are shaped and reshaped—or translated—while being circulated (Czarniawska and Sevón 1996; Gherardi and Nicolini 2000; Latour 1986). As an idea such as a specific model, an experience, a form of practice, or a general piece of advice is circulated, certain aspects of the idea may be described, passed on, or imitated, while other parts are ignored. Models are not, as DiMaggio and Powell (1991: 29) phrased it, "imported whole cloth." This might be the result of a conscious decision to attend to or adopt only certain aspects of a model. It might also be because some practices and models may not be fully understood or are impossible to account for or imitate. In addition, the models may be integrated with other models and traditions as they are adopted in new settings (Westney 1987; see also Boyer *et al.* 1998).

Most commonly, ideas are circulated in the form of written presentations or oral communication. Thus, what is being transferred is not practice as such but accounts of this practice. Such accounts undergo processes of translation as they spread, and we may find various local constructions of diffused knowledge (Czarniawska and Sevón 1996; Latour 1986). The distance between the source and receiver of an account provides scope for translating, filling in, or editing these accounts in various ways. Such accounts are often subject to editing, not only once but repeatedly, and they are edited differently depending on the context in which the editing is done and the use that the writer sees for the text (Sahlin-Andersson 1996). Various contexts, in other words, provide different editing rules according to which ideas tend to be edited so that they appear possible to circulate and consider.

Through the process of editing, an idea may be formulated more clearly and made more explicit, but reformulation may also change not only the form of the account but also its focus, content, and meaning. Hence, as knowledge circulates it may be fundamentally transformed in this way, so that knowledge is constructed and reconstructed during the processes of circulation (Gherardi 2000). Thus, the carriers who are circulating management ideas are co-constructing these same ideas (Czarniawska and Joerges 1996; Sahlin-Andersson 2001). Even small reformulations of a certain idea, which may follow as the idea is transferred from one context to another, may change the meaning or focus of this idea fundamentally. Thus, it is only *ex post facto* that one can distinguish revolutionary or fundamental shifts from smaller or detailed steps of translation. Some aspects of an idea may remain stable as the idea circulates, whereas other aspects of the idea are transformed. Labels often diffuse easily between settings, but this does not necessarily mean that technologies and programs remain the same as an idea flows. Even in a globalized world, differences among continents, countries, sectors, and industries do have an impact on how widespread knowledge is translated and used. Models that are placed under the same label may attain different local flavors as they are adapted and developed in different settings. This points to the importance of close and comparative studies of how knowledge flows into different settings.

As experiences are accounted for and transferred from one place to another, overly unique and local-specific aspects of this experience tend to be discarded; the practices are turned into models that are distanced and disconnected from time and space and rendered general (Czarniawska and Joerges 1996; Giddens 1990). In this way, ideas and experiences are made available for others to imitate or adopt (Greenwood *et al.* 2002; Røvik 1998). Stripping models of their local context tends to take place in several steps. It may start when someone, for instance, reports on her own practice or experience. This person may want to shape her presentation in a way that will make this experience interesting to others, disregarding aspects that seem too unique and too time- or local-specific and emphasizing those that seem to be general and generalizable. Those who mediate ideas, experiences, and models then do further editing, and the cycle repeats when the model is adopted in a new setting.

Accounts are subject to theorizing, which makes them appear to be trustworthy, universal, and relevant (Strang and Meyer 1994). In the course of the editing, accidental or coincidental circumstances are removed, as are aspects of practices and their effects that cannot be explained and accounted for in simple terms. Ideas that attract the interest of others and are deemed to be worthy of imitation are those whose implementation seems possible in another setting. Thus, practices, experiences, and ideas that are being spread are edited into models with clearly expressed intentions, procedures, and effects. They are packaged and commodified with labels such as BPR, MBO, SPC, and TQM. Many such widely circulated ideas are formed like general recipes, sometimes in the form of advice. Through such editing local practices are formed into models for others to adopt (Sahlin-Andersson 2000).

When examining the circulation of ideas and experiences in terms of editing processes, we can see how and why ideas are transformed when they are transferred from one place to another. The importance of the carriers of such ideas and experiences becomes evident. To a large extent global management trends are constructed and pursued transnationally. When carriers of management knowledge act globally, they also tend to construct the management knowledge they carry as global. In this way, management knowledge that is circulated tends to be formulated in universal and general ways. Moreover, knowledge that is circulated by organizations dedicated to management (such as business schools and other management program providers, management consultants, and management publications) tends to be formed and framed as management knowledge.

This brings us back to the concept of circulation. The concept of circulation not only points to the routes through which knowledge travels but also to how knowledge is shaped as it travels. The term *circulation* does not indicate a specific direction; it may well be that news or ideas are passed on in circles, so that the message—usually more or less transformed—may return to one who previously passed it on to someone else. Also, ideas may be recirculated so that old ideas reappear in new settings or are reshaped and recirculated (Furusten and Lerdell 1998). This means that the spread of ideas is not a linear process but involves overlapping, circular processes whereby ideas as well as sources and adopters may be shaped and transformed (Czarniawska and Joerges 1996). This view of the circulation of ideas suggests that in order to explain the present shape and extensive appearance of management knowledge we need to follow the processes of circulation closely.

Sources of Management Knowledge

In the two preceding sections, we have emphasized that management knowledge does not flow automatically but flows through processes of activity. Hence, we have pointed to the importance of understanding the activities of carriers who circulate management knowledge extensively and widely. However, our previous discussion not only points to the importance of present activities but also shows that carriers and ideas of today are rooted in processes with a long history. The overview thus points to the importance of taking a historical perspective when following the flow of ideas. In this section, we briefly discuss the sources on which the present stock of widespread management knowledge draws.

Diversification and Integration

Two trends emerge as we follow how management ideas have developed over time. First, ideas concerning production, organizing, and business have changed from being framed by and having a focus on technical skills to becoming increasingly management oriented. Second, over time these ideas have developed from being sector- and local-specific to becoming global and universal. These trends both display the reciprocal relation we described earlier between institutional development and the transformation and flow of specific ideas.

These trends may be interpreted as diversification processes: a development from one specific and well-localized type of knowledge to a more general, universal, diverse, and widespread knowledge area. Concepts such as "Americanization," which have been applied to the expansion of management (see, for example, Djelic 1998; Kipping and Bjarnar 1998) as well as to other and partly connected trends in business (Boyer *et al.* 1998), may sometimes give the impression that ideas were formed in one setting and then the message spread. Likewise, historical studies of the expansion of management in the United States attribute the expansion to diversification—especially diversification and professionalization of American engineers who entered into the management field and subsequently developed and claimed management knowledge (for example, Shenhav 1999).

We do not question these accounts, but we find them somewhat incomplete. Management knowledge does not have one root but many, and it did not start to grow in one setting but in many. We gave a few examples of this earlier as we accounted for the development of the most salient carriers of management knowledge. Management consultancy firms have their roots in engineering and accounting. The large professional service firms have their roots in auditing, engineering, and many other types of expertise. The management knowledge they circulate therefore draws not only on auditing and earlier developed management knowledge but also on law, communication science, computer science, and other disciplines. Business schools were established both in Europe and the United States in the late nineteenth century by building on different traditions, from academia and business (Engwall 1992). As business schools and management education programs developed in Europe, they were formed partly as imitations of American management education programs, and partly as an outgrowth of a European business and education tradition (Hedmo 2001; Mazza *et al.* 1998). Media and large corporations also display diverse features in various parts of the world; hence, the knowledge that is shaped and reshaped in these settings draws on the diverse sources at hand in the different settings. In the previous section, we described the circulation and translation of ideas whereby certain aspects of ideas are erased as the ideas are being circulated while other aspects are added. In this way, too, management knowledge draws on many sources.

Creolization

Historical accounts of the development of management knowledge and the carriers of such knowledge portray dramatic changes but also continuity. Historical analyses that trace the roots of management knowledge show how diverse sources of knowledge have become integrated into what is now circulated as management knowledge. The many sources of management knowledge contribute to today's hybrid or *creole* nature of management knowledge, and we claim that these diverse sources constitute a further explanation for the expansion of management knowledge.

Creolization has been used as an analytical concept in linguistics (Bloomfield 1935: 474; Trudgill 1974), as well as in cultural studies (Hannerz 1996: chapter 6). Creole languages or cultures draw on and are formed in the interconnectedness of various languages or cultures. Creole language or culture does not replace the original one. Instead, creole cultures have been shown to be open, and their relation to the cultures from which they have evolved remain visible and clear (Hannerz 1996; see Galison 1997 for an analysis of the development of microphysics as a process of creolization). In addition, creole cultures have been described as vital, diverse, and innovative (Hannerz 1996).

The creole concept appears to nicely reflect some of the features of management knowledge that we have emphasized in this chapter. Management knowledge draws on and has formed and expanded at the interface of engineering, auditing, technical, and organizational understanding. This does not mean that management knowledge has replaced auditing, engineering, legal knowledge, and other such disciplines; rather, the management field continues to be inspired by these fields. It also means that management knowledge is used in relation to those fields and in a great variety of organizational problems and situations. The creole character of management knowledge both follows from and makes widespread circulation possible. The diverse sources of management knowledge mean that the body of knowledge easily expands but also appears to be coupled and applicable to a wide variety of fields. Moreover, the creole character of management knowledge suggests that the management field is vital and diverse. The many sources continue to influence and inspire knowledge development in the field, and diverse sources seem to be variously shaped and integrated in different contexts. When management knowledge is circulated in different settings, it is reshaped as it is integrated with knowledge and traditions featured in these settings. The expansion then has resulted in the appearance of management knowledge in many places. However, the fact that management knowledge appears in different guises in different settings is unlikely to be negated as expansion continues. The expansion of management knowledge, then, may lead to convergence and variations.

The implication of the foregoing discussion is that we need to go back to the diverse sources to see how the foundation was laid for the explosive expansion of recent decades. In so doing, we should not limit our search for sources to single places and settings. Therefore, this book will present studies from a wide geographical range.

Content of the Book

This book aims to explain the flow and expansion of management knowledge. In this introductory chapter, we have portrayed the flow and expansion of management knowledge as an active process that is partly shaped (1) by how the carriers of such knowledge develop, act, and interact, (2) by institutions, and (3) by the consequence of long historical processes whereby diverse knowledge areas have been integrated into what is now distributed as management knowledge. These arguments are expanded in Chapter 2, in which John Meyer shows how globalization has generated an expansion of management and organization. This has occurred by the growth of markets and myths of markets, and the weakening of the protective sovereignties of nation and state, thereby intensifying organization-level mobilization. It is also an effect of the creation of the rights, potentials, and mythology of the modern global human person, and by the rationalizing or scientizing of the whole physical and social environment.

The rest of the book is structured according to the three features of the expansion of management knowledge, which we have discussed in this chapter: carriers, flows, and sources of management knowledge. The second part of the book (Chapters 3 to 5) focuses particularly on consultancies and their interactions with other carriers and users of management knowledge. The choice of consultancies as the focal carriers from which interactions and dynamics in the field are viewed is motivated by the observation that these organizations have tended to orchestrate developments in the field. In Chapter 3, Berit Ernst and Alfred Kieser develop a model of interrelated explanations of why so many organizations seek the advice of a consultant. They offer a dynamic explanation of the "consulting explosion." Business companies seek advice from consultants to handle complex and uncertain environments, but consultancies also contribute to the complexity of the environment. In addition, consultants are key participants in the arena for the creation of management fashions. With such strategies, consultants are able to actively enhance the demand for their services. The model further highlights the importance of the nature of the service itself and the difficulties clients are facing when trying to evaluate the effectiveness of consultants.

In Chapter 4, Martin Ruef further analyzes the diverse roles of consultants and their relation to the expansion of management consultancies. Using career history data of graduates from a major business school, the author tracks two developments that help explain the occupational expansion of U.S. management consulting. The first is the role differentiation of management consulting from traditional purveyors of management knowledge in the engineering, accounting, and finance disciplines; the other is the expansion of management consulting within a broader institutional framework of externalized management. Empirical findings suggest that both developments have played an important part in channeling business graduates into management consulting.

In Chapter 5 Thomas Armbrüster and Matthias Kipping focus on the interaction among consultants and their clients, and they show how management knowledge is transferred and co-constructed in the interaction between these various groups of actors. The authors distinguish among three types of management knowledge—general management knowledge, regulation-oriented knowledge, and change-oriented knowledge—and show that consultants play important, although different, roles in the dissemination of all three types.

The second part of the book (Chapters 6–8) analyzes how ideas flow and how they are shaped and reshaped as they flow. Each chapter in this section deals with the circulation and development of *quality concepts*, ideas that have been at the core of the expansion of management knowledge. In Chapter 6, Kjell Arne Røvik outlines elements in a theory about management ideas that flow. Røvik claims that the "winners" are not selected by coincidences and accidental processes; rather, there are common features among winning ideas that make it possible for them to travel quickly and widely. Based on a comparative study of the literature on three of the most popular super standards of our time—management by objectives (MBO), development dialogue (DD), and total quality management (TQM)—the author outlines elements in a general theory about the secrets of the "winners."

Peter Walgenbach and Nicholaus Beck in Chapter 7 give further insights into the quality movement, from another geographical location and with other methodological tools. They argue that in order to understand the dynamics of this movement fully, institutional explanations should be combined with resource mobilization theory. They show how and why the quality movement in Germany developed from having a main focus on technical skills to a broader management approach as the quality movement became institutionalized. The first part of the study consists of a historical analysis of the quality management movement in Germany. The historical analysis serves as the basis for the deduction of hypotheses concerning the institutionalization of quality management, which are tested in a quantitative analysis of the changes in the authorship of articles in the most important journal on quality management in Germany.

In Chapter 8, Nick Tiratsoo explores the quality movement further by analyzing why virtually identical American quality programs were received differently in Britain and Japan. The author rejects economic and essentialist explanations and instead argues that change was largely dictated by the interplay of political and cultural factors, and in particular the extent to which carriers of management knowledge and indigenous modernizers were able to combine in pursuit of their goals.

The third part of the book (Chapters 9–11) turns the spotlight on the diverse sources of management knowledge by analyzing how these sources have been integrated into the hybrid body of management knowledge as we know it today. The first two chapters in this section deal with training and education. In Chapter 9, Xiaowei Luo documents a largely ignored trend in employee training in U.S. organizations in the twentieth century. Not only has the content of training expanded, but its focus has also shifted from specific technical skills during the 1920s to human relations skills between the 1930s and the 1960s to personal development after the 1970s. The author reports on a systematic examination of the training discourse in a major journal in the U.S. personnel management field. The author shows that the increased orientation of employee training to "personal development training," including training in creativity, leadership, presentation skills, and career management, is explained by the rise of a more participatory view of organizations and a decline of bureaucracy and community.

In Chapter 10, Haldor Byrkjeflot argues that management knowledge does not solely stem from American engineering. A national comparison concerning differences in engineering education and its relation to management knowledge in Germany and the United States reveals that managers and management knowledge were strong in both countries, but management knowledge had different roots, features, and dissemination patterns. Germany and the U.S. industrialized between 1870 and 1930, but the two countries developed different management models and systems of technical education. The author accounts for the different educational systems and managerial ideologies by emphasizing differences in organizational resources and worldviews among four groups: teachers and academics, engineers in professional associations, politicians and civil servants, and business managers.

In Chapter 11, we return to some of the dominant carriers that have appeared throughout the book—the large professional business advisory firms. Eva Wallerstedt examines how these firms grew out of the more specialized auditing firms in Sweden. She analyzes the development that has led auditors to become important carriers of management knowledge. Market entries, professionalization, and diversification characterize the development. Needs for auditing created a market for auditors. Soon the established actors, strongly supported by the state, managed to control entries through a process of professionalization. Eventually this control has declined as the big international accounting firms, through both internal growth and acquisitions, have expanded their territories both nationally and internationally. In this process, consulting work has assumed a vital importance in their activities, making auditing firms today significant competitors to international management consultant firms.

The analyses throughout the book have portrayed the dynamics of knowledge management expansion. In the concluding chapter, Chapter 12, we elaborate on these findings. First, we discuss significant characteristics of the expansion processes. Second, we explore ways in which the expansion leads not only to homogenization but also to variation. Third, we elaborate on the effects of management knowledge expansion on organizational practice and institutional change. In this chapter, we relate our findings to neoinstitutional theory and show how actors, activities, and change interact with institutional developments. We have spelled out an extended research agenda in our introductory chapter, and even though the studies have answered some of the questions, major lacunae remain. We comment upon these and spell out crucial questions for further research.

2 Globalization and the Expansion and Standardization of Management

John W. Meyer, Stanford University, United States

Introduction

The chapters in this book have common roots in a striking phenomenon observed in recent decades in the world of organizations. Cultural models of expanded organizational management spread rapidly around the world (and perhaps especially around Europe), with ideas, rules, and practices flowing more freely than in the past. The contrast with the situation a few decades ago is notable: Guillén (1994) can write about past management ideologies and cultures as fairly distinctive to the political and social structures of the national societies he treats as his cases, though with some processes of diffusion and influence. Now, and in the chapters here, however, the center of gravity shifts to ideas about management as flowing generally around the world. National characteristics are now seen as operating to restrict or facilitate the flow (see, for example, Røvik in Chapter 6 or Tiratsoo in Chapter 8), rather than as constitutive determinants of principles of management (but see Byrkjeflot in Chapter 10).

This shift describes the observable realities of the management theories carried by the worldwide—and perhaps especially European—spread of consulting firms (Ruef in Chapter 4), social movements (Røvik in Chapter 6), or training systems and principles (Luo in Chapter 9). It also describes the social science models put forward to explain the changes. These tend to shift from "particle theories" of diffusion, which emphasize the histories and motives of the polities and firms to which ideas do or do not flow, to "wave theories," which emphasize the immersion of particular entities in a general context or medium that supports diffusion (Czarniawska and Sévon 1996).

What has changed in the broader context that makes a worldwide diffusion of management ideologies seem routine and central rather than surprising and peripheral? Behind their diversity, the chapters in this book have a common picture, not just of the phenomenon they are dealing with but of a basic explanatory variable: globalization (and its close relative, Europeanization). The rapid diffusion of management ideology is facilitated by the rise of a conception of society as transcending national boundaries.

Globalization, of course, has many meanings or dimensions. The aim of this chapter is to spell out some of the different aspects of globalization that are involved, and some of the different pathways through which these differing dimensions work to make a world that is safer for a worldwide McKinsey (Armbrüster and Kipping in Chapter 5; Ruef in Chapter 4).

Two Meanings of the Spread of Management Ideas

The expanded diffusion of management ideas around the world has two related aspects, which it is useful to distinguish. Each, in turn, is complex.

First, there is the intensified diffusion of standardized models of organization. Ideas about organization flow more rapidly across countries in the world, so principles of proper organizational supervision, accounting, structure, training, and so on apply everywhere. And ideas about organization flow more rapidly across social sectors or arenas, so the principles of proper business organization extend quickly from one industry to another, and outside the business system to public agencies, hospitals, schools, prisons, and so on (Olson *et al.* 1998). Clearly, this situation helps us understand the causal forces behind the diffusion: the ideas spread faster because organizations in different countries and different business and public sectors are seen as ultimately more similar than they were in the past (Strang and Meyer 1994).

Second, and closely related, there is a general intensification of focus on management as a common core element to all forms of structuring (Brunsson and Sahlin-Andersson 2000). The contrast is with older concerns with formal structuring as authoritative bureaucracy, ownership, or specific professionalism (for example, schools, hospitals, or shoe manufacturers). This shift, indeed, is partly captured in the modern preference for the general term *organization*, rather than *bureaucracy* or *association* and rather than substantive specification of the work involved. Thus, the head of a hospital or school is increasingly defined as a manager rather than a doctor or educator: the leaders of a utility company are seen as managers rather than electrical engineers, and so on.

The key to conceptions of *organization* as the crucial entity and *management* as core to organization lies in the extraordinary agentic actorhood attributed to organized entities in the modern system (Meyer and Jepperson 2000). They are no longer passive, trustworthy servants of the king or the public or their owners: they are rational bounded decision-making actors, with purposes and technologies and free resources of their own, with the sovereign authority to decide and act and the capacity to control their internal structures to conform to their decisions.

Hence, public agencies are to become privatized or decentralized or autonomous managed organizations to more efficiently meet their responsibilities (Olson, *et al.* 1998). Shoemaking organizations are to be managed and to such an extent that they may decide no longer to make and sell shoes. Even schools, which may be privatized and which may contract out teaching services, are in any case to become organizations that make decisions about how to serve their publics and enter into contractual relations with these publics.

The explanatory problem, therefore, is to explain how globalization produces a world of agentic, empowered, and managed organizations that function as rational and dramatic actors.

Dimensions of Globalization

Enlarged Markets: Experiences and Myths

A conventional and widespread notion is that on every side, from suppliers to regulators to consumers, organizations face with globalization (and especially the new Europe) markets that are much larger than before. The idea is that these expanded markets pose many new uncertainties and require much more effective decision making, control, and activity than were needed in the old village societies. The phrasing of the idea may emphasize the threatening character of the expanded markets (a common theme in pessimistic European interpretations) or stress the positive opportunities involved (as always, the American story), but the arguments are essentially the same.

In either case, it is essential to note, the idea of expanded *markets* is involved. This idea carries the implication that the new globalized world, although very complex (one meaning of the term uncertainty), is nonetheless very highly ordered, so the uncertainties can in principle be resolved by improved efficacious actorhood. Were globalization to imply simply disorder and anarchy (another meaning of uncertainty), expanded organization and management would not be likely consequences—prayer and defensive passivity would be wiser. Reliance on God and the state would be wiser than attempts at rational planning and action.

Expanded markets may be experienced by organizations, or with varying degrees of intensity, they may be anticipated. People may see European or global competition coming down the line. Or associated organizations may be experiencing it. Or advisors and business associations may predict it. In all these cases, the globalization involved brings in new uncertainty, but uncertainty of a highly rationalized sort, which responsible organizations need to mobilize to deal with.

At the extreme, globalization functions as a myth—a generally new and expanded picture of a standardized world with high expectations. In this sense, it can confront any organization even in the absence of any effective direct competition. Hence, modern public school organizations, even with effective monopolies, begin to envision a world of expanded educational competition (or economic competition to which their training must respond). Hospitals confront larger standards, perhaps carried by their real or imagined clientele—the old local people are now national and European and global citizens, carrying (in themselves or by attribution) high expectations for treatment. The old locals are now members of world society, and are understood to require treatment in light of the best practices obtaining anywhere. In the expanded global world, markets and market standards are part of a myth of enhanced rationalization.

Thus, the inputs, technologies, and outputs of modern organizations come to be seen against the background of a much larger, more complex, and more rationalized world than in the past. This requires more effective organizational structures, empowered to make the needed complex decisions and to take a broader range of actions across a much wider front of uncertainty.

But other elements of organization require similar mobilizations. Not only technologies but also sovereign decision-making capabilities and coordination and control systems need to be upgraded in the globalized world.

The Sovereign Organization in a Weakened State and National Community

Globalization, and especially Europeanization, has dramatically undercut the old sovereignties and protections provided to organizations by the national state and the national community. This development provides changed experiences for organizations but even greater changes in anticipations and in myths.

In the past, many organizations could effectively function as subunits of the national state and community rather than as autonomous entities. This is most obviously true of public agencies, which could often claim to simply be bureaucratic components of the national state, controlled and protected by its laws and regulations. The answers to questions about, say, the efficacy of a school could simply be that this school is in complete compliance with, and a dedicated professionalized servant of, the national state. In the same way, a hospital might be seen as the proper embodiment of the rules of the national professional medical community (Brunsson and Sahlin-Andersson 2000). In neither case does the organization posture as an autonomous decision maker or actor. The decisions are to be made in a ministry or professional community, not in the organization, which is more a faithful trustee than an organized actor. Mobilization as a bounded actor for such an organization would unreasonably sacrifice the protections of its monopoly position and would be in violation of its sworn responsibility. Secure under the umbrella of the nation and state, the proper posture is professionalism in Weber's sense—the loyal and competent servant, not the decision maker.

The same mentality describes much traditional private business organization, too. The organization is not a mobilized decision maker or actor, but a servant or trustee of owners or occupational communities or a local community. Demobilization is a more appropriately humble posture than is mobilized empowerment under such conditions.

One can see the traditional embeddedness of organization in national or local control systems in several ways. For instance, it can be seen as constraining possible choices, which are ruled out by national law or policy, professional authority, and so on. From this point of view, modern globalization represents a great expansion in organizational freedom and empowerment, since for the first time all sorts of new decisions can be made and new actions taken. However, the new freedom can be seen to have destroyed a mass of old protections that provided a secure and certain—however depressingly constrained—environment. In any case, the old monopolies are weakened, whether they are seen as protective or constraining.

In the new globalized system, sovereignty devolves on organizations, which are now to confront directly the problems of decision and action. They can no longer hide behind the state or local or national communities (for example, professional ones) but must become more rational and rationalized actors on a grand scale. The constructed space created in this expanded vision, of course, is one in which many new social movements supporting expanded managerial capacity spread rapidly.

Globalization and the Expanded Person

Organizations organize people. And globalization changes the practices, rules, and myths defining what people are, what they are entitled to, and what they can do. On all these dimensions, the changes amount to expansion of the personhood that organizations can and must deal with.

It is easiest to see this as creating new constraining uncertainties. If the old rules of local and national communities applied, fairly passive persons could be managed bureaucratically or with even more traditional mechanisms of the sort used to manage peasants. Now, with great expansions in principles of individual citizenship and the translation of this onto a global scale with principles of human rights, major new problems for organizing are created everywhere. Old technologies violate safety or medical or environment principles, which are now rationalized worldwide. Old control systems violate (worldwide) human rights, as do old exercises of organizational sovereignty. Old adaptations to market uncertainty violate modern employment principles. Old principles of employment or promotion violate the human rights of individuals or groups or both (for example, gendered employment). And the new principles sweep around the world, so that an organization doing customary labor control in Southeast Asia can generate a consumer strike on human rights grounds in San Francisco.

However, the new globalized persons provide new possibilities for organizing, too. They have extraordinary capacities and can be educated or trained to become part of the new expanded management system, having learned to create their own jobs, manage their own time, engage in their own proper human relations, and so on (see Luo in Chapter 9). So all sorts of new organizational forms become possible, far beyond traditional bureaucracy or professional community or family firm structures. The global citizen can be part of the new enhanced and empowered organization, which may be achieved by decentralization, weekend therapy sessions, or complex new computer systems. And with the rise of organization comes the rise of management possibilities—and then the social movements that spread expanded management ideologies everywhere.

The Rationalized Global Environment

It is common to see globalization as involving forces that break down the basis and autonomy of the state and liberate demonic forces of irrationality and localism in new tribalisms. And certainly events occur (for example, in Rwanda, Columbia, or Indonesia) that make such a view seem plausible. The view, however, is of no help to our present purposes. The "risk society" would not be likely to generate expanded organization and expanded management if the new risks were essentially arbitrary and anomic (Beck 1992). Rather, it would generate senses of powerlessness and meaninglessness that promote lower, not higher, levels of organizational mobilization.

But the view of globalization as breakdown is fundamentally in error. As I have stressed, contemporary globalization involves the construction of new domains of rationality, not only the collapse of some old ones. The new economic world is imagined as a market with expanded rationality. The new polity and society expand worldwide, with common models of societal organization and development reflecting a great deal of social scientization and rationalization (Meyer *et al.* 1997). The new persons are empowered and rational, with expanded human rights and capabilities (Frank *et al.* 1995). And all this occurs in a physical and technical and human environment increasingly scientized—in principles of engineering but also in ecological, biological, and medical analyses.

All this rationalization occurs on a worldwide basis, penetrating most societies, sectors, and organizational settings. It provides fertile ground for the mobilization of organization and management and for the rapid diffusion of new models and fashions for both. Perhaps the term *risk society* carries the wrong image, and we should employ the phrase *opportunity society* in parallel (Beck 1992).

To deal with all the expansions in the domains of rationality, organization must rapidly expand, and managerial capability must especially expand (Meyer 1994). And since the new rationalities are worldwide in character, the models of how to properly manage may be found everywhere and spread to everywhere. Thus, whole new doctrines spring up—here a new accounting system (Wallerstedt in Chapter 11), there an information one (Walgenbach and Beck in Chapter 7), over to the side a new system for training employees (Luo in Chapter 9) and new mechanisms for making decisions. And everywhere, new forms of standardization, measurement, and data (Tiratsoo in Chapter 8).

Carriers of Models for
Expanded Organization and Management

In many ways, as discussed above, globalization creates a new space or vacuum—the possibility and necessity for rapidly expanded organization and management capability or responsibility. This space—a greatly expanded, unfilled domain of rationalized uncertainty—has been filled with rapidly evolving promoters of managerial ideology. These are discussed extensively in the chapters of this book and may simply be noted here.

First, we may note the expansion in numbers and importance of the academic clergy—the intellectuals creating new management ideas and models. Institutionally this involves the rapid expansion and worldwide spread of business schools, which provide not only training but also intellectual centrality for the movement (Luo in Chapter 9). It also involves the production and spread around the world of academic publications supporting the new fashions.

But second, these business schools increasingly provide a training base from which managers are recruited. The shift from technical training (for example, in engineering, education, medicine, or other occupations) to generalized management training is a core indicator of the whole expansion in conceptions of organization and management that we are concerned with here. One indicator of the diffusion of management ideology is the spread of the MBA, or business training in general (Luo in Chapter 9). But this is not only an indicator—it is a cause of further diffusion, since each executive who obtains his position because of "management" education rather than training in substantive matters is likely to be a permanent node facilitating further diffusion. Dependent on faith in the existence of generalized management capabilities, he or she is especially susceptible to further expansions or developments of such doctrines. So presumably the expanded employment of people trained as generalized managers in overarching business schools directly increases the subsequent diffusion of new ideologies of expanded management.

Third, a whole set of specialists arises, translating more academic models into practical form and penetrating local organizational practice. Here we have the explosion of the consulting industry that is noted in many chapters of this book (for example, Ruef in Chapter 4; Wallerstedt in Chapter 11; Ernst and Kieser in Chapter 3).

Fourth, but less discussed in the chapters here, is the dramatic rise in organizational linkages to all sorts of associations. These associations may be general business groups or specialized to specific industries and activities. They may also be professional associations to which particular managers (for example, personnel or safety managers) belong. In any case, such associations of organizations become major carriers of general management information. For instance, they clearly provide the basis for the rapid expansion of standardized personnel practices in response to American affirmative action pressures (Dobbin and Sutton 1998; Edelman *et al.* 1992): the same process operates on a worldwide basis, too.

Finally, we may note that the rise of generalized conceptions of management as an activity—and of this management as going on in a rather standardized and globalized world—creates a strong tendency for organizations everywhere to look at an array of other organizations as potential models. If, on the one hand, an organization sees itself as an entity unique to a particular country, community, business setting, and so on, it is unlikely to look for (or be exposed to) management models drawn from around the world. If, on the other hand, it is seen as a modern organized actor, models are everywhere and the possibilities for diffusion are endless. The entire communication system around such an organization changes: its own elites look elsewhere, as do its ordinary participants. But so do customers and suppliers giving advice, and even members of the general public. If everyone within and without an organization examines it from the point of view of universal rationalities rather than local community, there is a great deal of exposure to expanded ideologies of organization and management. In practice, attention goes to the successful—Apple or IBM are models when things go well, and massive publicity in academic, professional, and mass media promulgates their organizational forms. And it is organization and management, more than technical accomplishments, that now circulate most widely (Røvik in Chapter 6). These, indeed, are the kinds of changes generated by modern globalization.

Dimensions of Global Organizational Rationalization: Some Speculations

Worldwide changes in recent decades strike at some dimensions of management and organization more than others, providing some focal points for further changes.

In many kinds of organized activities, global rationalization has been going on for a long time. This may especially describe technologies dealing with the physical world, since such matters have been rationalized for centuries. Thus engineering technologies and production management may have been diffusing rapidly for a long time. It is probably not reasonable to see special globalization going on in these areas in recent decades (Schofer 1999).

In contrast, in the pre–World War II world there was a considerable tendency to see people and organizations as local—tied to distinctive patterns of national citizen-membership and state structure. Thus it was reasonable, until recently, to imagine that managerial patterns for different national societies might be very different and the possibilities for diffusion very limited (Hofstede 1980). With the rise of scientized modern psychologies, and of human rights systems extended worldwide, and with the decline in the special sacred meaning of national citizenship, we may suppose that there have been rapid expansions in those aspects of organization and management concerned with persons and many diffusing and contending ideologies in the area.

In exactly the same way, recent globalization has hit hard in standardizing the meaning of social value and values—briefly, money in some of its various meanings (especially finance, credit, and investment, which have rapidly globalized). We may assume that there has been great expansion in standardized organizational control and management in areas related to monetary value—accounting, finance, measurement, and the like (Fligstein 1990). Social movements to improve management on these dimensions can flourish.

The point here is simply that the diffusion of cultural material on organizations and management is enhanced by the rise of standard models in these matters but also by rapid change in the areas, since this generates the space in which consultants and theorists and new training systems blossom.

Conclusion

Globalization has a variety of meanings and dimensions. Many of these operate to create more standardized pictures of organization across the boundaries of nations or social sectors. And they operate to create stronger pictures of organizations as empowered and managed actors.

One causal pathway, here, is through the expansion of all sorts of markets and myths and ideologies of markets. New uncertainties confront organizations (even in supposedly monopoly situations such as state educational systems). The market idea implies that these expanded environments have a rationalized character of a kind that demands and legitimates expanded organization and management, rather than the sort of threatening chaos that might undercut expanded organization. Even if the new world is threatening, it can and must be dealt with. So much structuration results.

A second causal pathway lies through the weakened control and legitimacy of the national community and nation-state. Organizations are no longer so protected (or constrained) by their position as subunits in national professional and bureaucratic structures. They are more exposed—and again, exposed to a highly rationalized environment of markets and standards. More organization and more management is called for and legitimated.

Third, globalization has produced a kind of natural law expansion in models of the persons that make up organizations—their rights, their capacities, and their ability to be organized. The new organizational forms must and can incorporate these people in dynamic participation, but in doing so must become more mobilized and more managed. Whole domains are created or expanded having to do with personnel, decision-making participation, safety, the environment, and all sorts of rights connected with employment and promotion.

Finally, globalization has expanded the overall scientization of the world, with great schemes defining the physical environment, the nature of social development, and indeed the capacities of human persons. Scientization generates the kinds of rationalized uncertainties that are recipes for organizing.

In the space created by all these rapid social changes, many new movements and institutions are created to diffuse new and expanded models of organization and management. New training institutions built around management provide the employment base, and expanded post-employment training is created. All sorts of academics generate new models expanding management capacity, and all sorts of consultants arise to diffuse them. And in a world in which disembodied organization is seen as subject to the same standards of high managerial capacity, models and exemplars are discussed in all sorts of media. All these processes greatly intensify diffusion and break down the boundaries (of nation, or social sector) that might restrict it.

3   In Search of Explanations for the Consulting Explosion

Berit Ernst and Alfred Kieser,
University of Mannheim, Germany

The Consulting Explosion

Banks do it. Energy providers do it. Consumer goods manufacturers do it. Even universities and art museums do it. They all seek the advice of consultants. Even if definitions of what is to be considered consulting remain blurry and reliable statistics are hard to come by, observers agree that the management consultancy industry has enjoyed a spectacular growth for the past two or three decades. Most estimates accredit a double digit increase in yearly revenues that ranges between 10 and 30 percent, varying by source and country (Hasek 1997; Rassam and Oates 1991). Compared to most industries' or to GDP growth rates, this means that advisers often grow at least twice as fast as their clients. The entire market volume is now estimated to be $62 billion worldwide (*Consultants News* 1999).

Whereas in 1980 less than five consultancy firms with more than a thousand consultants existed, in 1997 there were more than thirty. In simple terms, this implies that 80 percent of all consulting experience was generated in the years between 1980 and 1997 and only 20 percent in the period from 1886 (when the first consultancy was started) to 1980 (Canback 1998). We are facing a veritable burst of consulting activities.

This consulting explosion is impressive enough by itself. What makes it even more remarkable, however, is the fact that nobody actually *has* to employ a consultant: unlike lawyers or accountants, consultants may be contracted or not, and although many companies seem not to be able to do without them, a few (such as General Electric or Procter and Gamble) pride themselves on hardly using them at all (Wooldridge 1997). What we are observing is a growth phenomenon that seems to exhibit a self-sustaining, inherent dynamic—one that is puzzling many observers.

In the following, we will try to shed some light on this "tale of mystery and imagination" (Wooldridge 1997: 3). More precisely, it is our aim to identify reasons to explain the increased demand for consultants. In developing our argument we primarily focus on general management and strategy consulting. Therefore, we are not claiming that our arguments apply to all sorts of consulting. Taking rationalistic arguments as a point of departure, we will consider what mechanisms beyond such explanations might play a role in pushing the demand for consultants.

Starting at a macrolevel, we will first consider the dynamics and complexity of the environment that are often assumed to play an important role in creating demand for advice. To gain a better understanding of what consultants do, we will then zoom in to analyze the functions consultants fulfil for their clients during the course of a project. In a third step, we will consider which strategies consultants employ to increase the demand for their service. It is then argued that the very characteristics of this service make it extremely difficult for clients to evaluate the consultants' work. Finally, managers' need of control as a motivation for the use of consultants is explored from a psychological perspective. The result is a model in which all of these factors are combined to offer a possible explanation of the consulting explosion.

Experts and Supra-experts for an Increasingly Complex and Dynamic World

A frequently discussed explanation of the consulting explosion points to the continuously increasing complexity and dynamics of the environment businesses are operating in. Developments such as globalization, new technologies, notably information technology, the deregulation of markets, and the intensification of competition are some of the most important factors generally associated with the consultancies' growth (for example, Hasek 1997; Jackson 1997). It is argued that this increase in complexity forces management to seek professional advice. We believe that this explanation merely touches upon the surface of the consulting phenomenon, as it hardly takes into account how environmental complexity and dynamics (and the perception of these) are created in the first place.

Taking the ideas of Spencer (1876), Durkheim (1893), and Parsons (1951) as a point of departure, modern sociology embraces the notion that the process of societal modernization can be explained in terms of social differentiation (Alexander 1993; Rüschemeyer 1985). According to Luhmann (1980), functional differentiation represents an attempt to reduce the world's complexity by dividing a problem into subproblems, which are then tackled by specialized groups of people. This leads to the creation of subsystems that operate autonomously and are dedicated to the selective fulfillment of a specific social function. Although at first sight, complexity split in parts seems to imply reduced complexity, exactly the opposite is the case: as each subgroup is devoted to only an aspect of the entire problem, more capacities become available to create a specific complexity for each subproblem. In this case, the overall complexity (defined as the number of possible problem definitions and solutions that exceed those that can be realized) has grown (Luhmann 1980). As paradoxical as it may sound, functional differentiation implies that complexity is increased through efforts aiming at its reduction. And as we will see, consulting owes its enormous growth to this paradox.

With this concept of functional differentiation, Luhmann seeks to explain the "peculiar growth dynamics of modern society" (Luhmann 1987: 169). Growth in this sense is propelled by functional systems, such as politics, economics, and science (and their respective subsystems), that through their aims and structure are disposed toward a differentiation from given states of being. They all follow a rationale of increase and improvement. Science, for example, represents a system that in its striving for truth constantly produces new findings, which expand and put into perspective existing knowledge. It lies at the core of scientific activity to generate new solutions to existing problems *and* to create problems that were formerly nonexistent. Science is critical by definition, and *kriteion* means nothing else than "to distinguish" and "to differentiate": science takes part in the dynamics of growth by creating distinctions, categories, and subcategories (Kieser 2001).

Similarly, Habermas (1981: 484) observes an "unstoppable inherent dynamic," particularly with regard to the differentiation and autonomous operation of the economic and political subsystems, that results in a fragmentation of everyday consciousness (Habermas 1981) and, ultimately, in a great insecurity in almost all aspects of life (Luhmann 1987).

Human Resource Departments as an Example. Let us reconstruct the described dynamic by using an example: the existence of a human resource department nowadays represents a standard in virtually every corporation.[1] Some of the tasks of human resource specialists consist in ensuring a steady inflow of high-quality personnel, creating schemes of remuneration and career paths that motivate and commit employees, and controlling the costs associated with the human factor. Analogous to other functional departments, human resource experts specialize in providing solutions to one specific aspect of managing an organization. The establishment of these departments is meant to serve the purpose of absorbing insecurity (March and Simon 1958).

When functional departments are established by companies of a certain importance or visibility, other companies are triggered to draw level in a process of mimetic isomorphism (Powell and DiMaggio 1991). The rationale behind such processes lies in the fact that the risk of decisions under uncertainty is reduced by monitoring and imitating the actions of other companies. On the one hand, one can never be certain whether particular design features have lead to a competitive advantage. If they have, the imitating company has not fallen behind. If, on the other hand, a decision leads to negative effects, the imitating company is not alone in having to bear these. In short, the advantage of adopting lies in not being at a disadvantage. At the same time, a public discourse of rationality evolves around the establishment of certain functions (Baron *et al.* 1986, 1988).

The specialists working in human resource departments of different companies eventually begin to develop professional or quasiprofessional activities. These encompass the formulation of standards and the promotion of opportunities for specialist training, which in turn ensure the supply of new experts for the extension of the profession's influence. Professional associations, such as the European Association for Personnel Management (EAPM), are founded to advertise the importance of the functions performed by their members and to publicly legitimate their activities. They also support the development of specialized methods, as well as their dissemination.

At a more advanced level of institutionalization, institutions of tertiary education such as colleges and universities react by making the specialization subject of their research and by establishing specialized degrees. In the case of human resources, this has led to the establishment of departments in human resource management in business schools and the possibility to elect a human resource specialization within a business degree. A scientific discourse is thus added to the discourse of practice. These interlocking discourses unfold a particular dynamic, as all parties involved have a natural interest in expanding the specialization they serve and as they are able to mutually support these interests. A multitude of ever more complex techniques that are supposed to lead to advances in effectiveness are produced; the speed of innovation is continuously accelerated.

From the perspective of top management, it becomes more and more difficult to understand and control the complex and highly specialized systems of knowledge created through functional differentiation. As a result, the question of allocating resources to a particular function or technique proposed by certain functional experts is laden with insecurity. Although functional departments have come into existence to buffer the company from the complexity of its external environment, they have created an internal environment that tends to be even more complex and dynamic.

In this situation, a need emerges for an agent who is able to make decisions based on a holistic understanding of a given problem. This requires the possession of sufficient knowledge to judge the advice given by experts, but it is also necessary to be independent of the interests of specialized departments. We argue that in many cases, external consultants are expected to fulfill this need.[2] Consultants, however, do not lead to a solution of the complexity problem and the resulting insecurity. Rather, as we will aim to show, consultants are quite likely to aggravate the problems.

Supra-experts. Thus far, we have elaborated on the notion that experts increase complexity. Consultants of the kind considered in this chapter—those dealing with broad strategic and organizational issues—also fit into this category insofar as they develop, store, and transmit specialized management knowledge. However, these consultants draw and judge on previously autonomous knowledge generated by experts in subsystems in order to develop a comprehensive view of managerial problems. With this general and process-based orientation, consultants fall into a category that could be termed *supra-experts.*

Supra-experts are called in by managers in order to provide help in regaining control of the perceived complexity that is, as we have seen, caused by functional differentiation. However, it would be wrong to assume that the consultants, in the long run, are always able to bring about the desired reduction of complexity. On the contrary, consultants may add to complexity in several ways, although this increase in complexity may not necessarily be perceived by the manager, since it affects the macrolevel—the level on which we are focusing.

- Although they are perceived as supra-experts and market their services accordingly, consultants form a subsystem within the subsystem of the economy. The system of consulting is, as we will point out later, subdivided into many specialties. As a result, the dynamics associated with functional differentiation apply in a similar manner as in functional departments. Although consultants are called in to reduce complexity, they are bound to contribute to its increase as management becomes aware of the possibilities that the field of management consulting has to offer.

- In particular, consultants as supra-experts have infinite possibilities to combine and make sense of existing expert knowledge (which is dynamic in itself). The process of sense-making ultimately magnifies the problem of complexity, as every new interpretation links the elements of knowledge in a different way. This development, however, is not felt by the individual client who, at least under the impression of a recently completed consulting project that he considers successful, is more likely to perceive a reduction in complexity, at least for some time.

- Consultants have an interest in a highly dynamic production of knowledge, as this guarantees managers' need for orientation and, as a result, a source of demand for consultants. It is thus not surprising that consultants are active players in the creation of management knowledge and fashions (Kieser 1997). These fashions usually also play into the hands of the internal specialists. Thus, once management starts to pay attention to the consulting market, it is confronted with a plethora of concepts that do not seem easily applicable without the help of consultants.

- Environmental dynamics and complexity are constantly dramatized by the "siren voices of management commentators and consultants" (Clark 1995; Deutschmann 1997). Consultants not only instrumentalize *existing* complexity, they also attempt to intensify managers' *perception* of overall complexity.

In the following step of our analysis, we will try to shed further light on this phenomenon by examining in some detail the functions consultants perform for their clients.

How Consultants Transfer Knowledge—
and Other Official and Unofficial Functions

Knowledge Transfer and Commodification

Most definitions of management agree that the main *raison d'être* of consultants is to provide knowledge that their clients do not have (for example, Greiner and Metzger 1983). Consultants stress that they do not transfer ordinary knowledge but they transfer knowledge of "best practices." They create the expectation that they are able to extract knowledge on practices from the "most successful companies," store it, and use it to solve their clients' problems. This is in line with their role as supra-experts, which implies that they know how to select superior and appropriate knowledge from a confusing variety of possibilities. However, it is not at all clear what a practice is, how a "best practice" can be identified, and how a "best practice" can be transferred, for example, from a General Electric plant in North Carolina to a small company in the Black Forest. A thorough analysis reveals that the knowledge that is used by consultancies falls into the following categories (Werr *et al.* 1997): (1) *values, "visions" (Leitbilder), general approaches, or "philosophies,"* (2) *procedures* (for example, procedures for setting up project teams or training programs), (3) *tools* (for example, tools for the graphical representation of processes and for the simulation of alternative organizational processes), (4) *knowledge on individual projects that is documented in information systems* (Sarvary 1999; Werr *et al.* 1997).

So when consultants talk about the transfer of "best practices" they implicitly refer to all these categories of knowledge. However, it remains an issue for empirical studies to find out to what extent knowledge from these categories is actually brought into play in consulting projects. It also remains to be seen whether the consultancies' information systems live up to their promises in practice.

Consultancies strive to "commodify" the knowledge that they use in transfer processes. That is, they try to transform unstructured problems and problem solutions into standardized problems and solutions (Elkjær *et al.*

1991; Fincham 1995; Werr *et al.* 1997). They offer their clients "package approaches." This tendency is acknowledged in the profile of Arthur D. Little:

> Part of our job is continuously to retrieve, absorb, and fine-tune the latest and best methodologies. Our approach is eclectic and our criterion simple: we use what works. Often the techniques we employ are the ones that we ourselves have developed over the years in the course of doing business with our clients. (quoted after Dichtl 1998: 149)

However, by no means should the clients get the impression that the solution that is finally implemented is "off the shelf." The consultants claim that they apply standardized instruments in order to tailor customized solutions for each client.

Commodified or packaged approaches offer a number of advantages for consultancies:

1. *Greater potential for attracting clients.* Clients favor "package approaches" for a variety of reasons. The common assumption with offers of this kind is that they have been tested and proved successful in many organizations and, therefore, the risk of failure is comparatively low. Package approaches frequently become part of the discourses around management fashions. For consultancies it is easier to convince clients of the value of specific products than simply their competence with regard to specific management concepts, philosophies, or areas. Commodified products appear more tangible.

2. *Greater potential for marketing.* A "package product" can be marketed like a branded article. In the consultancy's communication the product usually has a catchy label like OVA (Overhead Value Analysis), Zero Base Budgeting, or Value Chain and is linked to certain quality assurances.

3. *Facilitation of coordination within the consultancy.* An exchange of personnel between projects in different client organizations is much easier when the consultants of a consultancy work with the same schemas and instruments. It is also easier to transmit knowledge to new personnel. Finally, the task of building up an effective information system for case histories is much easier if a number of cases follow the same standardized procedures (Hansen *et al.* 1999).

4. *Substitution of work by experienced consultants through work by less experienced consultants, the clients' employees, and computers.* Teams of experienced consultants produce procedures and tools into which they "program" parts of their knowledge and experience. Many procedures are designed as computer-assisted tools. Robust and easy to handle procedures and tools can be administered by less experienced consultants, even by the clients' employees who, after having received some training, cooperate with the consultants.

Other Official Functions

Consultants have more to offer than just the transfer of knowledge:

Legitimization: The separation of ownership and management created a problem of legitimization (Faust 1998). Analysts, shareholders, and an increasingly critical public need to be convinced that management efficiently uses state-of-the-art practices and acts in the interests of all stakeholders. It is perhaps no coincidence that in the United States the growth in the number and size of consultancies and the development of managerialism occurred parallel to one another (McKenna 1995).

Consultants increasingly take over the role of certifiers of rationality. They signal internal and external constituencies that expert knowledge is being applied to all functions and at all levels of an organization. Certificates of this kind, to a certain extent, buffer against the consequences of failure. Of course, management has to justify the choice of a consultancy. However, as long as the chosen one enjoys a reputation—and all the bigger ones do—it is not too difficult to defend this choice. The demands of constituents are often contradictory. The recourse to consultancies with a high reputation can be a means of handling conflicts of this sort. A periodical control of management quality also dovetails nicely with the popular discourse on quality control and on audits as a means of reducing far-reaching risks such as fatal environmental impacts (Power 1994, 1997).

The management system is both audited and repaired by consultants. This implies that consultants certify standards of rationality that they have set and implemented themselves. But it is surprising that whether this double function can be carried out by consultants in a reliable way is hardly considered. The use of consultants has traits in common with those observed by

Power (1997: 123) in the general context of auditing: it exhibits "the character of a certain kind of organizational script whose dramaturgical essence is in the production of comfort." And the "consultancy explosion" can be connected to the "audit explosion," which "suggests that audit is emerging as a powerful institution of risk processing" (Power 1997: 139).

Providing Temporary Management Capacity: Consultants can help clients overcome bottlenecks in management capacity or carry out tasks for which it is not efficient for the client organization to invest management capacity, since these tasks do not have to be performed regularly (for example, assessing the public image of the organization). The client organization is, in principle, capable of performing the respective task itself, so in this function knowledge transfer is not the point.

Communication and Stimulation of Acceptance After Top Management Has Decided on a Change Process: Consultants have well-tried presentation techniques and rhetoric at hand that enable them to overcome resistance to change by members of the client organization and to motivate them during the implementation process. They can also mobilize expert power for this purpose. This knowledge is distinct from problem solving knowledge in a narrower sense.

Latent Functions

Providing Weapons for Politics: Consultants are instrumental for increasing the power of groups of managers to have their projects accepted and to undermine the projects of rival groups. It is not uncommon in larger organizations for different groups of managers to employ different consultancies— not only to get advice on the company's problems but also to become equipped with arguments for the improvement of their own unit's status and to increase the expert power behind these arguments. Consultants can also take over the role of scapegoats.

Consultants promote the careers of managers who sponsor them. They are always trying to put their sponsors in a favorable light so that the managers who brought the consultants into the organizations can claim a good deal of the praise for themselves if a project is declared successful.

Interpretation, Simplification, Reassurance: Consultants offer "ideas, metaphors, models, and words that impose order on a confusing world, thus reconstructing our appreciation of experience" (March 1991: 29). The value of this sounding-board function increases if the consultant, as a discussion partner, offers management philosophies that top management finds useful; for example, the philosophy that internal exchange relationships should be defined as relationships between internal suppliers and customers (du Gay and Salaman 1992).[3]

Of course, the interpretation function can become instrumental for getting managers to accept problem definitions for which the consultant has packaged, standardized solutions. Consultants "do not so much target themselves at a particular niche as they seek to create a niche and persuade clients that they are within" (Bloomfield and Danieli 1995: 28; see also Bloomfield and Best 1992). This problem is also known as "biased problem definition" (Armenakis *et al.* 1990; Maclagan 1989).

The (demand producing) skill of the consultant consists in recognizing the distribution of power in the client organization, sounding out the expectations of the powerful actors, and handling these expectations in such a way that client satisfaction is maximized while the interests of her company are also being taken care of. Maximizing client satisfaction is the dominant long-term goal of consultants, since the satisfied customer is likely to prolong the cooperation with the consultancy. Consultants not only teach their clients how to establish long-lasting customer relationships, they also use this knowledge for themselves. The consultants who are successful in selling additional projects to a client receive incentives.

In this section we added a number of arguments to our explanation of the consulting explosion: consultants create new knowledge that they commodify into products and effectively market. Moreover, they offer a number of additional functions, official as well as unofficial ones, that managers find most useful. In the next section, we will consider how consultants actively create and expand the market for these products.

Creating Demand by Defining New Problem Areas That Are in Need of Expertise and by Creating Management Fashions

The consultancy industry is in constant motion, and its latest developments impressively demonstrate how consultants explore new areas of business that serve to secure their highly contested market share and expand their influence. The pressures for the individual consultancy are high, as a growing number of competitors are forcing their way into the market. Firms that were formerly concentrating on selling software, such as SAP, for example, now try to address all aspects of the organization, including general strategic issues (Lindvall and Pahlberg 1999). The big accountancy firms, which are experiencing stagnating growth in their traditional field of expertise, have already established themselves as an important supplier in the lucrative field of management consulting and are generating more income from consulting than from either auditing or tax (Wooldridge 1997). As a result, it is important for all players to create new demand to secure the firm's survival and the growth it needs in order to offer its employees the careers they are expecting and that are necessary to keep them from signing up with competitors. In the following, we will briefly explore three mechanisms of creating demand for consulting: the definition of new groups of clients, the expansion of scope, and the creation of management fashions.

To start with, consultancy firms exhibit an insatiable appetite for new clients. They increasingly find them in the bureaucracies of the public sector and not-for-profit organizations such as hospitals, theaters, and churches, which especially in Europe would still have been considered rather exotic consulting targets only a decade ago (Faust 1998). Nowadays, these organizations are expected to follow a rationale of efficiency similar to that of private sector enterprises, and consultancies have played an important role in promoting and establishing these norms as appropriate (Galvin and Ventresca 1999). Ultimately, the large consultancy firms have also recognized that small and medium-sized companies (which they previously neglected almost entirely) represent a vast terrain of opportunities for selling their advice, especially the kind of advice that has been developed into standardized packages and can thus be transmitted relatively easily and at a low cost for the consultancy, as we have pointed out above. Some of the large firms are even reported to now offer inexpensive consulting on the Internet (Wooldridge 1997). In all these cases, suppliers actively create demand by convincing organizations hitherto unaware of their need for consultants that they exhibit just those problems for which consultants happen to have the solution and are eager to solve.

Consultants are not only seeking new clients, they also try to expand the scope of their services by colonizing new areas of knowledge. As companies undergo functional differentiation, so do consultancies who propose solutions for new areas of specialization, such as new practices in human resource management or, most notably, information technology (for example, Biswas and Twitchell 1999). However, it would not be enough to consider consultants as followers of differentiation processes within client companies, as they themselves are acting as catalysts of differentiation by pointing to new possibilities of specialization. Each new specialization is a claim that a function that hitherto has not been subjected to professional expertise has now become one and that companies should take advantage of. Usually, it is emphasized that enormous gains in efficiency can be realized by subjecting this function that has been neglected so far to a thorough professional analysis. Simultaneously, it becomes more and more difficult for clients to decide what competing practices to adopt and which consultancies' recommendations to follow as the consulting industry differentiates. It is this context that fosters a trend toward a dualistic industry where huge one-stop suppliers cater to the need for supra-experts, on the one hand, and small consultancies occupy specialist niches, on the other (Wooldridge 1997). Internal differentiation and specialization of companies and specialization as well as consolidation of consultancies are mutually reinforcing each other.

As we have discussed, the targeting of new clients as well as new fields of consulting both lead to a constant differentiation of consulting supply, which, in turn, increases demand. Management fashions represent a third and highly important mechanism to boost the demand for consulting even further (Abrahamson 1996; Kieser 1997). A management fashion develops out of a discourse around a buzzword such as scientific management, Fordism, lean production, or reengineering. This discourse is triggered by and produces texts in many different forms—management books, articles in manager magazines, talks, workshops, comments in Internet forums, and so forth. Usually, many texts on management concepts simultaneously compete for the attention of managers. In this sense, they increase the complexity of the environment as it is perceived by managers. Concepts that relatively speedily gain large shares in the public management discourse are called *management fashions*. Whether texts are able to attract the attention of managers to a large extent depends on their rhetorical quality (Furusten 1998; Røvik in Chapter 6) and their timeliness—they must hit a nerve (Abrahamson and Fairchild 1997; Barley and Kunda 1992; Swanson and Ramiller 1997).

In the majority of cases consultants are the originators of texts of this sort. Usually the texts contain a number of expressions or principles that are vague, such as "empowerment," "internal customers," or "process ownership." Vagueness is a strength, since it triggers discussions among the recipients of the texts and increases their desire to learn more about the concept in question. At certain points in time, it appears inevitable to consult experts, and the best experts are the creators of the texts who usually also claim to possess knowledge from successful implementations of this concept. The skill of the experts—the consultants—is to increase the plausibility of the concept while maintaining the impression that outside help is necessary to implement it.

The wave of a management fashion gains momentum through adoptions. The more companies that are reported as having achieved competitive advantages through the implementation of a management concept—and the consultancies are eager to spread success stories—the higher the propensity of nonadopters to get onto the bandwagon until saturation and disillusionment sets in (Loh and Venkatraman 1992; Strang and Macy 1999; Zbaracki 1998).

In their attempts to spread new management concepts consultants can count on the assistance of other actors such as university professors, publishers, editors of management magazines, or commercial seminar organizers. Consultants strive to increase their control over other actors by organizing or co-organizing management seminars and congresses, which they regard as superb marketing instruments for a highly complex service. They cooperate with business schools in the setting up of executive trainings (Kipping and Amorim 1999). They also establish and cultivate "old boys'" networks with their former consultants who became managers in other companies (Byrne and Williams 1993).

Management fashions increase the complexity of the environment by their multitude, their vagueness, and their short life cycles. Managers face the difficulty of constantly having to choose whether to adapt to the current wave, and, if they decide to do so, how to apply a given concept in the context of their organizational realities.

The strategy of increasing demand by creating management fashions proves highly effective. Michael Hammer refers to a market research organization that estimated the world market for reengineering projects could reach a volume of $7 billion. The consultancy business of his coauthor, James Champy, CSC Index, has increased its turnaround from $30 million in 1988, before *Reengineering the Corporation* (Hammer and Champy 1993) appeared, to $150 million in 1993 (Jackson 1996). However, the principal creator of a fashion does not get all the additional demand, since after some time all the major consultancies sell packages for the implementation of the fashion.

Implementing a fashion is also a highly attractive strategy for the individual manager. Managers who innovate with the help of consultants along the principles of the current fashion early enough can distinguish themselves from the crowd, while still belonging to a worldwide, accepted group of managers who share the practice of the new management concept (Simmel 1957). This greatly reduces the danger that the projects associated with the implementation of a fashion are rated a failure. As we will see in the following section, however, there are serious hindrances to judging the success of such projects and the quality of the consultants' work. We therefore contend that the available approaches for evaluating consultancy projects are not suited to curb the managers' increasing demand for consultants' services.

All That Glitters Is Not Gold—
Difficulties in Evaluating Consultants' Performance

An organization that finds out that a consulting project did not improve its performance would probably not give this consultancy another contract. If this experience was repeated with other projects and other consultancies the organization would probably stop hiring consultants altogether or would at least reduce its budget for consulting considerably. The problem is that it is extremely difficult for clients to evaluate the performance of consulting with regard to effectiveness and efficiency.[4] This has strong implications for the demand for consultancy services.

The difficulty of evaluating consultants' performance results from three underlying problems, which can be summed up as follows:

1. *The problem of judging organizational effectiveness*: How is it possible to know whether a new concept is worth something or that an organizational decision is right?
2. *The problem of judging consultants' effectiveness*: How can clients assess whether a consultant is performing well?
3. *The problem of effectiveness as a concept applied to consultancy work*: Is effectiveness the appropriate concept to address the performance of consultants?

Judging Organizational Effectiveness

Management theorists have yet to agree on the question of how any organizational decision can be judged in terms of its effectiveness. The more complex the effects of such a decision, the more unsatisfactory simple models become, yet multivariate instruments have proven difficult or even impossible to handle (Meyer 1994). Blurry and conflicting goals, complex causality relations, and an uncertain long-term perspective are but some of the stumbling blocks encountered (Lewin and Minton 1986; March and Sutton 1997).

This unresolved struggle for reliable and valid criteria has led some theorists to reject the notion of effectiveness completely (for example, Hannan and Freeman 1977). Even though practitioners apply less vigorous methodological criteria than researchers and are able to navigate with the help of heuristics, the nature of the difficulties encountered remains fundamentally the same.

Judging Consultants' Effectiveness

Consultancy work exhibits the characteristics of a highly complex service that involves first of all, as we have seen, the transfer of knowledge. For our purposes, it is useful to focus on consulting as a knowledge intensive service (Alvesson 1993). This focus allows us to highlight the traits that have an important impact on evaluation: the difference in qualification between consultant and client, their interaction during service delivery, and the intangibility, singularity, and indeterminability of outcomes (Kieser 1998). As we will see, these characteristics are responsible for the problems faced in evaluation.

Difference in Qualification: If consultants are considered supra-experts who provide and transfer selected knowledge that the client lacks, it becomes evident that

> buyers of expertise itself [. . .] often have difficulty assessing their purchases. Clients often consult experts because they believe their own knowledge to be inadequate, so they cannot judge the experts' advice or reports mainly on substance. Clients may be unable to assess experts' advice by acting on it and watching the outcomes: the clients do not know what would have happened if they had acted otherwise. (Starbuck 1992: 731)

Even if the client is able to identify the "right" philosophy (which in itself represents a major obstacle because a lack of orientation in the jungle of management concepts often triggers the use of consultants), she is still facing the problem of distinguishing whether the combination of different forms of knowledge is appropriate; that is, whether the vision offered by a consultant is flanked by procedures and tools that will lead to its realization in the client company. In addition, as we have seen, it is difficult to assess whether the consultant is really knowledgeable or only knows how to manage impressions.[5]

What we have called a difference in qualification exhibits significant parallels to the concept of information asymmetry emphasized in agency theory (for example, Arrow 1985; Eisenhardt 1989; Ross 1973). Information asymmetry implies that the principal who delegates a job does not know exactly *what* the agent does, which bears the danger that the principal is not receiving an optimal service. When, as in the case of consulting, a difference in qualification exists, the principal (that is, the client) does not even know *how* the job that is delegated to the agent (that is, the consultant) could be performed (Sharma 1997).

A difference in qualification, or knowledge asymmetry, limits the possibilities of an *ex post* evaluation, but it also makes it difficult for the client to determine *ex ante* how much consulting will be necessary. In other words: the consultant not only decides *how* he will perform a task but to a certain degree also decides *which* tasks are to be performed (Wolinsky 1993). Theoretically, this bears the danger that the consultant stays longer with the client than it is wished or required, as it is only natural that the consultant, who is interested in selling his services, will be inclined to find new problems to fit the solutions he can offer (Armbrüster and Schmolze 1999). He is even more motivated to follow this course of action when—and this is often the case— he receives incentives for the acquisition of new contracts.

Interaction: The "product" of the consultancy process is created jointly by members of the consultancy and the client company. This reflects a feature commonly recognized in the literature on services: "[O]utput emerges from the coordinated efforts of both service employee and customer; it comes from a social situation that involves at least an exchange of information" (Mills and Morris 1986: 727).

The implications for evaluating the consultancy service are twofold: first, the responsibility for success or failure becomes blurred. As both consultants and clients are involved in an interaction process that frequently encompasses not only the exchange of information but also, for example, the joint definition of problems and goals in a mixed team, the outcome of this process is dependent on both the service supplier and the client. If the client wants to evaluate the consultant's performance, he encounters the problem of not being able to separate his own contribution, as the interaction creates highly complex interrelations. As a consequence, the evaluation of consultancy projects becomes a highly subjective and interpretative matter.

The second implication is contained within the word *social* of the above definition, which points to the importance of issues such as social influence, interpersonal attraction, and trust (Sharma 1997) during the consulting process. In the absence of reliable and accessible evaluation criteria, the perceived quality of the relationship often becomes a dominant factor in pre- and post-purchase evaluation (Clark 1995).

For consultants, managing client relationships thus turns into an important task. On the one hand, a good relationship with key members of the client company will enhance cooperation and acceptance, which can be considered an important prerequisite for the success of a particular project. On the other hand, a positive perception through the client opens up the possibility of repeat business and ensures a good reputation, two factors that have been identified to be of vital importance in the consultancy business (Dawes *et al.* 1992; Patterson 1995).

However, the social aspect of the interaction between consultant and client is highly problematic, as a good relationship between client and consultant does not necessarily imply that the client company actually benefits from the consultant's services. In many instances, quite the opposite may be the case. Conversely, some consultancy techniques require a confrontation with the client system in order to attain the desired goals. Client satisfaction based on positive relations cannot automatically be considered an indicator for successful consultancy.[6]

Intangibility: The notion of intangibility basically implies that consultancy services, unlike tangible products, are not receptive to assessment by the senses (Clark 1995). In other words, the service delivered by consultants, which fundamentally consists in giving advice, does not have a physical existence in itself. This makes it difficult to establish simple, obvious, and commonly shared (or at least readily communicable) criteria for judging its quality. Especially in the pre-purchase stage, there is a "total lack of perception of the service's characteristics" (Flipo 1988: 286), simply because it does not yet exist.

When a highly intangible service is performed, the predictability of its outcome is low and depends upon the personal discretion of those who are involved in the delivery (Larsson and Bowen 1989; Levitt 1981). For example, even if a particular consultancy as a whole has a good reputation, individual consultants may not live up to this standard and thus may deliver a service below the client's expectations.

Singularity: No consulting project can be reproduced in an identical manner (Clark 1995) because each combination of consultants, clients, and problems at a particular point in time is unique. From this strict point of view, the client has no possibility to compare the performance of consultants contracted by him to any other case that might deliver indications for possible evaluation criteria. Singularity also results from strong client involvement and the consultants' possibility for personal discretion, which we discussed above. The commodification of knowledge and consulting approaches, however, somewhat reduces the singularity of consulting projects. But in all cases a package product has to be customized to the client organization to some extent.

Indeterminability: Consulting, especially the kind dealing with organizational and strategic issues, which we focus on here, has an effect on a large number of variables throughout the client organization. To a certain extent, this impact cannot be controlled, mainly for two reasons.

First, external factors such as economic cycles or technological innovations influence the outcomes and evaluation criteria of consulting projects. These factors are largely beyond the consultants' or clients' control (Armenakis and Burdg 1988). Consequently, it is ambiguous whether a consultant intervention can be made responsible for changes observed in these criteria:

> Environments are unstable, and their dynamics are not well understood. Many things, not controlled by . . . actors, change simultaneously. Evidence and causal relationships are unclear. The significance of events and actions, their relevance for the future, and their implications are not well understood. (March and Olsen 1995: 202; see also March and Sutton 1997)

Second, the effects of a consultancy project are not only produced during the course of the project (temporal indeterminability) or by the interaction between clients and consultants (personal indeterminability) (Selchert 1997).

Temporal indeterminability, on the one hand, means that some consequences might only become visible long after the completion of the project. Immediately after completion, which is usually when an evaluation is carried out, the client will have difficulties in assessing whether and when the intended (or unintended) impact will show. *Personal indeterminability*, on the other hand, implies that the members of the client company directly participating in the consultancy project interact with others. This may lead to unprecedented modifications of the initially set goals and the formation of interest groups that were unaccounted for at the beginning of the project. Such dynamics make an evaluation extremely sensitive.

Effectiveness as a Concept Applied to Consultancy Work

Thus far, we have been discussing the difficulties in evaluating the consultants' work with respect to the notions of effectiveness and efficiency. Implicitly, an understanding of consulting as rational problem solving has been the basis for these considerations. This appears reasonable because an evaluation can only measure the achievement of goals that have been laid open. In the case of consulting, one could assume that these correspond closely to at least the official functions discussed above: the transfer of knowledge, legitimization, the provision of temporary management capacity, communication, and stimulation of acceptance.

At a closer look, however, the functions carried out by consultants are seldom purely official ones. *Latent functions* are perceived by managers as highly valuable; however, they cannot be admitted or included in official evaluation statements. An additional obstacle arises because the evaluation is often carried out by persons who are responsible for the consultancy project and who used the consultants for their own micro-political goals.

This leads to the conclusion that an objective evaluation of consultants' performance in terms of organizational effectiveness is not only impossible to achieve in most cases but might also not be desired. Paradoxically, effectiveness does not capture the real essence of what the high priests of rationality are doing. Consultancy as a subsystem to the economy cannot be measured in terms of economic values and goals—that is, in terms of effectiveness. This has strong implications on the demand for consulting services, whose dynamics will be explored in the following section together with the factors that we have analyzed in the previous sections.

Why Managers Increasingly Need Consulting

To achieve control over events that impinge on the realization of one's plans can be regarded as one of the strongest human motives (Adler 1929; deCharms 1968; Malinowski 1955; Nietzsche 1912; White 1959). As a consequence, the perception of a loss of control is experienced as an undesirable state of being and leads to intensive efforts to escape this situation (Thompson 1981). This should especially hold for managers, since to "have things under control" is what everybody expects from members of this species. Successes and failures of organizations are generally attributed to the managers at the top. The favorite motto of Jack Welch, the most successful manager of present times, expresses what all managers are supposed to believe: "Control your destiny or someone else will" (Tichy and Sherman 1995). However, managers' need for control is, as we have shown above, confronted with the perception of an increasingly complex and dynamic inner and outer organizational environment.

According to Thompson (1981) individuals have, in principle, four possibilities to enhance their perception of control: (1) They can identify new control options, that is, courses of action that appear suitable to restitute or increase control (behavioral control). (2) They can resort to reevaluations, that is, to cognitive strategies that reduce the stress associated with a loss of control (cognitive control). Strategies of this kind help one to ignore, deny, disassociate, or distract oneself from loss of control. (3) They can try to get hold of information that signals losses of control and thereby enables them to prepare for their occurrence (preventive control). (4) They can reduce the stress-associated events involving loss of control by finding plausible explanations retrospectively (retrospective control). Individuals usually find a loss of control that they can explain less menacing than one that is unexplainable.

Consultants can serve as facilitators for all four strategies: (1) Consultants offer managers new approaches such as reengineering, total (!) quality management, or target costing that promise to secure their control over organizational processes. Instruments such as the BCG "share-growth matrix" that most effectively simplify complex management problems create the impression that processes that hitherto appeared difficult to manage are kept under control. (2) The sheer presence of experts is often sufficient to heighten managers' perceptions of controllability. A consultant is seen as an experienced repairperson who will install powerful control instruments. Consultants also usually provide the information that the situation of the client organization is not worse or is even better than that of most competitors. They point out that the organization has specific strengths on which it can build. Thus, consultants strengthen or even restore managers' confidence. Moreover, they introduce new frames of reference and a new language that symbolically expresses the notion of control. As a manager comments: "Sometimes you need a new set of terms, a new framework—something you can get hold of" (cited after Watson 1994: 903). (3) Managers who associate with consultants are often convinced that they profit from their ability to foresee the threats of the future, as this will ensure that they will be prepared. (4) The approaches that are propagated by consultants are usually based on descriptions of typical management problems. Managers who read publications by consultants or listen to their presentations usually can easily project the problems they have identified in their organizations into the general problem scheme provided. Averse situations in the past that managers had difficulties explaining to themselves and others now make sense as a clear relation between cause and effect is established by consultants. Also, managers often learn that the problems they were facing did not represent anything unusual and need not be attributed to personal failure.

Whether managers experience their situation negatively as a threatening loss of control or positively as a need and an opportunity to act in order to secure control can be seen as depending upon the perceptions of their ability to exercise control over the environment.[7] The construct of locus of control (Rotter 1966) suggests that individuals who believe that external factors (which they cannot influence) are accountable for their successes are more likely to experience distress in situations of change, whereas internally controlled individuals attribute outcome to their actions and adopt a more positive and proactive stance. Research in organizational settings shows that an internal locus of control is associated with problem-focused coping strategies (Anderson 1977; Callan et al. 1994; Judge et al. 1999). Accordingly, it is likely that internally controlled managers resort to the behavioral and preventive strategies of control enhancement, whereas externally controlled ones will tend toward retrospective and cognitive strategies associated more with interpretation than with action. As a result, consultants will be used in very different ways by different managers.

We argue that managers' need to maintain control vis-à-vis the perception of an increasingly complex inner and outer environment, on the one

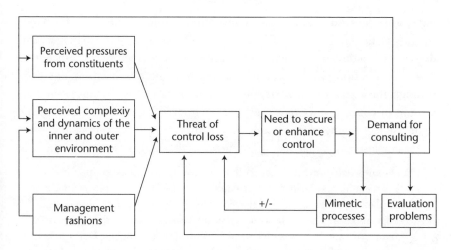

FIGURE 3.1   A model for the explanation of the consulting explosion

hand, and the consultants' reputation as experts for the reconstitution of management control, on the other, are the most important factors in explanations of the growth of the consulting market (Figure 3.1). However, this relationship alone does not suffice to explain the dynamics of the market for consulting, and its explosion, that we have sketched in the introductory section. We have to include the specific effects that consulting creates for the conditions that produce demand for consulting. In other words, we have to include feedback loops.

Let us now introduce a little thought experiment. We assume that the management of an organization has come to the conclusion that a consulting project—a reengineering project, for example—has been completed successfully. An "impact analysis" shows that key processes have significantly been speeded up, overhead costs have been reduced, and customer satisfaction has been increased. After some time, the management of this organization learns that competitors have also implemented or are about to implement reengineering with the help of consultants. Reengineering has become a common practice. *Mimetic processes*—that is, copying of practices, in our example reengineering practices—take place (DiMaggio and Powell 1991) and consultants act as brokers.[8] The observation that the organization did not succeed in out-competing its competitors with regard to market shares, profit, and growth rates is interpreted as an indication that the competitors have, also with the assistance of consultants, improved their performance roughly to the same extent. Of course, in the perception of the managers this does not at all deflate the success of the consulting project. Everybody agrees that the situation would be much worse had the organization not been through this exercise. *Mimesis*, the copying of practices, enhances the perception of control, since managers get the impression that they are "on the right track." At the same time however, they experience the feeling, with increasing insecurity, that lasting competitive advantages cannot be achieved:

> As knowledge spreads, factors that previously distinguished high performers from low performers tend to disappear; and the more powerful the explanatory mechanism is believed to be, the faster the diffusion of knowledge about it. This imitative mechanism does not require that the performance advantage or disadvantage attributed to a particular factor necessarily be 'real,' only that it be generally accepted and acted upon. (March and Sutton 1997: 699)

Of course, as we have already stated, they also lower the risk that competitors who are initiating similar projects will achieve a competitive advantage. They even can nourish the hope that they will be better at implementing the current fashion than their competitors and will thus be able to establish a competitive advantage themselves—a small one at least.

So the problem is that the perception of an enhancement of control does not last. As soon as the consultants are gone, questions come up that are bound to trigger insecurity: Has the project led to a lasting improvement vis-à-vis competitors, the majority of which have implemented similar projects? A proper evaluation of the project is, as we have seen, not possible. The perception of increased control did not last because the wave of projects along the current fashion is likely to have intensified competition with regard to criteria that had been in the center of this fashion. Most competitors have, for example, improved quality, reduced personnel costs, speeded up processes, or increased customer orientation. What now? In this situation, receptivity toward a new management fashion tends to increase again. It will be launched by consultancies, and for those managers who needed consultants to come to grips with the last fashion it is pretty obvious that they will need consultants again in order to implement it. They have gained the impression that consultants are necessary to keep up with competitors that increasingly engage consultants. They have become dependent on consultants.

The situation the managers have maneuvered themselves into is comparable to that of a driver in stock car races who learns about a garage that does a terrific tuning job. She buys this service and gets the impression that her car really has improved after this treatment. She is convinced that she goes into the next race with a big advantage. But then she gets the information that her competitors also had a tuning job done by the same or some other garage. Her good feeling disappears. In the race, a higher average speed was reached than in the races before, but the distances between the finishers were as close as always. All drivers are now convinced that tuning by real experts is indispensable. It is also clear for them that tuning will become increasingly sophisticated and, hence, increasingly expensive. Their insecurity about their chances for future races has increased because tuning that they cannot really control has become such an important factor for competitiveness. New techniques of tuning then come on the market and new tuning companies. . . .

This is more or less the situation the managers are in. They get the impression that they are becoming increasingly dependent on consultancies, even though, or just because, they evaluate past consulting projects as successful. However, there is an important difference between the tuning of cars and consulting: the effects of car tuning are much easier to measure than the performance increases that are due to a consulting project. These evaluation problems tend to increase the insecurity of managers as compared to that of racing drivers after having tuning jobs done to their cars. The feedback loops lead back into the system, creating ever more dependence. Consulting is addictive.[9]

The implicit assumption of our examples is, of course, that managers and drivers are equally incapable of extracting the knowledge from their respective experts. In the case of management this assumption appears realistic with regard to the dynamics of management fashions. Managers may succeed in learning from their consultants how to run a reengineering project or how to implement and handle target costing. However, when consultants pull a new management concept out of their magic box, many managers are flabbergasted again. It takes some time for a management fashion to become common knowledge.

That means that consultants can rely upon their clients' becoming increasingly dependent on them. This in turn means that managers are demanding consulting services at increasing rates. Consultancies only have to come up with new approaches from time to time that promise quantum leaps in performance. Consultancies fulfill this requirement by continuously inventing new management fashions and selling them with remarkable rhetorical skill (Abrahamson 1996; Kieser 1997). Managers have extreme difficulties finding out—in advance as well as in retrospect—to what extent new approaches really live up to their promises. As we have shown, subscribing to the latest fashion seems less risky for many managers than holding onto the old practices, especially if they have acted as fashion followers in the past and have always come to the conclusion that the situation would be worse without the help of consultancies.

Consultants also increase demand for their services, as we also have shown above, by positioning themselves in the eyes of the public as legitimators and auditors—to be more precise: as legitimators and auditors with a connected repair shop. Another phenomenon that can be observed is that after a management function has been downsized or outsourced (frequently following the advice of consultants), consultants offer to step in if the available management capacity is perceived as insufficient to handle the workload (Caulkin 1997).

Consultants also try to build up personal links with managers of their client organization. They establish personal relationships of mutual protection (Sturdy 1997a). As we have discussed, they usually foster the careers of managers who sponsor them. Since the quality of consulting is difficult to assess, a high level of trust is required on both sides. The more consulting projects prove beneficial for certain consultants and their sponsors, the more trust builds up and the more the relationship evolves into an open-ended affair. "Over the long term, service KIFs [knowledge intensive firms, to which consultancies belong] try to convert clients' satisfaction with specific projects into long-term relations" (Starbuck 1992: 732). Most consulting projects are follow-up projects (see, for example, BDU 1996). Consultants not only teach their clients how to practice customer retention management, they also apply this knowledge to their own customers.

Conclusion

Consultants sell a remedy for a situation that they have in part caused themselves—this becomes clear from the dynamics of differentiation in general and in the consulting industry in particular. Our model also points out that perceptions—of the environment's complexity and dynamics, different kinds of pressures, insecurity—play a central role in the demand for consultancy services. This should have implications for how consultants are dealt with by managers. If one can acknowledge that the need for consultants is to some degree caused by constructions instead of objective requirements, it should be possible to take a more critical stance toward the final decision of whether consultants are called in for help. An awareness of how these perceptions come into being may be a clue in assessing the potential benefits of a particular consultancy project in general terms.

For managers, it might also be helpful to give up the desire of achieving total control and to accept that unresolved issues, dilemmas, and paradoxes will always remain when managing an organization. As we have seen, consultants are able to offer temporary relief, but they cannot eliminate the underlying problem of lacking total control. We are not denying that the use of consultants can be highly beneficial in certain situations; however, the dynamics of demand can quickly turn into a vicious circle of addiction when the feedback loops we have discussed are not interrupted or at least weakened.

We have tried to explain the consulting explosion by generating assumptions on the basis of a number of theoretical frameworks as well as descriptive findings about the consultancy industry. It was our aim to create a basic model that opens up a new understanding on the growing demand for consultants by integrating various perspectives in a dynamic way. As we have worked in a deductive manner, it is clear that the proposed framework can only be considered a possible (and, we hope, plausible) explanation that does not claim validity or completeness. These limitations can only be overcome through the provision of empirical evidence, which despite a growing scientific interest in consulting-related issues is still scarce. Accordingly, empirical analyses should be high on the agenda of researchers focusing on management consultancy in order to substantiate and redefine the large number of highly interesting theoretical propositions that have been made by different contributors to date.

4   At the Interstices of Organizations:
     The Expansion of the Management
     Consulting Profession, 1933 – 1997
     Martin Ruef, Stanford University, California, United States

Introduction

Over the past two decades, a growing literature in organization theory has come to recognize the role performed by professionals (and professional associations) in promoting the interorganizational diffusion of practices, innovations, and fads (DiMaggio and Powell 1983; Baron, Dobbin, and
Jennings 1986; DiMaggio 1991; Galaskiewicz and Burt 1991; Ruef and Scott
1998). With some notable exceptions (for example, Suchman 1994), much
less analytic attention has been paid to the emergence and expansion of new
categories of professionals that operate at the interstices of formal organizations, acting specifically to promote flows of routines and norms. Insofar
as professionals have generally become "the great rationalizers of the second
half of the twentieth century" (DiMaggio and Powell 1983: 147), those
interorganizational actors dedicated to the spread of legal-rational principles
among modern organizations—consultants, advisors, policy experts—are of
special importance. The present chapter focuses on the historical expansion
of management consultants, a category of professionals that has slowly
become institutionalized since the early part of the twentieth century and
now exercises an increasingly pervasive influence on the behavior of formal
organizations (Hagedorn 1955; O'Shea and Madigan 1997).

The status of management consulting as a profession can be debated
on substantive grounds (For example, to what extent are consultants simi-

lar to physicians or lawyers?) and theoretical grounds (What constitutes the definition of a profession and why do consultants match this definition?) (see Abbott, 1988). A broad delineation of the term is employed here, based primarily on historical attempts by consultants to draw analogies with the traditional professions (*Fortune*, 1944), develop principles of ethical conduct (Shay, 1966), and build a cognitive base of abstract knowledge. Two characteristics distinguish management consultants from other professionals engaged in the interorganizational diffusion of practices and make them especially relevant for analysis. First, consultants are often charged with the responsibility of instituting dramatic change—either proactive or reactive—in the organizations that they serve (Hagedorn 1955: 165; Moore 1984: chapter 1). By applying legal-rational norms to a process traditionally thought to be the domain of entrepreneurs and "intrapreneurs" (firm-internal change agents), management consultants have attempted to routinize one dynamic often exempted from Weber's iron cage—organizational innovation. This feature differentiates management consultants from corporate accounting and legal professionals, who are typically less interested in introducing innovations in organizations and more interested in ensuring conformity to extant legal and normative frameworks. A second characteristic that distinguishes management consultants is their frequent emphasis on sociocultural rather than material innovations to be adopted by client organizations. Gathering inspiration from early consultants such as Elton Mayo (1945), a pioneering figure in the human relations school, American management consulting practice places heavy emphasis on the social, economic, and political context within which high-level managerial decisions are made.[1]

Given the ostensibly entrepreneurial character of the management consulting enterprise and its emphasis on sociocultural rather than product or service innovation, the profession can be seen as a principal carrier of so-called "paper entrepreneurialism." The term was coined by former U.S. Labor Secretary Robert Reich, who noted that paper entrepreneurialism "employs the mechanisms and symbols developed to direct and monitor high-volume production, but . . . involves an even more radical separation between planning and production" (Reich 1983: 141). Paper entrepreneurialism is associated with a broad social movement in modern business practice away from manufacturing, sales, or marketing views of organizations to more abstract conceptions of organizational control (Fligstein 1990). The growth of management consulting, now estimated to be close to a $62 billion industry worldwide (Kennedy Research Group 1999), is indicative of this historical decoupling between managerial attention to "rationalizing myths" and technical attention to production activities (Meyer and Rowan 1977).

To explore the development of management consulting, this study proceeds in stages that address the emergence and expansion of the profession, respectively. First, the emergence of a management consulting profession in the United States is considered via a qualitative, historical lens that extends back to the turn of the century. This discussion proceeds at a societal level of analysis. Next, theoretical arguments are developed to explain two social processes that have operated to expand management consulting and legitimate it as a career path: (1) role differentiation from engineering, accounting, and finance functions (accompanied by role integration around a multifunctional core of management expertise) and (2) the institutionalization of "externalized" management among formal organizations. Applying event history techniques, I analyze the career histories of a large sample of MBAs graduating between 1933 and 1997 to consider how these two factors have encouraged individual-level entries into management consulting.

The Emergence of Management Consulting

Although other precursors can be found, many academic and nonacademic accounts trace management consulting back to the scientific management movement of the early 1900s (Moore 1984; Kipping 1999a; see McKenna 1995 for a critique). According to the canonical history, pioneering industry consultants such as Frederick Taylor, Henry Gantt, Harrington Emerson, and Frank and Lillian Gilbreth led the way, endorsing time-motion studies and an ethos of rationalized management, largely within manufacturing contexts. Like organization theory itself, management consulting can thus be seen to have its roots in turn-of-the-century engineering ideology (Shenhav 1995; Scott 1998: 38–40). This movement yielded one major occupational forerunner of the modern management consultant—the so-called "consulting management engineer." The professional recognition of this occupation was both advanced and transformed in 1929, when the Association for Consulting Management Engineers (ACME) was created to oversee the accreditation of consulting organizations (Washburn 1996: 50). Later renamed the Association of Management Consulting Firms, the ACME issued influential standards on professional ethics for management consultants (Shay 1966), consultant qualifications (Association of Consulting Management Engineers 1959), and practice guidelines (Association of Consulting Management Engineers 1954–55).

Aside from industrial engineering, prominent forerunners of modern management consulting can also be found in accountancy. In the United States, the professionalization of accountancy was given a considerable boost in 1913, when the sixteenth amendment to the U.S. Constitution instituted the corporate income tax (Previts and Merino 1979: 135–136). During the following decade, one by-product of the sizable data collection mechanism created by the tax was that accountants began to move into the arena of management services (Washburn 1996; Previts and Merino 1979). Consultation on corporate budgeting and implementation of standard cost systems was added to the accountant's previous portfolio of tax and audit services. This close alignment between management consulting and accountancy is evidenced to this day in the management advisory service wings actively maintained by many of the largest accounting firms.

Although management consultants were plentiful in the first three decades of the twentieth century (Chandler 1977: 468), the profession itself was not clearly differentiated from accountancy or engineering (nor, for that matter, from commercial banking and finance). However, several processes were operating to change this lack of differentiation. In representing themselves to clients, consulting practitioners were increasingly forced to acknowledge their hybrid work identities, that is, their reliance on combinations of skills and routines not readily captured by traditional disciplinary boundaries. The boundary between engineering and accounting became especially fluid, with the result that consulting firms such as McKinsey and Company began to put "accountants and engineers" on their corporate letterheads in the late 1920s (McKenna 1995). Another process operating to support the differentiation of management consulting was the expansion of general management education between the 1880s and 1920s. As business schools were founded at a number of elite U.S. institutions—the University of Pennsylvania (in 1881), Dartmouth (1900), Harvard (1908), and Stanford (1925)—a labor force of young professionals emerged with interdisciplinary skills that generalized across previously separated business domains. Not necessarily accountants or engineers, these professionals would later become desirable recruits with the expansion of management consulting firms in the post–World War II era.

As sociologists have observed, the process of professionalization tends to extend through a number of stages—the creation of professional associations; the renaming of a profession; the development of training schools, university programs, and licensing procedures (Caplow 1954; Wilensky 1964)—though the sequencing of these stages may deviate considerably from a universal pattern and proceed at multiple levels of analysis (Abbott 1988, 1991). A number of these stages of professionalization can be identified for management consultants between the late nineteenth century and the beginning of the Great Depression. Nevertheless, informed historical accounts date the emergence of a truly distinctive management consulting profession in the United States quite precisely to events in the early 1930s (McKenna 1995). In 1931, James O. McKinsey—the professor of accounting who had founded McKinsey and Company just a few years earlier—developed the general management audit, a procedural template that allowed inexperienced management consultants to conduct analyses of client firms (Neukom 1975; Washburn 1996). Up to this point, relatively seasoned professionals with backgrounds in accounting, engineering, management, or banking had dominated the consulting enterprise. Entry-level positions were virtually nonexistent. McKinsey's tool promised an avenue for young college-trained professionals to become management consultants. As a result, management consulting came into its own as a viable professional career path, no longer just a source of income for experts in other fields.[2]

Regulatory changes in the United States operated as the other catalyst that supported a professional jurisdiction for management consultants. In 1933, the passage of the Glass-Steagall Act prohibited commercial banks from engaging in a variety of nonbanking activities, including management consulting (McKenna 1995; Rose 1987).[3] Commercial banks had previously served as an important source of advice and organizational analysis for a large number of firms. Not only did these firms now have to turn elsewhere for counsel but the commercial banks themselves were also obligated by Securities and Exchange Commission (SEC) regulations (beginning in 1934) to employ outside consultants to monitor new publicly traded firms and organizations undergoing bankruptcy proceedings. These regulatory events opened a sizable market niche for independent management consulting firms. Between 1930 and 1940, the organizational population grew from an estimated 100 to an estimated 400 firms in the United States (Association of Consulting Management Engineers 1964). In conjunction with McKinsey's general management audit, the tremendous demand sparked the beginnings of management consulting as a distinctive professional career path.

The Expansion of Management Consulting

By the mid-1930s, some observers could already identify management consulting as a specialized business profession. Its occupational expansion as a significant component of modern business enterprise, though, had only just begun. In 1938, the economist Joel Dean pointed out that, "almost unnoticed, professional management counsel has become an important institution in our business world" (Dean 1938: 451 [as quoted in McKenna 1995]). Half a century later, management consulting could hardly be called "unnoticed." An estimated $25 billion was being spent on management consulting services in the United States alone (O'Shea and Madigan 1997: 10), making the sector larger in revenue terms than television and radio broadcasting or such industrial-age powerhouses as railroad transportation. Some public policy analysts noted with alarm that management consulting—"where the specialty is rearranging assets and shuffling corporate boxes" (Reich 1983: 159)—was among the most sought-after careers for business school graduates. Whereas the proportion of business school graduates entering consulting had only been a trickle in the 1930s and 1940s, a number of elite business schools reported that 20 to 40 percent of their MBA graduates were taking first jobs in management consulting by the 1990s (Zich 1996; David 1999).

What factors have encouraged the tremendous expansion of the U.S. management consulting profession over the past sixty years? Previous research by business historians often relies on structural-functional explanations, pointing out that the growth of the profession has paralleled the decentralization, diversification, and globalization of modern organizations (David 1999). Theoretical versions of this argument point to the tendency of social systems to become functionally differentiated over time, contributing to escalating internal and environmental complexity and feeding the psychological need to reduce uncertainty (Ernst and Kieser, this volume). The expansion of management consulting can thus be tied to the growing complexity of administrative structures in the for-profit, nonprofit, and public sectors.

Such structural-functional considerations tend, however, to ignore the contentious early history of management consulting. As noted above, a large number of professionals—for example, engineers and accountants—provided counsel to complex organizations during the early twentieth century. First, why did a new profession of management consultants emerge and expand in lieu of alternative sources of advice? Or to place the issue within a competitive framework (see Abbott 1988), how were management consultants able to defend a professional jurisdiction given the system of other professions that were already active in this arena? Moreover, why did formal organizations rely increasingly on *external* management counsel? After all, the demands of greater structural complexity could be met, in theory, by growing the managerial ranks and administrative apparatus *within* formal organizations.

Role Differentiation and Integration

A preliminary answer to the first question is provided by the "imprinting" conditions involved in the emergence of management consulting. The hybridization of various roles (engineering, accounting, banking) offered an initial impetus to differentiate management consulting from well-categorized disciplines. By the late 1920s, role strings such as accountant-engineer were already becoming increasingly common. The events of the 1930s provided further opportunity for role differentiation. New tools such as McKinsey's general audit encouraged the packaging of management advice in a manner that separated it from traditional disciplines, while the Glass-Steagall Act placed regulative prohibitions on the involvement of some older occupations (commercial bankers) in consulting practice.

One can suggest that the successful expansion of management consulting required a final—and more radical—stage of role differentiation, involving the career structure of management consultants and their pattern of recruitment into consulting firms. Specifically, the argument holds that many business professionals with primary functional expertise in accounting, engineering, and finance were actually *discouraged* from entering management consulting in the decades following World War II, especially when compared to those professionals with multifunctional expertise (involving various aspects of marketing, strategy, human resources, finance, and so forth). This process of role differentiation was catalyzed by the shifting conception of management consulting in the 1930s, when "the United States had seen the emergence of a new kind of consulting company, no longer interested in efficiency improvements on the shop floor or in offices, but focusing on wider organizational and strategic issues" (Kipping 1999a: 207). The redefined nature of management counsel eschewed both the engineering contributions of Taylorism and the bookkeeping contributions of traditional audits, which were seen as excessively myopic. An emerging emphasis on package solutions (see Ernst and Kieser, this volume) called for counsel that addressed the entire enterprise. In the process, a new breed of management consultants was able to defend its jurisdiction from interlopers and integrate its professional role around a purview of multifunctional expertise.

From the standpoint of a sociology of the professions, the argument that management consultants were able to make their jurisdictional claims through the redefinition of management knowledge is itself significant. Lacking recourse to the conventional structural mechanisms used to secure professional closure (for example, licensure, associations), management consultants could only rely on cognitive strategies to effect what Abbott (1988: 98–102) has referred to as a "jurisdictional shift." In part, the purely cognitive—as opposed to structural—foundation of jurisdictional claims in consulting practice can be seen as driving the waves of management fads and fashions in this arena (see Barley and Kunda 1992).

Externalized Management

The second dynamic supporting the growth of management consulting—*externalized management*—refers to a fundamental transformation of corporate governance. During the twentieth century, conceptions of corporate control increasingly favored the separation of technical production and marketing from management tasks, as evidenced in the changing backgrounds of chief executive officers (moving from manufacturing and sales to finance) and the product and service diversification of large firms (Fligstein 1987, 1990). As management was removed from the technical particularities of various divisions and departments under its purview, there was a tendency to outsource managerial responsibilities to external consultants. Consistent with arguments in transaction cost economics (see Williamson 1981), the declining asset specificity of human capital in management favored corporate governance structures that contracted with outside management consultants rather than those that maintained large in-house staffs.

The institutionalization of externalized management can be traced to two underlying dimensions: (1) the cognitive abstraction of administrative

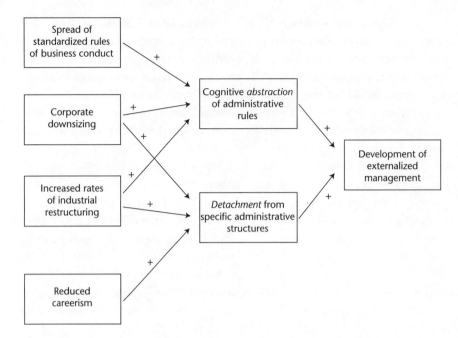

FIGURE 4.1   Processes affecting the development of an externalized managerial workforce

rules and (2) the detachment of managers from specific administrative structures. Both dimensions have been affected by a number of historical processes
(see Figure 4.1).

Standardized Rules of Organizational Conduct. The spread of standardized
rules of organizational conduct is evident in numerous developments, including the diffusion of total quality management (TQM) principles (see Walgenbach and Beck, this volume), the adoption of industry-wide managerial
guidelines (Ruef and Scott 1998), and the efforts of professional management
schools to package standardized scripts for their graduates. All these developments have fed into a process of "theorization," in which management
techniques are lifted from specific organizational contexts and are made to
generalize across them (Strang and Meyer 1994). This process of cognitive
abstraction, in turn, encourages the development of a cadre of managers that
are not wed to specific formal organizations.

The impact of standardized organizational rules can perhaps be witnessed most tangibly in the spread of governmental regulations. As early as

the 1940s, commentators in the United States suggested that the increasing scope of state regulation was stimulating a need for management counsel— "with more and more government regulations, [the business manager] became willing and even eager to ask questions and listen to answers" (*Fortune* 1944: 142). Whereas legislative efforts at the federal level produced 26 major regulatory statutes in the 1950s and 53 in the 1960s, the banner decade of the 1970s saw the passage of over 130 major regulatory statutes affecting business enterprise (Chilton 1984: table 6-1). The implementation of legislation such as the Occupational Safety and Health Act (1970) and the Equal Employment Opportunity Act (1972) confronted formal organizations with a host of new regulative prescriptions and proscriptions to which to conform. Outside consultants were often called in to advise top management on the reorganization of work practices and structures to accommodate these "rationalized myths." According to accounts stressing the impact of this regulative transition, the growth of U.S. management consulting was affected significantly by the new boundary-spanning requirements imposed by federal rule systems.

Corporate Downsizing. A second factor affecting the development of externalized management involves corporate governance. As trends toward investor capitalism have combined with decentralization, U.S. corporations have sought to reduce the size of their managerial workforce (see Useem 1996). The resulting corporate downsizing has produced an important supply-side (push) factor that expands the potential pool of management consultants. The new system of corporate governance leads to layoffs of experienced middle- and top-level managers, who often seek subsequent employment in management consulting firms (Henkoff 1993).

Corporate downsizing may also affect the work motivation of managers in two important ways. First, it can reduce their normative commitment to specific formal organizations, which become seen as fickle or fallible, unable to sustain traditional employment contracts. And second, it may encourage managers not to rely on organization-specific knowledge but instead to develop more abstract expertise and routines that are common to a large set of organizations. Both dimensions support the development of externalized management.

Industrial Restructuring. Other conditions affecting the externalization of management can be derived from the structure of labor mobility among organizational fields and industries. As noted previously, the growth of management consulting has been undergirded by an increasing separation of technical and managerial functions. Before this separation can proceed from tight to loose coupling (and from loose to decoupling), the rational abstraction of rules governing management must also have proceeded to a point where these rules no longer depend on the technical particulars of any given industry. In other words, the managerial principles must become *industry generic*. This cognitive orientation has, of course, been motivated by the development of modern administrative science itself, which—insofar as it seeks to develop universal rules of administration—serves as a crucial handmaiden to the legitimacy of management consulting (Moore 1984: chapter 1). With the aid of administrative science and transposable tools such as McKinsey's general management audit, consultants can claim expertise in the strategy, finance, human resource, and marketing routines of a client firm without knowing many of the details of the organization or the industry within which it is located.[4]

At the individual level, this cognitive capacity for abstraction is likely to develop when business professionals have limited enculturation within the context of particular industries. Reductions in industry tenure have been encouraged by the substantial job mobility of business professionals during the 1970s and 1980s, part of a larger industrial restructuring in the United States "propelled by unequal rates of technological advance across industries, by changing patterns of demand, and by an emerging global economy" (DiPrete 1993: 74). As industry tenure and enculturation decline, business professionals will become likely to abandon industry-specific managerial principles in favor of the more abstract generalizations advocated by management consulting practice.

Reduced Careerism. A final factor affecting the externalization of management can be traced to the culture of business professionals themselves. In the classic Weberian account of bureaucracy, managers are characterized as having a motivational commitment to clearly defined career ladders and rules of promotion (see Weber 1968). A recent study of work values by Robert Wuthnow questions this simple characterization. As Wuthnow (1996: 18) notes, "having moved securely into the professional-managerial class, [Americans] want more than simply an above-average standard of living. Working harder just to climb the corporate ladder and acquire more economic resources no longer seems as appealing as it once did." Quantitative evidence supports this trend: longitudinal survey results from alumni of one large MBA program indicate that a rising number of business professionals are leaving old jobs for lifestyle reasons—21.6 percent in 1995 as opposed to 12.2 percent in 1970 and only 4.5 percent in 1950 (Ruef 1999).

The relative increase in the salience of lifestyle compared to career motivations among business professionals has implications for the expansion of management consulting practice. On the demand side, firms feel compelled to hire human resource consultants in order to structure nonmaterial incentives among their managerial ranks and whitewash employee morale problems (see Machan 1988). Following the early human relations work of Mayo and Frederick Herzberg, this emphasis on motivating managers has assumed a key role in modern management consulting. On the supply side, increasing numbers of management experts are likely to abandon staid careers within large internal labor markets (ILMs) for the more flexible lifestyle offered by management consulting. In this respect, a reduced emphasis on career advancement also feeds into the detachment of managers from specific administrative structures.

Data and Methodology

In order to flesh out these historical dynamics, the following event history analyses examine the influence of role differentiation and managerial externalization on individual entries into the management consulting profession. All living alumni from a large graduate business school in the western United States were surveyed to obtain full career histories. Survey questions requested information on industry and organizational transitions, demographic characteristics, job roles and responsibilities, and motivational characteristics of respondents (job satisfaction and, when applicable, reasons for leaving a job).

The population frame included 12,069 targeted alumni. A response rate of almost 41.7 percent yielded usable surveys for 5,028 business professionals and 102,134 split job spells (that is, spells having any possible change in covariates) during the period from 1931 to 1997. For purposes of analysis, the starting year was fixed at 1933, reflecting the fact that prior to that year, the professionalization of management consulting had not proceeded to the point where new business graduates were really "at risk" of occupational entry (see section, "The Emergence of Management Consulting"). After removing foreign alumni and career spells prior to 1933, a dataset of 4,504 professionals and 93,530 split job spells was available for analysis.[5]

Dependent Measure

I conceptualized the dependent measure as the rate of entry into management consulting on the part of business professionals with MBA degrees. In order to qualify as a valid career path, consulting must be seen as a primary work activity by the respondents. Professionals are considered to be at risk of entry as soon as they graduate from business school; pre–business school employment or internships between the first and second year of business school are not considered. Professionals are removed from the risk set during the time that they are employed as management consultants but may otherwise reenter the field, given prior employment in some other industry. Entry into management consulting is thus considered to be a repeatable career event.

Between 1933 and 1997, some 1,345 entries into management consulting were reported for the survey sample. Plotting the resulting proportion of MBA alumni involved in consulting positions over time, one can note a steady secular rise since the mid-1940s (see Figure 4.2). In 1945, a mere 2 percent of the surveyed respondents were employed as management consultants; by 1995, this proportion had increased more than six-fold to around 13 percent of the surveyed business professionals. When the first jobs of MBA cohort members are considered as they leave school, these historical differences are even more dramatic. During the 1950s, only 1.6 percent of the respondents entered management consulting as their first job out of school; during the 1990s, that proportion had risen to a substantial 22.3 percent of respondents. Consulting had become the most popular field of entry for these newly minted MBAs, beating out other expanding areas such as investment banking and high-tech management.

The growth of MBA job placements in management consulting from this particular business program is all the more surprising when one considers that it is likely to *underestimate* the number of consultants with advanced degrees as a whole. Over the historical period being analyzed, the number of MBA programs and degrees conferred in the United States has swelled. Dur-

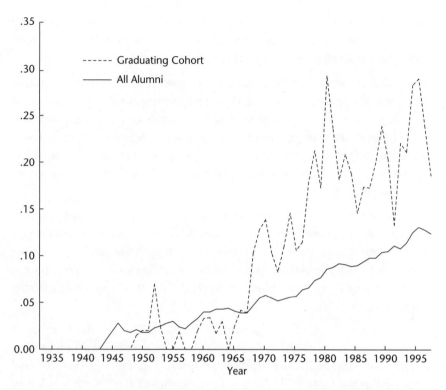

FIGURE **4.2**   **Proportion of sampled business school graduates employed as management consultants, 1933–1997**

ing the mid-1960s, some 36,000 prospective business students took admission tests for MBA programs; by the 1990s, that number had risen nine-fold (Shelley 1997). In conjunction with the growing representation of MBA graduates in consulting, these figures suggest that the number of consultants with professional business degrees may have increased by as much as a factor of thirty between the 1960s and the 1990s.[6]

Independent and Control Measures

Independent measures of theoretical interest derive from the previous discussion of influences on the expansion of the management consulting profession. Two main clusters of variables will be addressed: those linked to the role differentiation and integration of management consulting and those linked to the development of externalized management.

Role Differentiation: Respondents were asked to identify the primary functional focus during each of their employment spells, with functions including engineering and operations, accounting, and finance. Insofar as radical role differentiation has occurred, those business professionals listing one of these three functions as an area of primary expertise are expected to have lower rates of entry into management consulting than those not listing one of the three functions.

Role Integration: The integration of the management consulting role around a multifunctional focus is operationalized in the same manner as role differentiation. Specifically, those respondents reporting that their job focus could not be classified into a single functional category are expected to have higher rates of entry into management consulting than those emphasizing individual functions.

Standardized Rules of Organizational Conduct: The standardization of administrative rule systems was conceptualized as an environmental characteristic affecting individual career histories. Federal regulations were employed as the most visible proxy of standardized rules, with regulatory acts being considered in three statutory areas: Title 15 (Commerce and Trade), Title 29 (Labor and Employment Law), and Title 11 (Bankruptcy). The U.S. Federal Code of Regulations (U.S. Superintendent of Documents 1940–1997) was consulted for statutory listings. An index of regulatory intensity was calculated as a two-year moving average, including statutes passed each year and in the previous calendar year.

Corporate Downsizing: The effect of corporate downsizing was assessed at the individual level by considering patterns of involuntary termination within managerial career histories. Respondents reporting a loss of a previous position due to involuntary separation or company acquisition are expected to be at greater risk of entry into management consulting.

Industrial Restructuring: The rate of entry into management consulting is expected to decrease as business professionals become enculturated in the practices of a particular industry. At the individual level, the enculturation process is operationalized in terms of years of industry tenure. Industry experience is considered separately from the overall labor force experience of respondents, as well as job tenure.

Careerism: Business professionals who are motivated by their devotion to a particular career ladder or ILM are expected to have lower rates of entry into management consulting than those who dismiss such motivations. Survey respondents were asked to give three reasons that they left each job in their career history. Those reporting that they left for the sake of career advancement were coded as exercising this type of motivation.

Control Variables: The analyses control for demographics, years of labor force participation, span of responsibility, and job roles. Demographic variables distinguish male and female business professionals, as well as whites and minorities. The span of responsibility is measured in terms of the number of subordinates reporting to a respondent.[7] Job roles are assigned to three generic categories: technical roles (for example, functional or technical specialist), managerial roles (general, business unit, or functional manager), and owner roles (equity stakeholders or founders).[8]

Cases with missing values on any of the independent and control variables were removed by listwise deletion. This reduced the total number of entries into management consulting to 1,189 events and the total number of split spells to 81,378.

Statistical Methodology

I used an event history strategy to analyze career transitions into management consulting. Exploratory analyses revealed a decrease in job transition rates with the time spent by an individual in a given formal position. The following Gompertz model was employed to capture this effect of job tenure:

$$r(t) = \exp(B'X)\exp(Ct)$$

where r(t) is the transition rate into consulting, t indexes the job tenure clock, X is the matrix of independent variables, B is the vector of coefficients indicating the effects of the variables in X, and C is a constant term indicating the rate at which transitions into management consulting decrease with job tenure.

Because simple estimates of the career transition model may conflate the rate with which respondents tend to change jobs in general and the rate with which respondents have moved into management consulting, all hypotheses were tested using Wald statistics that evaluate whether significant coefficient differences exist between transitions into consulting and other kinds of job changes. For this purpose, a job change is defined as (1) moving to a new position in a different organization, (2) moving to a new position in a different subunit of one's current organization, or (3) moving to a new position in the same subunit of one's current organization but with a major change in work scope or content. Wald test statistics were generated based on a *competing risks* formulation (Blossfeld and Rohwer 1995) that considers management consulting and other job trajectories to be alternative career outcomes.

Results

To separate the effects of role differentiation and managerial externalization, event history estimates were obtained for two nested models: one excluding the cluster of variables capturing role dynamics and one including that cluster. I used Rohwer's (1999) Transition Data Analysis (TDA) program to estimate all of the event history models.

The first specification (Table 4.1, Model 1) shows a very substantial improvement in model fit over a null model that excludes variables linked to managerial externalization (likelihood ratio $\chi^2 = 297.88$, $\Delta df = 8$, p < .001).[9] The variable associated with increased federal regulation is positive and significant, as expected, suggesting that standardized regulative rules have sparked entries into management consulting by imposing new boundary-spanning responsibilities on administrators. The finding is supported by a Wald test statistic, which indicates that business regulations have had a markedly greater effect on rates of entry into consulting than into other business careers.

Involuntary separation is a motivational influence associated with the trend of corporate downsizing. We find that rates of entry into consulting increase significantly for managers who have lost their former positions due to involuntary termination or corporate acquisition (with a transition rate multiplier of $e^{0.207}$ or 1.23). Nevertheless, these entry rates are not affected to a greater extent than those leading to alternative career paths (the Wald test is insignificant). As a result, we must conclude that the effect of corporate downsizing on career entries into consulting is generally indirect—it operates

TABLE **4.1**   Influences on Career Entries into Management Consulting, 1933–1997

Variable	Model 1	Wald Tests	Model 2	Wald Tests
B Vector constant	− 2.613 (0.107) **	—	− 2.687 (0.112) **	—
C Vector constant	− 0.574 (0.027) **	—	− 0.565 (0.027) **	—
Demographics				
Gender (1=female)	0.494 (0.071) **	(+) 35.975 **	0.481 (0.072) **	(+) 31.948 **
Ethnicity (1=minority)	0.312 (0.089) **	(+) 7.869 **	0.352 (0.089) **	(+) 10.191 **
General Experience				
Years in labor force	−0.014 (0.005) **	(ns) 0.058	−0.016 (0.005) **	(ns) 0.376
Span of responsibility	−0.002 (0.003)	(ns) 0.030	−0.007 (0.004)	(ns) 1.200
Technical role	0.175 (0.077) *	(ns) 3.478	0.271 (0.077) **	(+)9.808 **
Managerial role	0.017 (0.077)	(ns) 1.333	−0.005 (0.077)	(ns) 0.850
Owner role	−0.275 (0.109) *	(ns) 0.662	−0.391 (0.111) **	(ns) 3.777
Specialized Experience				
Industry tenure	−0.056 (0.009) **	(−) 79.640 **	−0.053 (0.009) **	(−) 75.315 **
Motivational Influences				
Involuntary separation	0.207 (0.082) *	(ns) 1.942	0.225 (0.082) **	(ns) 2.498
Careerism	−0.367 (0.063) **	(−) 32.521 **	−0.346 (0.063) **	(−) 29.307 **
Regulative Influences				
Business regulation	0.042 (0.015) **	(+) 12.310 **	0.048 (0.015) **	(+) 14.447 **
Role Differentiation				
vs. Accounting	—	—	−0.346 (0.141) *	(−)7.034 **
vs. Banking and finance	—	—	−0.457 (0.093) **	(−) 20.951 **
vs. Engineering	—	—	0.111 (0.091)	(ns) 0.001
Role Integration				
Multifunctional focus	—	—	0.431 (0.075) **	(+) 34.721 **
Number of events	1189		1189	
Log likelihood (d.f.)	−29545.01 (26)		−29488.91 (34)	

* $p < .05$; ** $p < .01$ (two-tailed tests). $N = 81,378$ split spells.

by churning the labor pool of available business professionals while exercising no direct influence on managerial externalization.

Business professionals that embark on consulting careers do display motivations that depart in one important way from other job hoppers: they are less inclined to embrace careerism. In particular, respondents who report that they are leaving their old jobs for reasons of career advancement are only 0.69 times as likely to enter management consulting as those who do not report this reason (Wald test significant at the $p < .01$ level). Given the sometimes ad hoc character of consultant job ladders (at least, outside of the largest consulting firms), this motivational orientation is consistent with the typical cultural demands of externalized managerial hierarchies.

The duration of tenure in any given industry also tends to reduce the likelihood of moving into management consulting, as business professionals become enculturated within a system of specialized administrative rules and beliefs. By contrast, business professionals who avoid extended industry tenures may be able to reflect more abstractly on the rules associated with different organizational fields. Thus, respondents with five years of industry tenure have an estimated rate of entry into consulting that is more than double that of their counterparts with twenty years of industry tenure.

The effects of several control variables are worth noting in Model 1. First, the second constant (C) of the model indicates negative duration dependence over job tenure. In other words, the longer respondents remain in a given job position, the less likely they are to change to another job (this holds for management consulting as well as other career paths). Second, both women and minorities are significantly more likely to enter management consulting than their white male counterparts. Given that female and minority managers have historically faced "glass ceiling" effects in seeking promotion within large internal labor markets, they may hope for greater professional advancement by developing their careers in consulting practices that operate within an institutional framework of externalized management.

Model 2 adds the effects of role dynamics to the specification, improving model fit in the process (likelihood ratio $\chi^2 = 112.20$, $\Delta df = 8$, $p < .001$). In general, the results reflect considerable role differentiation between management consulting and traditional consulting professions. For instance, respondents with a primary functional expertise in banking or finance are only 0.63 times as likely to subsequently become management consultants as respondents lacking such expertise. To some extent, this effect may reflect the long-standing influence of the anticonsulting legislation leveled at commercial banks during the 1930s. For specialists in accounting, the equivalent rate multiplier is 0.71. Business professionals with engineering or operations research backgrounds show slightly less role differentiation. These respondents do not have a significantly greater or lower rate of entry into consulting than business professionals without a functional focus in engineering.

Role integration for management consultants clearly occurs around a multifunctional focus. Business professionals with job responsibilities across a variety of functions are 1.54 times as likely to be recruited into management consulting firms than professionals with primary expertise in individual corporate functions. A separately conducted Wald test also reveals that recruitment rates for professionals with multifunctional backgrounds are significantly higher than those for professionals with engineering backgrounds (p < 0.01), supporting the contention that management consulting has become packaged around a far more diverse set of concerns than its origins in scientific management would indicate.

Discussion

The proliferation of management consultants as central intermediaries of organizational norms and routines has been supported by a number of institutional developments in the United States. The intervention of the federal government in the market realm—as an overseer of securities and exchange transactions, occupational safety, labor rights, and commercial law—has stimulated demand for management consulting: first, in the 1930s, with the passage of the Glass-Steagall act and SEC amendments; and again in later decades (most prominently in the late 1960s and 1970s) with the passage of standardized rules of business conduct. To a somewhat lesser extent, the impact of changes in corporate governance has likewise been apparent. The restructuring and downsizing of middle management in corporate America has expanded the available pool of recruits for management consulting, but has not generated more direct effects on the career choices of business professionals.

These influences have been accompanied by factors linked to the composition, culture, and job mobility of business professionals. The rising representation of women and minorities in the managerial workforce has created a milieu in which business professionals are increasingly likely to operate at the interstices of organizations rather than within formal management hierarchies. The rise of consultancy has also been promoted by changes in the job tenure of business professionals, reflecting less enculturation in specific industries and a greater propensity to abstract experiences across administrative contexts. Shifts in the culture of business and work—away from a traditional bureaucratic ethos of careerism—have encouraged more flexible, arms-length relationships between business professionals and the organizations they work for.

All of these trends can be seen as reducing the attachment shown by managers to particular firms, industries, and job ladders and increasing the cognitive abstraction achieved by managers with respect to administrative and strategic rules. Both dimensions are crucial to the institutionalization of externalized management and, by implication, the expansion of management consulting. The process of managerial externalization, though, tells only half of the story involved in the expansion of management consulting. The other half involves the role differentiation of management consultants from traditional carriers of business recipes—industrial engineers, accountants, and bankers—who dominated the industry in the early twentieth century. The historical development of consulting and the changing nature of client relations have since led to an integration of the profession around a more abstract, multifunctional view of formal organizations.

Conclusion

In writing this chapter I have sought to fill a lacuna in the organizational literature, which has generally failed to account for the expansion of new professions that spread norms, fads, and fashions through organizational fields. The diffusion of "rationalized myths" is most often taken to be the outcome of interest in such analyses, and the existence of carriers responsible for diffusion is taken for granted. The growth of management consultancy during the twentieth century challenges the notion that the diffusion of new organizational routines has remained comparable throughout the period. As large corporations such as AT&T have started spending an average of $100 million dollars a year on consulting services (see O'Shea and Madigan 1997: chapter 1), interorganizational diffusion itself has become formalized, ritualized, and imbued with value. The content of institutionally approved structural elements that are incorporated by modern organizations may now be less important for their legitimacy than the process of hiring institutionally approved agents, such as management consultants, who act to promote "rational" diffusion.

Further research is required to parse out the salience of carriers and content in the spread of new institutional recipes. My analysis has also been bounded by its treatment of a particular national context: one in which management consulting has enjoyed remarkable success during the last half century. Although the early emergence of management consulting was most clearly marked in the United States (and, to a lesser extent, Great Britain, France, and Canada), the profession has long since become a global phenomenon. The international spread of consulting beyond the Anglo-American context is of considerable substantive interest in and of itself, since consulting firms have often been seen as primary cultural carriers of American-style management in the industrialized world (Kipping 1999a). From a more theoretical standpoint, the heterogeneity of different national contexts offers greater variability in the institutional influences identified previously and can probe the generalizability of the present findings concerning the expansion of management consulting.

5   **Types of Knowledge
and the Client-Consultant Interaction**
*Thomas Armbrüster, University of Mannheim,
Germany and Matthias Kipping, Universitat
Pompeu Fabra, Barcelona, Spain*

Introduction

In spite of all the rhetoric on business reengineering and radical transformations, organizational change can in most cases be understood as a continuous process of transmission and reception of management ideas and procedural innovations—hence, as the transfer of some sort of "management
knowledge." Consultancies are widely seen to play a particularly important
role in this process (Havelock 1969; Barley and Kunda 1992; Fridenson 1994;
Guillén 1994; Bessant and Rush 1995). Hagedorn (1955), for example, conducted a case study of an independent management consultant during the
interwar period as a "transmitter of business techniques." For the postwar
period, Servan-Schreiber (1967) pointed at the role of the three U.S. consultancies, Booz Allen & Hamilton, Arthur D. Little, and McKinsey, in spreading American management concepts in Europe. Other research has shown that
consultancies contributed to the diffusion of scientific-management methods
during the first half of the twentieth century and to the introduction of decentralized, multidivisional corporate structures in large European corporations,
even though their impact and significance varied considerably between countries (Littler 1982; Kipping 1997; McKenna 1997; Whittington *et al.* 1999).

In this literature, and even more so in the wave of publications on the
knowledge economy and society, the term "management knowledge" is in
many cases treated with a hierarchical connotation and thus in a potentially
misleading manner. The widely used term "knowledge-intensive company"

inherently assumes a ranking, that is, it paints the picture that some companies possess a high and others a low intensity of knowledge. Management consultancies, in particular, are often labeled "knowledge-intensive," assuming a knowledge-related superiority toward their clients. In many cases, however, the first task of consultants in an assignment is actually to gather information and knowledge *from* the client organization. Only in later phases, that is, after the consultants have gained enough knowledge about the procedures in the client organization, can consultants come up with suggestions.

As opposed to defining a degree of knowledge intensity, in this chapter we suggest distinguishing between different *types* of knowledge. We attempt to carve out the institutionalized, or activity-system-related, type of knowledge consultants possess in relation to the knowledge types of other actors. On this basis, we examine the consultant-client relationship and attempt to shed some light on why both consultants and client managers often perceive their interaction as distressing. We have divided the chapter into four parts. After this introduction, we examine the institutional differences of knowledge between consultants and other actors in order to present a typology of management knowledge. We employ this typology in the third section to identify the specific roles of consultants in processes of organizational change. In the fourth section we look at the intervention of management consultants in client organizations and analyze potential and actual difficulties arising from these institutional differences of knowledge. In the conclusion we reflect upon the usefulness of an ideal-type approach to management knowledge as suggested here.

Although the umbrella term of *management consulting* addresses a variety of services, our focus in this chapter is on strategy-and-organization consultancies that have attained international recognition and influence. Within the consulting industry they have held the longest tradition, and although information technology–related consulting in terms of revenue has overtaken them, they still typify what is generally considered management consulting (for their origin and expansion see McKenna 1995; Kipping 1996, 1999a). Strategy-and-organization consultancies are employed by all fields of economy and society; that is, they do not only work for private corporations but also for the public sector, including government departments, public administrations, and so forth (Saint-Martin 2000). Considering the ample growth rates, the continuing demand, and the often taken-for-granted use of consultants (Faust 1998), it seems evident that their input plays a central role in processes of organizational change. Few organizations dare to engage in change ventures without the aid of consultants.

Three Kinds of Management Knowledge

If consultants are allotted to the significant economic role as discussed above, a discussion of their kind of knowledge seems more than appropriate. Blackler (1995) points out that individuals obtain their knowledge through culturally located systems. Based on an extensive literature review of knowledge in organizations, he suggests that more attention needs to be drawn to the dynamics of the systems through which knowing is accomplished, since knowing is not only provisional and pragmatic, but also situated in and mediated through activity systems (that is, "located in time and space and specific to particular contexts"; "manifest in systems of language, technology, collaboration and control"; Blackler 1995: 1039–1041). In addition, it has been suggested that the acquisition of knowledge coincides with processes of identity formation, for which the inherent goals, language, logic, and power relations of the activity system in which knowledge is acquired are most relevant (Lave and Wenger 1991; Contu and Willmott 1999). The language managers speak, and the socialization they acquire in their organization, does in the long run hardly allow them to maintain a cognitive identity independent of their setting within the organization.[1] The argument is that different institutions and organizational contexts bring about different types of knowledge.

Our suggestion is to broadly distinguish between three institutions, or activity systems, in which managing is taught and learned and in which individuals inevitably become familiar with the topics and terms circulating in the public sphere of management. We suggest distinguishing among

- Business schools
- Practice within nonadvisory businesses such as manufacturing companies, banks, insurance companies
- Consultancies as business-to-business advisory institutions

For the activity system of business schools, needless to say, it is neither possible nor the goal to train students for a specific task within a specific company. Rather, business schools aim to prepare students for a variety of potential employers and business activities. The first kind of management knowledge developed in business schools is hence a broad familiarity with managerial discourses, dilemmas of decision making, and general ways to approach business problems. This kind of management knowledge is not only taught in business schools but is also conveyed through the immense number of management books, mostly written by academics. Although most books are concerned with one specific topic, they cannot deliver more than a broad acquaintance with the issue. Even if a book is written in the most practitioner-oriented style, additional familiarity with the procedures, tasks, and clients in a specific context is necessary in order to use this kind of knowledge. In addition, it is striking that large parts of the management literature are not concerned with advice related to the functional domains of a corporation but with general aspects of how to run a company. In this field, some publications and their authors have attained guru status and have coined terms that belong to the general knowledge of a large number of managers. Hence, since detailed knowledge with regard to the functional domains of corporations is hardly relevant, we suggest identifying a first type of management knowledge as *general management knowledge*, which refers to a familiarity with concepts circulating in the public sphere of management.[2]

We suggest that the second type of management knowledge is what practitioners develop over time through a long-term familiarity with the processes and issues within a particular organization and domain at non-advisory businesses. What we would like to point out is the type of management knowledge that is primarily concerned with the *regulation of the existing structures and procedures* in a given context, which is closely related to experience, expertise, and local know-how and to the notions of tacit and embodied knowledge that have recently been suggested (Collins 1993; Nonaka 1994; Blackler 1995). Roughly speaking, engineers, for example, be it in software or mechanical engineering, can become middle managers without having much of what we call general management knowledge. They can manage a department perfectly well without being familiar with such concepts as organizational culture, TQM, business process reengineering, and the like, and without much exposure to general discourses such as lean management in the 1980s or knowledge management in the 1990s. Of course, the same is true for other lines of business such as financial management, marketing, production management, human resource management, and information technology (IT) management. A deep familiarity with the processes in a particular domain and an acquaintance with "how to run things here" without much reflection upon the relation to prevalent management concepts may suffice. Such knowledge represents knowledge that can only be learned over time in a certain position and domain, independent of an education in a business school, and can thus be labeled *regulation-oriented management knowledge*.

The third activity system that brings about a potentially independent type of business knowledge, management consultancies, earns fees by changing current procedures in client organizations. Based on their interview study of five Swedish consultancies, Werr *et al.* (1997) point out that the dominant theme around which consulting revolves is organizational change. In order to prompt change, consultants structure and simplify problems in order to render them decidable. The inherent logic is that change is always necessary, and consultancies' business is to induce and accompany it. In this respect the employment and training practices of consultancies are of crucial importance. A defining characteristic of consultancies is that they hire young, often inexperienced graduates and develop their skills by assigning them to assorted management areas and various industry or service sectors (Berry 1991, Nevins 1998). Whether or not they have acquired function- or industry-related knowledge in previous work experience, they develop managerial competence through on-the-job training in the consultancy and the methods of change employed there. They learn how to carry out the different processes employed by the consultancy, for example, overhead-value analysis, the implementation of an enterprise resource planning (ERP) system, or approaches to post-merger integration. In most cases, these *change-oriented* skills have to be taught in-house in a more formalized way, because they cannot be easily acquired either outside or purely by observing more experienced consultants (Kipping and Amorim 1999). As Werr *et al.* (1997) found, the methods of change conveyed to individual consultants are "part of the general institutionalization of competence, which has the double function of facilitating the introduction and socialization of newly recruited consultants and of increasing the organizational component in the 'product' sold to the client" (p. 303). Change-oriented skills, therefore, are the governing characteristic of consultancy knowledge.

This distinction between regulation- and change-oriented knowledge resembles the traditional sociological separation between a sociology of regulation and a sociology of radical change (Burrell and Morgan 1979). The sociology of regulation is concerned with "the need for regulation in human affairs; the basic questions which it asks tend to focus upon the need to understand why society is maintained as an entity. It attempts to explain why society tends to hold together rather than fall apart. It is interested in understanding the social forces which prevent the Hobbesian vision of 'war of all against all' becoming a reality" (Burrell and Morgan 1979: 17). The sociology of radical change "is often visionary and Utopian, in that it looks toward potentiality as much as actuality; it is concerned with what is possible rather than what is; with alternatives rather than the acceptance of the status quo" (Burrell and Morgan 1979: 17). We are by no means implying that management consulting has anything to do with the sociology of radical change, to which Marxism belongs.[3] But Burrell and Morgan's spectrum refers to a dimension along which the different ways of thinking in management consultancy and managerial practice can be distinguished. To put it crudely and potentially oversimplify, consultancy focuses on what is possible, on potentials and visions, rather than on what is given; managerial practice tends to focus on actuality, social order, or at best on modifications of the status quo rather than substantial change.

Individuals in organizations obtain their management knowledge predominantly in these activity systems and are shaped by the system-immanent logic that differs from those of the other systems. Even if, over time, most managers go through more than one of these institutions (the majority of consultants, and many managers with regulation-oriented knowledge, underwent an education in a business school; a number of practitioners with regulation-oriented knowledge used to work in a consultancy), the present-day activity system of individuals still forms their way of thinking and thus their development of knowledge. If the acquisition of knowledge is situated in, and mediated through, culturally located activity systems (Blackler 1995), and if processes of learning coincide with processes of identity formation (Lave and Wenger 1991; Contu and Willmott 1999), then the affiliation to the activity system "consultancy" or "management practice" in the long run hardly allows them to develop knowledge independent of the change- or regulation-oriented activity setting.

In summary, we suggest distinguishing between three imaginary "ideal types" of individuals whose management knowledge can be distinguished as follows:

- An individual possesses *general management knowledge* if he is communicatively familiar with concepts well known in the public sphere of management and conveyed by the literature, such as business reengineering, total quality management, management by objectives, organizational culture. The imaginary ideal type of person with *only* general management knowledge would be a business-school graduate with no or little work experience.

- An individual has *regulation-oriented knowledge* if she has developed and accumulated expertise in the regulation of the existing operations within a particular domain of management. The hypothetical ideal type of individual who embodies this kind of management knowledge would be a software engineer or bank manager who did not undergo business school education but is deeply familiar with the process of running the respective domain along the established procedures of her respective company.

- An individual possesses *change-oriented knowledge* if he knows how to analyze an organization with regard to potential changes, how to convince organizational members of the need for change, how to trigger new business processes, and so forth. The ideal type of individual who embodies this kind of knowledge would be a consultant in a strategy-and-organization consultancy. Particularly significant for change-oriented knowledge is the awareness of, and acquaintance with, methods of change, which is a momentous feature of individuals in these consultancies (see in this regard Werr *et al.* 1997; Werr 1999).

The fact that individuals with regulation- or change-oriented knowledge also possess general management knowledge is not harmful for these distinctions. On the contrary, it allows us to model the circulation and adaptation of different types of knowledge (see next section), and the distinction between regulation and change orientation enables us to discuss the interaction between consultants and clients in the light of conflicting knowledge types. These distinctions allow us to identify the institutionally bound mindsets of their members and hence the inherent difficulties that must be undergone when individuals embedded in different activity systems come together in a consulting project. These difficulties will become more obvious when we discuss institutional roles in the dissemination of knowledge, which are related to the knowledge types' differing ways of transmission, tradability, and speed of dissemination.

The Circulation of Knowledge and the Role of Consultants

We have discussed that the *origins* of management knowledge are institutionally bound and suggested that business schools, management practice, and management consultancy produce different types of knowledge. With regard to the *dissemination and transmission* of knowledge, however, the differences between activity systems lose significance. Publications in the field of *general* management knowledge, for example, address the public sphere of management as a whole. But interests differ with regard to the dissemination of general management knowledge. Consultants, for example, encounter a permanent resistance of clients in processes of change, and thus have a constant need for legitimization—independent of whether the resistance is justified or not. General management knowledge and publications in this field provide opinions about market developments and trends in the form of texts, terms, and concepts, that is, something one can communicatively refer to. For consultants, these texts and concepts are welcome justifications of change-related actions, and hence consultants contribute to discourses in the public sphere.

For consulting firms, therefore, the transmission of general management knowledge is an important issue. If the role of consultants is to adjust clients to and prepare them for changing market conditions, and thus to translate general trends into the day-to-day operations of client organizations, then the familiarity with general management issues plays a considerable role in consulting assignments. The communicative use and thus the transmission of these concepts becomes an inherent part of the consulting business. It is expected that consultants are familiar with the terms and concepts of the general discourse and, because of their constant use of these terms and concepts, also become one of the main *transmitters* of general management knowledge.

Regulation-oriented knowledge originates in managerial practice. Management practitioners who possess this knowledge have little interest in its dissemination, since it is related to the competitive situation of the company and the micropolitical situation of the individual within the firm. Management consultants, however, are not only dependent on this local, regulation-oriented knowledge for the particular assignment, but their business as a whole is highly dependent on learning from their clients. The more local knowledge consultants have collected, the easier it is to understand the operations of the next client. A firm-wide dissemination of experiences and their application in new assignments helps consultancies achieve stronger impacts on client businesses. The self-concept of consultants is the application of methods of change in client corporations. Consultants, therefore, do not act as the creators but rather transmitters of client practices. Only with regard to *change-oriented* knowledge, management consultants theoretically function as both the creator and the transmitter of knowledge. The transmission of knowledge does not render them dispensable, since their "otherhood" (Meyer 1996), their externality, remains a fundamental feature to induce change. Table 5.1 summarizes these results.

This tabular juxtaposition does not mean that the dissemination of knowledge stops at the disseminator's place, or that the borders between the different kinds of knowledge are impermeable. In fact, the transformation of one kind of knowledge to another is in the consultants' interest: to transform general and regulation-oriented knowledge into change-oriented knowledge means to render it usable for them. The reason we believe that this schematic juxtaposition makes sense is that it indicates the circulation and adaptation of management knowledge between different carriers. General management knowledge is transmitted by management publications, business schools, and consultants; received by practitioners in corporations; and turned into regulation-oriented and change-oriented knowledge by practitioners and consultants. The latter types of knowledge are transmitted by consultants and, at least to a certain extent, received by managerial practitioners, academics,

TABLE **5.1**   Types, Origins, and Disseminators of Management Knowledge

	General Management Knowledge	Regulation-Oriented Knowledge	Change-Oriented Knowledge
Origin	Management gurus; business school professors	Practitioners in corporations	Consultants
Disseminator or Transmittor	Management publications; business schools; consultants	Practitioners who change employer; consultants	Consultants

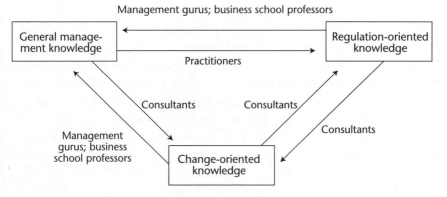

FIGURE 5.1   The circulation of management knowledge

and gurus. The loop closes when it has been converted into general management knowledge by the latter two. Figure 5.1 illustrates this.

This circulation cycle shows the supposed economic role of consultants from a functionalist viewpoint. It is often assumed that a high circulation of management knowledge is also dependent on the intensity of management consulting. The argument goes that if a rapid development of information technology and means of communication, and an increasing globalization of markets, cause a continuous demand for new knowledge, then consultants become indispensable for the transfer of knowledge and practices. The above discussion of knowledge types and transfer does not question this functionalist view at this point. The transfer of all kinds of management knowledge would be more difficult without consultants. Their function as transmitters of management knowledge and their role in transforming one type into another helps to explain their economic *raison d'être* and, in the current context, their high growth rates. However, the origins and circulation of management knowledge must also be put into the context of the economics of the consultancy business. If the consultants' trade is the dissemination of knowledge, then we need to consider that the tradability of their product is highly dependent on its communicability. The speed of the dissemination of knowledge is based on its elevation to a communicative level, which would parallel a spiral turn from tacit to explicit knowledge in Nonaka's (1994) sense.

However, the ease with which these different types of knowledge are transferred differs considerably. General management knowledge is based primarily on the attention to communicative processes and is able to travel fast. Regulation-oriented knowledge, in contrast, is closely connected to the details of value chains and the day-to-day operations within a company. Hence this kind of knowledge travels much slower. Lillrank (1995) has highlighted this in a study of the transfer of Japanese management innovations to Europe and North America. Taking quality control circles (QCC) and time-based competition (TBC) as examples, he distinguished among abstract management principles (for example, the idea of "quality first" or "zero defects"), organizational vehicles (structures required for carrying a principle, such as the organizational capability to handle short cycle times), and concrete management techniques and tools (for example, statistical process control, linear optimization). Lillrank concludes that QCCs first failed because of the initially low abstraction level of the transfer, and TBC only succeeded after a new generation of thinking, business reengineering, had emerged into which it could be packaged. Hence, as opposed to more abstract principles, the concrete level of techniques and tools requires a complicated process of learning and adaptation to country- and company-specific circumstances. It is not surprising that the transformation of concrete concepts into a new context is fraught with considerable difficulties and quite often fails completely, especially if the cultural gap is rather large (see in this respect also Florida and Kenney 1991; Hill 1991).

As it is in the business interest of consultants to disseminate knowledge—which, as we have discussed, is easier for general, communicable knowledge—a certain reluctance to get involved in regulation-oriented issues can be assumed. The generation of change-oriented knowledge, and the dissemination of all types of knowledge, therefore, requires a tradability of the consulting products. Fincham (1995) has drawn attention to the commodification of management knowledge taking place in the consulting industry. According to this account, the actual contents of management knowledge are wrapped in tradable concepts and given a label (such as business reengineering, lean management, total quality management). In the sense of the above model of knowledge circulation, these labels can then be used for a variety of tasks and procedures in such a manner that their circulation precedes the circulation of the contents and fosters the demand for consulting independent of the contents. An example for this process is presented in the study conducted by Benders *et al.* (1998) regarding the role of consultants in the dissemination of business process reengineering (BPR) in the Netherlands. The consultants interviewed did not agree on the contents of BPR, interpreted it in different ways, and openly admitted that the term *BPR* was mainly used for communicative purposes. As a result, Benders *et al.* (1998) concluded that the term *BPR-project* has little or nothing to do with contents such as those suggested by Hammer and Champy (1993). Czarniawska-Joerges (1990), Watson (1994), and Jackson (1996) have drawn similar distinctions between the actual contents of management knowledge, on the one hand, and labels and metaphors for management concepts, on the other. In summary, the model of different types of knowledge suggests that there is an inherent conflict between the economic role of consultancies in the functionalist sense and the logic of their business activities.

Difficulties Inherent in the Client-Consultant Interaction

A recent survey among alumni from the London Business School indicates that, for example, 68 percent of clients agree that consultancy projects make a valuable contribution to most of their clients, but 74 percent agreed or strongly agreed that consultants are better at fleshing out clients' ideas than suggesting new ones, and more than 50 percent of clients agree or strongly agree that consultants' first loyalty is to themselves and their firm rather than to the clients (Ashford 1998: 267–271). These contradictory perceptions regarding consultants are not new and point out how ambiguous the clients' attitude to consultants is. A recent series of interviews with the CEOs of the ten largest Swedish companies confirms this dilemma managers face regarding the decision of whether to hire consultants (Engwall and Eriksson 1999). Most of the CEOs express highly critical thoughts about consultants, but at the time of these interviews, all of the companies employed at least one, usually several consultancies. In spite of their concerns, the CEOs apparently consider consultants to be valuable.

Managerial practitioners, and especially consultants themselves, know that the group effort between clients and consultants does not take place without friction. And anybody who ever worked in top consultancies knows that partners of the firm are often haunted by the fear of being shown the door during an ongoing project or, more likely, of not receiving a follow-on assignment (see in this regard Sturdy 1997a; Kipping 1999b). More important from an economic viewpoint are those cases in which the implementation of consulting advice led to failure. Among the historical examples is Midland Bank in the United Kingdom that, following the advice of a well-known consultancy, expanded to the United States in the 1970s but soon withdrew again in the face of mounting losses (Holmes and Green 1986). The family-owned French edible oil producer Lesieur had a similar costly experience when it diversified into other areas, implementing the recommendations made, incidentally, by the same consultancy (Gaston-Breton 1998). A more recent case in which the extensive, possibly excessive, use of consultancies might have played a role in the subsequent bankruptcy is the large privately owned U.S. conglomerate Figgie International (O'Shea and Madigan 1997). Such discords between consultants and their clients have recently attracted considerable attention in the popular management literature (for example, Shapiro *et al.* 1993; O'Shea and Madigan 1997; Kesner and Fowler 1997).

Based on the framework of knowledge types suggested above, it would be misleading to blame malpractice of consultants for this outcome and for the problems in the relationship with clients. From this viewpoint the difficulties in the consultancy-client interaction can primarily be understood in terms of clashes of knowledge types and differing interests regarding knowledge transmission rather than in terms of malpractice. An illustration of the significance of the knowledge-based view is the case of the introduction of the multidivisional structure in Europe. As mentioned in the Introduction, in many cases this was done with the help of top consultancies. By screening earlier research on this issue, Kogut and Parkinson (1993) found that many European companies adopted a decentralized organization only "on paper," that is, they maintained their original structure in terms of the actual processes and interaction, be it a loose holding in Britain or highly centralized management in France. In such cases of on-paper-only implementation the consultants' change-oriented knowledge might have overrun the regulation-oriented knowledge of clients. The processes and behavior of the actors in the client organization were not sufficiently taken into account; the result orientation of the consultants' change approach was not applied to the internal functioning of the organization. And on the surface the consultants succeeded: client companies did adopt a new structure—only the structure no longer reflected the internal functioning of the organization. These cases confirm the early neo-institutional view that formal structures are sometimes no more than myth and ceremony (Meyer and Rowan 1977) or the finding of Brunsson (1989) that companies incorporate different structures, processes, and ideologies for internal and external use—a phenomenon he calls hypocrisy. They are also paralleled by a number of historical case studies that highlight that the divisional organization was widely perceived, namely at the middle management level, as "too radical" (for example, Holmes and Green 1986; Pugh 1988; Public Histoire 1991; Cailluet 1995).[4] The reorganization plans were often implemented only half-heartedly, or even just shelved. With the model of knowledge types in mind, one could conclude that the intervention of the consultants consisted largely of carrying *general* management knowledge into the client organization (the communication of new concepts such as the multidivisional form),[5] and pushing change-oriented knowledge through the assignment with too little regard to the established practice in the client organization. Individuals with embedded, regulation-oriented knowledge, therefore, were likely to resist. These examples suggest that using the above distinctions between the different types of knowledge can make the inherent difficulties in the client-consultancy relationship more explicit.

Conclusion: How Useful Are Categorizations of Knowledge?

Many authors have highlighted risks in purchasing consultancy services and have produced checklists to avoid the associated dangers (for example, Kubr 1993; Mitchell 1994; O'Shea and Madigan 1997; Ashford 1998). We do not want to repeat this here but would rather like to point out that popular speculations about consultants' malpractice may lead to a deadend. Our objective in this chapter has been to bring some clarity to the variety of difficulties between consultants and clients, and to this end we have suggested a potentially crude categorization of types of management knowledge. We have highlighted the different institutional logics of management consulting and management practice, and suggested that consultants and clients act within their specific logic of knowledge. Based on this conceptual framework and some historical illustrations, we have pointed out that the knowledge transfer from consultants to clients does not and cannot function in a frictionless manner.

Distinctions of this kind, such as presented here between regulation- and change-oriented knowledge, are always on the brink of oversimplification. Knowledge is put into boxes and to an extent treated as a commodified asset. In a debate with Blackler (1996), Prichard (1996) pointed out that the discourse on knowledge work and especially the categorization of knowledge types may lead to a normalization of practices that legitimates a division of labor and downplays the relation of knowledge and power. Yet by referring to the activity system and institutional logic within which knowledge types emerge in different social systems, we have tried not to reify knowledge as an objective asset but to give way to socialization processes, social relations, processes of identity formation, and thus to power relations within which knowledge is shaped in social systems. We have chosen an ideal-type approach in order to facilitate comprehension rather than simplify the argument, downplay aspects of power, or normalize practices. This lens offers a view that individuals with different knowledge types, professional identities, and intra-organizational logics may speak different languages and induce misunderstandings that hamper a productive cooperation (Kieser 2002). In addition, it has drawn attention to institutional interests of consulting firms (knowledge codification, communication, commodification) and thus allows distinctions between the often-suggested malpractices, on the one hand, and institutional and cognitive circumstances within which consulting transactions take place, on the other. Conflicts about which way is right, which pace of change is appropriate, and which circumstances must be taken into account in developing a solution belong to the normal business of consulting projects. An awareness of the different institutional logics and knowledge types may foster comprehension of these issues, and the redirection from degrees of knowledge intensity toward types of knowledge based on activities and institutional logic may be of help in this respect.

III   *Flows of Management Knowledge*

6   The Secrets of the Winners: Management Ideas That Flow

Kjell Arne Røvik, University of Tromsø, Norway

Introduction

What does it take to turn a management idea into a popular organizational recipe that spreads fast and wide? In other words, what are the secrets of the winners—that is, the most popular ideas such as business process reengineering, management by objectives, balanced scorecard, development dialogue, or total quality management? These are the research questions addressed in this article. This approach is motivated by numerous observations indicating that there is some kind of selection of ideas going on among the world's organizations. Whereas most ideas about management and organizing hardly get any attention at all, a small and rather exclusive set of ideas, which include the above mentioned, flow rapidly and obtain an almost global dissemination. I will term these management ideas *organizational superstandards*. For a period of time they may dominate organizational discourses in various arenas and trigger numerous organizational reform processes worldwide. Further, although most ideas about management and organization are never published, or even put down in writing, the organizational superstandards have their own distinct and rapidly growing literature containing a large number of practical how-to-succeed publications as well as academic works in many languages.

There is no doubt that some types of organizational ideas, or recipes, "travel" better than others (Meyer 1996: 250, Røvik 1998). But are the "winners" selected by coincidence and random processes, leaving no clear patterns for researchers to disclose, or do they have some crucial qualities in common that make them travel fast and wide? And most important, if such common features can be revealed through research, is it possible to use the insight gained to work out a general theory about what makes certain management recipes popular and moves organizations to implement them? These questions are discussed in a comparative study of the literature on three of the most popular superstandards of our time: management by objectives (MBO), development dialogue[1] (DD), and total quality management (TQM). I have analyzed both the recipes and their presentation in order to identify common features that may help explain their status as organizational superstandards.

Theoretical Approaches

Two theoretical approaches have inspired a search for explanations. The first is the rationalistic-instrumental approach, which includes insights from different schools of thought, among them scientific management (Taylor 1903, 1911), administrative theory (Fayol 1950/1916; Gulick and Urwick 1937), classical theory of bureaucracy (Weber 1968/1924), contingency theory (Lawrence and Lorsch 1967), and new rationalism (Egeberg 1989; Donaldson 1996, 1999). This camp views organizational recipes as tools in the hands of rational actors (managers) attempting to design effective and efficient organizations. Hence, the quality of an organizational idea, or a recipe, is evaluated solely on the basis of how it works, that is, from the results produced in the organizations where it is applied. Documented results, preferably from a large and representative sample of organizations, are, according to this perspective, the decisive criterion for a recipe's reputation and thus for its potential to flow. Consequently, it can be hypothesized that an organizational recipe with wide acceptance and use is one proven to be instrumental in bringing about radical improvements in a large number of organizations when it comes to effectiveness and efficiency.

The second theoretical approach reflects insights mainly from new institutionalists (Meyer and Rowan 1977; DiMaggio and Powell 1991; Scott and Meyer 1988,1994; Meyer and Jepperson 2000) but also from symbolists (Czarniawska 1997; Goodman 1999; Rogers 1999) and social contructivists (Berger and Luckmann 1966; Latour 1986; Knorr-Cetina 1994).

Viewed from this theoretical perspective, widespread and popular organizational recipes have key properties in common other than simply being a well-calibrated tool for enhancing organizational effectiveness and efficiency. Here the focus is on legitimizing processes: in order to travel, an organizational idea must be linked to, and thus legitimized by, central values of the modern world such as rationality, efficiency, renewal, development, democracy, individuality, and justice (Strang and Meyer 1994; Meyer 1996).

To highlight this argument, one might reconsider Talcott Parsons' seminal article, "Suggestions for a Sociological Approach to a Theory of Organizations," in which he claimed, as one of the first, that modern organizations are unlikely to proceed and survive by being efficient in the technical-economical sense only (Parsons 1956). Organizations also need legitimacy. Hence, they have to incorporate and demonstrate their approval of widely accepted societal norms and values in their environment. This insight has been a cornerstone in the new institutionalism of the 1980s and 1990s in organization theory (Meyer and Rowan 1977; DiMaggio and Powell 1991).

Parsons' perspective, from which he outlined his famous argument, was the individual organization. From this position he observes its environment, a typical *inside-out perspective*, which has become very common in organization theory since the late 1950s. However, we will argue that a similar reasoning may be asserted when the focus is shifted to ideas and recipes that flow within institutional environments and sometimes "travel into" a number of organizations. This is an *outside-in perspective*, or a "reversed Parsons," which is organizations observed from their environment. The outside-in perspective highlights that it is not only the individual organization that has to obtain legitimacy, that is, by incorporating norms and popular recipes from institutional environments. If organizational ideas and recipes are to gain approval and be adopted by many organizations, they too must be legitimized in terms of norms and values that are widely accepted among the world's organizations. Consequently, one can predict that successful *definition* and *presentation* of an organizational recipe as one with strong links to eminent societal norms and values will be decisive for whether or not it will flow. The better a recipe is justified in terms of a wide range of such values, the better it travels.

Against this background, a couple of propositions can be stated. First, a management recipe's capacity to flow may depend on whether it is clearly associated with typical rational values in modern society. Thus a recipe should be seen as a means to generate efficiency, profit, and prosperity. According to John Meyer:

> It seems obvious that organizing ideas linked to central rationalistic values travel better than ideas less linked to these highly legitimated goals. Organizations are to produce outcomes rationally, efficiently, and effectively: this is centrally legitimated in terms of the Western, and now world, project of progress. Thus ideas justified in terms of enhanced organizational outcomes travel better that ideas justified in other terms. (Meyer 1996: 250)

That an organizational recipe is legitimized through rationalization may also mean that it has been successfully linked to what Habermas (1987), among others, claims to be modern societies' dominant ideology: the deeply rooted belief in science and technology. In this ideology lies an enormous potential for the legitimization of various organizational ideas. Hence, recipes that claim to be based on science and research may have a greater potential to flow than others.

Second, modern societies celebrate—and try to imitate—individuals, organizations, and even nations that are looked upon as particularly successful, that is, creative, productive, and efficient (Sevón 1996). Such actors usually become authorities and models with great potential to legitimize and authorize an organizational recipe. Thus the popularity of various ideas and recipes and the range and speed of their diffusion may depend on whether they have been socially authorized, that is, clearly associated with those actors who are celebrated as particularly successful.

Third, renewal and progress toward higher levels and standards—the vision of a continuous movement toward something better and of a higher order—are cornerstones in the modern Western schema and are thus central values in modern societies (Berger et al. 1973; Bauman 1995; Giddens 1991). Organizational recipes that are defined such that they symbolize "the new" and are associated with what is thought to be the latest stage of development or with future-oriented solutions will probably flow better than ideas and recipes associated with bygone days.

Fourth, the idea of the sovereign individual has for a long time permeated political as well as economic and religious Western institutions. This is the belief that each individual is endowed with certain fundamental and inviolable rights, with intellect, creativity, and responsibility for his own actions (Meyer et al. 1987; Meyer and Jepperson 2000). Since the late 1970s a new and very powerful wave of individualism has surged over Western institutions and reinforced these values (Nozick 1974; Scott and Meyer 1991). Thus we can presume that organizational recipes that are successfully defined as means to realize contemporary Western individualism will have an increased capacity to flow.

According to this theoretical perspective, one might assume that the better an organizational recipe is justified in terms of a wide range of celebrated values, such as renewal, progress, individualism, effectiveness, and efficiency, the better it travels.

Method and Data

Management by objectives (MBO), development dialogue (DD), and total quality management (TQM) are all prominent examples of popular management ideas that have experienced a rapid and almost worldwide dissemination.[2] The question raised here is whether they have anything in common that may explain their success. Although these are all very popular management ideas, there are variations among them. Whereas MBO and TQM have gained almost global popularity and dissemination, DD has been more of a "regional hero," that is, its dissemination has been largely concentrated among Scandinavian organizations. One may say that this recipe, compared to the two others, to some extent has "failed," meaning that it has not gained the same popularity and dissemination outside Scandinavia. Hence, I will also look for possible explanations of the variation: for example, are there any systematic differences in the presentation and attempted legitimization of MBO and TQM, on the one hand, and DD, on the other, in the management publications, differences that may account for the variation in popularity?

The method chosen to carry out research on this question is an examination of books and articles in the missionary, prescriptive literature where these three recipes are outlined and presented. The term *prescriptive* is operationalized to publications where the bottom-line of argumentation is that organizations *should* adopt the recipe in question. There are two main reasons for this methodological approach. First, organizational recipes such as MBO, DD, and TQM are not physical objects but ideas. They are often formulated and expressed in speech but most precisely and coherently in writing. Hence, management literature is probably the best source of knowledge about the contents of popular organizational ideas. Second, management literature is probably the single most important medium for the diffusion of organizational recipes. This insight is also the basis for the increasing interest among organizational researchers to study texts, mainly journals, annual reports, and newspapers to investigate the origin, authorization, and diffusion of various management ideas in time and space (see, for example, Astley and Zammuto 1992; Shenhav, 1995, 1999; Fenton and Pettigrew 2000; Furusten 1998, 2000; Mazza and Alvarez 2000; Benders and Van Bijsterveld 1997; Mazza 1998). Managers as well as employees often become aware of new organizational ideas and recipes through easily accessible publications, especially best-selling books (Clark and Greatbatch 2001). And in the case of the three very popular recipes being compared in this study, we know that the way in which they have been interpreted and advocated in these publications has been particularly successful, in the sense that the message has, within a relatively short time, attracted attention and inspired actors in many organizations all over the world. Consequently, by examining how the most widely read management publications advocate MBO, DD, and TQM, we might learn something about the codes that have been so successful in making the recipes flow. In other words, we may learn what kind of arguments and justifications are required for a recipe to be regarded as a highly appropriate tool by numerous organizations all over the world. However, since recipes are not physical objects but ideas that are expressed as texts in prescriptive publications, it may be hard to differentiate between what is a recipe (how to act) and what is an argument in favor of it. Recipes and their justifications are often intertwined in "packages of language" (publications) and will also be analyzed as such.

Two sets of publications have been examined. The first comprises 150 publications written in Norwegian, which is a significant proportion of the total available Norwegian prescriptive, or "missionary," publications dealing with these three recipes. MBO is featured in 42 percent; DD in 30 percent; and TQM in the remaining 28 percent of this sample. The other sample comprises 170 key publications in English, equally divided among the three recipes. These were selected because they (1) have status as a classic, (2) are written by authors regarded as pioneers or gurus in the field, or (3) are among the most frequently cited in the literature.

Each publication has been examined by two researchers (one is the author of this article). The content is registered and analyzed on the basis of a classification scheme that gives special attention to patterns in the presentation, that is, to what extent and how (1) the recipes' origins are discussed and (2) the organizations' experience with them is presented and discussed. From the two analytical perspectives we have derived different expectations about what kind of arguments will be applied in the publications to justify the recipes. From the rationalistic-instrumental perspective, popular recipes are highly effective tools producing successes in most organizations where they are applied. Hence, one could expect that the literature will argue in favor of the recipes mainly by referring to documentation of such effects. From the sociological-institutional perspective, one could expect that the publications will justify the recipes by referring to well-known, prestigious actors who use them and by arguing that application of them will enhance renewal, progress, and individualism. However, our examination of the literature is also characterized by an open-minded, explorative approach. We attempt to identify *all* the types of arguments that are frequently applied in favor of these ideas. In the next sections findings from the literature survey are in part held up against the expectations derived from the two theoretical camps, but we also present other frequently applied arguments that have come to light.

Findings

Organizational Superstandards as Super-Efficient Management Tools

Viewed from the rationalistic-instrumental perspective, organizational superstandards, that is, widespread and frequently applied recipes, are management tools that are particularly well suited for increasing organizational efficiency and effectiveness. Hence, the speed and range of an organizational recipe's diffusion is supposed to depend on its capability to enhance efficiency and effectiveness, and on whether such effects have been clearly documented. Consequently one might assume that superstandards—such as MBO, DD, and TQM—are tools that have generated extensive and well-documented positive results in a large number of organizations. Inherent in this perspective is also the assumption that organizations normally act as rational consumers. This means that organizational decision makers are expected to critically evaluate information about various management tools in order to choose the best. Hence, decision makers will primarily be interested in information about the recipes' documented results in different organizations.

Given the fact that management literature (including the publications examined in this study) probably is the single most important medium for spreading information about organizational recipes, one should also expect that it is mainly through such publications that potential customers will find *documentation* of the recipes' actual effects. This fact, in turn, may lead to more specific expectations about the content of examined publications on MBO, DD, and TQM. First, one should expect that considerable space will be used to describe and comment on the results achieved by organizations that have adopted the recipes. Second, if the assumptions about organizational superstandards as *particularly* efficient tools are correct, this should be clearly expressed in the literature; for example, in reports of extensive positive effects from a large, representative sample of organizations. Third, viewed from the rationalistic-instrumental perspective, organizational decision making about the adoption of popular recipes is supposed to be a rational process with much emphasis on calculating effects and on learning from experience. Hence, one could expect management publications about MBO, DD, and TQM to be written with a view to documenting the achieved results as thoroughly and objectively as possible.

The Presentation of Results in Management Publications

Examination of the selected publications reveals that quite a lot has been written about the alleged positive effects of TQM, MBO, and DD. In most cases, however, the effects are described in rather general terms, without reference to specific studies or specific organizations. In the presentations of the results, future and promised effects are often more thoroughly discussed than the past situation and the effects already achieved. Another striking characteristic of the literature is the almost total absence of discussion of failures. The few failures that are reported are rarely explained as being caused by imperfections in the management recipe.

The idea that the superstandards are super-efficient management tools also implies that they have generated particularly *impressive* effects. How great, in fact, are the reported effects? A closer examination of the publications modifies the impression of many great successes, revealing that a rather limited number of success stories from specific organizations keep cropping up and are retold in many different publications and in slightly different versions. Thus one might get the impression that the great successes are more frequent than what is really the case. Stories about dramatic improvements are most frequent in the TQM literature. The literature on Development Dialogue stands out as containing the fewest success stories on adoption of this recipe.

One might have expected that management publications, in accordance with the rationalistic-instrumental approach, would contain *documentation* of the three recipes' various effects on organizations, and further that potential customers evaluate the recipes and decide on whether they should adopt or not primarily on the basis of such documentation. To what extent, then, are these success stories in fact substantiated and documented?

There are some examples of well-documented effects (see Bank 1992; Kennedy 1994). But these are the exceptions. In about three-quarters of all cases referring to positive effects in one or more organizations, the documentation is insufficient, that is, it does not fulfill ordinary methodological requirements. The weaknesses may be divided into two types: (1) positive effects are claimed without making clear whether the conclusion is a result of investigation and (2) the effects are presented in an inaccurate and exaggerated manner, leaving much room for various interpretations of the recipes' actual effects on the organizations.

Although there are some examples of documented success stories in the examined publications, most of the stories are substantiated by applying soft data and soft logic. Reports focus on single cases only, and the sample size is rarely taken into consideration. The lack of data is often compensated for by anecdotes and examples that appear convincing because they often involve well-reputed and successful organizations. The main conclusion is that the more stringently one applies methodological principles of social science (that is, sample size, validity, and reliability) to the reports, the weaker and more insignificant the actual effects of the management recipes seem, and the more complex and indirect the causal relationships become. This conclusion is supported by quite extensive academic research carried out in the 1970s to clarify the effects of MBO (Ivancevich 1972, 1974; Caroll and Tosi 1973; Wofford 1979; Locke 1978; Taylor and Zawacki 1978), more recent work attempting to evaluate the effects of TQM (Heverly 1991; Fricke 1992; Reger *et al.* 1994; Hackman and Wageman 1995; Chabaud and Rot 1997), and other work investigating the effects on organizations applying various performance appraisal systems (Meyer *et al.* 1965; Beer 1981; Fletcher 1986; Girard 1988). Far fewer attempts have been made to evaluate systematically the effects of development dialogue.

We do not claim, however, that it is *impossible* to document positive effects from adoption of any of the three recipes. But the main point is that popular management literature, which probably is the most important medium for the diffusion and presentation of these ideas, rarely does so. This implies that the thousands of organizations around the world that have adopted these and other popular management recipes either are not *interested* in documentation of the recipes' actual effects (see, for example, Guion 1975), or they have been *persuaded* about their effects by convincing success stories from well-known organizations; in other words, they consider anecdotes as sufficient documentation of success (Tversky and Kahneman 1974).

Social Authorization

From the institutional-symbolic perspective a proposition is derived about the importance of social authorization of organizational recipes. The proposition, precisely formulated, is that an organizational recipe's capacity to flow depends on whether it is clearly associated with organizations or individuals who are widely recognized as authoritative actors and models. There are many such authoritative actors that have influence on organizational decision making when it comes to choice of management ideas and recipes. The reasons for their authority and status as models vary a great deal. Consequently it may be assumed that organizational recipes that have obtained extensive dissemination—such as the three examined—have been very successfully authorized by being linked to *several* and particularly *influential* model organizations or individuals.

The popular management literature is perhaps the most important source for understanding the logic of the social authorization of management ideas. It is primarily in this literature that the social authorization actually takes place. Hence, in the examination of the publications we have focused upon two questions. First, if social authorization really is an important premise for whether a recipe will flow, we expect it to be clearly reflected in the publications—for example, by leaving ample space for stories about the recipes' origin as well as accounts of well-reputed previous and contemporary users. Second, who are the organizations and individuals that have obtained the status as models in stories about the recipes? Where in the social and geographical landscape are they located, and how *stable* is their authorizing power in the long-term? The answers may shed some light on the source of the model organizations' and individuals' authority, that is, what gives them the power to authorize organizational recipes.

Stories About the Recipes' Origins. A full 85 percent of all publications examined contain stories of individuals and organizations that are claimed to be either *originators* or successful *users* of the recipe(s). Thus, such stories are almost obligatory elements in management literature, especially in TQM publications (94 percent). First we will analyze published stories of the origins of the three recipes.

One should bear in mind that MBO, DD, and TQM are based on three very *simple, general,* and *timeless* ideas: that (1) all activities within modern organizations should be structured and directed toward the achievement of specific goals (MBO), (2) that there should be good communication between managers and workers (development dialogue), and (3) that managers have particular responsibility for making sure that all members of an organization are committed to and engaged in producing high-quality products and services (TQM). Obviously these ideas have been around as long as formal organizations have existed. It is therefore difficult—and from a researcher's point of view, a waste of time—to try to date and locate the origin of these general ideas more precisely. Although these basic ideas are very old and very general, the surveyed literature presents and interprets MBO, DD, and TQM as *new* and *distinct* management tools; hence the numerous stories about where, when, and how these timeless and general ideas have been molded into distinct recipes. A common feature in the stories about the recipes' origin is their presentation as *inventions* and organizational *innovations* and as the accomplishments of some very talented individuals, that is, pioneers. Usually one, but sometimes two or three individuals are presented in each publication as the recipe's pioneer(s). The DD literature distinguishes itself in the sense that it contains very little storytelling about great pioneers and gurus.

Pioneers have some distinct features in common. Although most of them are not researchers but consultants, their links to research and science are emphasized in the publications through reference to their academic titles (such as Ph.D.) and to academic institutions where they have earned their degree. This confirms our point that the relation to science is a powerful and important means in the authorization of organizational ideas and recipes (Meyer 1997). Hence the very successful pioneers of MBO, DD, and TQM gain authority by combining two powerful roles: the academic, whose knowledge and ideas are based on scientific evidence, and the consultant, whose advice is based on practical experience (Crainer 1997).

Alternative Stories About Origin. During the examination of management literature, we made an interesting observation: the circulation of *alternative*—and often contrasting—stories about where, when, and by whom the recipe was originally designed. In the case of TQM, the story about W. E. Deming who went to Japan as a consultant in the early 1950s and coined the concept there is paralleled by that of another American guru, Dr. Joseph Juran. He, too, was a consultant to Japanese top executives at almost exactly the same time as Deming, and introduced what he termed *company wide quality management* (CWQM)—a recipe whose content might be mistaken for that of TQM (Juran 1988; Feigenbaum 1983; Kennedy 1994). The origin of MBO is most often linked to Peter Drucker and his book *The Practice of Management* from 1954. However, at approximately the same time this work was published, another American management consultant, Edvard Schleh, published two articles in the management journal *Personnel*, launching a recipe that he called management by results (Schleh 1953, 1955). Its content was almost identical to Drucker's management by objectives.

These examples might imply that popular organizational recipes, rather than having *one* authoritative source, crop up at different places at approximately the same time—although in slightly different versions—just like mushrooms in the fall (Brunsson 2000). In other words, they are *ideas whose time has come* (Czarniawska and Joerges 1996). The "mushroom model" might be considered as an alternative to the pioneer or entrepreneur model, which holds that the management tool is invented by a certain individual at a certain time and place. It is difficult, however, to determine whether the "mushroom model" really explains the origin of popular recipes. It may also be that once a brilliant idea has been hammered out, it spreads so rapidly from its "place of birth" that in retrospect, it could seem like a massive "outbreak" cropping up in different places simultaneously.

Stories about Users. In addition to stories about recipes' birthplaces, the literature also contains references to organizations and individuals who have adopted and used the recipes with success. These are important for understanding the logic of social authorization. A full 79 percent of the selected publications contain stories of contemporary and previous users. However, leaders and employees who hope they can use these stories as a basis for successful implementation of the recipes are bound to be disappointed, since the stories rarely contain information about the trial-and-error processes that we *know*, from several studies, are part of the implementation process (Røvik *et al.* 1995; Erlingsdottir 1999). Quite often, the authors limit themselves to listing several well-known and successful users and to brief accounts of the successes achieved. This type of presentation would seem to be deliberate attempts to authorize the management ideas.

Who, then, are the successful users who are held up as models? The greater part, 89 percent, are private companies. The remaining 11 percent are various public organizations. Looking exclusively at the English-language literature, this pattern becomes even clearer. Only 6 percent of the success stories are reported from public organizations. Hence the possibility of an organization's acquiring the status of a model with the power to authorize management ideas decreases dramatically if the organization is a public one. Also, nonprofit organizations are rarely held out as examples of successful users. This reflects, of course, the global trend at the turn of this century: organizational forms associated with business firms generally rank above those associated with public administration and nonprofit organizations.

The Nordic-language MBO literature differs from that in English in the more frequent reference to public organizations as success stories. This is a reflection of MBO's great popularity in public administration in Scandinavia, particularly in the second half of the 1980s. It also reflects, however, that the public sector in Scandinavian countries on the whole has a better reputation than in most other countries (for example, the United Kingdom or United States). Consequently, it is to a greater extent possible to authorize organizational ideas and recipes in Scandinavia with reference to successes in public organizations.

Deauthorization. The social authorization of a recipe does not have an everlasting effect. Like other sources of energy, there is also an end to the "fuel" that comes from social authorization. The effect of a recipe's social authorization may deteriorate if the organization or individual with which it has been associated loses its status as an authoritative actor or model for one reason or another. The SAS airline, for example, enjoyed a good reputation throughout the 1980s and thus lent important authority to a number of contemporary management ideas popular in Scandinavia, such as MBO and corporate culture (Røvik 1992). However, when the company's economic problems increased dramatically in the early 1990s, leading to a large deficit and the resignation of Jan Carlzon as CEO, SAS's status as a model organization with extensive capacity to authorize organizational recipes decreased markedly. This loss of authority is reflected in the Scandinavian management literature from this period. Attempts to authorize popular ideas and recipes, such as business process reengineering, business ethics, and learning organizations in Scandinavia, were made mostly with reference to other organizations that were regarded as successful and exemplary during this period (for example, large information technology firms, such as Sweden's Ericsson, Norway's Telenor, and Finland's Nokia).

The idea of corporate culture, which had been largely authorized in Scandinavia in the 1980s by reference to SAS as a model organization, experienced a sudden decrease in popularity parallel to the increasing problems of SAS in the early 1990s (Røvik 1992). This points to a possible relation between *deauthorization*—that a model organization for various reasons loses its power to authorize organizational recipes—and *deinstitutionalization*, that is, a decrease in the popularity of the organizational recipe itself, which for some period has been widely perceived as a modern way of organizing (Røvik 1996).

Universalizing

An important observation from our study of management publications is that MBO, DD, and TQM are described as *panaceas*, meaning that they are claimed to be tools that work successfully in all kinds of organizations, regardless of location, size, culture, the members' educational level, or type of industry or sector. This means that a garage in Lisbon, a directorate in Copenhagen, a high-tech company in Silicon Valley, and a fish plant in northern Norway all receive the message that they need and will profit from adopting MBO, DD, and TQM.

The recipes' image as universally applicable tools is expressed in management publications in various ways. Often it is indirectly communicated: the publication does not discuss—and consequently does not make any limitation of—the recipe's applicability. However, Badawy (1976) is only one of many who explicitly argue the universality of one or another recipe. He states that MBO can be used by any organization for the simple reason that formal organizations are more or less similar systems.

When particular *types* or *groups* of organizations are mentioned, this is in order to *extend* the range of application—such as when Peter Drucker (1976) argues for employing MBO not only in private companies but also in public administration. In fact, we never came across any attempt by authors of management publications to restrict the range of application of the three recipes, for example, by considering types of organizations or industries where they are not likely to succeed.

How Dissimilarity Becomes Similarity. As noted, the claim of universal applicability is frequently found in the surveyed publications. But how is it possible that a state department in Copenhagen, a car factory in Tokyo, a fish-processing plant in northern Norway, and a health care institution in London require—and will benefit from—exactly the same organizational recipe? It implies at any rate that a certain similarity is perceived among these highly different entities. Strang and Meyer (1994) claim that a fundamental condition for an idea to spread to many units is that the units themselves are believed to have a great deal in common. In other words, different units must be transformed from the concrete level—for example, car factories, restaurants, fish plants and hospitals, where they appear as completely different—to a more abstract level before they can be perceived as relatively similar. And a very important premise for the construction of this perceived similarity is the successful development and diffusion during the past thirty to forty years of the concept of *formal organizations*. The belief has become firmly established that highly different units, such as the above-mentioned factory or hospital, share an overarching identity as formal organizations. This is an incredibly powerful abstraction and concept (maybe the most successful in the twentieth century!) in that it plays down an enormous number of actual variations while emphasizing the similarities.

The breakthrough and the pervasive power of the concept of formal organization have many consequences. Turning dissimilarity into perceived similarity, it has paved the way for the idea of a world of organizations that all display, or at least *should* display, more or less the same *components*, such as a formal structure (principles of coordination and specialization), leadership, recruiting system, organizational culture, personnel department, quality control systems, and budgeting and accounting routines (Brunsson and Sahlin Andersson 2000). Thus a huge global market has emerged for the production and mediation of recipes for the successful design and function of formal organizations. Strang and Meyer (1994), partly inspired by Mead (1934), use the term "theorization" to depict the processes whereby the richness and variations of the real world are transformed into categories and units (for example, organizations) that are perceived as being similar:

> By theorization we mean both the development and specification of abstract categories, and the formulation of patterned relationships, such as chains of cause and effect. Without such general models, the question of similarity is unlikely to arise and gain force. And without such models, the real diversity of social life is likely to seem as meaningful as are parallelisms. (Strang and Meyer 1994: 104)

How Organizational Recipes Are Universalized. Although the image of a world society of more or less similar formal organizations has been established, and thus a very important premise for the creation and diffusion of organizational recipes is fulfilled, it does not automatically follow that any of the three recipes in this study will be widely perceived as effective management tools that can be applied by all kinds of organizations. The idea of a world society of organizations is, in other words, a necessary but insufficient condition for any of "our" recipes (MBO, DD, and TQM) to obtain the status of a panacea. The recipes *themselves* must also be universalized. This involves, among other things, being defined and presented in such a general and abstract form that they will be perceived as tools every organization needs. And this kind of universalizing process takes place first and foremost in the prescriptive management literature. The publications we examined show the following three devices.

First, the image of organizations as basically similar systems paves the way for claims about the elements constituting these systems. It is frequently argued that MBO, DD, and TQM are important components in all organizations and are, or at least should be, present regardless of time and place. Notice, for instance, the self-evidence of the following statements stemming from the examined publications: "[All] organizations have—or should have—clear *objectives*." Consequently they need tools to secure a constant focusing on objectives and results. This could be turned into a quite irresistible argumentation in favor of MBO and related recipes. Or "[All] organizations may be perceived as production systems that make their living by satisfying customers," which implies that a tool such as TQM is required to make high-quality products as effectively and efficiently as possible. And finally: "The members of an organization are usually divided into two main groups, leaders and workers, and the two groups must be able to communicate." If this premise is accepted by most of the world's organizations, DD and related recipes are likely to be widely perceived as indispensable.

Strang and Meyer explain the underlying logic in this way:

> If flows are more rapid when units are theorized as similar, so also the actual social elements that flow are creatures of theorization. A theory of social form emphasizes certain features as central and relevant, while treating others as variable, or unnecessary, or derivative. The social elements marked as theoretically relevant are then privileged candidates for diffusion. (Strang and Meyer 1994: 105)

Second, management publications attempt to define the recipes as standard components and panaceas by insisting that they are based on knowledge about cause and effect, which is claimed to function in the same way no matter where and when applied. The prospect is held out, then, that the effect you get if recipe (x) is implemented in organization (a) will be basically the same as that in organizations (b) and (c), provided the recipe has been correctly implemented.

Third, the authors are generally concerned with emphasizing that the recipes they provide are not biased toward any specific cultures or nations. This is often done by stressing that the recipes' range of applicability is not limited to the particular culture or nation in which they have been developed.

There are nonetheless subtle distinctions among the recipes on this point. Many publications about DD claim that this is a tool especially adapted to Scandinavian working life traditions and egalitarian values (Wollebæk 1989; Holt-Larsen and Bang 1993). The main impression, however, is that recipes, through universalizing processes such as those shown above, are defined as general tools with an almost unlimited range of applicability.

To summarize, an important premise for the diffusion of recipes is universalizing, that is, creating images of similarity and worldwide applicability through abstractions and simplifications. The idea that different organizations have a lot in common if they are seen as formal organizations—that is, that they are almost identical units—must be developed, and the recipes must, in order to spread, be brought onto an abstract, theoretical level and presented as components that are both useful and vital to most organizations.

Commodification

From the early 1960s, Western organizational thinking has been heavily influenced by a phenomenon that may be termed the *commodification* of organizational ideas, that is, the transformation of organizational ideas into products that are marketed to organizations all over the world. Thus important aspects of this trend may be explained with the logic of the *market*. During the past twenty to thirty years, specific roles have emerged for producers, mediators, and buyers of organizational success recipes. The competition for the attention of the organizations as potential customers is tough. New ideas and recipes are constantly introduced to the market, while "old" ones fade. In many respects, this phenomenon resembles modern consumer society.

This observation underlies the proposition that the capacity of an organizational recipe to flow may depend on whether it has been successfully commodified, that is, the idea is transformed so that it can compete with others in attracting a vast number of organizations that want to acquire this type of product. Based on theories of marketing (for example, Miller 1956; Gummesson 1996) one can assume the following three elements to be very important in a commodification strategy of transforming management ideas into a marketable product:

- The idea or recipe should be designed as an easily communicable message.
- The recipe should be presented as a user-friendly product.
- Potential customers should be assured of an effective output in proportion to the costs and efforts of implementation.

Communicability. An important measure of the communicability of an organizational recipe is whether the general message can attract the attention of—and appeals to—a large number of potential customers. A frequently repeated statement is that modern leaders do not have the time, the competence, or the will to acquaint themselves with material that is presented in a tedious manner and formulated in complex technical language (Miller 1956; Lyttle 1991; Huczynski 1993). In order to overcome this problem and capture the attention of potential customers, the recipe must be correctly packaged, that is, it must be clear and simple, minimizing exhaustive argumentation and phrases such as "on the one hand . . . on the other hand. . . ." Above all, the message must be brief—the content condensed into as few words as possible so that it is easily recognized when repeated in speech and writing.

Judged by these criteria, the three examined recipes must be said to be very well packaged. They are recognized in numerous organizations simply by reference to *one* word. In addition, the communicability of MBO and TQM is facilitated by their acronyms. Because they do not have to be constantly translated into new phrases or expressions, acronyms can more easily acquire the same meaning across language barriers. This argument is well illustrated by reference to development dialogue. Unlike MBO and TQM, this recipe is not generally identified with an acronym, and it has also been difficult to arrive at a precise English translation of the original Scandinavian term *medarbeidersamtaler* (Holt-Larsen and Bang 1993). This has obviously been a barrier to diffusion of this organizational idea.

The communicability of a recipe also depends on whether the message is packaged such that it tickles people's curiosity and thus motivates them to unwrap it. Thus, the contents of the package should not be too obvious, and the message should not be delivered in dull phrases but in words that appeal to the potential users' intellect and spirit of inquiry (Huczynski 1993). Management ideas packaged in acronyms such as MBO and TQM might be attractive to curious people, partly because behind such precise trademarks (almost like chemical formulas) many might expect to find precise, even scientifically based, management tools.

User-Friendliness. A requirement for any successful modern product is that the customer is able to make use of it almost immediately without wasting any time, a principle known from marketing as "ready-to-wear." When the products are *ideas*, as is the case MBO, DD, and TQM, user-friendliness implies that both producers and salespeople should be capable of demonstrating to the potential customer how simply the idea can be implemented in the organization and thereby be transformed into programs, actions, desired results, and, not least, profits.

Consideration for user-friendliness is clearly reflected in the examined publications. For instance, the authors are usually very particular about describing the steps and principles to be followed in the process of implementing the recipes. A full 81 percent of all publications examined contain practical instructions (often very specific) for "installing" the recipes. There are several reasons for this. A set of basic principles and steps helps managers know how to act, makes the recipes seem more tangible and useful rather than abstract and theoretical, is easily remembered, and appeals to impatient leaders because the steps plot the course from the present position to the desired position.

The Prospect of Returns. Informing potential customers about the advantages of adopting a product is fundamental in all marketing strategies (Miller 1956; Kotler 1994; McCarthy 1994). Potential customers must be convinced that the returns will exceed the efforts and costs of acquiring the product. This important premise for successful commodification is also attended to in the reports we examined. Most publications contain comments on the positive effects that can be expected by adoption of the recipe in question.

What, then, are the projected positive effects? Both the TQM and MBO literatures are mainly concerned with improvements in efficiency—and above all economic profits. The TQM literature stands out by suggesting *considerable* effects. The literature on DD, however, is quite different when analyzed in light of this feature. Generally the DD publications are the most cautious when it comes to accentuating or promising any effects. The following quote from one of the recipe's Scandinavian pioneers is typical:

> The development dialogue is not at all an open sesame. But correctly employed it might turn out to be a useful and practical tool that can lead to fewer difficulties, the release of latent resources, and to the development of the individual's as well as the organization's level of competence. (Jorem 1985: 91)

The above discussion points out that *commodification* is a common feature of MBO, DD, and TQM: all have been deliberately transformed into successful products on the vast market of organizations in search of recipes for success.

Timing

A frequently noted but poorly defined notion is that an organizational recipe must be *well-timed* in order to become popular (Huczynski 1993). This means that the capacity to flow may depend on whether the recipe captures the spirit of the time in some way. Viewed from the rationalistic-instrumental perspective, a widespread recipe is a very effective management tool, or solution, that successfully matches the dominant problem definitions for organizations within a given period—that is, an idea whose time has come. The important question, however, is *how* and *why* a particular organizational recipe comes to be perceived as a timely message. Not by itself, we suppose, or by the help of any magic spirit of the times! What is required is a thoroughly executed social construction—the work of *defining* and *presenting* the recipe as timely. The *timing* of an organizational recipe is a process of actively locating and defining it in relation to stages of development and modernization in the past, present, and future. We became aware of the significance of such definition processes during our close reading of management publications. We were struck by the amount of space used for defining the recipes as timely (see, for example, Garmannslund 1994; Wollebæk 1989; Tofte 1993). This indicates that timing is an important part of strategies and efforts to make organizational recipes flow.

We have been looking for possible common features and patterns in how the publications have attempted to define MBO, DD, and TQM as timely recipes. Two that we have identified will be discussed below. Briefly, these are what we call decadism and an orientation toward the future and the "new."

Decadism. Timing is about interpreting a recipe into a context, a frame of developments and changes that are claimed to unfold over a period of time. But which time and how far into the future and back into the past do the authors of prescriptive management publications look? The time horizon referred to in the literature is relatively short. Comments on the development are most often limited to the recent past, within the past ten to twenty years. The future is even more limited, rarely exceeding ten years. A number of observations reveal a clear pattern in these time-framing attempts: their unit of reference is usually a decade. Development trends and change processes are most frequently grouped and classified as belonging to the 1980s, the 1990s, and so forth, a phenomenon that may be termed *decadism*. The underlying belief seems to be that the arrival of a new decade means fundamental economical, technological, and sometimes political changes, which consequently call for new ways of managing and organizing. This logic thrives on managers' fear of being left behind. A frequent element in the timing of a recipe is a prophesy of dramatic changes in the near future (usually the next decade); this message is particularly prominent in literature on MBO and TQM. The impression is that the recipes—rather than being solutions to the problems of today—are tools designed to handle problems that are likely to arise in the near future.

Decades are without doubt becoming a popular time unit for describing current as well as future trends in organizational and management thought. But even if this unit is a social construction and, seen from the historical record, not very precise, it will probably become an increasingly accurate description of the development within this area, because the more the decade is referred to (for example, in management publications) and becomes institutionalized, the more leaders, consultants, and other actors in the field will experience—and probably also become sensitized to—signals of what the next decade will bring. Their expectations will develop in accordance with such signals, and consequently their *actions* will be based on these expectations. Hence, the ten-year-prophesies—or the social construction of the next decade—often become a reality.

Orientation Toward "the New." Another important element in the timing of a recipe is the attempt to present it as a *novelty*, that is, something brand-new and distinctive from previous solutions. The amount of space given to such interpretation in management publications certainly reflects the norms and demands in numerous organizations. At the turn of the millennium most modern organizations are permeated by a strong ideology of change and renewal, echoing deeply rooted beliefs in the Western project of modernization. Consequently, organizations have to demonstrate that they *are in motion*, constantly seeking improvements in order to reach even higher stages of development. This can be done by expressing willingness to replace "old" solutions with those defined as brand-new. Hence the attractiveness of an organizational recipe depends on whether, among other things, it is presented in such a manner that it becomes a symbol of the new and modern. One frequently applied strategy in the publications to define recipes as novelties is by *contrasting*.

Contrasting statements point out how and why a particular recipe is different from previous ones. One such example is found in Peter Drucker's seminal piece of 1954, *The Practice of Management*. Drucker uses much space arguing that MBO clearly breaks with the principles of Fordism, which is

described as the old and traditional way of managing large industrial organizations in America (Drucker 1954: 141–153). About forty years later, however, in the 1990s, many authors of TQM publications find it vital to define
this recipe in contrast to the "old" MBO recipe. An example is Tofte (1993),
who argues for the necessity of implementing TQM in kindergartens. The
author uses pairs of opposite concepts, systematically labeling what she
claims is the "old" MBO recipe in negatively charged linguistic labels, while
presenting the "new" TQM recipe in just as systematically positive terms. The
pairs of contrasting labels include (the first associated with MBO, the second
with TQM) technical thinking–people oriented, profit oriented–customer oriented, the importance of gaining sudden profit–the importance of long-term
strategy, formalized control structures–process-oriented structures, competition–cooperation, hierarchical organization–organic organization, importance of formal rules–importance of values, and static system–orientation
toward continuous improvements (Tofte 1993: 67–68).

Obviously, contrasting such as the above often involves dramatic simplifications, especially of the richness of the ideas that are depicted as the
"old" ones.

Harmonizing

A number of researchers have described organizations as arenas for
the display of power and conflicts. The importance of the conflict perspective is clearly demonstrated in numerous studies (for example, Cyert and
March 1963; Coleman 1975; Perrow 1986; Gouldner 1954). Organizations
have typical flash points where conflicts are frequently displayed, such as in
the borders among leaders and workers, internal subunits, subcultures, professions, and occupational groups. However, the power and conflict perspective is clearly downplayed in the examined management literature.
Instead there are numerous attempts to *harmonize* the recipes by defining and
presenting them in a way that does not provoke or challenge any of the
above-mentioned dimensions of conflict. This is another important common
feature of the three recipes.

Let us take a closer look at how the harmonizing of MBO, TQM, and
DD is expressed in the literature. Most publications emphasize that the recipe
is designed to facilitate the interest of the organization as a *whole*, not that
of particular subgroups within the organization. When particular internal

groups or units are mentioned (for example, leaders, professions, departments, women), the recipes are rarely described as "weapons" that one group can use against another to gain advantages. Hence, the authors of management publications are usually very cautious not to fall down on either side of the recognized conflict dimensions in modern organizations.

The Scandinavian literature on DD contains a great number of excellent illustrations of attempts to harmonize this recipe in order to make it acceptable to various groups within the organization. Most interesting are the numerous attempts to define development dialogue in ways that avoid a mobilization of people along the most classical of all borders of conflict: the cleavage between leaders-owners and workers. Many influential publications claim that an important reason that the American-inspired counseling and appraisal system did not have any success in Scandinavia was that this recipe was perceived as a tool for managers to control their workers—in other words, it was not considered neutral in relation to this highly important conflict dimension (Wollebæk 1989; Holt-Larsen and Bang 1993). In Scandinavian DD publications, harmonizing means, among other things, emphasizing that development dialogue is a "dialogue between two *equal* actors," the manager and the worker (Wollebæk 1989), and that the dialogue should *not* include discussions about traditional conflict material, such as negotiation of salary. Thus, in order to gain acceptance of development dialogue in Scandinavia, it is essential to avoid favoring either one of the two main parties in work life.

Harmonizing sometimes means presenting the recipes in such a *general* and *ambiguous* form that groups with various—and often also conflicting—interests may give them their support. This is clearly demonstrated in many MBO publications. This is a recipe that, on the one hand, easily gains the support from top managers because it is promised, for example, in management publications, that implementing the recipe means that managers can concentrate on devoting all their intellectual capacity and energy to strategic questions, while delegating "minor work" to subordinates. On the other hand, MBO might also have a strong appeal to ordinary workers because it is claimed—and widely believed—that the application of this recipe leads to more autonomy and hence to more interesting jobs for the frontline personnel as well as for the workers at the lowest levels of the organizational hierarchy.

Management literature often presents an image of organizations as complete, integrated systems that nonetheless are often threatened by external dangers, for example, technological innovations, competitors, and political regulations. Thus, a frequently voiced message in publications is that all groups within the organization should be united in an effort to pull in the same direction and thereby secure the organization's success and survival. This is also an important feature of the harmonizing process.

These observations indicate that the probability that an organizational recipe will gain popularity and flow will increase if it is successfully harmonized, that is, defined so that it is perceived as neither favoring nor provoking specific interest groups known to exist within organizations.

Dramatizing

A strikingly common feature of MBO and TQM (much more prominent than is the case with DD) is that the stories about their origin and diffusion, as they are outlined in recipe literature, very often contain numerous and quite *dramatic* elements. We know from drama and theaters about the methods for dramatizing a story. A central idea in dramaturgy is that the story should be *exciting* and contain a fundamental contrast between sharply profiled actors (or *characters*) representing conflicting ideas. In the course of the story, both ideas and actors are expected to be met with obstacles and resistance, with a few highlights and dramatic turning points thrown in.

Such dramatic elements are relatively easy to spot in literature on MBO and TQM. Stories about exceptional "characters" are presented, such as the ones about Peter F. Drucker, W. Edwards Deming, and Joseph Juran. The stories about their lives and careers have some clear dramatic features in common. These pioneers are described as strong and outstanding personalities who early in their careers discovered and launched new and provocative management ideas and tools. They are, however, met with resistance by contemporary, dominant management gurus and their ideas. Consequently the pioneers have to fight against conventional knowledge and the ruling management doctrines. And as in real dramas, the stories contain dramatic turning points whereby the pioneers and their ideas and recipes are "victorious" at the end.

Probably the most dramatic story (which incidentally is referred to in numerous publications) is the one about W. Edwards Deming and his influence on the birth and success of TQM, first in Japan, and later in the United

States and Europe. The story starts in the United States in the second half of the 1940s when W. Edwards Deming had developed a sophisticated quality control system. He and his colleagues had great confidence in the potential of this system to improve the competitive power in contemporary American industry. However, this early recipe for quality improvements was largely disregarded, the story goes, because Deming—in much the same way as Dr. Stockmann in Henrik Ibsen's famous drama *An Enemy of the People* (Ibsen 1882/1967)—partly was ignored, and partly was met by resistance and imprudence by his fellow countrymen (Kennedy 1994). In the swinging and booming 1950s there were few in the United States that realized the necessity of Deming's ideas. But what does this misunderstood and rejected person do in response? Around 1950 he turns his back on his country and heads for Japan. And here—from his country's recent enemy—he gained a warm reception and great respect. In the following months Japanese top executives received a thorough instruction in Deming's principles for quality control and quality leadership. And these particular insights, which the Americans according to the story so casually and arrogantly had renounced, now become the seed of what in the next act, about ten years later, returns to the United States as a boomerang. By that time Japan had become the great victor of the industrial and economic race. Another important turning point in the story takes place in 1980. In the final act of the drama—and in the nick of time for the then eighty-year-old Deming—he is rediscovered in his own country. In June 1980, the TV-company NBC broadcast a documentary with the title "*If Japan Can, Why Can't We?*" In this program Deming and his ideas about TQM were broadly presented for the first time to the U.S. population. Consequently, the previously rejected and ignored Deming, during the remaining twelve years of his life (he died in 1993), received the status of a guru and nothing less than a potential rescuer of the U.S. economy. This story, if in slightly different versions, has made its rounds in numerous TQM publications. It contains, as shown, all the typical ingredients of a dramatized story.

There are distinct dramatic elements also in many interpretations of the origin of MBO. One is the frequently cited story about the "fight" between the MBO inventor, Peter Drucker, and probably the greatest of all giants in American economic life, Henry Ford. MBO is held up as an alternative to Ford's more aristocratic form of leadership. And although Drucker later obtained a status of a giant, or "the guru's guru" (Micklethwait and

Wooldridge 1996), the part he played in 1954 was more like David's fight against Goliath. This dramatic point is often referred to, especially in the early MBO literature.

Is it possible, then, that dramatization does have an effect on the capacity of organizational recipes to flow? The answer is probably *yes*. Although it may not be one of the most important factors, there is much evidence that the potential for a recipe to flow increases if the stories about the recipe's origin and its pioneers contain dramatic elements. The connection between dramatization and flow can be explained as follows. Dramatic messages flow more easily than others, simply because they are more *exciting* to tell and because dramatic stories attract more attention. Not least, dramatic stories are easily *remembered*, hence the chances of their being retold and spread increase. Thus a dramatized message often has a "life of its own"; it becomes a story, in the true sense of the word, that spreads rapidly, often without any costs, and with the dramatic element as an important driving force.

Individualizing

The three examined recipes, MBO, DD, and TQM, also have in common that they are *individualized*—the message is defined such that it represents an appealing offer to the individual organizational member. There is no doubt that individualization adds to the recipes' capacity to flow, partly because it reflects the present tendency to emphasize individualism. This phenomenon is observed by other organization researchers. John Meyer states:

> Much modern rationalization is around worker, citizen, and human right considerations that directly derive from ancestral Western celebration of the individual soul. Ideas legitimated in terms of such rights—to equal treatment, to the celebration of individual merit, and so on—probably travel fairly rapidly. (Meyer 1996:251)

The movement toward increased individualism in Western society as a whole—aptly formulated by Scott and Meyer (1991) as the arrival of the "The Heroic Individual"—has gathered momentum especially during the postwar period. A new, strong wave of individualism has surged over both the United States and Europe since the late 1970s and is reflected in politics, economics, and religion (Nozick 1974; Meyer and Jepperson 2000). Consequently, contemporary organizations have to cope with individuals who have acquired an increasing number of rights, are better educated, and are more and more conscious of career and personal development (Legge 1995). Developing and securing human capital—the intellectual, analytical, and creative resources of the work force—has become an increasingly important part of modern organizations' strategic efforts. Such efforts to cope with the modern individual include, among other things, establishing personnel departments, hiring expertise on human resource management, and adopting various personnel training programs (Monahan *et al.* 1994; Meyer *et al.* 1987).

These tenets are also clearly reflected in the interpretation of each of the three management recipes. The publications present them as means to create more exciting jobs, increase the autonomy and empowerment of the individual members, and enhance learning and personal development. To illustrate, one of the cornerstones of MBO, as formulated by Drucker in the early 1950s, is the idea that the individual worker should not be tied to detailed instructions (as in the Taylor system) but rather—by delegation— be given confidence and autonomy to solve problems using his or her own judgment (Drucker 1954).

A great concern expressed in many TQM publications is that organizations must encourage the individual worker's personal development and creativity:

> The TQM "post-Fordism" or "post-modernism" context calls for a management environment where human dignity and independence of the individual worker are respected . . . TQM is decidedly people-centered and might equally be called Total People Management. (Morgan and Murgatroyd 1994:15)

There are interesting differences on this point between American-English literature and Scandinavian literature. The former is considerably more concerned about individualizing the recipes than is the latter. Obviously this reflects differences between the Anglo-American individualistic culture and the more egalitarian Scandinavian culture. It clearly illustrates the relevance of the "reversed Parsons" argument outlined in the Introduction: the recipes' capacity to flow depends, among other things, on the extent to which they correspond to basic norms and values in society.

A general proposition may be derived from the above: the probability of an organizational recipe to obtain popularity and wide dissemination increases if it is individualized. Hence, ideas and recipes that do not fulfill this "requirement"—that is, that are not aimed at the contemporary "heroic" individual as means of creating more exciting jobs and enhancing personal development—will most likely be limited in their capacity to flow.

Toward a Theory of Management Ideas That Flow

This chapter attempts to identify possible common features of some of the most popular and widespread management ideas, features that may explain their enormous capacity to flow. In this final section the insights are synthesized in seven propositions.

The rationalistic-instrumental perspective in organizational analysis assumes that the most widespread recipes are those that have proven to be most suitable management tools for improving organizational effectiveness and efficiency. Consequently one might expect that management publications advocating these ideas would contain documentation of such effects. This study's sampling of such publications does not bear out this expectation. Thorough documentation of a recipe's positive effects across a range of organizations is rare. There is, however, a general *concern* about the recipes' effects, and stories of great successes are frequently presented and interpreted. It is not altogether impossible that the three examined recipes are indeed efficient management tools. But the point is that the literature, which is a very important medium for the presentation and diffusion of these ideas, is definitely not the place to find effects documented. Obviously, the appeal of popular organizational recipes, and hence their capacity to flow, lies elsewhere.

The analysis of management publications on MBO, TQM, and DD reveals that their presentation has common features that may explain the enormous appeal of these recipes. They have all undergone, and successfully project, social authorization, universalizing, commodification, timing, harmonization, dramatization, and individualization. Development dialogue differs from MBO and TQM in some of these features. This recipe is, in contrast to the two others, socially authorized by references "only" to Scandinavian organizations. Nor has the commodification of DD been as thorough as that of MBO and TQM. For example, the stories about its origin and diffusion are devoid of any dramatic or exciting elements. This might help explain why DD has not obtained the popularity and extensive dissemination of the other two.

The insight gained from comparison of the three organizational superstandards—or "winners"—should inform any attempt to outline a general theory about factors that can influence a recipe's capacity to flow. More specifically, such a theory should consider the following seven propositions based on this study:

1. *Social authorization*: The capacity to flow increases if the organizational recipe is socially authorized, that is, is clearly linked to and associated with one or more widely reputed and successful organizations or persons.

2. *Universalizing*: The capacity to flow increases if the organizational recipe is universalized, that is, if it is defined as a panacea with a universal range of application. It involves attempts to win acceptance of the ideas that (1) all organizations are more or less similar systems with similar needs if perceived as formal organizations and (2) the recipe itself is based on knowledge about cause and effect that allows it to produce positive results almost independent of where and when it is applied.

3. *Commodification*: The capacity to flow increases if the organizational recipe is commodified, that is, if it is transformed into something resembling a product. Successful commodification means, among other things, that the recipe is formulated as an easily communicated message that catches the attention of a broad audience, it must be perceived as a user friendly product, and the potential user must be given the prospect of positive effects in return for implementing the recipe.

4. *Timing*: The capacity to flow increases if the organizational recipe is properly timed, that is, it is interpreted in relation to stages of development in the past, the present, and the future and is presented as a new, modern, and future-oriented answer to ongoing processes of environmental changes.

5. *Harmonizing*: The capacity to flow increases if the organizational recipe is harmonized, that is, is defined and presented in such a way that it does not provoke or challenge any of the typical conflict dimensions in modern organizations.

6. *Dramatizing*: The capacity to flow increases if the organizational recipe is dramatized, that is, interpretations of its origin, develop-

ment, and path to popularity are presented as stories containing dramatic elements.

7. *Individualizing*: The capacity to flow increases if the organizational recipe is individualized, that is, it is defined in such a way that the individual organization member sees it as an appealing offer of exciting jobs, a career, and personal development.

Obviously these seven factors may co-vary; for example, a recipe's capacity to flow probably will increase in proportion to the number of above-mentioned requirements that are fulfilled. It may also be assumed that organizational recipes that are not successfully defined in accordance with any—or at least a few—of these factors will be clearly limited in their capacity to flow.

This study has demonstrated the weakness of the two most common explanations of why some organizational ideas gain great popularity and wide dissemination but others do not. The first is the rationalistic-instrumental inspired belief that the recipes that obtain the greatest dissemination are those that have proven to be the best management tools. The second is the metaphysical-inspired belief that organizations are more or less helpless captives of the *Zeitgeist*, and consequently, that a recipe that gains wide acceptance is *an idea whose time has come.* Underlying both explanations is the assumption that some organizational ideas and recipes spread almost of their own accord, either by virtue of simply being the most effective management tools or by being an idea whose time has come.

Unlike the rationalistic-instrumental and the metaphysical explanations, the seven propositions generated by this study are rooted in a sociological-institutional paradigm. A common denominator of these propositions is the belief that social construction and reconstruction of organizational recipes through processes of definition and presentation are decisive for whether the recipe will flow or not. Thus, organizational recipes, such as the three examined, do not become organizational superstandards or "winners" by virtue of their intrinsic qualities but rather as a consequence of processes of social construction and reconstruction.

A well-known insight from institutional theory is that organizations must adopt ideologies, routines, and structures that are congruent with broader social norms and values in order to obtain legitimacy, and hence to increase their capacity to exploit resources and services—an argument Parsons was one of the first to outline. This article, however, emphasizes another insight, the "reversed Parsons." An important condition for organizational ideas and recipes to become popular and adopted by a great number of organizations is that the recipes themselves have been legitimized according to widespread norms and values among the world's organizations. Such legitimizing work is mainly carried out by the authors of prescriptive management publications.

The Institutionalization of the Quality Management Approach in Germany
Peter Walgenbach, University of Erfurt, Germany and Nikolaus Beck, University of Erfurt, Germany

Introduction

The body of management knowledge has grown significantly since the beginning of the industrial revolution. New management concepts have continually been developed and many of them are now seen as taken-for-granted elements of modern management even if doubts are repeatedly expressed as to whether they can contribute to an improvement in performance generally, that is, in all organizations. Nevertheless, organizations often cannot avoid adopting such institutionalized management concepts. They have to signal to their environment that they match up to the perceptions of modern management, that is, they use institutionalized management concepts.

New institutionalism in organizational analysis focuses on this problem. Its core argument is that the elements of organizational structure are less a technical means of coordinating and controlling production and exchange efficiently and more a reflection of institutionalized demands and expectations in the organizational environment (Meyer and Rowan 1977; DiMaggio and Powell 1983; Powell and DiMaggio 1991; Scott and Meyer 1994; Scott 1995). External constituents or stakeholders regard certain elements of formal structure as rational means to achieve certain desirable goals. These elements of formal structure are adopted by organizations irrespective of their effect on the performance of the organization. They serve merely to increase the legitimacy of the organization in its institutional environment (Meyer and Rowan 1977; DiMaggio and Powell 1983). An important source of fundamental demands concerning the design of the formal structure of an organization are the professions (Abbott 1988). They often demand organizations to comply with their respective values and standards and to implement their corresponding concepts and techniques of organization. In addition, professions are frequently supported by other external claimant-groups who also regard these elements as a means of enhancing the efficiency of organizations. As a consequence, organizations adopt these elements in order to achieve legitimacy in their institutional environment. The adoption may, in fact, become a prerequisite for the survival of the organization.

Despite its prominence, institutional theory has a number of shortcomings (Donaldson 1995; Walgenbach 1999). An important critique is that the process of institutionalization remains unexplained (Zucker 1987; Tolbert and Zucker 1996). Thus, a "metaphysical pathos" seems to be attached to the emergence of institutions (DiMaggio 1988). There have been several attempts to solve this problem conceptually (DiMaggio 1988; Oliver 1991), and there are also numerous empirical studies that identify a number of different factors influencing the process of institutionalization, such as the interests of actors (see the studies in Powell and DiMaggio 1991; Scott and Christensen 1995). However, even prominent institutionalists (Tolbert and Zucker 1996) concede that the conceptual problem remains. The discrepancy, however, lies mainly in the rejection of the rational actor model, as well as the negation of the concepts of strategic behavior and power (Oliver 1991). We want to concentrate on this problem in this chapter. We want, through an example, to investigate how a new management idea develops, how management knowledge that is linked to the idea spreads, and how the management concepts linked to the idea develop into an institution.

We propose that the process of institutionalization may be more accurately accounted for if institutional theory is combined with resource mobilization theory, as formulated by McCarthy and Zald (1987). Resource mobilization theory was developed to grasp social movements conceptually. Its core idea is that social movements are less a spontaneous than an organized phenomenon. Organizations within a movement try to ensure and increase the transfer of resources such as, for example, money, manpower, and legitimacy. Social movements attempt to ensure their existence and growth.

We argue that resource mobilization theory is particularly suitable as a complementary approach to institutional theory in order to explain the emergence of institutions. This is substantiated by the fact that the conceptual understanding of organizations, as well as the basic assumptions of both approaches, correspond. Resource mobilization theory enables processes of institutionalization to be understood, both conceptually and empirically, without having to refer to an almighty or rational actor. However, resource mobilization theory concedes much more leeway to the actor than institutional theory.

Furthermore, we will provide empirical evidence that supports the fruitfulness of resource mobilization theory as a complementary approach to institutional theory. We will present a concrete example illustrating the fruitfulness of resource mobilization theory, namely, the institutionalization of quality management (QM) in Germany. Thus, we will attempt to explain how new management ideas are developed, how they are expanded, how they are spread and become institutionalized.

The study is divided into two parts. The first part is a historical analysis in which we will present the strategies and activities of the quality-management movement that were used to anchor the value-system of the quality engineering profession in important subsystems of society. Findings from the study show that the anchorage of the movement's value system in society cannot be traced back to the activities of the quality-management movement alone but also to a weakness in the governmental system of the European Community. The European Commission considered certain management concepts and techniques developed by quality engineers as methods for overcoming those weaknesses. Due to the involvement of the European Commission, the concepts and techniques of the quality-management movement have become legitimized. As a consequence, they have become increasingly supported by other subsystems of society, such as business and science.

Our presentation of the interplay of the strategies and activities of the quality-management movement and the European Commission serves as the basis for the deduction of a number of hypotheses on the resulting process of institutionalization of QM in business and science. We will test these hypotheses in the second part of the study. We will provide a quantitative analysis of the changes in the authorship of the most important and most influential journal on QM in Germany, namely *Qualität und Zuverlässigkeit* (QZ, Quality and Reliability). The debate on quality control, quality assurance, and QM is essentially reflected in this journal, which is the organ of the quality-management movement in Germany. We assume that changes in the concepts, techniques, and understanding of QM itself, as well as in the composition of the groups providing resources for the quality-management movement are reflected in this journal.

We assume that changes in the authorship of this journal show the evolution of the institutional field. If the strategies of the quality-management movement have been successfully realized, the pursuit of legitimation should have resulted in an increasing number of authors who are willing and able to award legitimacy to QM and the quality-management movement. If members of particular groups, such as academics, invest part of their working time, make their qualifications available, and place their reputation at the disposal of the quality-management movement by promoting QM, QM and the quality-management movement will be legitimized. Furthermore, we expect the changes in the authorship of the journal to be particularly reflected in articles on ISO 9000 and total quality management (TQM), as these approaches were used and promoted by the European Commission and had, therefore, already been legitimized.[1]

Both empirical sections are preceded by a description of the respective database and the applied methods. At the end of the paper we will discuss the results of the study.

Resource Mobilization Theory

Many authors have recently referred to theories of social movements to explain the emergence of new industries and institutions (Carroll 1996; Barnett 1995; Olzak and West 1991; Carroll and Hannan 1995; Hannan 1995; Barron 1995; Strang 1995). The resource mobilization theory (McCarthy and Zald 1987; Tilly 1978, 1984; Olzak 1992) is one of those; it is understood as a partial theory to conceptually depict the phenomenon of social movements. A core argument of this approach, which distinguishes it from other theories of social movements, is that social movements should be regarded as organized. Organizations within the social movement aim at ensuring and increasing the flow of resources to ensure the social movement's maintenance and growth, as well as their own.

McCarthy and Zald (1987: 20) regard social movements as "a set of opinions in a population representing preferences for changing some elements of the social structure or reward distribution, or both, of a society." For them, as for many other authors, social movements are "nothing more than preference structures directed toward social change . . ." (McCarthy and Zald

1987: 20). However, in some important aspects McCarthy and Zald (1987) diverge from traditional theories of social movements. First, according to McCarthy and Zald, a social movement may or may not be based upon the grievances of the presumed beneficiaries. Second, those who provide money, facilities, and even labor may have no commitment to the values that underlie a specific movement. Third, McCarthy and Zald argue that opportunities for social movements are created by regime weaknesses on the one hand, as well as regime support on the other. Furthermore, they point out that social movements are organized. Rather than seeing organization and movement as contrasting phenomena, they emphasize that they are embedded. They focus attention on the fact that social movements, counter-movements, and authorities are organized.

McCarthy and Zald (1987: 20) define a social movement organization as "a complex, or formal, organization that identifies its goals with the preferences of a social movement or a counter-movement and attempts to implement those goals." The targets of social movement organizations are very much like those of economic and other organizations. Social movement organizations try to ensure the flow of resources, such as money, manpower, reputation, or legitimacy. Like economic organizations and other organizations, social movement organizations attempt to ensure their existence and growth. To ensure the flow of resources, it is important for these latter organizations to mobilize supporters, neutralize counter-movements, transform the mass and elite public into sympathizers, and achieve changes in general values and targets. This is why they often emphasize that the realization of the values, targets, and concepts of the movement benefits wider groupings of citizens through notions of a better future or society.

The environment of a social movement organization is populated with other purposeful actors who are deliberately trying to influence, control, or even destroy it (Gamson 1987). The environment of the social movement organization is active, not passive. Thus, a social movement organization does not interact primarily with other such organizations within the same movement, but with organizations who control the decisions they want to influence, or with organizations in the counter-movement, which oppose the changes it is promoting. The strategies and activities of the respective actors with which the social movement organizations interact cannot, however, be fully foreseen by the social movement organizations. Therefore, the result of the interplay of the strategies and activities of a social movement organization and various other actors cannot be fully anticipated.

It is our intention to utilize this theory of social movements to make the process of institutionalization of quality management concepts and techniques in Germany intelligible to the reader. Concepts such as ISO 9000 standards or TQM are increasingly being adopted by companies all over the world. The adoption of these structural management concepts, however, often seems to be triggered more by the demands of external claimants (customers, governmental organizations) than by concerns of how to increase the efficiency of an organization (Hackman and Wageman 1995; Walgenbach 1998). Thus, we are addressing a phenomenon regarded as being typical in institutional theory (Meyer and Rowan 1977; DiMaggio and Powell 1983).

Data and Methods of the Historical Analysis

In the first part of the study we will analyze the process of the institutionalization of QM in Germany after World War II. The focus, however, is on the period from 1972 to 1997 because in 1972 the *Ausschuß Qualitätssicherung und angewandte Statistik* (AQS, Committee for Quality Control and Applied Statistics) was set up in the *Deutsches Institut für Normung e.V.* (DIN, German Standards Institute). This committee played a decisive role in developing standards for quality systems such as ISO 9000 (see Walgenbach 2000). The development of standards for quality systems marked an important change in the quality-management movement. It represented the crystallization of a development that began with the use of techniques of statistical quality control in the production departments of U.S. companies in the early 1920s and ended with quality systems. These systems came to be seen as a universal management approach to control the work processes of an organization in its entirety.

Furthermore, we analyze the interaction between this committee and German industry and its associations, because the associations were important representatives of the counter-movement to the quality-management movement. Moreover, the activities of the *Deutsche Gesellschaft für Qualität e.V.* (DGQ, German Society for Quality), which is an important organization in the quality-management movement, and the strategies and activities of the European Commission and the European Council are of relevance for an understanding of the institutionalization process of QM.

We contacted a number of important organizations and institutions that influenced the process of the institutionalization of QM in Germany from 1972 onward, such as the *Bundesverband der Deutschen Industrie e.V.* (BDI, National Confederation of the German Industry), the German Standards Institute, the *Deutsche Gesellschaft zur Zertifizierung von Managementsystemen mbH* (DQS, German Society for the Certification of Management Systems), the *Trägergemeinschaft für Akkreditierung GmbH* (TGA, German Association Body for Accreditation), and the *Deutscher Akkreditierungsrat* (DAR, German Council for Accreditation). Most made comprehensive data available upon request. We analyzed the following documents:

- Minutes of meetings of the Committee for Quality Control and Applied Statistics in the German Standards Institute and of the National Confederation of the German Industry, which refer to the development of standards for quality systems
- Correspondence of the Committee for Quality Control and Applied Statistics in the German Standards Institute and the National Confederation of German Industry, which refers to various drafts of standards for quality systems
- Comments of the National Confederation of German Industry, other industrial associations, and a number of companies referring to various drafts of standards for quality systems

Furthermore, we analyzed the 1972 to 1997 editions of the journals *DIN-Mitteilungen,* the organ of the German Standards Institute, and *Qualität und Zuverlässigkeit,* the organ of the German Society for Quality. We considered that these journals are very likely to document the strategies and activities of the social movement organizations, as well as the institutionalization process of QM. We also analyzed publications and (working) papers of the European Commission and the European Council, which can be linked to the increasing spread of quality systems, quality system certification and TQM. In addition, we studied the general literature on quality control, QM, and TQM.

Attempts to Anchor the Concepts and Techniques of Quality Management in Society

In this section we will describe attempts of the quality-management movement in Germany to anchor its concepts and techniques to society.

These attempts can be divided into three streams of activities. These concern, first, the gradual broadening of the field of activities; second, attempts to professionalize the body of technical knowledge of the quality-management movement and activities aimed to establish quality management as an academic discipline; and third, attempts to institutionalize quality management in for-profit organizations. The historical analysis presented in this section is used to deduce hypotheses that are tested in a later section.

The Gradual Broadening of the Field of Activity

The Origins of Quality Management. The trigger for the emergence of the quality-management movement, which has almost been forgotten, was the increasing diffusion of the methods of "scientific management." The methods of controlling the process of production and a definite product quality, as developed by Taylor (1911) and his colleagues, were subject to inevitable fluctuations in performance of people entrusted with the tasks of quality control. Controlling outputs and picking out faulty products, especially when producing large masses of products with a low market value, thus proved to be as awkward as it was expensive. This procedure could never be completely satisfactory from the point of view of efficient quality assurance. The problem could have been solved to a large extent during Taylor's time through the methods of applied or technical statistics, which were already fairly developed (Lerner 1988). However, the application of statistical methods was slow to win recognition in management practice (Tuckman 1995), primarily because the qualifications required to use these methods were nonexistent in most companies (Masing 1978).

In 1931, a book regarded today as a classic in statistical quality control was published. It was Shewhart's *Economic Control of Quality of Manufactured Product*, which discussed suitable sampling plans and methods for their development. The first systematic access to the use of statistical quality control in industrial production was thus created. Subsequently, managers in production departments gradually began to use statistical methods to process large numbers of data (Lerner 1988). However, it was application in U.S. industry by the Statistical Research Group during World War II and the enormous success achieved through the application of statistical methods that led to the establishment of statistical quality control in mass production (Tuckman 1995).

Development in Germany. In Germany it was not until the late 1940s that the methods of applied statistics spread (Daeves and Beckel 1948; Bücken 1949). The reason for the delay was that the qualifications required for their utilization were initially almost nonexistent in German industry. In response to this situation, and promoted by a visit from Deming, "father of the quality-movement" (Mann 1989), considerable activities in German industry were started in the early 1950s (Altenkirch 1972; Stumpf 1972; Kirstein 1989). On October 24, 1952 the *Ausschuß Wirtschaftliche Fertigung* (AWF, Committee for Efficient Production) founded the subcommittee *Technische Statistik* (Technical Statistic). Statistical quality control became a core activity in this subcommittee. The idea was to open up considerable potential for industrial rationalization. In many German cities, task forces were set up to exchange the experiences made in applying the methods of statistical quality control. Booklets summarizing the outcomes of the task forces had begun to be published by 1954. In 1956 the journal *Qualitätskontrolle* (Quality Control) was launched. In 1969, it was renamed *Qualität und Zuverlässigkeit.* In 1956 the subcommittee was also renamed *Deutsche Arbeitsgemeinschaft für statistische Qualitätskontrolle* (ASQ, German Working Group for Statistical Quality Control). The focus of the activities of this working group remained initially narrow. Until well into the 1960s, the interest of quality engineers in Germany was concentrated on statistical methods (Fuhr 1993; Orlemann 1995).

From 1960 onwards, the field of activity was broadened. Topics such as organization, expenses, cost effectiveness, suppliers, customer service, and liability for defective products were issues that gained attention. It seems that the extension of the range of topics addressed by quality engineers was valued positively, as reflected in the circulation of the journal edited by members of the quality-management movement. At the end of the 1960s, circulation was more than four thousand, which is an impressive number for a professional journal. Today it is more than twenty thousand (Masing 1996).

In 1968 the former committee *Technische Statistik* changed its name again to *Deutsche Gesellschaft für Qualität e.V.* (DGQ, German Society for Quality). This organization founded in 1952 by only nine representatives of German industry had 1,200 members by 1972 (Altenkirch 1972) and it has more than 7,600 members today. Since the founding of the German Society for Quality, the development and diffusion of the values, concepts, and techniques proclaimed by the quality-management movement in Germany have been closely aligned with this organization (Altenkirch 1972; Masing 1978; Pfeifer *et al.* 1991a).

The field of activity of the quality-management movement not only broadened with respect to the topics discussed, but also the concepts and methods of the quality-management movement gradually began to penetrate the entire organization, initially in production and continuing all the way up to top management. Quality control in production had been the focus of quality engineers into the 1970s. After this time, opinion spread among quality engineers that production departments were by no means the only source of defects, but rather that the reliability of products was primarily determined by other factors, namely leadership, administration, research and development, construction, purchase, distribution, customer services, accounting, and training (Altenkirch 1972). Subsequently, the emphasis shifted from quality assurance in production to methods of planning and organizing (Masing 1978). At this time and in the following years, the approach corresponded to the international development of QM, to which the names of Deming (1982), Juran (1990), Feigenbaum (1991), and Crosby (1986) are connected.

From the 1970s onward, the field of activity was also extended in another respect. The documentation of quality-related activities was now regarded as an important responsibility of quality assurance departments (Masing 1978). The core idea was that quality-related activities must be planned, documented, and inspected. This was led by the thought that production should be based on authorized technical documentation and should be documented on the basis of continuous nominal and actual comparisons. The intention was to create a combination of quality planning and quality control, with documentary proof of compliance to the prescribed procedures and quality standards (Kilian 1984; Stumpf 1976). The concept of documented quality assurance systems, or quality systems, had become discernible.

Quality engineers in Germany established the Committee for Quality Control and Applied Statistics in the German Standards Institute in the 1970s. This committee—based on earlier standards for quality systems created by the British and Canadian Standards Institutes—made several attempts to develop industry standards for documenting quality systems. All these attempts were rejected by German industry, which was represented by industry associations and large enterprises and had formed a counter-movement to prevent the initiatives of the quality engineers. The standardization of quality systems was resisted because German industry feared organizational inter-ference, as well as a standardization of management (Walgenbach 2000).

The European Dimension. In the mid-1980s, it became clear that the European Commission intended to change its policy of technical harmo-nization. Due to massive problems and delays in harmonizing technical char-acteristics of products in Europe, it planned to use the ISO 9000 standards to hasten the realization of the single European market (Sauer 1987). Tech-nical specifications were no longer to be integrated into the directives of the European Community. Moreover, a system of certifications should be used to ensure that products would be in line with the demands of the directives (Zuckerman 1997). The European Commission, however, pointed out that the changes in its attempt to technically harmonize the European market should not lead to an area-wide product certification, but rather the manu-facturers' declaration that the products comply to the demands of a directive should be accepted on par. The declaration of the manufacturer, however, should be supplemented by independent tests of types and specific aspects of the products or by externally approved (certified) quality systems if necessary. As a result of these measures, the European Commission expected a consid-erable speed-up in the process and schedule of technical harmonization and realization of the single European market.

German industry, which was supported by representatives of the Ger-man government, was not able to push through its reservations for the use of ISO 9000 standards at a European level. The reference of the European Commission to ISO 9000 standards seems, from a German point of view, to be a result of the influence of Great Britain, which had focused on quality sys-tems such as BS 5750—a forerunner to the ISO 9000 standards—in its national industrial policy. The reference to quality systems in directives that have to be implemented at a national level by member states of the European Community led to a virtually forced acceptance of the ISO 9000 standards in Germany (Walgenbach 2000).

Furthermore, the European Commission made use of the ISO 9000 standards in its quality promotion policy in those areas not regulated by directives. Several programs were started to promote the use of ISO 9000 standards and certification. Among the measures implemented was the sub-sidization of the certification of quality systems in small and medium sized companies. The Commission signaled plainly that it regarded the ISO 9000 standards as a means of increasing the competitiveness of European companies (Walgenbach 2000).

Subsequently, the certification of quality systems spread at an accelerating pace. Whereas at the end of 1988, German certifiers had not even issued ten certifications, there were more than seven hundred certified quality systems in Germany by 1992 and more than five thousand by 1995. The number continues to increase. By 2000 more than twenty thousand certifications had been issued.

TQM has recently become popular, as is manifested in the Malcolm Baldrige Award, the European Quality Award, and a number of related national and regional quality awards. TQM seems to be the temporary end of the expansion of the field of activity of the quality-management movement. The adoption and encouragement of TQM by quality engineers in Germany, which has hardly any technical components but is rather a comprehensive management concept, was due primarily to the increasing spread and success of TQM globally.

TQM and the European Quality Award were again promoted by the European Commission (Qualität und Zuverlässigkeit 1992). In using a concept of the quality-management movement for its industrial policy, the Commission once again hoped to increase the competitiveness of Europe's enterprises with a management approach proclaimed by the quality-management movement (European Commission 1995).

The recourse of the European Commission to ISO 9000 and TQM legitimized these concepts. We argue that this legitimacy should be reflected in an increasing number of articles that refer to ISO 9000 or TQM in the organ of the quality-management movement. Thus, we hypothesize:

> Hypothesis 1: The probability that an article in the organ of the quality-management movement, namely the journal Qualität und Zuverlässigkeit, refers to ISO 9000 or TQM increases over time.

The latter expansions of the field of activities in particular implied a distinctive shift in the main focus of the concepts of the quality-management movement. The ISO 9000 standards replaced "quality *assurance*" with "quality *management*" in 1987. The ISO 9000 standards were seen as a management tool that should not only be applied in production departments. From that point on, QM was understood as a *universal* approach that should be used in every department of every company in every industry. The ISO

9000 standards also meant a clear break in another aspect. They signified—
at least in Germany—a fundamental expansion of the area of standardization. Besides the technical standardization of product characteristics, the
standardization of management systems had now become a field of activity
of the German Standards Institute. The re-orientation in industry policy and
technical harmonization of the European market induced by the European
Commission through its reference to the ISO 9000 standards made the break
even more significant. We argue that these concurrent events have had far-
reaching effects. One would expect that it should have become increasingly
attractive for members of other nonengineering professions to enhance their
own legitimacy by referring to the concepts and techniques of the quality-
management movement. Consequently, they should have provided resources,
such as labor or their reputations, to the quality-management movement.
Thus, we hypothesize with respect to changes in the authorship of the journal *Qualität und Zuverlässigkeit*:

> Hypothesis 2a: The proportion of articles in the organ of the quality-
> management movement written by nonengineers increases over time.

The legitimization of the ISO 9000 standards and TQM by the European
Commission should have had the effect that nonengineering professions in
particular provided resources to promote these concepts. We assume:

> Hypothesis 2b: The probability that an article is related to ISO 9000 or
> TQM increases over time more strongly for articles written by nonengi-
> neers than for articles written by engineers.

From Training for Practitioners Toward an Academic Discipline

Training Practitioners. Besides the expansion of the field of activity and
the changes in the content of the concepts promoted, other activities and
strategies were helpful in the institutionalization of QM. It is noticeable that
from the beginning, quality engineers tried to build and expand a system of
training and instruction simultaneously. As early as 1954, the German
Working Group for Statistical Quality Control, later renamed the German
Society for Quality, provided elementary training and courses for practitioners (Sattler 1972). The courses found approval. Until 1972 more than
23,000 qualified employees were trained in various courses of instruction and
seminars (Altenkirch 1972). From the beginning, attempts to professionalize

the educational system were obvious. The level of the courses gradually increased. Examinations were introduced and certifications issued (Stumpf 1972). The training courses were encouraged by employment offices, which provided grants to participants. The content of the training courses and the certifications issued by the German Working Group for Statistical Quality Control were acknowledged by the state, and thus received an official and legitimized status.

The course offering was soon complemented by a crash course with written and oral examinations. After having attended the course, participants were expected to be able to explain the methods of statistical quality control to their colleagues and bosses. Moreover, it was their responsibility to ensure the spread and utilization of the methods in the companies where they were employed (Stumpf 1972). Many graduates became lecturers of the German Working Group for Statistical Quality Control themselves. They now taught the "unified body of knowledge," which they themselves had acquired in the training courses they attended. The unification and systematization of the body of knowledge of the quality-management movement was an explicit target (Stumpf 1972; Fuhr and Stumpf 1993) and indicates the attempts to institutionalize an approved profession (Hartmann 1972). By the early 1990s, more than 250,000 participants had attended the training courses of the German Society for Quality (Fuhr 1993).

Until the 1970s, the focus of the training courses was on the application of statistical methods of quality control. In the early 1980s, the accent shifted to techniques and processes of organizing. The intent of diversifying the courses was to address management and even top management. Since the publication of the ISO 9000 standards, these standards have served as a basis for management training (Stumpf and Franke 1986; Kampa 1996). From 1985 onwards, the German Society for Quality offered courses on QM (Fuhr and Stumpf 1993). Participants who successfully passed the exams acquired the title "Auditor," and since 1995, the international certification "Quality Systems Manager" (Kampa 1996). Meanwhile, the German Society for Quality has diversified its courses again. Today, seminars and courses covering topics such as "EQA (European Quality Award), from ISO to TQM, How the Utilization of the EQA-Concept Leads to Business Excellence" or "Integrated Management Systems—What Comes After the ISO 9000 Certification?" are offered (DIN-Mitteilungen 1996). Since spring 1996, a course on TQM is also being offered. Participants are trained to become assessors of the TQM-model, which is based on the criteria of the European Quality Award. Participants should become familiar with the TQM model and methods of performing a self-assessment of their company's management system. As soon as a participant has successfully applied the methods of "self-assessment," a certification "TQM-Assessor" can be issued by the German Society for Quality (Kampa 1996).

"*Quality Science.*" The successful integration into the lectures of technical universities in Germany from the late 1960s onward was beneficial for the accelerating diffusion of the concepts and techniques of QM. Quality assurance gradually came to be seen as a "science." As of 1964, the chairman of the German Working Group for Statistical Quality Control taught an elective class on quality management to graduate students at the Technical University of Berlin; in 1971 he became honorary professor. A year later, lectures on quality management were held at the Technical University of Hannover (Stumpf 1972); in the following years, other universities followed suit. In 1984 the German Society for Quality changed its statutes in order to advance the anchorage of quality assurance in universities: "In § 2 it is now stated: 'The German Society for Quality aims to promote scientific studies in the area of quality assurance'" (Pfeifer 1986: 57).

At the same time, the quality-management movement attempted to mobilize further resources in order to anchor QM in the system of education. The strategies and tactics employed to achieve this aim included descriptions of international competitors as having an increasing competitive advantage, allusion to an actual or potential economic crisis (for a more detailed description of these tactics see Kieser *et al.* 1998), and, as is typical for social movements, emphasis on the enormous potential societal benefit that may be achieved through the realization of the movement's value system and techniques.

This strategy appears to have been successful. In 1988 an important goal was accomplished when QM became an academic discipline. The first chair for "*Qualitätswissenschaft*" (quality science) was established at the Technical University of Berlin (*Qualität und Zuverlässigkeit* 1989; Malorny and Kassebohm 1994). By 1989 there were three chairs at German universities containing the term and a fourth was planned (Pfeifer *et al.* 1991a, 1991b). In the mid-1990s the activities were intensified once more. In December 1994, eight professors established the *Gesellschaft für Qualitätswissenschaft e. V.* (GQW, Society for Quality Science). The objectives of this society were to promote *Qualitätswissenschaft* in theory and research, facilitate the transfer of quality-management knowledge to companies, and ease its utilization in industry (*Qualität und Zuverlässigkeit* 1995). This development was and still is supported by the European Commission (European Commission 1995, 1996; Storp *et al.* 1991).

It appears likely that the increasing attempts to professionalize quality-management knowledge, as well as the effects that resulted from the European Commission's programs to promote QM, should have led to increasing support of the quality-management movement by another of society's already established and legitimized subsystems, namely science. We thus hypothesize:

> Hypothesis 3a: The proportion of articles in the organ of the quality-management movement written by academics or with participation of academics increases over time.

The support from the scientific subsystem should become particularly clear in concepts encouraged by the European Commission to harmonize the European market and increase the competitiveness of European enterprises, which thus already appeared to be legitimized concepts:

> Hypothesis 3b: The probability that an article is related to ISO 9000 or TQM increases over time more strongly for articles authored or coauthored by academics than for articles written by nonacademics (practitioners).

*Attempts to Institutionalize Quality Management
in For-Profit Organizations*

A further objective of the quality-management movement was to institutionalize quality-management knowledge in the upper levels of management hierarchy in companies. Behind the increasing efforts to make quality an issue at the top-management level (Müller-Rossow 1972; Franzkowski *et al.* 1984) lies the attempt to establish QM as a self-evident aspect of "modern" companies. This attempt can already be identified in an article published in 1972 by a cofounder of the subcommittee of the Committee for Efficient Production, *Technische Statistik*, from which the German Society for Quality originates (Altenkirch 1972). If the attempt to institutionalize QM as a management approach in organizations was successful, it should be reflected in the authorship of the journal analyzed. The proportion of managers (practitioners) with high formal qualifications and extensive experience who place resources at the disposal of the quality-management movement should have increased over time. The level of formal qualification can be regarded as a predictor of the rank or future rank in the managerial hierarchy in German companies. The age of the authors can be interpreted as a measure for work experience (Eberwein and Tholen 1990; Wuppermann 1989; Walgenbach 1994). So we assume:

> Hypothesis 4a: The proportion of articles in the organ of the quality-management movement written by authors with high levels of education increases over time.

> Hypothesis 5a: The proportion of articles written by older authors increases over time.

The accelerating diffusion of the ISO 9000 standards was useful for the attempt of the quality-management movement to anchor QM at the highest possible level in corporate hierarchy in order to gain influence in companies because the standards contain clear requirements regarding the tasks and the division of labor in the management of an organization:

> The supplier's management with executive responsibility shall appoint a member of the supplier's own management who, irrespective of other responsibilities, shall have defined authority for ensuring that a quality system is established, implemented, and maintained in accordance with this International Standard . . . [Further,] (t)he supplier's management with executive responsibility shall review the quality system at defined intervals sufficient to ensure its continuing suitability and effectiveness in satisfying the requirements of this International Standards and the supplier's stated quality policy and objectives.

However, exactly who should become management representative remains unspecified in the standards. Hans (1992: 251), auditor of one of the largest German associations for certification states: "It should always be the CEO of the corporation or the head of a business unit." The president of the German Society for the Certification of Management Systems, Hansen (1994), is less demanding. His interpretation of the standards is that the representative of management may be a member of the board, but he does not regard this as a prerequisite.

Nonetheless, the ISO 9000 standard's claim of being an approach for company management is modest. QM is only declared to be *one aspect* of management (Saatweber 1994). QM is understood to be the aspect of management that defines quality policy and the means for its realization. The claim is much more comprehensive in TQM. Here, QM is not only one aspect of management "but the entire management system per se which encompasses all other activities" (Grabert *et al.* 1993: 269).

It was also attempted to anchor QM at top hierarchical levels by conveying QM as one of or even *the* management concept already being used by companies. Petrick (1995) ascertains that today a (certified) quality system is sometimes seen as being on a par with systems of finance management, cost management, or environmental management; he argues that it is more frequently seen, however, as the core of the entire management system of a company.

If attempts to institutionalize the values of the quality-management movement at higher levels of the managerial hierarchy were successful, then this should be reflected in the authorship of the journal *Qualität und Zuverlässigkeit*. The proportion of more experienced and formally highly qualified managers making resources available to the quality-management movement for the promotion of ISO 9000 and TQM should have increased over time.

> Hypothesis 4b: The probability that an article refers to ISO 9000 or TQM increases over time more strongly for articles by authors with higher levels of formal qualifications than with lower levels of formal qualifications.

> Hypothesis 5b: The probability that an article referring to ISO 9000 or TQM over time increases more strongly for articles by older authors than by young authors.

Data and Methods of the Quantitative Analysis

As we noted in the introduction, we tested our hypotheses by analyzing articles published in the journal *Qualität und Zuverlässigkeit* between 1987 and 1997.[2] We selected this time frame because the publication of ISO 9000 in 1987 led to a shift in the contents of the journal toward a stronger consideration of management aspects.

Within this time frame, we identified 1,515 articles, many of which were written by more than one author. Since in almost every article there was ample information about the author(s) and the subject, we could easily build the necessary variables to test the hypotheses. However, some articles did not provide the necessary information and had to be excluded from the data set. Therefore, the data set was reduced to 1,314 observations.

We divided the eleven years of observation into six time periods, five of which covered two years of publication and the sixth only one year. We measured the content of the articles by registering whether they referred to ISO 9000, TQM, or any other item.

We then identified five sectors from the articles. These were the chemical industry; the service sector, including the software industry; the metal industry; the electrical industry; and articles that were not related to any specific industry. We also measured the occupational fields of the authors. We distinguished among articles written solely by practitioners (nonacademics), articles written solely by academics, and articles written by both practitioners and academics.

Moreover, we distinguished between articles having at least one author with a diploma in engineering and all other articles. Then we measured the authors' education by registering the author's highest formal qualification. We used three categories: articles written by at least one professor,[3] articles written by at least one author who had obtained a Ph.D. (without being a professor at a university or polytechnic), and articles written by authors whose qualification was a university diploma or lower.

Finally, we distinguished among three age categories of authors: articles written by older authors (aged more than fifty-five years), articles written by middle-aged authors (aged thirty-five to fifty-five years) and articles written by young authors (younger than thirty-five years). Where an article was written by more than one author, the age of the oldest author was taken.

We tested Hypotheses 2a, 3a, 4a, 5a by bivariate means in order to study the development of the different attributes of the articles over time. We calculated χ^2 values and contingency coefficients. We tested the other hypotheses (Hypotheses 1, 2b, 3b, 4b, 5b) by multivariate means. We estimated the different effects on the probability of an article being related to ISO 9000 or TQM with binary logit-models (Agresti 1990). These models have the form:

$$P(Y = 1) = \frac{\exp(\beta_0 + x'\beta)}{1 + \exp(\beta_0 + x'\beta)},$$

with P(Y=1) describing in our case the probability that an article is related to ISO 9000 or TQM. The dependent variable of such a model is calculated as

$$\log\left\{\frac{P(Y = 1)}{1 - P(Y = 1)}\right\} = \beta_0 + x'\beta,$$

which describes the natural logarithm of the ratio of the probability that an article is related to ISO 9000 or TQM and its complementary probability. This expression is called logit and is calculated as a linear function of the covariates.

Results

Before we come to the analysis of the change in the contents of the journal (Hypothesis 1), we want to consider the changes in the attributes of the authors over time.

In Hypothesis 2a we stated that the proportion of articles written by nonengineers increases over time. Although this hypothesis is supported, the support is not very impressive. The first column in Table 7.1 shows that there is not a continuous increase in the proportion of articles written by nonengineers. This proportion was at its lowest in 1989 and 1990 at 7 percent. In 1997 15 percent of the articles were written by nonengineers, but the χ^2 value is significant only at the 10 percent level. Hence, the most common profession of the authors remained technical, although differences over time are detectable.

According to Hypothesis 3a, the proportion of articles written by academics or with the participation of academics should increase over time. As we can see in the second column of Table 7.1, this is clearly the case. There is a continuous decline in articles written solely by practitioners. In the first period, almost 90 percent of the articles were authored by practitioners. In 1997 this was the case for only 50 percent of them. The increase of articles written by academics stopped after the fourth period. However, there is a continuously growing tendency for articles to be written jointly by practitioners and academics. In 1997, almost a quarter of all papers were written jointly by authors from both occupational statuses. This can be seen as a successful strategy to gain legitimacy for QM and the quality-management movement. By gaining the coauthorship of academics, practitioners underline the importance of their subject.

Hypothesis 4a stated that the formal qualifications level of the authors should increase over time. The third column in Table 7.1 confirms this assumption. The proportion of articles written by authors whose highest educational qualification was a diploma decreased notably and continuously from 64 percent in the first period to 36 percent in the fifth period. In 1997, there was a very slight increase in articles written by authors with the lowest levels of formal qualifications. However, the percentage of papers written by professors grew from 10 to 33 percent. As a consequence, the three formal qualification levels of authors are almost equally distributed among the articles that were published in the two last periods. Furthermore, the statistics underline the descriptive results. Since time period and education are both on ordinal levels, Somers d with level of formal qualification as a dependent variable could be computed. Like the χ^2 value, the positive value of this coefficient is significant at the 1 percent level. These results are in line with our assumption that the efforts to gain legitimacy of QM by winning the support of people with high levels of formal qualifications should increase over time.

Finally, we will take a look at the development of the age structure of the authors. We stated in Hypothesis 5a that the percentage of articles written by older authors should increase. As can be seen in the fourth column of Table 7.1 this hypothesis is supported. The proportion of articles written by at least one older author (aged over fifty-five years) increases from 16 percent in the first period to 33 percent in the fifth period—with a small reduction in 1997. The proportion of articles written exclusively by young authors remains fairly stable at about 12 percent over the six periods. The percentage of articles written by at least one middle-aged author decreases from over 70 percent to 56 percent in the fifth period. This percentage remains about the same in 1997. This pattern leads to a highly significant χ^2 value and a highly significant Somers d coefficient.

To sum up the results of the bivariate analyses, there are clear indications of increasing professionalization within the quality-management movement. We will refer to these indications in more detail in the discussion at the end of the chapter.

Before we come to the multivariate analysis of the probability that an article is related to ISO 9000 or TQM, we want to take a look at the development of the contents structure of the articles. Overall, 323 articles (25 percent) are concerned with ISO 9000 and 54 (4 percent) are concerned with TQM. The fifth column in Table 7.1 shows that there is an increase in articles dealing with ISO 9000 over the first five periods up to 42 percent. However, in 1997 this decreases to 32 percent. The number of articles concerning TQM is virtually nonexistent at the beginning of the observation and increases to 9 percent in 1997. As a consequence, these results seem to clearly

TABLE 7.1   The Development of the Attributes of Authors
and the Contents of Articles over Time

	Engineer	Non-engineer	Practitioners	Academics	Practitioners and Academics
1987–1988 (n=196)	91.3%	8.7%	87.2%	11.2%	1.6%
1989–1990 (n=250)	92.8%	7.2%	79.2%	7.6%	3.2%
1991–1992 (n=244)	91.8%	8.2%	71.3%	24.6%	4.1%
1993–1994 (n=225)	87.6%	12.4%	62.2%	29.8%	8.0%
1995–1996 (n=264)	87.5%	12.5%	56.8%	28.8%	14.4%
1997 (n=135)	85.2%	14.8%	50.4%	25.9%	23.7%
χ^2	9.8		125.8		
DF	5		10		
p	0.08		0.00		
Somers d					
S. d.					
p					

support Hypothesis 1. However, this hypothesis will be tested in a more precise manner by the multivariate logit-models.

In the next step, we analyze how the different attributes of the articles influence the probability that an article is related to ISO 9000 or TQM. We estimated three hierarchical binary logit-models in which the relatedness to ISO 9000 or TQM was the dependent variable. Since there are few articles referring to TQM, and TQM is very much connected to ISO 9000, we decided to put these categories together and estimate binary rather than multinomial models. The first two models in Table 7.2 display the main effects of the periods, the attributes of the authors, and the different industries to which the articles were related. The industry dummies were included as control variables.

TABLE **7.1**   *(continued)*

Diploma or Lower	Ph.D.	Professor	<35 Years	35–55 Years	>55 Years	TQM	ISO 9000	Other Items
64.3%	26.0%	9.7%	13.3%	70.9%	15.8%	0.5%	5.1%	94.4%
54.8%	30.8%	14.4%	12.0%	68.0%	20.0%	0.4%	8.4%	91.2%
44.3%	32.4%	23.3%	13.9%	59.9%	26.2%	2.0%	24.2%	73.8%
40.4%	31.6%	28.0%	10.2%	60.0%	29.8%	5.3%	34.7%	60.0%
35.6%	33.7%	30.7%	11.0%	56.4%	32.6%	8.7%	42.4%	48.9%
37.0%	30.4%	32.6%	12.6%	57.8%	29.6%	8.9%	31.9%	59.2%
	69.0			25.6			196.5	
	10			10			10	
	0.00			0.00			0.00	
	0.16			0.07				
	0.02			0.02				
	0.00			0.00				

To test Hypotheses 2b, 3b, 4b, and 5b we included interaction effects between the attributes of the authors and the periods in Model II. Since in the first years of observation there were only a few articles related to ISO 9000 or TQM, interaction effects were only built between the last three periods and the referring attributes of the authors. Our hypotheses suggest that we should find positive effects of the interactions.

The first model in Table 7.2, which measures the influence of the different periods, corresponds with the fifth column in Table 7.1. We took the third period as the reference category because the proportion of ISO or TQM articles in this period reflects the mean percentage of these articles quite well. In the first two periods, the logit of an article being concerned with ISO 9000 is significantly lower than in the third period, with a stronger effect in the first

TABLE 7.2 Binary Logit Models of the Articles' Content

	Model I	Model II	Model III
Constant	−1.034***	−0.767***	−1.852***
Period[a]			
1987–88 (P1)	−1.788***	−1.771***	−1.790***
1989–90 (P2)	−1.304***	−1.248***	−1.295***
1993–94 (P4)	0.629***	0.566***	1.849***
1995–96 (P5)	1.080***	1.031***	2.598***
1997 (P6)	0.659***	0.627***	2.556***
Industry[b]			
Metalwork		−0.892***	−0.933***
Electrical		−1.042***	−1.024**
Chemical		−0.362	−0.475
Service sector		0.797***	0.700***
Authors' Profession[c]			
Nonengineer		0.105	0.423
Authors' Occupational Fields[d]			
Academics		−0.519**	−0.339
Academics and practitioners		−0.150	−0.208
Authors' Level of Formal Qualification[e]			
Ph.D.		−0.331**	−0.451
Professor		−0.037	−0.177
Authors' Age[f]			
Middle-aged (35–55 years)		0.078	1.252***
Older (>55 years)		0.181	1.523***

TABLE **7.2** *(continued)*

	Interaction Effects		
	Model I	Model II	Model III
Nonengineer*P4			−0.545
Nonengineer*P5			−0.591
Nonengineer*P6			−0.050
Academics*P4			−0.410
Academics*P5			−0.064
Academics*P6			−0.595
Academics and practitioners *P4			0.387
Academics and practitioners *P5			0.384
Academics and practitioners *P6			−0.873
Ph.D.*P4			−0.633
Ph.D.*P5			0.935**
Ph.D.*P6			0.258
Professor*P4			0.087
Professor*P5			0.291
Professor*P6			0.775
Middle-aged*P4			−0.897
Middle-aged*P5			−2.207***
Middle-aged*P6			−2.038***
Older*P4			−1.517*
Older*P5			−2.112***
Older*P6			−2.381***
Log-Likelihood	−682.8	−660.5	−643.5

*$p<0.10$ **$p<0.05$ *** $p<0.01$

Omitted Categories:	a: 91 – 92 (P3)	d: Practitioner
	b: No specific industry	e: Diploma or lower
	c: Engineer	f: Young (<35 years)

period. In the fourth and fifth periods the effect is positive and increases. In 1997, the logit drops to the level of the fourth period. This pattern remains quite stable in Model II, where all of the main effects were included.

In Model II, the effects of the different industry sectors show that articles referring to the metal or electric industry have a significantly lower logit of being concerned with ISO 9000 or TQM than articles with no relation to any specific sector, which were taken as the reference category. Articles for the chemical sector also have a lower logit of being related to ISO 9000 or TQM; however, this effect is far from being significant. However, articles for the service sector, including the software industry, display a positive and highly significant effect. This is remarkable, as standards for quality systems had not originally been designed for the service sector and the software industry. However, this effect represents institutionalization as described in institutional theory.

Apart from these main effects the following significant influences of the attributes of the authors are also detectable: the logit of an article referring to ISO 9000 or TQM is significantly lower when it was written by academics than when the authors were practitioners. When articles were written by authors who had at most a Ph.D., the probability of their being concerned with ISO 9000 or TQM is significantly lower than for those articles whose authors had at most a diploma. It is interesting that when at least one author is a professor there is no detected effect.

By looking at the interaction effects in Model III we detect only very slight support for our hypotheses concerning the changing probability of articles being related to ISO 9000 or TQM. Articles written by nonengineers do not display a stronger affinity to ISO 9000 or TQM over time than articles written by engineers. Also there is no stronger consideration of ISO 9000 or TQM over time for articles written by academics compared to articles written by practitioners. For both of these interactions, negative effects, although not significant, could be detected. For articles written both by academics and practitioners, one finds a stronger increase in the tendency to deal with ISO 9000 or TQM in the fourth and fifth period compared with articles written by practitioners. However, these coefficients are not significant. In the sixth period the coefficient turns negative. Thus, Hypotheses 2b and 3b cannot be confirmed.

However, the results suggest at least some support for Hypothesis 4b, however slight. Compared to articles written by authors who had obtained, at most, a university diploma, articles whose authors had at least a Ph.D. display a significantly stronger increase in the tendency to be related to ISO 9000 or TQM in the fifth period. The interaction effect between the last period and articles written by authors with a Ph.D. is still positive but much lower than that for the fifth period. This interaction effect is not significant. But articles with at least one author who is a professor display a continuously stronger increase in the tendency to be related to ISO 9000 or TQM, although these interaction effects are not significant.

For articles written by older authors, the referring interaction effects are not positive as expected. On the contrary: articles written by older authors have a significantly smaller increasing tendency to refer to ISO 9000 or TQM over time than articles by young authors. For articles by middle-aged authors there is also a significantly smaller increase in the tendency toward ISO 9000 or TQM for the fifth and sixth period. The highly significant and positive main effects of author's age show that in the first six years of observation, articles by older and middle-aged authors are actually more concerned with ISO 9000 or TQM than articles by young authors. However, this pattern changes thereafter.

To provide a closer look at the differences in the development of the probability of an article being related to ISO 9000 or TQM between articles of the different age groups, Figure 7.1 displays these probabilities for articles of young and older authors. A presentation of the period-specific probabilities for articles by middle-aged authors is omitted in order to avoid making the figure too complex. The probabilities were calculated by taking into account the period and age effects and the referring interaction terms, while holding all other influences considered in Model III constant. This means that the period-specific probabilities of articles by young and older authors were calculated for all modal categories (which are also the reference categories) of the remaining covariates.[4] Note that the differences in the probability of an article being related to ISO 9000 or TQM in the first three periods could only be calculated by taking the main effects into account, since interactions were not constructed until the fourth period onward.

One can see that the stronger increase in the tendency toward ISO 9000 or TQM for articles by younger authors leads to a leveling of the referring probabilities for young and older authors in the period 1993–94. In the

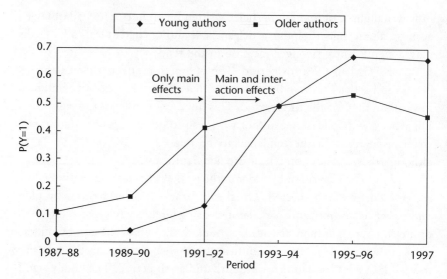

FIGURE **7.1**   Development of the probability that an article is related to ISO 9000 or TQM for articles by young and older authors

periods thereafter, articles by young authors display a higher probability of being related to ISO 9000 or TQM. We will discuss this finding in the following section.

Discussion

In this study we have endeavored to unfold the institutionalization of QM by using resource mobilization theory. Our aim was to show that resource mobilization theory is a suitable complementary approach to institutional theory in explaining the emergence of institutions. The process of institutionalization is influenced or at least accompanied by a process of resource mobilization. Thus, the process of institutionalization can be explained by drawing on resource mobilization theory. Institutional demands on organizations are the result of the interaction of the activities of different actors whose strategies and activities are institutionally defined.

In our study, we have depicted the activities and strategies of the movement that aimed to anchor its own system of values and thus its own concepts and instruments within the different subsystems of society, particularly the business and scientific subsystems. Three basic streams of activities could be clearly identified:

- The gradual broadening of the field of activities of the quality-management movement
- The increasing professionalization and attempt to establish the movement's own knowledge within the scientific subsystem
- The attempt to anchor the concepts of the quality-management movement within firms

The process of institutionalization was encouraged by the European Commission, which referred to ISO 9000 and TQM and tried to use these concepts for its own purposes. We assumed that this activity resulted in an increased legitimacy toward the quality-management movement and its values, instruments, and especially the above-mentioned concepts of ISO 9000 and TQM. The historical portrayal of the interplay of the activities of the quality movement, its counter-movement, and the European Commission provided the basis from which several hypotheses about the course of the resource mobilization process were derived.

In the second part of our empirical study we tried to uncover the striving for resources and the process of institutionalization within the quality-management movement by analyzing change in the authorship of the journal *Qualität und Zuverlässigkeit* between 1987 and 1997. Our results show that the movement succeeded in gaining more and more authors who were able to provide important resources for the field of QM. These resources, such as qualifications or experience, provide a high degree of legitimacy. Within the time frame of observation, the proportion of articles written by academics or with the participation of academics increased. Moreover, the proportion of professors and older, that is, more experienced, authors increased. In addition, articles were increasingly written by nonengineers. This indicates that the topic of QM has been recognized outside the profession of quality engineers.

The change in the composition of the journal's authors was then expected to be connected with an especially increased commitment of "new" authors toward the items ISO 9000 and TQM. We believed that this should be the case because authors with high formal qualifications and ample experience should be especially interested in concepts that have already received external legitimacy. We argued that the willingness of these authors to provide resources should be higher, since these concepts had already been legit-imized by the European Commission and the European Council. However, the results of our multivariate models showed that the probability of an arti-cle being related to ISO 9000 or TQM only increased more strongly over time, that is, after an initial period of six years when the article was written by authors with a higher level of formal qualifications. Apart from this find-ing, a stronger commitment toward ISO 9000 or TQM by authors with spe-cific qualifications was not detectable.

For articles by older authors, the increase in the probability of the arti-cle being related to ISO 9000 or TQM is distinctly smaller than for articles by young authors. This contradicts the hypothesis that the process of resource mobilization should have led to an especially increased commitment of older and, therefore, more experienced authors toward these concepts. A possible explanation for this unexpected finding is that the concepts of the quality-management movement had already been legitimated to a sufficient degree to attract younger authors to write and submit articles to *Qualität und Zuverlässigkeit*. Another possible explanation is that the responsibilities of QM and the associated tasks of public relations were delegated to younger, less experienced employees in the organization. If this assumption is correct, supported by the fact that the proportion of articles that address ISO 9000 decreased in 1997 after having continuously increased for a whole decade, one has to conclude that the aim of the quality-management movement to establish QM at the upper level of the managerial hierarchy and to mobilize these resources was not achieved.

8   **The American Quality Gospel
in Britain and Japan, 1950–1970**
*Nick Tiratsoo, Business History Unit,
London School of Economics, United Kingdom*

Introduction

During and just after World War II, American experts began to
develop new ways of controlling product quality. They believed that they had
found the secret of making goods that would conform rigorously to specifications and thus allow consumers much greater levels of satisfaction. Unreliability and outright product failure were to be things of the past.

As the Cold War developed, the U.S. government decided that its allies
should share in the benefits of this breakthrough and accordingly made great
efforts to popularize it in both Europe and Asia. Indeed, the quality gospel
became an integral part of the technical assistance programs that were so
much a feature of the succeeding years. American missionaries toured widely,
explaining what needed to be done, and financial assistance was given to
local organizations that wanted to concentrate on the issue.

This chapter looks at what happened when the quality gospel arrived
in Britain and Japan. It first examines the American innovations and then
outlines how they were received in the two national contexts. The evidence
shows that the Japanese were more enthusiastic about U.S. methods than the
British, and the second half of the discussion reviews some of the ways in
which this contrast might be explained. Broad cultural or economic theories,
it seems, cannot account for the whole story. Most emphasis, it is argued,
needs to be placed on the particular political configurations of the postwar
period—and, in particular, on the way in which U.S. experts and their indige-

nous allies interacted with key British and Japanese institutional players, both governmental and industrial.

The Development of Quality Control Best Practice

Between the 1920s and the 1960s, conceptions of best practice in quality control moved through three broad (though overlapping) phases (Ott 1953; Feigenbaum 1956; American Management Association 1958; Thomas 1964; Nixon 1971: 26–38; Butman 1997). At the beginning of the period, virtually all firms used inspection methods. Specifications were stipulated for each article to be produced and then inspectors weeded out defectives, either during or at the end of the manufacturing process, by using visual tests as well as measurement devices such as rulers, gauges, and calipers. Then from the 1930s there was a growing realization that statistical methods could enforce compliance more rigorously. Much of the impetus for change came from experiments at the U.S. Western Electric company, while the publication of W. A. Shewhart's seminal *Economic Control of Manufactured Product* in 1931 was a major step forward in communicating these innovations to industry. The core of statistical quality control (SQC) involved the calculation of frequency distributions in order to reveal when output deviated from pre-set norms and thus allow corrective intervention. The SQC approach spread widely during World War II, with operators on the shop floor in a wide range of engineering sectors typically using the simple control chart to determine machine settings (Shewhart 1931; National Industrial Conference Board 1949: 7–11).

The final phase began in the mid-1940s and hinged around the development of what came to be called total quality control (TQC). This change was propelled by two developments. First, laboratory experiments showed that inspection was inherently unreliable. Factors such as lapses in concentration or poor eyesight meant that a significant number of defectives always went undetected. However hard inspectors tried, they could never provide a satisfactory level of screening (McKenzie and Pugh 1957). In addition, it was increasingly recognized that to institute control procedures of any kind *after* processing had begun was inherently wasteful, in that it always led to some degree of either scrapping or reworking. Far better to ensure that there were no mistakes made in the first place. On the basis of these insights, it was concluded, quality control measures should be completely reoriented. Several new principles were enunciated. First, quality concerns must be pushed back through the organization. For example, getting things right in machining was impossible with low-grade or flawed raw materials, so purchasing departments had to be just as attuned to quality requirements as anybody else. Second, and following from this, quality therefore had to be given the utmost priority within management decision making. It was no longer acceptable to leave the issue to production managers or inspectors. Chief executives must take active responsibility. Moreover, all section heads needed to be involved in order to create a virtuous feedback loop, whereby information about product performance was circulated constantly from sales to design to production and around again, with requisite modifications being introduced whenever and wherever required. Finally, it was observed that since workers could either make or break performance targets, depending on their dexterity, mental agility, and commitment, they too must be fully integrated into the overall strategy. The new approach was encapsulated in the slogan, "Quality—where do we get it? It walks into our plant every day on two legs" (Anglo-American Council on Productivity 1953: 58).

The Quality Gospel in Britain

The Americans first started to push the quality gospel in Britain in the immediate wake of World War II. The U.S. government had decided that one of Britain's main problems was low productivity and so embarked upon a program of technical assistance, in conjunction with the Attlee administration, in order to provoke reform (Tiratsoo and Tomlinson 1993, 1998). The focus on productivity led to scrutiny of quality and the realization that this, too, needed attention. A number of British companies had adopted SQC techniques as part of the wartime armaments drive, but there had subsequently been a lull in applications. The existence of a temporary seller's market and the government's export drive meant that many companies were turning out goods without worrying about their character or performance (Tippett 1962: 15; Richardson 1954: 50). There was no doubt that a gap had opened up between U.S. best practice and the British norm, and it was this that the technical assistance personnel became determined to plug.

The American initiatives proceeded on several levels. An Anglo-American Council on Productivity (AACP) team visited the United States in 1951, investigated twenty-two manufacturing plants, and met with acclaimed experts such as Joseph Juran (Anglo-American Council on Productivity 1953: 1–5; Barnett 1953; van Rest 1953). In addition, American consultants toured Britain at various times in the ensuing decade, often under the auspices of U.S.-inspired organizations like the European Productivity Agency (EPA). Finally, the prompting from across the Atlantic led directly to spin-off activity—conferences, seminars, publications, and films on quality organized by the British Productivity Council (BPC), the successor to the AACP; similar campaigning by specialist organizations ranging from the Institution of Engineering Inspection (IEI) to the Institution of Production Engineers (IPE) to the Royal Statistical Society to a plethora of trade associations; and the eventual foundation of the National Council for Quality and Reliability (NCQR) as a dedicated crusading organization in 1961 (*Inspection Engineer* 1956: 3; *Inspection Engineer* 1957: 1; Green 1957: 64–65; Institution of Production Engineers 1958; *Inspection Engineer* 1959: 57; Nixon 1960: 46, 1963: 50; Rafts 1964: 83).

What did all this effort accomplish? Measuring impact is very difficult because of (among other things) the multiplicity of influences at work and the scarcity of data about actual practices on the ground. But it seems clear that the U.S. missionaries were only able to achieve limited gains. To begin with, it is noticeable that few of the organizations involved in spreading the quality gospel really prospered. Both the IEE and the IPE expanded steadily, with the former, for example, increasing its membership from 1,600 in 1952 to about 4,000 in 1970. Yet both were beset by monetary difficulties and struggled to make much of a wider impression (Caplen 1969: 20; Caselton 1971; Morrison 1981: 22). Elsewhere, the situation was even less prepossessing. The BPC and the EPA were each dogged by more general problems, which limited their effectiveness (Tiratsoo and Tomlinson 1998: 48–49), and the NCQR proved particularly disappointing. The scale of involvement during the organization's "Quality and Reliability Year," launched in October 1966, was indicative. For although some 8,000 companies took part in one way or another, the "general run" of their peers were conspicuously indifferent (British Productivity Council and National Council for Quality and Reliability 1967: 3–4). Indeed, by the early 1970s, the NCQR's plight had, according to one contemporary, become "something approaching a national scandal." It could no longer afford to maintain an adequate headquarters and was reduced to operating out of a small single-room office in London, kept perilously afloat only by the unstinting efforts of a handful of enthusiasts (Morrison 1981: 23). Thus, all told, the quality missionaries did not leave much of an institutional imprint.

Moreover, a range of evidence suggests that reaction on the shop floor was similarly muted. Some British companies, particularly in process industries and electronics, kept pace with best practice (Anon. 1956), but these were in a pronounced minority. Many firms remained wedded to inspection alone. Engineering concerns employed an average of one inspector for every seven production workers in the 1960s, though among specialists (for example, brake and clutch makers in the motor trade) the ratio could be as high as one to four (Nixon 1964b; Research Institute for Consumer Affairs 1965: 9–17; *New Society*, 18 March 1965; Nixon 1971: 188–189). However, there was relatively little experimentation with some of the newer techniques being promoted by the Americans. Writing in 1970, the chairman of the IPE's quality and reliability committee regretted that there was still "widespread lack of comprehension" regarding modern techniques, and little desire to introduce them, so that "progress on a broad industrial front" had been "disappointingly slow." When Lockyer, Oakland, and Duprey questioned 1,866 members of the Institute of Industrial Management twelve years later, they found that the situation had hardly improved, since less than half of their respondents reported using statistically based sampling at any stage within their firms' production processes (Institution of Production Engineers 1970; Lockyer *et al.* 1982; Oakland 1986). There were even fewer signs of TQC measures being adopted.

In these circumstances, British companies inevitably continued to manufacture a high proportion of defective products. Surveys by consumers' organizations were revealing. Half of washing machines sold in the early 1960s gave problems before they were one year old. No brand of condom, it was discovered in 1963, "could possibly be a certain way of preventing conception." Tests on fifty-two new British cars between 1962 and 1964 revealed that all were delivered with visible defects, thirty-seven had rain leaks, and as many as one-third had front wheel misalignment (Anon 1965: 15; *Which Contraceptives Supplement* 1971: 45; Research Institute for Consumer Affairs 1965: 6–7; Millar 1963: 147–176; Robertson 1974: 14–33). Similar findings emerged from more rigorous inquires undertaken by the armed forces. The Royal Air Force calculated that it had to deal with 1.25 million defective parts every year. Bombers averaged seven part failures per flight made. Some equipment was particularly unreliable. About 40 percent of alternators and 30 percent of generators failed within the first 100 hours of their operational lives (Cleaver 1963; Institution of Mechanical Engineers 1963). At an extreme, disdain for performance standards could produce what were known as "quality calamities." In the late 1960s, a consultant employed by the British Institute of Management (BIM) reported:

> The quality calamity has been revealed as a regular event in industry. Over half the participants at BIM seminars are ready to supply the details about a calamity of which they have personal knowledge. Each calamity refers only to a single incident, yet about a quarter of these . . . involve losses of £50,000 or more. Losses reaching £1/2 million—£1 million are by no means rarities.

In his view, such "major mishaps" were certainly "something more than mistakes" or "cruel blows of fate" (Belbin 1970: 8).

All told, the quality problem in industry meant considerable extra expenditure for producers and consumers alike. In the 1960s, the Royal Air Force was allegedly spending nearly half of its annual government grant on "servicing and the necessary ground equipment to deal with it." For civilian firms, it was credibly estimated that "quality costs" (the cost of defects— scrape, rework, and defective products—added to the costs of appraisal and prevention) ranged from 4 to 20 percent of gross turnover, depending on the sector. An economy-wide inquiry in 1978 suggested that this added up to as much as £10,000 million a year, equivalent to 10 percent of British industry's total sales (Cleaver 1963: 7; British Productivity Council and National Council for Quality and Reliability 1967: 3; Department of Prices and Consumer Protection 1978: 3).

The Quality Gospel in Japan

The quality gospel also entered Japan as part of a more general technical assistance effort. The U.S. government had become worried at Japan's balance of payments problems in the early 1950s and decided that the only way forward was to make Japanese industry more efficient. Accordingly, it had launched an ambitious productivity program in 1955 and prioritized quality control issues within this, as shoddy production appeared to be one of Japanese industry's greatest and most enduring difficulties (Tiratsoo 2000).

When they began their mission, American technical assistance personnel recognized that some measures were already under way to galvanize the Japanese over quality. Indigenous organizations such as the Japan Standards Association (JSA) (established in 1945) and the Union of Japanese Scientists and Engineers (JUSE) (established in 1946) had been actively advocating modern SQC techniques, organizing courses of various kinds to spread knowledge of specific methodologies (Koyanagi 1952; National Productivity Council 1963: 72; Miura 1964: 111–115, 118). Moreover, the American influence was already pronounced. The Civil Communication Section of the Occupation forces had campaigned on quality, while U.S. consultants such as W. Edwards Deming (ex-Western Electric) and Juran had engaged in lecture tours and seminars at the request of local manufacturers (Hopper 1985; Nonaka 1995; Tsutsui 1996; Dees 1997). Yet, as the technical assistance personnel also perceived, despite this activity the situation was still unpromising. Participation on JSA and JUSE courses was very limited (Koyanagi 1952: 6). Indeed, most Japanese producers apparently remained largely oblivious to the quality issue. For example, an Agency of Industrial Science and Technology survey of the mid-1950s, which focused on 1,078 enterprises in textiles, chemicals, and engineering, revealed that only 13 percent were actively using control procedures (Quality Control Specialist Study Team 1958: 20). Moreover, even where the importance of quality was recognized, the mechanisms for its regulation were often very rudimentary. An American expert visited the Canon Camera Co. in August 1955 and reported:

> My observations, in this plant reinforced by previous impressions, lead me to believe that the average Japanese inspector . . . is an unknown quantity motivated by conflicting emotions which might be summed up as follows: (1) Inability to understand specifications which are not always clear except as to physical dimensional tolerances. (2) Tendency to magnify insignificant imperfections which cannot possible [sic] affect the ultimate appearance or functional performance of a product. (3) Conviction that unless a reasonable percentage of rejects is detected (legitimately or otherwise) the suspicion is aroused that the inspector is not properly carrying out his or her assignment.
>
> So far I have not found any evidence of authentic spot re-inspection or checking of the regular inspection results, such as is practiced in the U.S. (Landes 1955: 4)

What this meant, inevitably, was that the proportion of finished goods with debilitating flaws remained unsatisfactorily high. There was certainly no doubt, as the experienced American consultant Charles Hatton discovered after visiting 150 plants of all sizes in 1956, that "variations in quality of final products" were "far more common than in the West" (Hatton 1957: foreword).

In this situation, the Americans concluded, the quality issue would have to be given greater salience, and in the late 1950s and early 1960s much was done to fulfill this objective. The U.S. technical assistance program provided consultants, relevant literature, and a range of seminars and conferences. In addition, a Japanese team visited the United States to study advanced methods at first hand. Headed by Noboru Yamaguchi, of the Tokyo Shibauru Electric Co., and including such academic luminaries as Kaoru Ishikawa of Tokyo University, this team spent two months talking to manufacturers as well as experts from such bodies as the American Quality Control Organization before returning home and engaging in a raft of promotional activities (Sasaki 1995: 64–67; Tiratsoo 2000).

The response to this new level of prompting was extraordinary. First, there was an effervescence of organized activity. Both the JSA and JUSE suddenly found that demand for their training courses was expanding, and as a result they grew significantly. By the mid-1960s, the former alone had more than 100 staff and an annual throughput of over 50,000 students (National Productivity Council 1963: 72; Ishikawa 1969: 425; Tsutsui 1998: 192–220). Moreover, a whole host of new agencies now entered the field—trade associations, universities, and even dedicated consultants (Quality Control Specialist Study Team 1958: 6; Nishibori 1969). Quality even became an object of public interest. The Japanese Broadcasting Corporation put on annual three-month radio courses, organized around fifteen-minute daily programs, which later turned into a successful television series; publishers took up the subject with relish, and there was an outpouring of guides and handbooks on SQC and TQC subjects; and after 1960 the whole country joined together in a "national quality month" each November. Managers, foremen, and workers, whether beginners or sophisticates, were all catered for (Ishikawa 1963a: 31–34; Miura 1964: 124–125; Mizuno 1969).

Second, there was clear evidence of innovation in actual practices. The situation did not change overnight. Reviewing developments in 1958, a group of experts complained of management indifference; their conundrum, they believed, was "how to lead an unthirsty horse to the river and make it drink water." Six years later, a comprehensive survey concluded that there were still "many top and middle management people" who did not yet comprehend quality control, and went on to point out that backwardness was especially prevalent in Japan's myriad small enterprises (Quality Control Specialist Study Team 1958: 53; Miura 1964: 149, 151). Yet there was no doubting the overall trend. For example, one investigation of nearly 400 companies in 1969 concluded that quality control measures were "enforced totally" in 78 percent of large firms and 68 percent of their smaller equivalents (Higashi 1969: 486–487). In addition, as the Americans had urged, quality control was becoming fully integrated into many companies' manufacturing strategies (Ishiwara 1966). Chief executive officers were increasingly likely to have taken over responsibility for the issue. At the same time, operatives on the factory floor were being involved through quality circles. The first of these was created in 1962, and within six years about 17,700 were in operation (Imaizumi 1969; Tsutsui 1998: 224–235).

Finally, there were also many who believed that all of this effort was demonstrably improving the quality of Japanese output. In late 1962, the editor of the American journal *Machinery* commented:

> Up until the Second World War "Made in Japan" stamped on a product usually conveyed to the buyer an impression of cheapness and inferior quality. Today the same words may have an entirely different connotation, as many purchasers of Japanese items will readily testify. While there are still products of inferior quality, the nation has become generally competitive as to quality in quite a few categories. (Anon. 1962)

British manufacturers who toured Japan made similar observations. Edward Turner, a senior director of BSA, told readers of the *Times* in 1960: "There is a myth still in existence that things Japan produces are clearly shoddy copies of western articles. That has gone forever. The Japanese are fully aware of their reputation and are insisting on quality" (*Times*, 4 October 1960). Well traveled and experienced industrialists such as Norman Kipping, director-general of the Federation of British Industries (FBI), and Sir Christopher Hinton, chairman of the Central Electricity Generating Board, were equally impressed (*Times*, 26 October 1961; Hinton 1963). By the end of the decade, consumer's organizations in Britain, at least, were often taking Japanese products very seriously. In 1968 the journal *Which* examined medium-sized family cars, including the Toyota Corolla. It noted that the latter was not perfect and had been delivered with, among other things, a rusty exhaust system, a harsh clutch, squeaky suspension, and a noisy transmission. But in a comparative framework, the Corolla shone. The journal's report on the British Triumph Herald provided a salutary contrast:

Most of the exhaust system was very rusty. There was a slight oil leak from the gearbox. The carburetor throttle spindles were worn, and the vacuum advance connection had split open. The front suspension was showing signs of considerable wear. First gear synchromesh was weak, the transmission was a bit noisy, and number one cylinder knocked at low speed. Overall condition was rather poor. (*Motoring Which* 1968)

Evaluated as a whole, therefore, it is clear that the American quality gospel met with very different responses from its allies on either side of the world. The British seemed indifferent and suffered the consequences, whereas the Japanese were very receptive, quickly built a movement that was largely self-sustaining, and gradually gained a well-deserved reputation for the soundness of their manufactures. Most observers readily acknowledged the winners and losers. Reviewing developments to 1980, one authority concluded bluntly: "Where does Britain stand in the international quality race? The writer's view is that we have been lagging behind where we should have been leading" (Morrison 1981: 28). What explains this contrast?

Understanding the Differential Responses

One hypothesis is that the pattern reflected Britain and Japan's contrasting cultural characteristics. The British, on the one hand, many have argued, historically celebrated the "practical man," who had little time for the arts. The Japanese, on the other hand, have often been described as traditionally valuing beauty and harmony in every facet of life. It seems quite plausible to suggest that these long-standing dispositions may well have shaped receptivity to the quality gospel. The British proclivity for pragmatism would have dictated caution. By contrast, the Japanese obsession with esthetics seems to explain why an initially limited search for product integrity rapidly turned into a national crusade.

Yet such an approach does not, in fact, stand up to closer scrutiny. The key flaw in the argument is that both Britain and Japan were considerably more complex than the often repeated stereotypes suggest. The British were by no means simply philistines and had a well-established reputation for the production of top-quality goods—from fine porcelain, fabrics, cutlery, and furniture to precision instruments of every kind. On the other hand, it needs to be remembered that until the late 1950s, Japan was notorious for manufacturing export products to the very lowest specifications possible.

There was little sign here of an intrinsic desire for beauty and harmony. An appeal to national cultures, therefore, simply leaves too much unexplained.

A second possibility is that this question (like so many others) was a function of the two countries' overall post-1945 experiences, and in particular of the fact that Britain, as victor, tended to complacency, whereas Japan, as vanquished, had little option but to take whatever was demanded by its American occupiers. Yet this proposition, too, is not consistent with some important evidence. Sections of the British economy were extremely dynamic in the postwar period—indeed in the early 1950s there was talk of an unfolding "New Elizabethan Age" of unprecedented technological advance and prosperity, animated by such world-renowned companies as English Electric, Hawker-Siddeley, ICI, Pye, and Rolls-Royce (Hopkins 1964; Montgomery 1965: 48–52). On the other hand, Japanese attitudes to America were far from monolithic. Many wholeheartedly accepted the American way, but others were much less convinced. Prejudice, antipathy, and contempt frequently lurked just below the surface (Dower 1999: passim). Significantly, too, it is striking that the Japanese did not accept everything that was proffered in the technical assistance program. For example, U.S. ideas about business education and labor relations had little impact on the other side of the Pacific (Tiratsoo 2000). So although the differential impact of World War II cannot be ignored entirely, basing an explanation on this factor alone is clearly unsatisfactory.

A third (though related) supposition is that what occurred was largely determined by market frameworks and the economic incentive to innovate. It has been insistently asserted that Britain suffered from a plethora of "cozy deals" in the postwar period—a numbing and enfeebling complex of business- and labor-restrictive practices, given oxygen by the fortuitous existence of sellers' markets at home and abroad. It is tempting to assume that there must have been contrasting features of Japanese corporate life, which in turn produced more positive responses to innovation.

However, this is by no means convincing, either. Dispute continues about both the extent of British collusive behavior and the longevity of favorable commercial circumstances (Tomlinson and Tiratsoo 1998; Broadberry and Crafts 1998). But what is more important, it is hard to see how Japan was somehow dramatically different from Britain in any of the respects that are said to be crucial. Indeed, Japanese "cozy deals" seem to have been *prima facie* if anything, more embedded. Business collusion was, after all, hardly unknown in Tokyo and Osaka. Moreover, the country maintained notoriously protected home markets. To hypothesize that Japan bravely exposed itself to the stimulating winds of competition while Britain cravenly sheltered behind restrictionist barricades is, therefore, completely at odds with the facts.

A second reason to doubt that economic factors were paramount relates more directly to the quality gospel itself. The innovations being advanced by the Americans were not technologies but techniques. They required little investment (perhaps some expenditure on training) and could be adopted incrementally. Many case studies showed that firms of all sizes could participate, and that returns were almost always likely to be substantial, while also confirming that continuing with existing practices imposed significant financial penalties—the direct cost of scrap and rework, as well as less quantifiable expenditure associated with factors such as the investigation of customer complaints (British Productivity Council 1957; Nixon 1962). Except in the very unusual immediate postwar years, it is difficult to see why British firms should have been any less subject to these calculations than their Japanese counterparts.

A final explanatory variable that can probably be safely discounted is the legal position in the two countries. For most of this period, British consumer law was based on the precept *caveat emptor* (buyer beware), which no doubt favored producers. But Japanese legislation was, if anything, even more biased against the complainant. Indeed, Japanese courts have arbitrated on only about 150 product liability cases in the whole postwar period, a tiny number compared with, for example, the 13,000 or so decisions that were being handed down *every year* in the admittedly unusually litigious United States during the early 1990s (Hamada 1996). It is little wonder that the *Economist* recently commented: "Japan looks like a consumer society. . . . Yet . . . it has failed to make the consumer king. Rather, it is a producer's heaven and a consumer's purgatory" (*Economist*, 27 November 1999).

A more fruitful line of inquiry involves focusing on the two assistance programs themselves, because there were some significant differences in size and content. The British program was the first attempted and so suffered from various "teething" troubles. Japan's program was costlier (though precise comparative financial data are lacking), involved a much greater number of people, and was generally better organized, in that American personnel had learned from their previous mistakes. Furthermore, the Japanese initiatives were more closely integrated, and this certainly helped develop thinking about the quality issue. For example, the simultaneous discussion of top management best practice, together with the circulation of new thinking about how to treat workers, two key components of the technical assistance package as a whole, no doubt eased the way for the creative implementation of TQM objectives (Tiratsoo and Tomlinson 1998; Tiratsoo 2000).

But accepting this, there is no doubt that the pattern of take-up was most profoundly shaped by internal political factors in the recipient countries. The Americans provided the impetus to quality control innovation, while indigenous organizations tried to spread and develop their ideas. Yet other institutions and actors—national governments, employers, and managers—ultimately dictated what happened next. And it was exactly here that differences between Britain and Japan were most pronounced. To substantiate this point, it is necessary to look at the two constellations of key players in a little more detail.

The Dispositions of Institutions and Interest Groups

Governments

To begin with, it is striking that for much of the period, the British and Japanese governments had very divergent views about whether intervening in the economy at a microlevel was in any way desirable. The Attlee administration in Britain was interventionist, of course, but the successor Conservative regimes from 1951 to 1964 took a broadly laissez faire line and were largely unprepared to do more than talk about the need for change. By contrast, the Japanese government never had any qualms about pursuing a vigorous industrial policy, seeing itself as in some senses responsible for generating a national economic strategy. These very different orientations shaped quite distinct policies regarding productivity in general and quality in particular.

The situation over standards offers a revealing illustration. Official intervention to enforce standards had a long history and was, in theory, one of the most important ways in which a government could try to uphold the integrity of an industry's products. Most advanced industrial nations had some kind of standards agency and an involvement in the burgeoning international standards apparatus. But Britain and Japan pursued policy in this area with very different degrees of vigor.

The British Standards Institution (BSI) had been established in 1903 and was part funded by the government. It was charged with formulating standards at the request of others (a stipulation that is in itself rather symptomatic). Some 1,000 standards had been published by 1939, though after the war activity increased, and there were about 3,400 standards in existence by 1962. However, this performance was rarely judged favorably. The BSI was criticized for all but ignoring consumer goods industries and for being too soft on manufacturers. Some went so far as to allege that it had been effectively "captured" by trade interests, a contention that was given some credence by at least one official investigating committee. Put in the best light, the BSI had established a reputation for methodical work rather than crusading zeal (Political and Economic Planning 1955; *Final Report of the Committee on Consumer Protection 1961–62*; Department of Trade and Industry 1971; Woodward 1974).

In contrast, Japanese government-led activity on standards was much more vigorous. The Japanese Industry Standards Committee (JISC) was established in 1949 as an adjunct of the Ministry of International Trade and Industry, and quickly proved itself to be a dynamic organization. By the early 1960s, JISC had formed 12,500 subcommittees and published 5,140 standards. On top of this, the administration also coordinated several other measures on similar lines. One interesting innovation was the Export Inspection Law of 1958, which stipulated that 165 categories of product had to be inspected before shipment abroad. This was not a wholly successful measure—for example, there were many instances where certification was gained through bribery—but it did at least amply demonstrate the official determination to improve quality (National Productivity Council 1963: 71–75; Manders 1964; Department of Trade and Industry 1971: 21; Hatton 1957: 3–8; Tano 1969; Kusakabe 1969).

Employers

Contrasts also existed among those who ran industry. The Federation of British Industries (FBI) was largely lukewarm to the American programs. British employers had been deeply scared by Labor's post-1945 nationalization measures and many continued to feel uneasy about any policy that even vaguely suggested state intervention. There was also a more diffuse feeling that the Americans were up to no good, perhaps intent on stealing Britain's markets (Tiratsoo and Tomlinson 1998: 97–98). On the other hand, Japanese employers were generally positive about the whole idea of technical assistance. Some argued that a proportion of American techniques would not work in a Japanese context, whereas others pointed out that the gap between the two countries' practices was not as wide as some suggested. But there was almost complete agreement that much could still be learned from America and that the various initiatives were therefore well worth supporting. Symbolically, one of the first teams to cross the Pacific was composed exclusively of so-called "top managers," and this was followed by seven other similar missions in the years to 1962 (Asian Productivity Organisation 1968: 97–98).

Given these different dispositions, it is unsurprising to find that the two sets of employers also held strongly contrasting views about the role that indigenous technical and educational organizations should play in augmenting the American crusade. In Britain, the FBI gave some credence to specialist technical societies (for example, the engineering institutions), but it remained deeply suspicious of bodies that were more self-consciously intent on wider reform. The fate of the British Institute of Management (BIM) provides a particularly telling example. This body was launched in 1947 to spearhead the drive for better management, but it consistently struggled to gain influence and in the end was condemned to a fairly peripheral role in national life. Several factors were to blame, but there is no doubt that the FBI played a less than helpful role. What the employers disliked was the BIM's belief that management could and indeed should be professionalized. Such jealousies and tensions were not unknown in Japan, but in general relationships tended to be rather more constructive. Bodies such as the politically progressive, intellectual, and pro-American *Nihon Keizai Doyukai* (Japan Committee of Economic Development) were allowed to enter mainstream debate about industrial matters. Moreover, Japanese employers were quite happy that, for example, the JSA and JUSE should play a major role in promoting the new techniques (Ishikawa 1963b: 12–16; Tiratsoo 1999, 2000). Thus, the Japanese coalition for change was much wider and more vibrant than its British counterpart.

Managers

Implementing the quality gospel required that managers should have three sets of interlocking capabilities. They needed to be numerate (to understand statistical techniques); willing to work in teams (to create a virtuous communications loop); and disposed to the view that their workers were assets (in order to free shop floor creativity and commitment). However, it was quickly apparent that British and Japanese managers were very differently placed to fulfill these conditions.

British management culture was well developed and revolved around a few clear-cut propositions. The British believed that "managers were born not made"; that management was essentially about the leadership of people; and that the really great manager would share the attributes of a military general like Montgomery. Technical knowledge about the manufacturing process was not particularly valued. In fact, British managers implicitly accepted a status hierarchy with "gin and tonic" specialisms like sales or marketing at the top and anything to do with production at the bottom (Tiratsoo and Tomlinson 1998: 95–96). Finally, there was strong underlying contempt for the working class in whatever form it was encountered. Employees were believed to be stupid and "bolshie" and thus in need of discipline. One fairly common management view was that the only choice when dealing with labor was between being "a bastard or a bad bastard" (Nichols and Beynon 1977: 34). Likewise, ordinary customers were frequently dismissed as overwrought and irrational. Marjorie Byrne served on various advisory bodies pressing for consumer rights during the 1950s and found many managements indifferent or even hostile to the public. When complaints were raised behind closed doors at trade conferences, she reported, the usual response was "a recital of the customer's crimes (of an unbelievable blackness) and a list of reasons for never doing anything in a different way" (Byrne 1957: 893). Fairly typically, the secretary of a trade association told a popular Sunday newspaper in 1961 that he was "awfully sick of the British housewife" because only one in three of the complaints his industry received about its products turned out to be "justified" (*Reynolds News*, 30 July 1961). Five years later, the consumer affairs writer Elizabeth Gundrey opined that manufacturers were changing, but only slowly. The prevailing stance reminded her of a traditional limerick: "An epicure dining at Crewe/Found quite a large mouse in his stew/Said the waiter 'don't shout/And wave it about/For the rest will be wanting some too!'" (Gundrey 1966: 115).

Such attitudes inevitably impeded adoption of advanced quality control measures. Ruminating in 1964 on Britain's tardiness in the field, the veteran quality enthusiast Frank Nixon of Rolls Royce concluded that one explanation was "the 'professional' nature of this work." According to a later authoritative study, the "major reason for the low usage of SQC techniques" was "lack of knowledge, particularly amongst senior managers." When investigators subsequently looked at why the move to TQC had been sluggish, they found that an important retardant was the fact that workers and customers were not sufficiently valued (Nixon 1964a; Oakland 1986: 31; *Observer*, 27 September 1998).

The established management culture in Japan was in some ways equally conservative. Various traditional nostrums regulated business and frequently contradicted American thinking (Gordy 1957). But there were also more progressive features, which certainly helped in relation to the introduction of quality control measures. For example, Japanese managers were quite familiar with the idea of collaborative work, since their firms had long used the *ringi* system for decision making.[1] Moreover, they did not look down upon technical specialists or undervalue their work. Finally, a well-established belief in the benefits of paternalism—lifetime employment, a seniority-based reward system, and heavy involvement of management in the lives of workers—eased the way for an approach that depended on seeing workers in a positive light (Yoshino 1968). Thus, the American initiatives partly flowed with the grain of existing practices in Japan, not against them, as in Britain.

Some Conclusions

The quality gospel presented practical solutions to the age-old manufacturing dilemma of producing goods to specification without deviation. It was not part of a drive to spread "the American way" regardless, but a carefully thought-out combination of ameliorative measures that could benefit firms of all sizes.

Elements in both Britain and Japan reacted positively to the American programs, but the two sets of modernizers varied considerably in their strength and influence. The British were held back by government indifference, employer politics, and an unhelpful if deeply rooted management culture. Their Japanese counterparts experienced some resistance, but not nearly enough to prevent ultimate success. Applications of new techniques languished in Britain but soared in Japan.

It is perhaps appropriate to close by pointing out that the decisions made during this period have colored developments right down to the present. Japan has not had an unblemished record over quality issues, as recent scandals and product recalls illustrate (Eberts and Eberts 1995; *Economist*, 26 August 2000, 16 September 2000). But Britain has consistently struggled to manufacture with anything like comparative results. The United Kingdom's Lex organization recently surveyed the mechanical reliability of its 88,048-strong car fleet, logging faults over a twelve-month period. It found that Mitsubishi came in on top, with just 5.8 breakdowns per 100 vehicles, followed by Jaguar (7), BMW (8.2), Honda (9.7), and Audi (10). Ford scored a lowly 31.9, Vauxhall did even worse at 32.2, while Rover's figure was an abysmal 34.7 (Rupert 1998).

IV   *Sources of Management Knowledge*

From Technical Skills to Personal Development: Employee Training in U.S. Organizations in the Twentieth Century
Xiaowei Luo, University of Illinois at Urbana-Champaign, United States

The only purpose of a training program should be to train the exact knowledge and methods which the employee will use on his particular job or the job just ahead of him.
>   —*Quote from the President, at the founding of Personnel Research Federation, 1921.*

Our success is more likely to depend on the quality of our conversations than on any other single factor.
>   —*Quote from the CEO of a Fortune 100 company, as preface to a one-day workshop, "Conversation Skills: the Art of Asking Great Questions," 1998.*

Introduction

Training programs have become widespread among U.S. organizations, involving more and more employees and expanding in content, since the beginning of the twentieth century and especially after World War II (Miller 1987; Monahan *et al.* 1994). In the 1910s, only a few big companies such as Westinghouse, GE, and International Harvester had factory schools that focused on training technical skills for entry-level workers. By the 1990s, 40 percent of the Fortune 500 firms had a corporate university or learning center (Meister 1997). According to the 1995 Survey of Employer-Provided Training, nearly 93 percent of U.S. organizations with fifty or more employees provide formal training, and close to 70 percent of their employees, ranging from executives to frontline workers, are involved. In recent decades, as the U.S. companies have been confronted with technological changes, various social problems at home, and global economic competition, training programs in organizations have received even more attention, touted as almost a panacea for organizational problems (Carnevale *et al.* 1990).

The enormous expansion in the content of training programs over time has now largely been taken for granted. To use the two quotes above as an illustration, rarely would people now question whether training in conversational skills fits the commandment for training pronounced by the Personnel Research Federation in 1921. Clearly, such skills were not part of the "exact knowledge and methods which the employee will use on his particular job or the job just ahead of him," and are arguably still not part of some jobs in a technical sense. The idea that organizations should devote resources to training employees in such skills would have been regarded as absurd in the 1920s. However, seventy years later, 11 percent of U.S. organizations deem communication skills training as the *most* important on their priority lists of training, and many more regard it as highly important (Hackett 1997). More than 300 training organizations or firms specialize in communications training (*Training and Development Organizations Directory* 1994).

Previous studies on training have largely focused on the incidence of formal training and the total amount of training offered (see Bishop 1997 for an overview of studies in employee training). This study draws attention to the enormous expansion in the content of training with an emphasis on the rise of personal development training, defined as training programs that aim at improving one's cognitive and behavioral skills in dealing with self and others. It is intended to develop one's personal potential and is not immediately related to the technical aspects of one's job tasks. Conversation skills training is one type of such training. Monahan *et al.* (1994: 261–262) describe the spread of personal development training programs based on their survey and interviews with more than 100 organizations in Northern California in the following way:

> Training programs became more elaborate; they incorporated, in addition to technical training for workers and human relations training for supervisors and managers, a widening array of developmental, personal growth, and self-management courses. Courses of this nature include office professionalism, time management, individual contributor programs, intrapreneuring, transacting with people, applying intelligence in the workplace, career management, and structured problem solving. Courses are also offered on health and personal well-being, including safe diets, exercise, mental health, injury prevention, holiday health, stress and nutrition.

The dominant theoretical approaches in training studies are either ahistorical (for example, human capital theory) or exclusively focused on the growing demands on training from changing technologies and work organization. These approaches cannot very well explain why training in organizations has expanded in such a direction, emphasizing self-development rather than proficiency in specific technical tasks.

The institutional perspective of organizations points out that organizations are constructed by the rationalization processes that are going on beyond specific organizations, and that the rationalization of organizing tends to lower the rationality of specific organizations (Meyer 1992). This study builds on such an institutional framework and argues that different types of training are outgrowths of the dominant organizational models in different historical periods. The secular trend of rationalization of the individual and organization has led to an evolution of the dominant organizational models from bureaucracy to community model and then to the participatory citizenship model. With it, training in organizations has expanded from specific-technical to human relations training and then to personal development training.

Therefore, the purpose of this chapter is to (1) describe the pattern of expansion in training content in the twentieth century and (2) explain why training has shifted its focus to personal development. With historical evidence of training practices, it will demonstrate that the rise of the participatory citizenship model of organization not only drives the general institutionalization of training but also changes the emphasis in training.

Growth of Training and Expansion in Its Content

This chapter discusses formal training programs provided or financed by organizations, excluding informal on-the-job training and apprenticeship programs. Formal training programs often involve structural and substantial financial commitment on the part of organizations.

For a long time after the industrialization in the latter half of the nineteenth century, formal training programs were not considered necessary. The apprenticeship tradition of learning by doing continued, and vocational education started to grow outside organizations to supply some basic technical skills. Further specialization and mechanization and the rise of scientific management for the first time initiated formal training in the form of specific

technical training. One historian of training describes the beginning of formal training in United States as follows (Miller 1987: 9):

> By 1910, when the Ford Motor Company moved into a new plant at
> Highland Park, they had established a production line concept. However,
> it was not until August 1913 that the first test car began its journey as a
> bare chassis on one end of the "moving assembly" line, and ended up on
> the other end of the line as a finished Model T. Thus began the need for
> special training of the production line worker for a specific job.

Only a few big companies invested in formal training in the early twentieth
century. Li (1928) visited the Ford plant and reported a variety of specific-
technical training in its corporate school, such as drilling, screwing, specific
electrical operations, and some basic literacy training. He also reported that
less than 10 percent of the Ford workers actually participated in these training programs, as most of the jobs were considered to be sufficiently learned
on the job.

The emergency demands for production during World War I stimulated specific-technical training. In 1917, the Emergency Fleet Corporation
of the U.S. Shipping Board set up an educational and training section to solve
the urgent need for ten times as many workers they already had. Charles R.
Allen, as the head of the program, promoted the four-step method of "show,
tell, do, and check" as the standard method of job instruction training and
ordered the supervisors to train the new workers accordingly. Such a method
became popularized during the years after World War I.

During the interwar years, training for supervisors on how to handle
workers became increasingly important. During 1940–1945, confronted
with World War II emergency production, the U.S. government set up the
Training Within Industry program to help all manufacturers with federal contracts train their workers and supervisors. In this program, not only was there
intensive specific-technical training such as Job Instruction Training, there
was also strong emphasis on human relations training to motivate workers
and build high morale.

In 1945, Kurt Lewin initiated the Training Laboratory in Group
Development. Several years later the Human Relations Research Group was
founded at University of California at Los Angeles. These two centers became
the engine for sensitivity training in the 1950s and 1960s, a quintessential program of human relations skills training. "T-group" and "group dynamics"
approaches were popularized to sensitize individuals to feelings and attitudes.

Training of managers gradually became accepted within organizations during this period. In 1946, only 5.2 percent of 3,498 companies reported that they had structured executive training programs (Habbe 1950). In the 1952 American Management Association (AMA) survey of 1,954 companies, 30 percent reported that they had structured management development programs, and 47 percent reported that they gave human relations training courses.

The period after World War II witnessed rapid adoption of formal training and the rise of personal development training. In a 1962 survey of 9,600 establishments conducted by the Department of Labor, about 20 percent of them sponsored or provided some type of formal training. In the most recent survey of employer-provided training conducted by the Bureau of Labor Statistics (Frazis *et al.* 1998), 92.5 percent of organizations employing fifty or more employees provide formal training.

Personal development training was first given to executives and managers as part of executive-management development programs. At the beginning, human relations training was given much more weight than personal development training in these programs. In the 1946 and 1952 surveys of management development programs, courses of the personal development type were not even listed as a choice. In the 1974 Bureau of Labor Statistics survey of selected metalworking industries, only 10.3 percent of the establishments provided structured training in leadership, and 13.7 percent in communication skills (Bureau of Labor Statistics Bulletin 1977).[1]

Since the 1970s, there has been a sharp increase in the kinds of personal development training, and employees from more levels have been given such training (Eurich 1985). Table 9.1 lists the training programs according to categories and the percentages of organizations that engaged in them in 1989. We see that (1) more varieties of personal development programs were offered in organizations than technical or human relations training and (2) more organizations were involved in personal development training than in technical, human relations, or remedial training. The 1989 training survey also reported that more money was spent in building interpersonal skills than technical skills (*Training* 1989). In a 1997 survey of 315 corporations conducted by the Conference Board, 92 percent of them regarded leadership development, one type of personal development training, as the most important type of training (Hackett 1997).

In recent decades, the American Society of Training and Development

TABLE 9.1   Types of Training Programs: Percentages of Organizations That Offered Training in 1989, According to *Training Magazine Industry Report*

PERSONAL DEVELOPMENT TRAINING		SPECIFIC-TECHNICAL TRAINING	
Leadership	60.4	New equipment	54.4
Interpersonal skills	56.6	Purchasing	22.3
Listening skills	53.6	Hiring process	54.6
Time management	51.5	Word processing	49.4
Decision-making	51.1	Planning	40.3
Motivation	51.1	Product knowledge	49.2
Goal-setting	50.1		
Stress management	49.6	GENERAL-TECHNICAL TRAINING	
Team building	48.5	PC application	49.6
Problem solving	46.8	Comp. programming	46.6
Public speaking	44.5	Data processing	40.6
Managing change	40.5	MIS	35.6
Negotiation skills	37.4	Marketing	33.8
Creativity	25.6	Strategic planning	33.8
Smoking cessation	32.3	Finance	33.0
		Quality control	29.9
HUMAN RELATIONS TRAINING			
Employee and labor relations	52.1		
REMEDIAL SKILLS TRAINING			
Reading skills	17.1		

NOTE: These numbers are percentages of U.S. organizations with 100 or more employees, over which the 1989 survey was conducted. There were nine types of training not included in this table as it is unclear how to classify them into the five types of training. Some examples are safety, new employee orientation, substance abuse, and ethics.

(founded in 1944), among other professional organizations, actively spreads success models through publications, conferences, train-the-trainer sessions, and consulting services. It periodically conducts benchmarking exercises of human resource and training practices for what it considers to be high-performance organizations, and recommends that other organizations compare their practices with those of the leading organizations. Personal development training programs, as a marker of success models, have spread across boundaries of industry and resources. For example, the 1994 National Employers Survey of U.S. organizations with twenty or more employees shows that in almost all industries (except for the construction industry), above 50 percent of the companies provide teamwork and problem-solving training (with around 70 percent of the companies in chemistry, finance, and insurance providing such training).

Alternative Explanations

There have been four theoretical perspectives that attempt to explain the incidence of training. The human capital approach in labor economics treats training as investment in human capital in exchange for greater productivity gains and economic returns. Because of the externality problem of training (Becker 1962), economists emphasize the disincentive for employers to provide general training that trains transferable skills. Training is provided only when the benefit from productivity gains is greater than the cost of training. Such an assumption does not hold firm ground, especially for nontechnical training, whose benefits are hard to measure or demonstrate and are in fact rarely evaluated by organizations themselves (Thayer 1989; Scott and Meyer 1991).[2]

The second perspective, the technology-based approach, views training as a skill-formation process, which is affected by increasingly complicated work (Lynch 1992). Barley (1992) describes how the introduction of computer-integrated technologies demands that workers "make decisions formerly reserved for occupations with higher status." Studies have found that companies employing flexible or high-performance production systems are more likely to provide training (Kochan and Osterman 1991; MacDuffie and Kochan 1995; Katz and Keefe 1993; Cappelli et al. 1997).

The technology-based approach demonstrates the *need* for different types of training based on different work requirements, and is therefore also functional in nature. Such logic is prevalent in popular and policy discussions. However, the need for training is not necessarily the same as the actual practice of training. A recent survey shows that 46 percent of U.S. organizations report the need for training in basic math and reading but only 12 percent of them actually offer such training (Olsten Corporation 1994). In addition, despite the admonition for "need analysis" as the first step toward training planning in numerous training handbooks (for example, Craig 1987), organizations seldom conduct any systematic need analysis for their training, especially nontechnical training (Thayer 1989; Monahan *et al.* 1994). Moreover, as will be demonstrated below, the perceived need for certain types of training (such as personal development training) is not only technically shaped but also constructed by the shared understandings about the individual and the organization. The fact that organizations *believe* personal development training can answer the challenges posed by complicated technologies and changed work organization, despite lack of demonstrated proof, is not problematized by the technology-based framework.

The third is the structuralist perspective. It emphasizes that the structure of work settings may shape individual job training opportunities. The development of a strong internal labor market within many big firms in the 1940s and 1950s called for more internal training so that lower-level employees would have competence to fill the higher-level positions (Baron *et al.* 1986). Knoke and Kalleberg (1994) show that large organizations, organizations with a strong internal labor market, and organizations with more formalized rules and procedures are more likely to engage in formal training. Such a perspective sheds some light on the spread of formal training but is less useful in explaining why training has shifted its *focus* over time.

The fourth approach, the institutional perspective, points out that organizational behavior is not always driven by conscious rational-choice calculations, but is an enactment of the cognitive and cultural schemes in society at large and among peer organizations, independent of efficiency considerations (Meyer and Rowan 1977; Scott 1998; DiMaggio and Powell 1983). Such a noninstrumental framework of organizational behavior not only helps us understand the rise of personal development training, which is not immediately related to job-specific technical tasks, but also directs our efforts to examine changing cognitive and culture schemes over time.

In studying training, Monahan *et al.* (1994) describe the evolution of U.S. personnel systems from the market model to the citizenship model. In the citizenship model, which became institutionalized after World War II, organizations regard their employees as citizens with increasing rights to participate and claim organizational resources. Consequently, training has become legitimized and diffused across many employment contexts as part of the generally expanding norms of organizational citizenship.

This chapter builds on such an institutional framework and proposes that changes in individuals' organizational role and organizations' societal role drove the diffusion of training *and* especially the shift in the focus of training. These changes were reflected in the evolution of the dominant organizational models promoted by management experts and practiced by organizations. Training, as an important aspect of organizational behavior and an enactment of the relationship between individual employees and the organization, has been powerfully shaped by these fundamental organizational models over time.

Definition and Typologies of Organizational Model

In this chapter, an organizational model is defined as the shared understandings about an organization's fundamental goals and means of organizing. The goals are exhibited in organizational reach in terms of an organization's responsibilities to society. The means are revealed in the role of the individual in an organization. Such a model is embodied in the formal and informal rules and structures of an organization and is at the same time reinforced through the latter. The organizational model sends out signals of expectation and shapes what is considered to be appropriate behavior and effective solutions. It can take on an "institution-like" character over time, largely taken for granted by the individuals who come into contact with the organization, thus powerfully affecting organizational behavior in many arenas, including training decisions.

The concept of an organizational model is built upon previous theories of organizations. Scott (1998) describes the rational, natural, and open organizational systems. Guillén (1994) uses scientific management (1900–1920s), human relations (1930s–1960s), and structural analysis (1970s) to depict evolving management models. Barley and Kunda (1992) describe the succession of managerial ideologies since 1870: industrial betterment (1870–1900), scientific management (1900–1923), welfare capitalism and human relations (1923–1955), systems rationalism (1955–1980), and organizational culture (1980–present). These paradigms all reflect different roles of individuals in an organization and different organizational reach.

Based on these two dimensions—organizational reach and individuals' role in an organization—four ideal types of organizational models can be constructed (Figure 9.1). What the bureaucracy and community models have in common is that individual employees are expected simply to conform to the preestablished organizational rules and minimize their own discretion. But the models differ in their organizational reach: whereas the bureaucracy

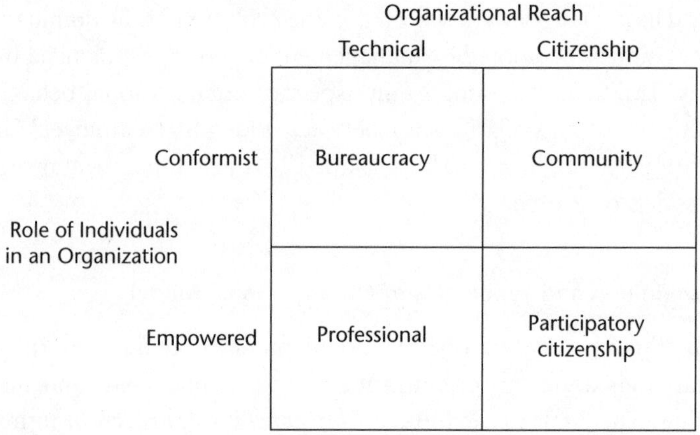

FIGURE 9.1   Ideal types of organizational models

organization is single-mindedly concerned with its core production or service, the community organization is broadly concerned about the well-being of employees and community. The professional and participatory models have in common that individuals are expected to be empowered actors, to bring their full capacity, initiative, and creativity into the organization. They differ also in their organizational reach: whereas the professional model organization is focused on its core production or service, the participatory organization can assume a wide range of social responsibilities from school endowments to relief efforts in third-world countries.

Two core historical changes in organizations can be abstracted based on previous organization theories (Perrow 1986; Scott 1998; Barley and Kunda 1992; Guillén 1994): one is that individuals play an increasingly enlarged role in organizations; the other is that organizations take on broader social roles over time as a result of pressure from state and civil society. These changes have been brought on by broad societal changes such as the increasing educational level of individuals; waves of labor movements; growing knowledge about engineering, human psychology, and management science; and the rise of the authority of science and the expert others, an institutionalized notion of proper statehood and actorhood, and industrialization and postindustrialization with increasingly complex and changeable technologies. With these changes, the dominant organizational model has evolved from bureaucracy to community and then to participatory citizenship.

How Organizational Models Shape Training

Organizational models shape the content of training by affecting (1) perception of individuals and their desired competencies, which in turn shape the goal and content of training, (2) perception of organizational solutions to problems, which involves different kinds of training or might not involve training, and (3) employees' right to demand what is beneficial to them.

Bureaucracy Model and Specific-Technical Training

The bureaucracy model characterized organizations in the early twentieth century. The average worker was depicted as coarse, unclean, unreliable, and prone to drunkenness, and simply an adjunct of a machine (Commons 1921), and was therefore needed to be remade according to preset organizational roles and structures.

The efficiency engineers were perceived as superior because they could specify cause and effect in the production process (Shenhav 1995) and find the best way to do each job *for* workers. The rationality of the organization was fully embodied in these scientific rules. The role of management was to closely supervise workers so that exact performance according to the rules could be realized. As carriers of the traditional control of organization by rules, efficiency engineers and functional managers became strong advocates for specific-technical training. For workers, it was in the best interest of efficiency that they minimize their own discretion and just follow the exact procedures of the simplified job tasks.

In organizations with the bureaucracy model, there was either (1) little training, as individuals were supposed to possess technical qualifications and competencies before they enter the organization and to pick up organization-specific knowledge and skills through learning by doing, or (2) a lot of specific-technical training but little general-technical training, human relations training, or personal development training, as conformity to specific roles, rules, and structures was emphasized and consideration of individual affect or creativity was outside the model.

The philosophy of training was to "mold the human material." In the first handbook for training, Greene (1937) laid down two principles for organized training: (1) technical skill deficiencies or business situations must be known in advance and training devised to meet them *specifically* and (2) the results of training should be *immediate* and in some cases can be measured in economic returns.

Although specific-technical training has continued to be demanded in organizations as new technologies are adopted, the emphasis on such training at the ideological level has declined over time as other types of training have become important.

Community Model and Human Relations Training

The community model during the human relations era (1930s–1960s) brought to public attention that the affect and morale of employees were at least as important as their technical skills in contributing to their performance (Mayo 1945; McGregor 1960; Barnard 1938). The prevailing logic was that happier workers were more productive. Organizations offered more employee benefits and engaged more in community-building partly for the purpose of having happier workers. But still, management and workers played a limited role in active thinking and contributing to the organization.

Management now had to make sure that these goals and rules were shared and internalized by workers. This became such an important task that personnel managers came upon the scene (Jacoby 1985). Personnel managers were qualified not because they knew the technical side of manufacturing, as efficiency engineers did, but because they knew and could handle workers thanks to their "great and evident human sympathy" (Commons 1921: 29). Personnel managers actively promoted human relations training in support of their philosophy of management and their newly established niche in organizations.

Supervisors and managers, for the first time, were subjected to training. The soldiering, absenteeism, and high turnover were addressed by strengthening rules and supervision under the bureaucracy model but by supervisory training in better human relations skills under the community model (Gaudet 1960). Supervisors and managers needed to know how to construct a nonauthoritarian environment in an authoritarian setting (Perrow 1986). They received human relations training such as how to handle grievances, how to have stable, satisfied workers, and how to improve working conditions to keep workers happy. Articles such as "Three Ways to Humanize Your Handling of Workers" appeared in the *Personnel Journal*.

Supervisors received most of the attention in human relations training, as this group was in closest contact with frontline workers, and their behavior affected the morale of workers most. In a 1937 handbook for organizational training (Greene 1937), supervisors and foremen were the only group discussed as trainees of human relations skills. A 1946 survey based on more than 3,498 companies showed a definite increase in formal training between 1939 and 1946; it increased most for supervisors at 81 percent, 50 percent for production workers, and 40 percent for top executives (Raube *et al.* 1947).

Workers were instructed about the history of their organization and the importance of their job to the whole organization in order to gain a sense of belonging. The human relations theorists emphasized the eager human desire for cooperative activity (Mayo 1945); motivation based on money was considered ill-advised and ineffective.

The goal of human relations training was not so much to develop individual potential as to ensure voluntary conformity to organizational rules. In fact, scientific selection of people with the right inherent traits was more emphasized in this period than was training, as the "right" types of people were easier to "contain." One article in 1942, *Personnel Journal*, encouraged selection of a particular type of clerk. The author described the characteristics of good clerks as follows: they dislike to assume responsibility, are dependent on others, are ill at ease socially, and dislike public speaking (Dodge 1942). In 1959, the California Merchants and Manufacturers Association conducted a survey to find out what methods employers used to reduce employee turnover. More employers answered that they relied on the sound employee selection than those who answered that they resorted to supervisory and employee training (Gaudet 1960).[3]

Human relations training started to become more important during the 1930s and reached its peak in the 1950s and 1960s. Since then, it has gradually declined. The ascendance of the professional model and especially the participatory model encouraged active socialization of individuals rather than catering to their affect and containing disturbing emotions. Human relations training was increasingly criticized as being too paternalistic, insincere, and ineffective. Some of its programs were transformed into personal development training.

Professional Model, Participatory Citizenship Model and Training

In both professional and participatory models, individuals are per-ceived as autonomous and rational actors and the ultimate competitive advantage of an organization (Pfeffer 1994). The competence projected on-to individuals according to the professional model is that they are Weberian professionals, capable only in their technical field (which is broader than job-specific skills). Therefore, the professional model tends to stress general-tech-nical training. From the organization's point of view, such a technical focus is sufficient for its functioning because of its narrow goals.

The enlarged organizational role for individuals and the broadened societal role for organizations in the participatory citizenship model led to the rise of personal development training. First, the participatory model regarded individuals as Wilensky professionals (Wilensky 1964) capable of thinking, suggesting, and deciding in many fields outside their technical expertise. The participatory model brought about a radical shift in the philosophy of train-ing. Training had been aimed to fit employees into the organization. Train-ers started to advocate that the philosophy of training be replaced by a phi-losophy of education (Stover 1964). Organizations started to regard personal development training as the best strategy for enlisting full employee partici-pation and preparing for market and technological uncertainties. Second, the growing government regulations about employees' rights and public pressure for socially responsible organizations cast doubt on the message implied in traditional training that the organization's good was superior to the indi-vidual good. Individuals now can more easily claim organizational resources for training and development of themselves, and organizations are more likely to perceive such training as fulfilling their citizenship roles.

There are three fundamental differences between human relations and personal development training, which reflect differences in community and participatory models of organization. First, their goals are different. Whereas the former aims to appeal to employees' wants in order to gain better con-formity to organizational goals and procedures, the latter attempts to develop individual potential to improve organizational performance. Second, the underlying causal assumption is different. Whereas human relation training assumes that increased morale and job satisfaction lead to better perfor-mance, personal development training assumes that a set of developed per-sonal qualities (such as critical thinking, management skills, and interpersonal skills) lead to enhanced performance, which in turn generates high morale and job satisfaction. Third, the emphasis is different. Human relations training emphasizes cooperation for the sake of cooperation, whereas personal development training emphasizes how one can accomplish more through strategically dealing with oneself and others.

The growing importance of management gurus and the management consulting industry since the 1970s has played an important role in the spread of personal development training. These expert others helped the internal management interpret problems (such as changes in technology and market competition) and formulate solutions. They helped push the waves of movements, such as organizational reengineering, quality circle, total quality management, quality of work life, and learning organization. Despite their faddish nature, these movements strengthened and enlarged individuals' role (including workers) in organizations and broadened the content of personal development training. Management consultants are also directly involved in the design and delivery of personal development training programs.

Personal development training was first given to executives and managers, as utilization of their potential and broadened commitment was perceived to be critical to the future of organizations. Some human relations training programs became transformed into personal development training. For example, leadership training used to focus on how to avoid mishandling of subordinates and how to make them happy and content. It shifted its focus to how to effectively influence people to get work done. With more levels of employees perceived as actors who think and choose as contributing organizational members, personal development training started to be given to more employees, including frontline workers, and the content of personal development training expanded. For example, leadership training is also given to employees who are not positional leaders, as every team member should also be a leader and self-manager (*Personnel Journal* 1990).

The involvement of almost all employees (at least in theory) in personal development training indicates the institutionalization of training. Under the bureaucracy and community models, to say that virtually all employees need continuing training implied that the wrong people were selected, and the word *training* had a condescending connotation. The way to deal with changes and uncertainties in the environment (admittedly the changes were slower than they are now) was to alter the organizational rules and structures (especially the periphery structures). Under the participatory model, training has gained legitimacy, as individuals are viewed as the most important source of organizational success, and investment in individuals is viewed as the best preparation for uncertainties and changes in the environment. Such training is development-oriented rather than conformity-directed. Therefore, we have seen the growth of investment in human resources through training and the rise of personal development training take place at the same time, driven by the same force of the participatory organizational model.

Conclusion

There has been an enormous expansion of training content in U.S. organizations during the twentieth century. Training has expanded from technical training specific for certain job tasks to human relations training during the 1930s to personal development training on a large scale since the 1970s. The wide spread of personal development training cannot be completely explained by the human capital and technology-based perspectives, because provision of such training does not entirely follow an instrumental logic in the sense of technical rationality. First, such training is not immediately or innately related to the technical aspects of specific job tasks. Second, prior need analysis is rarely conducted for such training. Third, organizations and trainers seldom conduct evaluation of behavioral or outcome changes brought out by such training. Fourth, the rapid expansion of personal development training has taken place in the absence of scientific evidence of a link between such training and improvement in the organizational bottom line.

Hence, the chapter has adopted an institutional perspective of organizations, and has regarded training as shaped by the dominant organizational models in addition to the cost-benefit calculation and technical requirement in specific work situations. The shaping force of these models has been best demonstrated in the historical shift of emphasis in training. As the dominant organizational model evolved from bureaucracy to community and then to the participatory citizenship model, human relations training grew to complement specific-technical training, and personal development training rose to overshadow both human relations and specific-technical training.

Analysis of the historical evidence of training practices in organizations suggests a link between the organizational models and the different emphases in training. First, the expansion of training content matches the shift in the dominant organizational models. In particular, the rise of personal development training took place after the 1970s, coinciding with the rise of the participatory citizenship model of organizations, as represented by the decline in human relations ideology and practices, the emergence of the contingency theories and open system theories, and a surge of organizational literature on commitment.

Second, the focus of training on specific-technical skills, human relations, and personal development has been associated with different groups of advocates. Since these groups obtained different notions about individuals' role and the organization's role, called the *organizational model* in this chapter, they became carriers of the dominant organizational models. And since they brought such notions with them when they advocated, designed, and delivered training programs, their association with the different training emphases supports the impact of the organizational model on training content. As non-personnel company managers and efficiency engineers were professionalized in the bureaucracy model and represented traditional organizational control, personnel managers came to the fore during the reign of community model, and management consultants were instilled in the philosophy of the participatory model, they promoted training in specific-technical, human relations, and personal development, respectively.

The importance of the shared symbolic understandings in shaping organization behavior has increasingly been recognized in organization research (Meyer and Rowan 1977; DiMaggio and Powell 1983). This chapter demonstrates the fruitfulness of such a perspective and sheds light on the classic question in the training field, Why do organizations provide general training? It also points to at least two directions for future research. First, there might exist a reciprocal relationship between the organizational model and training. This study has focused on how the participatory organizational model drives personal development training. Future research can examine whether training people to be empowered decision makers and leaders also reinforces the participatory model. Second, since investment in personal development training is largely driven by the participatory organizational model, there might be a loose coupling between such training efforts and productivity gains. Cognitive consistency brought by such training for employees in a participatory organization is certainly valuable, but it does not necessarily help the bottom line. Measuring the contribution of personal development training to productivity gains can further reveal the shaping force of such training and provide a healthy dose of skepticism for the popularity of such training endeavors.

10 Management Models and Technical Education Systems: Germany and the United States 1870–1930

Haldor Byrkjeflot, University of Bergen, Norway

Introduction

It has often been suggested that there is a link between the development of engineering and the emergence of a management ideology in the United States. The latest contribution in this literature is Shenhav (1999), who argues that the scientific management model and the ideology of rationality, systems, and organization were invented and advanced by engineers in order to promote their professional interests. Others have studied how these ideologies were transformed into hegemonic management models as American engineers came to be the first group to define the management function as a career and profession (Fligstein 1990; Guillèn 1994). What has been overlooked in such studies is that management, being a context-dependent function, has to be sustained by various kinds of arguments and competence. In most cases, it is not likely that managers may convince anyone about their superior abilities or legitimate their position in the long run by referring to a single source of management knowledge or by relying on one kind of competence, be it American engineers or any other professional groups. There may be a wide variety of sources of knowledge and personnel for managers to choose from, and the interesting question is what kind of management positions are legitimated by what kind of knowledge, and whether there is a trend toward convergence across social contexts in such matters. Rather than focusing on one profession in one country, then, one must study how parallel development processes in different contexts—for example, how engineers in Germany and the United States—use knowledge in different ways in order to develop a common identity and legitimate their actions. It is not sufficient, then, to focus on the role of the American engineering profession in the construction of modern management, and then look at European cases mainly as a laboratory for diffusion of Taylorism and other engineering-constructed American concepts of management. There is a need to study how European and other regions each developed their distinct systems for knowledge formation and legitimation of authority in management and also how they selected and educated their top managers. The focus in this chapter is on the contrast between Germany and the United States.

Although differently positioned, German engineers were equally influential in the development of organization practices in industry, but they provided a distinctly different kind of legitimation for management. The German engineering-executives (*Unternehmer*) came to see themselves foremost as experts in a technical field and representatives of family traditions and servants of national interests, whereas the American executives were *general managers* and legitimated their social role by emphasizing their scientific and organizational *status* (Hartmann 1959; Byrkjeflot 1998). The American engineering ideology was universalistic and with a managerial purpose, whereas the German ideology was more particularistic and linked to the nation-state. The American engineering ideas could travel more easily than similar ideas developed in Germany.

It was increasingly a requirement for industrial leaders both in Germany and the United States that they have a higher degree in education, and the industrialists in both nation-states were keen to arrange for their offspring to acquire an engineering degree. This was one of several reasons for the strong growth in technical education and the formation of engineering associations from 1870 to 1930. There was a stronger tradition for guilds and craft communities in Germany, and the movement for technical education would take a more collectivist character than in the American case.

Professions and professional associations, as well as education systems, are strongly influenced by states. States set the stage for the professional struggles for recognition taking place both in the workplace and within professions and occupational systems. The worldviews and actions of civil servants and politicians are responses to worldviews and actions taken by teachers, academics, businessmen, and professional practitioners. Such actors all influenced the construction of management models and technical education systems. I will put emphasis on differences in organizational resources and worldviews among such groups of actors. The conventional story tells us that educational systems develop in predictable ways, and that what needs to be "controlled for" are variations in technical and economic development. I will present some empirical data that has led me to question this assumption, and further move on to discuss alternative explanations that relate to the effects of contrasting worldviews, coalition-building, and strategies among the various actors. I ask what factors were most important in each case: educational philosophies and institutional arrangements within the education system, industrial structures and business interests, or professional and governmental strategies? The failure to develop a direct career-path from apprenticeships and vocational schools into engineering may be one of the major explanations for the "managerialist" worldview of American engineers and top executives. The German states, as well as other states in Europe, have developed a more comprehensive and multiple-layered system for technical education. I will discuss the reasons for this, and what may have been the consequences of this for management and organizational practices.

Why do I focus on Germany and the United States? These countries represent important contrasts in managerial models and professional ideologies. They also represent alternative international models for economic development, work organization, and education. The more recently industrialized countries in Asia and other European countries have emulated both systems. There has been a movement away from the traditional German model toward the American model of management in Germany and Europe. Ringer (1992: 36) has argued that the first educational revolution in the world occurred in Germany. Whereas the educational revolution preceded industrialization in the German states, it was taking place along with rapid industrialization in the United States. Both economies were large and their engineering-dominated industries were involved in international competition early on. Their internal markets and technologies, and their positions in the international marketplace and technologies, were not identical but similar enough to justify a comparison. Germany and the United States clearly took the lead in engineering education and research from 1910 on, both in numbers of patents and engineers. The engineers took very prominent positions in industry, a position that German engineers have continued to hold until the present. Until now, the most frequently compared cases have been European nation-states such as Germany, Sweden, France, and Great Britain. It may be useful to focus more on the contrasts between the German and American cases and between Europe and the United States (Müller *et al.* 1987; Ahlström 1982; Landes 1986; Torstendahl 1982, 1993; Lundgreen and Grelon 1994).[1]

The educational systems did not develop independently of each other. Germany was looked upon as a kind of "second mother country" in the United States because of the German university (Rheingold 1987: 130; Röhrs 1995). The "scientific" curriculum in German technical education was a model for American educators from around 1860. Likewise, as the American machinery industries demonstrated their competitive strength, the interest in the "practical" features of American engineering schools spurred a movement for closing the gap between theory and practice in German engineering (Gispen 1989: 115–121). Industrialists as well as teachers and academic entrepreneurs advocated a direct emulation of laboratory instruction and other practical teaching methods in American engineering schools. A comparison of the formation of systems for industrial education may therefore also give a better understanding of the processes of international borrowing of organizational models and reform ideas in education.

Outline of the Problem and the Argument

The term *engineering education* as used in the United States around 1925 had no direct equivalent in continental Europe, where *technical education* was used as a more inclusive term for the training of all ranks of specialists in industrial and building technology (Wickenden 1930: 751). *Technical education* was in Germany used to describe a wide variety of training and education institutions qualifying for jobs and specialties at several levels of the industrial hierarchy. Three quite distinct categories of technical education developed: higher, middle, and lower (Wickenden 1930: 751; Ahlström 1982; Lundgreen 1994). The American system also had a lower "vocational" and a higher "professional" level, whereas it was difficult to recognize a middle level. There was thus no link between the lower and higher levels and no alternative educational pathways into the higher ranks of the firm.

In two to three years the new middle schools for technical training in Germany were expected to produce the "connecting link between the university educated engineer, on the one hand, and the foreman on the other," as argued by the Cologne chapter of the Association of German Engineers (Kocka 1980: 105). The most impressive fact about the German system was "its comprehensiveness; it is applied to every occupation in which it is better for a workman to have it than be without it" (Dawson 1919: 103). A vocational orientation penetrated the school and corporation from the lowest to the highest levels, and there was also a great deal of horizontal specialization at each level. A nonacademic practical type of engineer competed with the traditional academic engineer for the same type of jobs at the upper hierarchical levels. In contrast to in the United States, both types of engineers originated in a school culture.

Higher technical education in Germany was the exclusive province of the technical universities (*Technische Hochschulen*) requiring the high school diploma (*Abitur*) from a nine-year high school and typically providing an eight-semester curriculum. At the other end was lower technical training, based on *Volksschule* and made up of part-time vocational schools for blue-collar workers and foremen. In between was a separate set of schools that had filled the gap between vocational and academic schools after the early 1890s. *Abitur* was not required for these schools. *Realschule* was the preferred track in secondary school, and it was a prerequisite for admission that the student had an extended period of prior practical experience (Gispen 1989: 216; *Datsch Abhandlungen und Berichte* 1910, 158–161). Employers had articulated a preference for the more practical and specialized nonacademic engineers. The teachers from these schools were involved both in the engineering association and the institutions associated with the development of technical education, and the influence of these schools in the German occupational and institutional structure was steadily increasing.

The American engineering education system developed later and the universities took a more active role. The "self-made" engineer-entrepreneur and mechanic therefore was able to establish a much stronger position in industry, and the conflict was more between a "shop" and "school" tradition than between various types of educated engineers (Calvert 1967; Layton 1986; Noble 1977; Meiksins 1988). Whereas industrialization led to a divide between practical and academic engineers in the United States, the nonacademic engineers educated at the middle level provided a link between manual and academic labor in Germany. The two kinds of engineers were also organized in the same major professional association. This meant that manual, administrative, and conceptual tasks were not separated into different cultures and careers to the same degree as in the United States (Wickenden 1930: 751; Chamberlain 1908: 8).

The Germans tended to dignify and even glamorize the engineer as a force for social unity and nationalism (Sorge and Warner 1986: 189; Locke 1989: 267; Lawrence 1980: 97, 1992: 89). *Technik* symbolized a common language that made it possible for people in various functional specialties and hierarchical positions to communicate and develop common understandings and identities. The notion of management and the discourse and metaphors attached to *system* and *rationality* may have played an equivalent role in American society (Shenhav 1999; Lawrence 1996: 21). The American engineers may have undermined their own power base by putting so much emphasis on the management function, however. If top management jobs were not about technology, manufacturing, and product development but a more general people-oriented and financial skill, then accountants, lawyers, and sales personnel could also do the job. The idea that management was a profession in itself opened the field of management to other professions, and it was particularly those with a background in law and business administration that would later take up the battle with engineers to enter the top positions (Byrkjeflot 1998).

Engineering education in the United States was based on the idea of a distinction between technology and art; the implication was that engineering (and management) was a collection of abstract principles and techniques that could be applied in industry. However, it was not established as a clear hierarchy among schools as was the case in France, where the theoretical approach to technology was linked to a hierarchical system among engineers in the workplace (Kranakis 1997: 258), and in Germany where it was developed as a hierarchy not among particular schools but among categories of schools. The aim was the same in Germany as in France: to establish a clear correspondence between workplace hierarchies and educational hierarchies (Kocka 1980: 104).

American engineers did not want to be associated with the notion of vocational training, since they feared that this would lead to a degradation of status. Progressive U.S. reformers had filled the concept of vocational education with a particular pedagogical and social meaning; the purpose was to improve motivation, recruitment, and career prospects for manual jobs. Manual training, accordingly, was associated in the public mind with the rehabilitation of criminals (Fisher 1967: 78–79). In Germany, on the other hand, the concept of vocational training was linked to the notion of industrialization and *Kultur*. Germany was much more of a "late industrializer" than the United States in the sense that civil society and the education system were much more penetrated with a "catch-up mentality" vis-à-vis Britain and the other more industrialized countries (Veblen 1954; Gerschenkrohn 1962).

Organization of Presentation

I will discuss why the organizational fields of technical education in Germany and the United States developed in their distinct ways. The model presented in Figure 10.1 will structure the chapter.

The four relevant actors in this scheme are (1) states, (2) business interests, (3) academic entrepreneurs and teachers, and (4) professional associations. The state is important both as a direct and indirect variable because it defines the interaction pattern among education, profession, and industry.

Different Perspectives on National Models of Technical Education

Let me present four conjectures about how the fields of technical education were shaped, and then discuss to what extent each conjecture may explain the various outcomes and ideologies in technical and industrial education.

1. It may be argued that it was the state apparatus and the strategies of actors linked to the state that most decisively set the pace for the development of technical education systems.
2. According to a more functionalist argument it will be assumed that it was industrial demands and particularly the increasingly powerful *business interests* that were the decisive forces behind the transformations and renewal of the existing educational systems.
3. Such patterns of transformation and renewal may have been driven by internal factors, that is, dynamics and conflicts within the education system itself.

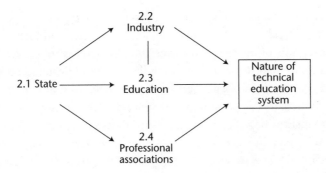

10.1   Actors influencing the formation of technical education systems

4. It may have been the technical and professional associations and strategies associated with the new professions that have most decisively influenced education systems.

Within the industrial argument one should be aware of how different industries with varying needs perceived of their interests in a given period, and to what degree industry developed internal education and training systems instead of attempting to influence the education system. According to the argument from education the important actors are those involved in scientific development, academic institution-building, and teaching. In the professional perspective it is important to be aware of the relationship among different segments in the profession, to what extent the profession was unified or diversified, and its program for technical education. Clearly, there is a great deal of potential for internal conflicts within each major group of actors, and this creates room for political actors and states to influence the shape and content of self-interested strategies and problem formulation among the major actors.

The State-Centered Argument

The special character of the state is that it has the power to define or "institutionalize" the relationship between the other organizations and actors in a society. "All the actors involved depend on the state," Burrage *et al.* (1990: 222) argue, and "the decisions and policies of the state towards professional knowledge and professional services are therefore a subject of particular importance." The state is a privileged actor because it may take legal and political action and thereby pick the winner and loser in conflicts over conception of control and governance structures in a given sector or organizational field (Campbell and Lindberg 1990; Fligstein and Byrkjeflot 1996). Legal traditions and certification procedures are important; for instance, whether it is possible to create cartels in industry, or whether an education institution or a professional firm must satisfy certain requirements in order to remain in business. The fundamental difference between Germany and the United States was that the German states promoted cooperation and cartels in industry, whereas the American states promoted competition and had several types of cooperation outlawed. This had important consequences for the educational system also, since the early American universities were corporations, and since the various academic groups were directly affected by the restrictions on cooperative arrangements in product and labor markets. The laws relating to cartels and industrial relations may also have had important consequences for the strength of industrial, occupational, and educational associations.

In continental Europe control over higher educational institutions was vested in ministries of higher education, which were assigned broad powers, including the right to determine who should be admitted, be allowed to teach and be promoted, and who should practice in the professions. The state in Germany did not see any reason to issue individual licenses for engineers, probably due to the strength of its technical civil service and the public status of technical education (Lundgreen 1990: 74). The major governance method was to bring the partners together in cooperative organizations and promote compromises between them. In the case of the United States the federal authorities and the states took another and less active role. Individual states started to require licenses from engineers employed in public service from around 1920 (Rothstein 1969: 83). In 1934 all American states still would allow a person to become registered without having graduated from an engineering school (Grayson 1993: 132). There was no agreement among the professional associations on licensing, and the state did not make any attempt to bring the partners together in order to establish a standard. The idea behind the emerging system of education in the United States was that the professions ought to set the standards for their own activities. The federal and state levels were more actively involved in the establishment of engineering schools than in law and medical and dental schools, however. The engineering schools would function at both the undergraduate and graduate levels as integral parts of the academic and administrative structures of the university (Grayson 1993: 26). National engineering societies were for the most part established after their respective curricula, and this means that the states and schools took a more active role in the formation of the engineering profession than in the legal and medical professions (Grayson 1993: 51).

The agencies that developed in the United States were of a more collegial kind, in contrast with the corporatist structures in Germany. There was a dramatic increase in the number of institutions offering university degrees between 1860 and 1920, and the American higher educational institutions gradually developed a unique but complex system known as *accreditation*.[2] The Association of American universities was engaged in such activities from 1914 on, and the Flexner report on medical education (1910) has been given much credit for the strong growth of accreditation associations (Zaret 1967: 178). The American Council of Education (1918), of which the Society for Promotion of Engineering Education (SPEE) was among the founding members, was another pioneer in accreditation activities. SPEE was the major governance agency in American engineering, at least until the establishment of the Engineers' Council for Professional Development (ECPD) in 1932. The establishment of ECPD was partly a result of the need felt by engineering societies to create their own accrediting agency. These two associations arguably took on some of the same tasks as educational ministries and governmental committees in continental Europe.

The industrial and state elites in Germany did not develop the same aversion against vocationalism and practical training as the British and the French elites (Sorge 1979: 52–53). The German states dominated at the higher levels in the technical education system, associations at the lower levels. The state was rather predominant at all levels in France, in contrast to the United Kingdom, where it was much weaker. This relates to the distinction between state-centered societies and stateless societies (Nettl 1968; Birnbaum 1988). Such a distinction may also be relevant in a comparison between Germany and the United States. It would be misleading, however, to argue that the formation of technical education in Germany was an outcome of state policies, and that the United States was a copy of another stateless society: Great Britain. Dawson depicts the development of technical education in Saxony as a social movement based on traditional craft and guild values, whereas Gispen argues that the engineering profession in Germany was a new and more liberal kind of profession, shaped in a struggle against the "old order." It is thus indicated that the state's role may have been indirect also in Germany, and that state actions may matter almost as much in nation-states with "weak" states (Gispen 1988: 568; Dawson 1919; Evans *et al.* 1985).

The state agencies in the United States took a greater responsibility for higher technical education than the British. The land-grant colleges developed as a direct response to a state initiative (the Morrill Land-Grant Act of 1862). The dislike of state involvement in vocational education was strong also in the United States, however. Fisher (1967: 114) notes that the corporation schools' association in the United States had a "rather astounding blind spot; until 1917 when the Smith Hughes bill (on vocational education) was passed, they hardly mentioned federal aid to vocational schools." The basic difference between the German and American states, at a federal and regional level, was that the German states were more instantly involved in the development of higher technical education and in agencies related to this purpose. The American Government was more inclined to let the professions, the industrial associations, and the educational institutions govern their own matters. This lack of state involvement was a problem according to a report on technical education from 1930, since "the leaving of all initiative to individual institutions, with no coordination of policy, has resulted in the failure to work out a well-rounded national system of technical education in its several natural divisions" (Wickenden 1930: 823). In Europe the stratification in the school system was "public, legal, and taken for granted" (Rubinson 1987: 523). The U.S. policy was to provide everyone with the same introductory education and leave the tracking decisions to the students:

> Our technical education is conceived as an aid to the progress of individuals of varying needs and tastes, and only secondarily as a process of recruiting well defined callings. Not so in Germany or elsewhere in Central Europe; there technical education is a definitely organized arm of the body economic, controlled by the brain of the system—the state. (Wickenden 1930: 997)

The Argument from Industry

It has been commonly assumed in the social sciences that change in industrial and economic arrangements causes educational change. Functionalists of various kinds have argued that schools merely develop the skills and attitudes needed at work; as work requirements change, so do schooling practices and the structure of education (Carnoy and Levin 1985: 3). In this perspective cross-national differences are explained simply by pointing out the contrasting industrial structures and growth patterns. Differences in industrial output, size of national markets, and position in the international trade would inevitably lead to different education systems. The larger markets and associated strategies for mass production in the United States indicated a higher demand for managerial-technical manpower at the higher end and more unskilled labor power at the lower end. Struck (1930: 91) argued that "specialization in industry had, by 1905, already progressed to the point where it had almost killed apprenticeship in all but a very limited number of skilled trades such as the machine shop, printing and building trades."[3] American industrialists were driven by market demands and it was rational for them to develop a top-heavy polarized technical education system as opposed to the Germans, who needed more skilled workers on the middle level and on the shop floor.

A prominent place in functionalist lines of argumentation is assigned to the increase in output from education systems, since these numbers are supposedly a function of the growth rate in industrial production. Tables 10.1 and 10.2 provide some support for this argument. The explosion in engineering education in the United States came between 1900 and 1915, with an increase from 17,000 to 55,000 engineering graduates. In the same period the production index jumped from 675 to 1,250 points. Germany did not match this growth pattern with an increase from 464 to 714 points only. Its population of engineers did not grow as fast (from 41,000 to 65,000, nonacademic graduates not included). The most rapid growth in engineering and production in Germany came a few decades earlier. The slower growth in engineering education in France as compared to Germany might also be "explained" by the comparatively slow production growth. What cannot be explained is why the number of graduates in the United States was so much lower than in France and Germany until 1890.

The functionalist perspective of education does not specify by what mechanism education systems adjust to changing skill demands in the workplace. According to critical functionalists such adjustment follows from the increasingly powerful position business interests have in society. It is assumed that changes in the orientation of institutions take place because capitalists

TABLE 10.1   Industrial Output in Europe and the U.S. from 1850 to 1913

	Germany	Great Britain	France	United States
1850	100	100	100	100
1870	129	129	131	138
1900	464	232	254	675
1913	714	294	385	1,250

SOURCE: Thanheiser and Dyas (1976: 44).

TABLE 10.2   Estimated Number of Engineers with Degrees in France, Germany, and the U.S. Between 1850 and 1914[a]

	France	Germany	United States
1850	6,687	3,343	n.d.
1870	12,050	11,856	866
1880	15,994	24,452	3,125
1890	21,504	32,166	6,962
1900	28,829	41,657	17,392
1910	38,317	59,738	38,392
1914[b]	42,850	65,202	55,392

SOURCE: Mann (1918: 6) (United States) and Ahlström (1982: 106–108) (Germany and France).

[a] The data on the United States are based on cumulative data on numbers of graduates from engineering schools. Ahlström's methodology is somewhat different (see Ahlström 1982: 70–71). Nonacademic engineers are not included in the German case.

[b] The basis year for the U.S. estimate is 1915.

impose their will on them as part of a strategy to control or discipline the working class (Rubinson 1987). An example of this kind of argument is Noble (1977), who tells the story about how engineering education was transformed into a "unit of the industrial system." *America by Design* (Noble 1977) is among the most quoted studies of engineering education in the United States.[4] Noble argues that industrialists were able to impose their views on the profession and the education system in three ways: first, by developing cooperative educational programs; second, by developing strong in-house training programs; third, he lists several new agencies that were created to coordinate activities between education and industry (1977: 169–170). I will now discuss these three arguments.

Cooperative Programs. Noble has put a great deal of emphasis on the introduction of cooperative programs between General Electric (GE) and Massachusetts Institute of Technology (MIT) between 1907 and 1920. His narrative centers on the actions of Magnus Alexander, who was in charge of the training department at GE. Carlson (1988), who has presented a more detailed study of this case, concludes that "it was not the leaders of GE who spearheaded the course but rather, Dugald Jackson, an "academic entrepreneur" at MIT. "From the outset," he says "Jackson strove to shape the course to reflect his vision of the engineer rather than simply serve GE's manpower needs" (550). "In Jackson's engineering philosophy the vision of the engineer as a leader and expert was fundamental, . . . and he pursued it even when it ran counter to what big business wanted or needed" (546). Whereas Noble portrays an almost conflict-free relationship between the representatives of GE and MIT, Carlson thinks the process was marked by constant tension and conflict. On the one hand, it was Alexander's purpose to educate "designer engineers and factory supervisors" that would fit in with General Electric's immediate manpower needs. Jackson, on the other hand, advocated that the MIT cooperative program should produce men "of larger vision and finer training . . . for the distinctively higher executive positions," and not just "better $2000–3000-men" (Carlson 1988: 550).[5]

Noble and Carlson also disagree fundamentally about how successful the cooperative programs were and how much backing Jackson and Alexander got in their respective organizations. Carlson argues that neither the staff at MIT as a whole or managers at General Electric saw the cooperative course as an integral part of their institutional strategies (Carlson 1988: 557). The plans were postponed because of the recession, and the first cohort did not graduate until 1922. The classes were much smaller than planned, due to lack of support from GE. The course did not satisfy the firm's demand for technical manpower. The graduates from the cooperative program were not regarded as better prepared for firm-specific jobs than other engineers and there was no special recruitment policy for graduates from the cooperative program.

By the mid-1920s the cooperative idea had been adopted by sixteen institutions, or about 10 percent of all engineering schools (Carlson 1988: 548). Several of the cooperative programs failed, and the movement for cooperative education was not able to establish a position as the major model for American engineering education. If the cooperative idea was the industrialists' model for engineering education, then this case contradicts Noble's claim that industry was able to "take over" the engineering schools. One might, of course, argue that these programs represented a major ideological alternative in education and that most institutions adapted to the business demand for more practical education by incorporating major elements from these programs in their curricula. This does not seem to have been the case, however. Wickenden (1930: 232) argues that the plan had gained mainly by establishment of new schools and that it was rarely introduced in already established schools.[6]

In-House Training Programs. If the emergence of cooperative programs demonstrated industry's increasing influence, then the question is why they did not become more widespread along with the rise of industrial power. An answer might be that industrialists would not take the risk of sharing the costs with education institutions, that they preferred to organize their own proprietary programs. This is what one would expect according to an argument put forward by many that skills are not treated as collective goods in the Anglo-Saxon economies, and that the threat of losing skilled employees to competitors poses a serious obstacle for investing in skill-creation (Streeck 1989; Rieble-Auborg 1996). If this was a major problem, then one should expect that employers sought to prevent their own graduates from seeking employment in other corporations. But Wise (1979: 173) found that GE took twice as many engineers than its expected needs into its "test" classes every year, and that placement interviews were arranged for those who did not continue for a second year not only with company components but also with other organizations. The major purpose with these classes was "not to educate, but to initiate, indoctrinate and select"(Wise 1979: 171), and the students that left the company did turn out to be good customers. Large companies, like GE, accepted a division of labor between engineering schools and corporations, and they developed in-house programs in order to identify candidates for staff jobs and top management positions. GE expanded their inhouse programs for graduate engineers in the 1920s. With the exception of the Depression years, some 400 to 600 men would enter "the test programs" annually (Wise 1979: 174–175).

A number of other large industrial enterprises, such as AT&T, General Motors, Chrysler, and IBM also developed schools of their own. Zaret (1967: 388) reports that the total enrollment for corporate schools was many times greater than that for all engineering technology institutes and engineering colleges combined, and that such schools were already an important and consistent part in the skill formation strategies of many larger American companies in the interwar period. It is difficult to believe that these firms would be willing to develop such costly in-house engineering programs if they could fill their skilled manpower needs through development of joint programs with engineering schools and by participating in associations for accreditation in engineering education. Lazonick (1991: 217) argues that American firms traditionally have depended heavily on recruitment of lower-level technical specialists, which were subsequently rotated from one department and function to the other in order to enable them to gain the experience necessary to move up the corporate ladder. In the long run, then, it might have emerged to both parties that academics and educators should have the responsibility for the content and structure of education, but that it would be necessary for the employers to define the needs for further training and management development.

Cooperative Agencies. The most striking fact with the development in the United States in comparison with Germany is the lack of cooperative agencies in which state and industrial interests were directly represented. SPEE, an organization of men teaching civil, mechanical, mining, and electrical engineering, was founded in 1893. SPEE was by then the only professional society devoted solely to education (Grayson 1977: 254). This association of educational interests was "able in a few short years to gain complete control of curriculum, admission standards, and other basic constituents of engineering education" (Calvert 1967: 58). Although it maintained close relationships with the four major engineering societies, the organization's membership and leadership were largely engineering educators, not practicing engineers (Zaret 1967: 54; McGivern 1960: 116). McGivern (1960: 254) and Grayson (1977: 254) both argue that SPEE was able to keep the control of engineering in the hands of engineering educators. David Noble has presented another opinion on this issue, according to which the industrial interests gradually took control over SPEE and its offspring ECPD. The major evidence he presents for this is an editorial from 1912 stating that there is a "great increase in teachers and businessmen."[7] The occupational distribution of the membership was published annually in *Bulletin of the Society for the Promotion of Engineering Education* (BSPE, later *Journal of Engineering Education*). These statistics show that the teachers continued to dominate the association between 1908 and 1923–1924, and that only 5–6 percent of the membership were "industrial officers."[8] There was a slight increase in practitioners among the membership after 1910, but teachers may have regained some of this position as SPEE began to admit educational institutions to membership in 1914 (Zaret 1967: 87).

Higher technical education in Germany was established as a separate system, independent from the traditional university. This was a result of a compromise between the liberals and the conservatives in the 1820s, after which the Department of Commerce and Industry in Prussia was allowed to set up its own system of specialized instruction. This marked the beginning of an era with conflict about the status of engineering education in relation to traditional education. The technical education system was built in a single movement against "the old order," represented by the state and the traditional education system. Modernization was thus achieved through a separate program of special education for private industry. Engineering education was only accepted as having the same status as the traditional academic education in 1899, when the *Technische Hochschule* was granted the right to issue doctorates.

The main conflict was between the state and the engineering professionals and educators before the 1870s and between the state and the professionals and industrialists after this decade.[9] A major compromise was reached around 1910, and as a result of this came DATSCH (*Deutsche Ausschuß für Technische Schulen*), the German committee for technical education. This was an association in which educational institutions, professional associations, industrial associations, and state representatives participated and among which the German Engineering Association—*Der Verein Deutscher Ingenieure* (VDI)—took the central position (Wickenden 1930: 802). If there had been anything like DATSCH in the United States, then Noble's argument that interests outside of engineering education were able to design the whole system in their image would have been more plausible. "There is no question that the managers of Germany's large engineering firms dominated the DATSCH," Gispen (1989: 211) argues. It was "through DATSCH, the managerial elite of the engineering profession was able to mold and subordinate the noneconomic functions of the engineering schools to its own needs." Gispen does not see any contradiction between this turn of events and VDI taking a commanding position, since he thinks that the industrial interests also were the predominant segment within the engineering association (Gispen 1989: 218).

A closer look at the membership lists and protocols of DATSCH and SPEE makes Gispen's claim more credible than Noble's in the case of the United States. Both DATSCH and SPEE had institutional as well as personal members. SPEE only granted educational institutions such membership, however, and the teachers were in overwhelming majority among the personal members. In the American context it is likely that the practitioners identified themselves more with the school they came from than their specialty and business. DATSCH was not primarily a voluntary cooperative agency or an accreditation institution as SPEE and later ECPD in the United States, but rather "a private body endowed with de facto public powers" (Gispen 1989: 212). Among the institutional members in DATSCH were the powerful association of the engineering industry, the VDMA, and the major technical and professional associations. Several state agencies participated although they were not listed as institutional members. The academics and teachers constituted a minority. As DATSCH developed further the representation of industrialists and state agencies expanded more than educational institutions. The implication of this according to Gispen (1989: 219) was that "the engineering society's leadership had now emerged next to the Prussian government as co-sovereign in the determination of technical education policy."

This remarkable *corporatist arrangement* is essential if one wants to understand how the German comprehensive system was governed relatively independently from the state. VDI took the initiative to DATSCH after having been urged to do so by the state. Using their own consultants and experts, DATSCH studied all forms and aspects of technical education. First on its agenda was the controversial question of nonacademic engineering. This question had led to a split in VDI. Professor Riedler, along with a group of engineer-educators broke out and founded VDDI— *Verband Deutscher Diplom-Ingenieure*, which was explicitly meant to be an association for academic engineers only. This was a protest against VDI's support of the nonacademic engineering schools in a period with overproduction of engineers. It was in the wake of this conflict that VDI reached a compromise with the state and the industrialists. The guidelines and recommendation following from the work of DATSCH became law almost exactly as proposed in

1910 (Gispen 1989: 215). After the successful resolution of this question, the DATSCH next turned its attention to academic schools and then to lower technical training. The result of this work was a nationwide coordination, consolidation, and standardization of a system for technical education. It was the reform program initiated by industrialists and VDI as part of a national movement for a more practical and specialized technical education that provided the guiding idea for DATSCH between 1908 and 1912. In the case of the United States there was no equivalent national agency for the governance of engineering schools and technical education. Different professional interests specialized in different fields. Industrialists were, for instance, more important in the association for promotion of industrial education than in engineering education (Fisher 1967). They also had an Association of Corporation Schools, set up to develop in-house apprenticeship programs and management training (Noble 1977: 170–185).

There are several indications that managers and industrialists in the United States actually wanted a more comprehensive type of education system similar to the German. Indeed, one of the most often repeated critical remarks in the trend-setting Wickenden report on engineering education was that the American system of technical education was "unbalanced and top-heavy." It was necessary to look to Germany and develop a more comprehensive and rational system.[10] According to Elbaum (1991: 208) the decline of the apprenticeship system in the United States was "by no means due to lack of employer interest. Indeed, during the later nineteenth and early twentieth century U.S. employers often bemoaned the decline of apprenticeship and a perceived association with skilled labour scarcity." The quality of engineering schools has been repeatedly criticized from a business viewpoint, and there has for the most part been a demand for a more practical orientation. This indicates that the prevailing inclination among American managers was not always to promote deskilling and to recruit "Taylor-made" engineer-managers directly from schools, as indicated by the trend-setting works by Braverman (1974) and Noble (1977). There are other ways of explaining the American industrialists' strategies than by referring to their Tayloristic attitudes. It is, for instance, possible that constant immigration of skilled personnel from Europe, and the abundance of engineering dropouts ready to take the position of technicians, was an important reason for the exclusive focus on academic education among American businessmen. If immigration was that important, however, then their strategies should have changed in the

1920s when immigration of skilled technicians was down to 51,000 from 180,000 in 1905 (Struck 1930: 68).

So far I have not found much evidence for Noble's theory of a corporate "takeover" in American engineering education. It is not possible to identify a clear program for this among American industrialists, who were less organized than German industrialists at the time. It rather seems like the traditional employers in the United States wanted a more stratified and vocational system like the one in Germany, the problem being that they were not able to get the politicians and the new engineering professionals on their side. What was different, according to Rubinson (1987), "was not so much the interest of the capitalist class but its ability to impose those interests." Could it be the case, then, that Shenhav (1999: 135) is quite to the point arguing that engineers had developed priorities that were different from capitalists or government and that they were better organized to impose their interests than either the state or the traditional capitalists? One may assume, contrary to the class imposition argument, that there is always an element of choice in managerial and professional strategies. The choices that are eventually made will depend, for instance, on the professional background and worldviews predominant among managers and professionals. American employers and managers may have lacked the organizational capabilities that would allow them to take the lead, and also a clear conception of what kind of engineering education they wanted. These organizational capabilities and conceptions may have been further developed in Germany. The academic brand of professionalism gradually won out in the technical associations in the United States in a period when *general managers* took over as role models in industry.

The Argument from Education

The argument from education is that educational systems develop autonomously from industry and professional associations. Schools have their own dynamics rooted in prevailing institutional and epistemological legacies and associated political arenas. Cross-national variations, then, might be understood to be a consequence of different educational traditions and worldviews among academic institution-builders, scientists, and teachers. Their strategies are not determined but constrained by the respective institutional frameworks and available economic and ideological resources.

These elements can be seen as "building blocks" for educational entrepreneurs (Meyer and Rowan 1977: 26). According to common knowledge about these societies, there was more room for institution building and entrepreneurialism in the educational sector in the United States because of the lack of any national regulations or standards (Rheingold 1987). American society was also more multicultural and had developed a value system and a mobility pattern based on achievement and ascriptive values (Parsons 1991).

The early impact of industrialization on American higher education has to be understood in relation to the host of forces gradually seeking governmental support to defend their professional territory. Academic entrepreneurialism exploded in the decade after the introduction of the Land Grant Act in 1862, which provided for the allocation of public lands to the foundation and support of colleges. The number of engineering schools increased from about a dozen in 1862 to 70 in 1872 (Grayson 1977: 250). The most prestigious colleges that came to function as role models, such as Columbia, Harvard, and Yale, were predominantly initiated by donations from wealthy businessmen. After the dramatic increase in the 1870s the coming of the engineering school in the United States was more of a continual trend. Between 1870 and World War I the number of engineering graduates swelled from 100 to 4,300 annually (Noble 1977: 24, 39). Just as remarkable, especially seen in relation to the high rate of organizational proliferation and entrepreneurialism, is the outcome of this process as reported in 1930:

> It is surprising to find so little variety of types of instruction and of levels of entrance and completion among the one hundred fifty colleges of engineering, and so few substantial technical schools of any other type. Tradition, the influence of early modes and imitative growth evidently may impose even greater uniformity than bureaucratic authority. (Wickenden 1930: 1,000)

In order to explain this outcome it is necessary to take a closer look at what had happened in the previous decades. It appears that the origins of the larger number of American colleges cannot be attributed to the industrial revolution or the demands of the economy (Collins 1979: 121). Religious ideas and an emphasis on discipline and piety, the education of a democratic citizen, and equality of opportunity were more important than the demand from employers and professions for provision of practical skills and licensing of qualified labor power. This traditional model, however, faced a serious crisis in the 1850s. Failure rates were high, the colleges too small, and financial difficulties were common. "Feverish entrepreneurship" in the educational sphere had founded perhaps 1,000 colleges before the Civil War, of which over 700 failed (Collins 1979: 121; Rudolph 1990: 219). The lack of any national regulations or standards and the variety in resources and ideologies continued to lure academic entrepreneurs into higher education. There were at least four types of actors involved: wealthy men of vision, pioneer educators, politicians, and college presidents (McGivern 1960: 164). Among these, the college presidents were most important until well into the twentieth century (Collins 1979: 120).[11] It was due to their administrative gifts and the unifying power of the ideology of professionalism and "science" that a system in crisis and disarray came to be stabilized and entered into a phase of expansion and consolidation.[12]

Wickenden locates a formative stage in American engineering education in the decades before 1870. This phase was marked by the creation of new and distinctive schools and programs: "its dominating personalities were more often scientists and publicists than engineers; and its chief aim had been the training of civil engineers" (Wickenden 1930: 818). Given the fact that the most preeminent institutional entrepreneurs did not have a practical background and that they imported a "science" model, it was no wonder that they alienated their clientele in the industry and the profession. The historical dominance of a shop culture in industry made the cooperation between the colleges and the elite in the professional associations difficult. The early academic entrepreneurs had to orient themselves toward practical and administrative engineering in order to gain acceptance for their graduates in the business community and in the professional associations.

The same type of crisis did not shake the German education system. This must be explained by the strength of the "old order." Whereas the industrial revolution and the development of a technical education system antedated the creation of large civil services in the United States, in Germany the situation was reversed. All the academic technical schools were state institutions, and the proprietary middle-level technical schools, which mushroomed between 1890 and 1910, were also gradually brought under state protection (Gispen 1989: 216–217).

The stability in the number of academic engineering education institutions was exceptional in comparison with the United States. The total number of technical universities and universities in Prussia increased from thir-

teen in 1875 to sixteen in 1920 (Lundgreen 1983: 151). In order to say something about the "impact" of the industrial revolution on higher education in
Germany, it is therefore necessary to concentrate first on the processes of
internal diversification in the technical universities. Second, it is necessary to
study the development of separate educational institutions at a lower level,
such as the nonacademic engineering schools. In contrast, it is the institutional proliferation of institutions at the academic level that is most striking
about the American case. There was an increase from four engineering
schools in 1860 to 126 schools of college level in 1918. Among the 126
schools in 1918 were forty-six land-grant colleges operating under the Morrill Act, forty-four professional schools in universities, twenty schools
attached to colleges, and sixteen independent institutions (Mann 1918). As
other American professional schools, these schools adopted the same degree
structure as the classical university departments (B.A., M.A., Ph.D.). The
inclusion of engineering schools in comprehensive universities became the
dominant model, in contrast to what was the case in continental Europe,
where there was a tradition for technical universities (Clark 1978; Collins
1979; Lundgreen 1990: 60).[13] Whereas horizontal differentiation within in
stitutions (curricula, chairs) and vertical differentiation among types of
schools (lower versus higher technical education) were the common pattern
in Germany, competition also took place among different institutions at the
same level in the United States (Lundgreen 1983: 49; Herbst 1982: 205). The
curricular diversification within German technical universities took place at
a quite early stage. Until about 1870 there were fifty to sixty technical and
scientific teaching subjects in institutes of technology. The number increased
to more than 100 by 1880, nearly 200 by 1890, and by 1900 there were
more than 350 subjects at the Berlin technical university (Manegold 1978:
153). Herbst (1982: 205) argues that the diversification among colleges in the
United States initially tended to hold back curricular diversification within
them, but that American universities later diversified also internally. The
major difference was that the American universities were more oriented
toward general education and teaching and that they were organized according to more egalitarian principles.

The need for setting qualifying standards in engineering education
was supported by reports of the high failure rates among students in the
United States compared to Europe. The Mann report published in 1918
revealed that 60 percent of freshmen failed to obtain their degrees (Mann

1918: 32–33). Accordingly, a large group of American technicians distinguished themselves from academic engineers not by type of schooling but by their failure at achieving a degree. This must have strengthened the trends toward relying on degrees and school ranking as criteria for a new status hierarchy in engineering (Collins 1979: 171). In the longer run the academic engineer was the only type of engineering graduate, and the strong drive toward standardization in engineering education strengthened the influence of the elite schools.

The major institutional framework in German and American technical education was in place around 1870, except the technical middle schools in Germany, which mainly were established from the 1890s. Growing from a few hundred in the 1830s and 1840s, the enrollment in the higher technical schools in Germany fluctuated between 1,000 and 2,000 in the 1850s. By the 1860s, enrollments shot up rapidly, reaching a total of nearly 5,000 in the academic year 1871–1872, and over 6,600 in 1875–1876 (McClelland 1980: 241). It then increased to 12,576 in 1903–1904 before leveling off at 11,541 in 1914. At the same time, student numbers in the nonacademic engineering schools increased from about 1,400 in the late 1880s to almost 11,000 by 1910 (Jarausch 1990: 18).

State responsibility for higher education in Prussia gave professors autonomy from private funds and professional contributions. This meant that they depended on the state and that they as civil servants were obliged to implement state policies. One might then have expected that the established civil service and *Bildung* ideal would have penetrated the early engineering schools in Germany. As mentioned above this was not necessarily the case. Engineering was developed as a science before industrialization took off. The dominant status group in Germany, at this early stage, was not the entrepreneurs as in the United States, but the academics, the state engineers, and other civil servants that predominantly had a legal education (*Bildungsbürgertum*). Industrial engineers and engineering professors were not usually allowed to advance into the German civil services. It was for this reason that they had to turn their attention to commerce and business occupations with a lower status: the *Wirtschaftsbürgertum* (Lash 1989: 70). It was their strategy to increase the status of the engineer through academization of technology and industry (Manegold 1978), and the struggle for approval of the *Technische Hochschule* as equivalent with the traditional universities continued after it had been granted the right to educate doctors in 1899. But as the industrial revolution took off in Germany, these engineer-educators encountered an increasingly strong reform movement among practitioners, teachers, and industrialists. Apparently they did not see it as a realistic and appropriate model for academic engineers to claim a monopoly on all qualified technical positions within the firm, and they gradually had to accept the formation of a new brand of technical schools at a middle level.[14] It was partly for this reason that German engineering gradually developed into a more practically oriented profession than its American counterpart.

The engineering-educators in the United States did not meet resistance from a broad movement of this kind, and the state had basically allowed for the engineering associations to govern their own matters. Like the engineering pioneers in Germany, the American engineers also aspired to establish their science as a pathway to elite positions in society. It was in confrontation with traditional industrial entrepreneurs and an elite of "gentlemen" from the shop culture in the professional associations that they established their own brand of *managerial professionalism* (Shenhav 1999). The conflict between shop and school had begun already in the late 1860s as the first engineering schools for mechanical engineers were set up. This conflict intensified until 1890 but was followed by a period of self-examination and compromise that led the school forces to get an upper hand from 1905 (Calvert 1967: 281).

The period from the 1860s through the 1920s was a golden age of prestige for the American engineers, precisely because so many of them were entrepreneurs. The men who founded the professional associations in the United States were secure in social status, and their associations served to lend the occupation of mechanical engineer the status they already possessed as individual entrepreneurs. It was a classical attempt to defend status by transferring economic capital into cultural capital (Calvert 1967: 131, 1972: 49; Bourdieu 1984). But this was also the start of the golden age for the large industrial corporation and the application of science to industry. The original entrepreneurial ideology was therefore increasingly outdated, and it was necessary to develop educational institutions. In Germany the renewal of the engineering tradition had to take other directions. The status of the entrepreneur had always been low, and the engineers had been actively pursuing a scientific agenda since the 1850s.

In the United States private funds were important in the establishment of a technical education system, but as was the case with the politicians in

Prussia, the providers of these funds seem not to have been able or willing to control the development of the school system. A parallel to the entrepreneurialism in higher education in the United States was found in lower technical education in Germany. There was one difference, however. The major institution-builders in Germany were not individual entrepreneurs but collective actors, such as associations and local state authorities. Dawson reported in 1912 that "disregarding altogether the regular schools—primary, continuation, middle, and higher—there were in this comparatively small country (Saxony), no fewer than 515 special schools exclusively engaged in imparting technical knowledge of one kind or another" (Dawson 1919: 105). He noted that there were a variety of schools and interests supporting them. The trade schools (*Handelsschulen*) were in the hands of the merchants and manufacturers' associations. The Industrial Schools (*Gewerk- und Gewerbeschulen*) had for the most part been established by trade guilds and other associations, among them several municipal and state associations. Chamberlain (1908: 9) also noted the role of guilds and corporate associations, which "may organize, equip and foster schools of such character as train directly for their particular lines of work." Such institutions for lower level technical education were not very developed in the United States. It was estimated by the Douglas Commission of Massachusetts in 1905 that technical education at the high school level was fifty times as extensive in Germany as in the United States (Struck 1930: 91).

Technical Education as Part of a Strategy for Professionalization

The argument from the profession, eventually, is that the formation of two models of technical education may be understood as part of a professionalization project among the new middle classes, and most preeminently among them the engineers. The implication of the argument from industry is that a profession in order to be a "real profession" should not identify too strongly with industrial interests. In the argument from the profession, however, a professional association is never exclusively an agent for an external principal, such as a business association or an educational organization, even if one segment may be predominant in its internal affairs. Since professional associations are coalitions of their respective competing segments, and since their leaders are elected, their policies tend to be a compromise between dominant coalitions and the leadership's interest in promoting their own interests. I will compare the collective strategies and the organizational resources among engineers in order to explore this argument. It follows that the policies and structure of professional associations may be of major importance. The success of these associations will depend on their agenda, their ability to unify distinct interests around this agenda, and to what degree other and more powerful organizations are engaged in the same issues and organizational fields. I have earlier noted that there was less opportunity for the corporate managers in the United States to influence higher education directly, since the states had left it to the educational institutions to develop standards and cooperative programs. It was the professional models advanced by these educators that won out in the United States, not those preferred by the employers or the "shop" models fostered by the early engineering associations. The American pattern of professionalization was school-based (Burrage *et al.* 1990: 219; Burrage 1993: 180).

The prevailing professional model among German engineers had its base in the professional associations, but was modified by the advancing industrial interests. The traditional brand of professorial professionalism oriented toward occupational closure partly "lost out" when it was faced with a strong reform movement among practitioners and industrialists. One reason for this failure was the historically weaker status of the German engineering profession in comparison with the American engineer-entrepreneurs. The status of German engineers increased, however, whereas it may seem as though the status of the American profession may have decreased as a consequence of academization. By focusing on the distinct role of *engineering associations* I want to account for the emergence of the new educational models and technological cultures. I will explore the impact of the professional associations—whether they acted as a force for unification or polarization in the workplace and how they influenced the self-perception (*leitbild*) of engineers.

The question of engineering professionalism has been subject to controversy in the literature on professions. There was a lot of interest for this in the wake of the perceived Soviet scientific advantage or the so-called "Sputnik" shock in the 1960s, and a discussion on whether the engineers qualified as a profession has been a standard exercise in the field of the sociology of professions since then. It has been argued that the engineering profession is an "open profession" (Rothstein 1969), a "profession without a community" (Perrucci and Gerstl 1969), and that it is a *weak profession* in comparison with the archetypal lawyers and physicians. Burrage *et al.* (1990: 214) argues that neither collective organization or ideology have been effective strategies for strengthening the engineering profession:

> It appears, in fact, that the upward, managerial "exit" route is the Achilles' heel of the profession, undermining both their solidarity and their ideology. . . . Strong professions on the other hand have no alternative career outside the profession, no such exit.

Similarly, Layton has argued that American engineers painted themselves as an industrial and managerial profession and that this accounts for their subordinate status. Business interests in the United States have favored technical societies built around single industries. A count in 1963 listed 130 national engineering and allied societies (Layton 1986: 56). The nature of engineering work itself is also used as an explanation for its weakness. Engineers do not have individual clients, and the engineering profession is one of the most occupationally assimilative of any profession: "its higher-level segment tends to merge with that of managers in general, its lower group into the class of skilled craftsmen" (Collins 1979: 174). But engineering can also be perceived of as the core occupation in the technical division of labor among craftsmen, technicians, and engineers, a perception that may be used to bolster the position of engineers, as the German case illustrates. This gives credibility to another perspective on professions, putting less stress on the nature of the work itself and focusing instead on the division of labor within organizational fields. This division of labor takes a different shape depending on what society we are talking about. It might be polarized or integrated in a hierarchy or skewed toward the managerial or the craft end of the continuum (Abbott 1988, 1991: 33; Armstrong 1984; Meiksins and Smith 1996). What is interesting about the suggestion that strong professions have "no exit" is that it implies that the strength of the engineering profession will vary with the degree to which they have successfully gained access to and occupied the managerial dimension.

Let me assume that *status* is a good indication of the strength of a profession. Evan (1969: 127) finds that the status of engineers decreases with the progress of industrialization and that it is higher in less industrialized societies. This thesis fits in nicely with the observed development pattern in the United States wherein engineering was increasingly defined as a preparation for a more prestigious but separate profession: management (Wickenden

1930; Rae 1955). The chances of ending up as a manager decreased as the number of engineers increased dramatically from 1900 to 1930. Professions with a background in accounting, finance, and business administration posed a challenge to the engineers' position in the field of management knowledge (Fligstein 1990). The perception of engineering as a preparation for management survived at the same time as the chances of reaching the top decreased. The engineers had sought to strengthen their position by "colonizing" the managerial function, but this strategy turned out to be an "Achilles heel" as they were losing out in the competition for control over the management function. The engineers in Germany and Japan may have been able to avoid status degradation because of their success in creating an overlapping identity between engineers and managers. At the time of Evan's study (1969) the lower level of industrialization in Japan and Germany was commonly thought of as an explanation for the higher status of engineers in these countries. This kind of argument clearly does not have the same kind of credibility today. Let me instead suggest the following alternative hypotheses:

1. The "exit" option was not used as frequently in Germany; engineers did not advance into management to the same extent.
2. Engineers did advance into management, but they were more successful at defining management as a technical dimension and a value-based calling, as opposed to a general management profession in which marketing and financial knowledge would matter more than technical knowledge. A career from technician to engineer to manager, then, was not perceived as an exit from the profession to the same extent as it was in the United States.
3. The one-sided emphasis on the academic engineering end of the technical spectrum in the United States and the neglect of the other occupations and specialties involved in technological development weakened the status of technology as such and therefore also engineers.

Hypothesis 1, that engineers did not advance into management to the same extent in Germany as in the United States, is apparently wrong. Academic engineers, indeed, were even more successful in management in Germany. The other two hypotheses, however, are supported by a great deal of literature (Hartmann 1959, 1967; Lawrence 1980; Locke 1984, 1989; Byrkjeflot 1998).[15]

Burrage's hypothesis about the relationship between an exit option and weak professions, then, has to be modified. Engineers are weak when they have to leave the engineering profession and enter the managerial profession as they climb into leadership positions, whereas they are stronger when it is possible to identify as manager and engineer at the same time. The engineering profession, then, is weak or strong depending on the social context. This modification actualizes the recurrent criticism against the literature on professions that it is too time and context-bound. Engineers are not weak everywhere because they are weak in the United States and Britain.

The major engineering association in Germany was the *Verein Deutscher Ingenieure* (VDI), which was established by engineering graduates at the technical institute in Berlin in 1856. None of the founders of VDI were industrial entrepreneurs. The purpose of the association was to promote "intimate cooperation for the intellectual powers of German technology for their mutual encouragement and continuing education in the interest of the whole of German industry" (*VDI-Zeitschrift* 1857: 4, quoted in Gispen 1989: 51). Gispen (1989: 55) reports that these early founders conceived of technology as "an autonomous intellectual-practical and national achievement, not an activity tied to profit or money." It was this conception of their role in society that drove the engineering professionals in VDI to unite with teachers and see education policies as a major strategy for professionalization. The initial marginality of both the engineering association and the technical school system in comparison with the state bureaucracy and the traditional university gave them a chance to develop alliances, and it has been argued that the VDI had a strong group-formative effect on German society.

The engineering professors who were predominant in the German engineering association until the 1870s promoted a conception of engineering as a science, and they also saw a classical secondary education as a precondition for becoming an engineer. They identified with quasi-aristocratic measures of social honor and sought to develop an honorable image of engineering. In contrast to the situation in the United States these engineering-professors had arrived on the scene well before the breakthrough of industrial society (Gispen 1989: 16). The various segments of the American associations were much more in conflict with each other. There were no membership criteria, and this meant that the industrial entrepreneurs were predominant. Calvert (1967: 55) classifies the Association of Mechanical Engineers (ASME) as a "gentlemen's club."

TABLE **10.3**   Membership in VDI 1856–1920

1856	172
1860	367
1870	1,821
1880	3,959
1890	6,925
1900	15,245
1910	23,952
1920	23,917

SOURCE: Ludwig and König (1981: 562).

TABLE **10.4**   Foundation Date and Membership Distribution Among the Four "Founder Societies" in the United States

		Membership	
	Founded	1900	1916
Civil engineers	1852	2,227	7,909
Mining engineers	1872	2,661	5,234
Mechanical engineers	1883	1,951	6,931
Electrical engineers	1884	1,273	8,212

SOURCE: Mann (1918: 19).

Only 866 engineers had graduated in the United States before 1870. There were 179 members of the American Society of Civil Engineers, as compared to the 7,374 listed as engineers at that date. McGivern (1960: 108) concludes that 88 percent must have received training by the apprenticeship method. This supremacy of the "shop culture" could well explain why there was a lack of interest in formal engineering education among the engineers themselves, and why technical education during the first half century developed independently of the engineering associations, which did not engage in educational matters.

As noted, there was one engineering association (VDI) that clearly took the lead in Germany, whereas there was a power balance between four associations in the United States (Tables 10.3 and 10.4). The more unchallenged status of VDI was one of the reasons for its strong influence in educational and professional matters. Wickenden wrote about the German association that "its publications on educational matters probably equal those of all the engineering societies of France, Great Britain and America combined" (Wickenden 1930, 802).

Conclusion

The focus of many studies of management and management knowledge is on the diffusion of American management concepts and practices to Europe. In this chapter, however, the focus is on the formation of systems for management knowledge and legitimation of management positions in Germany and the United States. The engineering professions took a central role in both cases as practicing managers and in the development of the knowledge that managers used in governance of firms and in the legitimation of their position in society. The institutions that provided managers with knowledge in Germany and the United States were structured very differently. American engineers developed a separate system of academic engineering schools and an ideology of managerialism and professionalism to advance their common interests. They distanced themselves from craft workers and other technical workers. They developed a managerial mentality and wanted to be at the core of a new managerial class. This strategy backfired, as they gradually lost out in the battle to colonize the managerial function. German engineers developed an ideology of technical competence and patriotism and saw themselves as representatives of the whole field of technical education and industry. They were more successful in management positions, probably because they did not develop an identity that separated them from other technical workers and engineers. The knowledge base of German managers was different from that of American managers, much less formalized and much less focused on defining management as a separate function and competence. German management knowledge was much less codified and much more embedded in local contexts, and it was for this reason less vulnerable for local colonization (that is, being attacked by alternative professions) and more vulnerable for distant colonization (that is, import of codified management concepts from the United States). The last kind of colonization did not take place in the period dealt with in this chapter, however; so let me concentrate on outlining the relationship between technical education systems and concepts of management in each case.

I have explained how the boundary of the field of technical education was drawn differently in Germany and the United States. German states developed a multilayered "estatist" system of technical education, whereas the American system for technical education was heavily centered on academic engineering education and oriented toward management. The movements for establishing technical education at a lower level were much weaker in the United States, and the ideology and the arguments of the associations involved in such activities were more individualistic and oriented toward uplifting of the disadvantaged. Missionaries, philanthropists, and social reformers were interested in vocational education in the United States, not artisans, state politicians, and industrialists, as in Germany. Manual training was developed for cultural and social reasons, not to serve industrial purposes. Although the industrial education system in Germany developed at a time when apprenticeships were still strongly supported by trade associations and guilds, it was presumed that the apprentice system was dying in the United States.

Secondary vocational schools and apprenticeships were not perceived as units in a system for technical education as they were in Germany. The failure to develop realistic career paths from apprenticeships and vocational schools into engineering might be one of the major explanations for the persistent and unbroken trend toward management dominance in American engineering. Engineering education in the United States was built on top of an existing, generalist model for secondary education. It is thus not a coincidence that the American education system "for all the talk of its vocational emphasis, is still the most massively non-vocational system of education in the modern world" (Collins 1979; 162).

In Germany a sharper line was drawn between the traditional university and technical and industrial education. The rise of the more technically oriented secondary schools and middle and top-level education institutions was part of a movement for industrialization and improvement of the status of industrial elites and professional middle classes in relation to traditional professionals and civil servants. A system of institutions was built up from the ground to serve this twin purpose, and the outcome was probably the most comprehensive and vocationally oriented technical education system in the world.

Each of the four actors presented above—professional associations, the state, the educationalists, and the industrialists—contributed to distinctive development patterns. The stronger state and the influence of the civil servant as a role model in Germany gave the professional association a powerful position in educational matters, since this association could serve as a mediator among industrial interests, academics, and workers. Wickenden (1930) argued that the industries provided the "motive power," while the technical professions were guiding the movement. The German engineering association took a central role. The emerging consensus among industrial, professional, and state elites around 1910 was the result of a long process of political negotiation and adjustment.

Wickenden put a strong emphasis on education in the American case:

> In no other country have the engineering schools been so free from outside domination. They owe little to statecraft other than the provision of means for their extension and support. They owe little to the organized engineering profession except the benefits of occasional criticism of their aims and methods. They owe little to the industries except an ever-widening field of employment for their graduates. (Wickenden 1930: 823)

The discussion above supports his argument. In the United States the industrial interests could not take the lead in the same way as in Germany, since they lacked the organizational arenas and resources provided by corporatism in Germany. The state legislated initiatives that spurred the development of engineering schools, but they left it to these schools to govern their own matters once they were established. Educational and professional entrepreneurs took the lead in associations for coordination and standardization. Professional associations were weakened by the emphasis on functional fields and specialized curricula among the early engineering schools.

In this account I have emphasized the different institutional framework and political constellations and the differences in organizational resources among academics, practitioners, states, and business interests. The boundary of each organizational field was drawn differently. The academization process started much earlier in Germany. It was for this reason that the industrial revolution was bound to have a different impact on the development of technical schools. The rise of the large corporations in Germany increased the influence of the practitioners and the industrialists in the educational system, not the teachers and academics, as in the United States.

11 From Accounting to Professional Services: The Emergence of a Swedish Auditing Field

Eva Wallerstedt, Uppsala University, Sweden

Introduction

Points of Departure

In 1990 Hopwood *et al.* (1990: 17) found that the professional accounting firms were experiencing higher rates of growth than the economy in general. Partly this expansion of professional accounting firms follows an expansion of auditing activities. The attraction that auditing now holds for many diverse interests has led to the creation of what Power (1997) has termed an Audit Society. This increased demand for the services of an auditor emanates from all kinds of private businesses as well as from local and national authorities. Over the years the word *audit* has been used with growing frequency, and the profession has expanded its domain beyond financial audits to include such things as environmental audits, management audits, value-for-money audits, teaching audits, and data technology audits (Power 1994: 1).

Partly, the expansion of the audit firms also is a result of a diversification of these firms into most management areas. Nowadays the accounting firms are competing with the big international management-consulting firms. In Sweden, for instance, the management consulting departments in four of the "Big Five" accounting firms rank (number of specialist consultants) among the eight largest such departments in the country (*Konsultguiden* 2002). Accounting firms have in this way developed into becoming the most salient carriers of management knowledge. In their traditional role as auditors they were already important carriers of management knowledge. When performing auditing assignments the auditors move between different kinds of private and public organizations. In this way they have genuine opportunities to get acquainted with different businesses and their specific problems. In the course of time auditors thus acquire considerable knowledge of management problems and the solutions required, and are then able to apply this experience to other organizations. In addition, as the professional service firms have increasingly taken on management consulting assignments, these firms have become carriers of some of the better known and widely spread commodified management ideas.

The point of departure for this chapter is the significance of history for understanding the present role of auditors. I will analyze how the auditors became such significant carriers of management knowledge by examining the evolution of the auditing field in Sweden in the period 1895–1999. This historical analysis traces the development from a situation in which just a handful of people in the country did auditing as a full-time operation to one in which auditing has become a recognized profession offering a variety of services. Parallel to this professionalization of auditing I point out an increased internationalization and integration of auditors into large multinational professional service firms. Following the long-term professionalization of auditors reveals driving forces that have turned auditors into such important carriers of management knowledge.

Professionalization

Processes of professionalization have long since attracted significant academic interest. As a result different perspectives have developed over time. Abbott (1988: 14–20) thus points out that research on professions has gradually moved away from (1) the study of professions as organized bodies of experts applying esoteric knowledge to their problems (Carr-Saunders and Wilson 1933) toward (2) an interest in seeking to identify a common pattern of structural regularities in the process of professionalization (Wilensky 1964) to (3) a view of professions as a means of acquiring influence over status and power (Larson 1977). Recent studies have emphasized the cultural authority of professions and have associated the professionalization process with individual decisions and opportunities for social mobility (Bledstein

1976; Haskell 1984). The importance of discussing professions in relation to one another has also been noted. Abbott (1988: 33) argues that professions must be treated as the ecology of an interactive system in which each profession has its specific tasks. These tasks are not permanent over time, however, and professions compete with each other within this system with a view to changing the jurisdiction, that is, "the link between the profession and its work," in their own favor (Abbott 1988: 20). This means that new tasks are created, whereas others are abolished or possibly reshaped from time to time. Professions thus compete with each other by taking tasks from one another. The work of any specific profession thus changes over time. Moreover, Abbott's analysis emphasized that professionalization is an ongoing concern for professional groups. Even groups that have come to be considered and treated as professions may face jurisdictional competition and have to defend and justify their jurisdictional claims.

In order to understand why the big Anglo-American international accounting firms got to play such an important and influential role in the world market economy, Strange (1996: 135) has pointed out that we have to look into the past and to the importance of the joint-stock companies in the industrialization process. When a growing number of joint-stock industrial companies needed qualified accounting assistance, commercial interests initiated the process of developing an auditing profession.

An analysis of auditors' long-term professionalization shows that they diversify their domain of expertise over time to include increasing shares of management advice activities. This diversification is not so much driven by the professional groups themselves, however, but by the large accounting firms that have come to dominate these professional groups. Partly, this development can be seen as a strengthening of the profession. However, another interpretation of this development is that as auditing services have come to be controlled by large multinational industrial firms and international organizations rather than by local professional bodies, the profession has become weakened and threatened.

In studying the professionalization of the auditing profession, it is convenient to use the notion of field in capturing how this profession has developed in relation and response to other professions and organized interests in society. This concept is central to institutional theory and bridges the organizational and societal levels (Scott 1995: 55–60). Individuals and organizations within a field respond in isomorphic ways, since the same rules, norms, and cognitive frames direct them. According to the classic definition used by many researchers, a *field* is "those organizations, that in the aggregate, constitute a recognized area of institutional life" (DiMaggio and Powell 1983: 148). As DiMaggio and Powell see it, the structure of an organizational field cannot be defined beforehand but must be defined empirically.

Fields emerge through stages of increased structuration (Di Maggio and Powell 1983; Greenwood *et al.* 2002). In its early stages a profession cannot exploit existing markets but has instead to "create them" (Larson 1977: 10). The development of the size of the market is thus of vital importance to the demand for the services offered, and market conditions will have a direct effect on the service suppliers' possibility of supporting themselves. During the structuration process organizations are set up to support the development of the profession.

Professional organizations are important for three reasons (Greenwood *et al.* 2002): as arenas in which organizations "interact and collectively represent themselves to themselves," as "negotiating or representative agencies," and for defining and enforcing collective beliefs. The kind of knowledge that each profession claims as its own is a strategic factor. Hence, professional services have to be standardized and professionals have to be trained to be able to produce "distinct services for exchange on the professional market" (Larson 1977: 14). The production of this specific knowledge is essential, and the organizations that produce this kind of knowledge are an important part of the field. The state, and the organizations set up by the state, have been key actors when it comes to regulating the auditing field (Wallerstedt 1999).

The development of the auditing profession in Sweden has to some extent followed its own track, but it has also followed a more general and global trend. Swedish auditors professionalized later than, for example, the British. As will be shown below, the Swedish auditors drew partly on British experiences and examples. By focusing on the development in one country, then, we can capture how relations develop among the important actors in the field and what impact this has on the development of auditors in general.

The Structure of the Chapter

In the analysis I have identified three phases: 1895–1931, 1932–1972, and 1973–1999. For each of these periods I will provide evidence of *external demands, responses in the field,* and *the structure of the field.* In addition to the references mentioned in the text, I have built my analysis on files from the archives of the Swedish Institute of Authorized Public Accountants (APA) (Föreningen Auktoriserade Revisorer) 1923–1999, Stockholm, and interviews in different accounting firms in Sweden. For the years 1912–1922, I have used files in the archive of Central Board of Auditing (CBA) (Centrala Revisorsamfundet).

The first period (1895–1931) is characterized by the emergence of an auditing field in Sweden. At the beginning of the period most audits were performed by laymen as a sideline to other activities. The market for auditing services was gradually growing, however, and regulations that controlled entry into the profession evolved. Laws and regulations that stimulated demand were passed, and organizations were established to support the development of a profession. At the end of the period, however, most audits were still being performed by laymen and professionals were still few, but an institutional field had emerged, complete with professional societies, professional training, legislation concerning the appointment of auditors, and regulations regarding entry into the field.

The Kreuger Crash in 1932 did much to promote the development of the profession in the second phase (1932–1972). The institutional field that had developed in the first phase—that is to say, clients, suppliers, professional societies, and state agencies—were involved in discussing the future direction of the auditing profession. In the wake of the Crash, actions were taken both inside and outside the field with a view to strengthening the jurisdiction of auditors. Auditorial independence became an important issue that had to be discussed and solved. This was a period of consolidation of the profession during which the professional organizations gained increased influence over their development. By the end of the period, however, the structure of the accounting firms had changed in such a way as to foreshadow future developments both in Sweden and internationally.

In the last phase (1973–1999) Swedish auditors came to follow a more general and global development. As in the first phase, new organizations were set up to support the development of the profession, and changes occurred in the jurisdiction that regulates auditing work. The big firms increased their merger activities and expanded their territories both nationally and internationally. During this period consulting work assumed a vital importance in the accounting firms, which even started to compete with other consulting firms for market share. In the last decade of the period the Big Five international accounting firms had established their positions in the Swedish auditing market, and Sweden became a member of the European Common Market. Both these circumstances influenced the development of the profession in such a way that accounting and auditing practices gradually were harmonized with international practice.

The Creation of a Profession

External Demands

Although the earliest evidence of regular auditing in Sweden is to be found in the accounts of Swedish trading companies and dates from around 1650, the first distinct sign of the emergence of an accounting profession in the country appeared in 1899—the year that the Swedish Society of Accountants (SSA) was founded on the model of the Institute of Chartered Accountants in London. As there were no more than a handful of full-time auditors in Sweden at the time, those who joined the society were laymen (Sillén 1949; Hanner 1963; *Archive* SSA: Styrelseprotokoll October 29, 1900, Section 3).

In the Companies Act of 1895 it was stipulated for the first time that limited companies should have auditors, although this had in fact been a tradition since the first half of the nineteenth century, when most limited companies began to include stipulations about auditing in their articles of association. In this way the 1895 Act can be seen as the confirmation of a long-established practice. In the Companies Act of 1910 it was stated that company auditors were not to be in the service of the company or of any of the members of its board. Until then it had been rather common in Sweden for auditors to be elected on account of their good relations with the owners or other stakeholders in the company, which means that their independence vis-à-vis those who were supposed to be audited must be regarded as questionable (Sillén 1949; Watts and Zimmerman 1978; Sjöström 1994: 29–45).

There were no formalized instructions in Sweden around 1900 as to how the auditing work should be performed. The situation was similar in the United Kingdom, the country from which those forming the first professional association had looked for inspiration. Laypersons such as bank directors and bank clerks, lawyers, businessmen, merchants, chief accountants, high-ranking officers, and so on all interpreted auditing assignments according to their own traditions or cultural beliefs. In this situation the Stockholm

Chamber of Commerce, founded in 1902 on the initiative of the Society of Merchants in Stockholm, authorized their first six auditors in 1912. Right from the start in 1899 the SSA had pleaded consistently in various ways for official recognition of the institution of auditors. Thus, contrary to the wishes of the SSA the authorization procedure in Sweden became a private business matter (*Archive* CBA).

The authorized public accountants were required to hold a degree in business studies from the Stockholm School of Economics, at that time the only business school in Sweden offering academic education, and to have had three years of documented practical service with an authorized public accountant.[1] It was also stipulated that an authorized public accountant should not have a business of his own, should not be allowed to audit companies in which he had a personal interest, and was not to be in either private or public employment (Sjöström 1994 *Bilaga 3*: 1–5).

At this time there were around 2,700 limited companies in Sweden with a share capital of over SEK 100,000. The potential market for the six first auditors was thus enormous, but as Hanner (1963: 3) put it, "it took time for the new profession to develop this potential market into an active market."

The authorization procedure just described is an example of "closure" in the Weberian sense, whereby entry into a profession becomes controlled. Those who were allowed to enter the profession met certain requirements: an advanced academic education, an apprentice period of three years, and a requirement not to do auditing as a sideline to other work but to work at it full time. Only a minority of the members of SSA met these requirements. Thus, from 1912 onward there were two competing groups of accountants in Sweden, the main difference between them being that the authorized group had a more advanced theoretical education and its members were prevented from taking private or public employment. From the start the independence of the authorized accountants vis-à-vis their clients was stressed in that they were not allowed to audit companies in which they had a private interest (Sjöström 1994 *Bilaga 3*: 1–5).

Responses in the Field

Even if the formation of a professional society does not actually create a profession it is an important signal of "movement" (Edwards 2000: xli). A significant step in the professionalization process was thus the foundation of the Swedish Institute of Authorized Public Accountants (APA) in 1923. In that year the authorized accountants in Kristiania (now Oslo, Norway) called a Scandinavian meeting for professional accountants. It was felt that this was an appropriate time to launch the APA. As soon as they had formed an institute of their own, the public accountants began to work out ethical norms for their profession (Sillén 1949; Wallerstedt 1988: 321).

In order to control the expansion of the population of authorized public accountants outside the capital of Sweden the Central Board of Auditing was created in 1919, and from then on auditors in different parts of Sweden were authorized. Thenceforth authorization procedures changed, in that each chamber of commerce submitted a list of applicants whom it judged to be competent for authorization from its own region, and the Central Board of Auditing then made the final decision as to whether a candidate should be authorized. Of the forty-eight authorized auditors belonging to the Swedish Institute of Authorized Public Accountants (APA) in 1931, ten were appointed outside Stockholm (*Archive* CBA; Sjöström 1994: 63).

From the establishment of APA until the end of the period the relations between the older SSA and the younger APA were somewhat ambivalent. At certain times they negotiated about cooperation, and at others they dissociated themselves from one another. The SSA auditors in 1921 even decided that they were going to authorize auditors of their own. In 1930, however, two openings were made for auditors who had not graduated from the Stockholm School of Economics: applicants could either apply for the title of approved examiner or they could take a special auditing exam to become authorized accountants. The difference between an authorized public accountant and an approved examiner was that the theoretical and practical requirements for the approved examiners were lower, requiring only good knowledge of accounting and several years of practical experience. The conditions for becoming an authorized public accountant according to this new system were that the applicant should be at least thirty years old and should have completed an upper secondary school education. The first entrance exam was held in 1932, when thirty-six people were accepted to take the exam. Exactly how many of them passed is not known, but it was certainly a very difficult exam. These measures did something to ease the tension between the SSA and the APA auditors, and to reduce the barrier to entry into the authorized auditor group (*Archives* SSA, CBA, and APA; *Revisorn* 1925; *Handlingar till 18:e svenska Handelskammarmötet* 1930).

The Structure of the Field

Once the accountants had taken up auditing on a full-time basis, the professionalization process began. Nonetheless the population of authorized public accountants grew very slowly. One important reason for this was the requirement regarding three years documented practical service with an authorized public accountant. The population of six authorized accountants in 1912 had only reached forty-eight by 1931, while over the same period the number of accounting firms in Sweden rose from five to thirty-one. The explanation is that most accounting firms were small, and the majority only had one authorized accountant. The three biggest firms had five or six authorized accountants.[2]

In addition to the low numbers of authorized accountants, other facts contributed to the small size of the accounting firms in this early period in Sweden. An authorized auditor could very easily set up his own company. There were no heavy investment costs. All that was needed was the authorization certificate from the Central Board of Auditing, an apartment, and a telephone. During the first decades of the 1900s even calculating machines were unusual. When several auditors worked together in the same premises, they did not register as a legal entity. The situation is described below by an assistant to the auditors in the oldest Swedish accounting firm, which started in 1912.

> They were four gentlemen [authorized auditors] who worked together under the name of STEO and who shared the same office. They did have common bookkeeping, in which each one's fees were entered and the overheads were split up, they each did their own income tax returns. There was nothing that could be called 'the firm.' Each one had their own assignments. (Sven Påhlgren, auditor 1932 at STEO, Stockholm in Wallerstedt 1988: 247)

Already at this time, the work of auditors was diverse. The auditors became well acquainted both with the companies for which they performed audits and the developments in the academic field. This made them well suited for doing consultancy work in addition to their auditing. A study of the activities of Oskar Sillén, one of the six accountants authorized in 1912, shows that from the time he became an accountant he received numerous consultancy assignments for companies and various local and government institutions. These were obtained alongside his ordinary auditing assignments and in addition to his work as the appointed accountant for several of the largest and most important limited companies in Sweden. His consultancy assignments dealt with the organization of accounting systems, cost accounting, investigations of financial matters, and an investigation of the supply of provisions in Sweden in 1914. In the early 1930s Sillén's most important client was one of the Swedish commercial banks, Svenska Handelsbanken, which like many other Swedish banks had faced serious difficulties during the period 1918–1923 as a result of its inability to evaluate the future prospects of Swedish companies. Credits granted by Svenska Handelsbanken to Swedish industry against collateral in shares had expanded very rapidly during the war. Consequently between 1919 and 1923 Sillén wrote several reports on the companies in which the bank had economic interests (Wallerstedt 1988: 257–286).

Considering that the number of limited companies had risen to around 16,000 by 1931 and that the auditor population was only forty-eight, it is obvious that most of the auditing in Swedish companies still had to be performed by nonprofessionals. Thus by 1930 only 8 percent of the largest limited companies in the country had appointed authorized auditors. An obvious reason for this low figure, of course, was that apart from the limited supply of authorized auditors it also took some time to change the long-established custom of appointing lay auditors (Sillén 1949). The market situation at the end of the 1920s, that is to say just before the international Great Depression, was auspicious. By this time, according to Dahmén (1950: 372), Swedish industry had prepared the ground for expansion in most industrial areas.

Discussion

In this first period (1895–1931) an auditing profession gradually emerged in Sweden. Even if, at the end of the period, the professionals were still few, a community of organizations that constituted important parts of an auditing field had been set up. The field comprised two professional accountancy societies (the Swedish Society of Accountants and the Swedish Institute of Authorized Public Accountants), one academic institution for the education of the candidates for authorization as accountants (the Stockholm School of Economics), and two organizations that were set up to regulate and handle applications for authorization as public accountants (the Auditing

Committee at the Stockholm Chamber of Commerce and the Central Board of Auditing). These five organizations interacted in the development of the field. The timing of the decision by the Stockholm Chamber of Commerce in 1912 to initiate the authorization process was certainly connected with the establishment of the Stockholm School of Economics, which was founded in 1909. Although a request from the Chamber of Commerce in 1912 that an auditing exam should be established at the school was turned down, the Chamber still made attendance at this school a prerequisite for authorization as a public accountant in Sweden. The fact that a university degree is stipulated for a new profession serves, according to Macdonald (2000: 37), two purposes for the "would-be profession." In this way a new profession can achieve both economic and status advantages. The university degree is good for business at the same time as it provides a warrant of the abilities of the new professionals. A university degree also carries "a certain social cachet" that raises the status of the professionals (Macdonald 2000: 37–38).

The stipulated university degree not only brought economic and status advantages to the authorized public accountants, however. The authorization procedure with entrance requirements in the form of advanced theoretical education, followed by three years of apprenticeship with an authorized public accountant, also became an effective closure mechanism for the profession. As an effect of these entrance requirements there were still only forty-two authorized public accountants in 1930, more than fifteen years after the introduction of the authorization institute. This scarcity complicated the relationship between the very limited supply of authorized public accountants and the potential market of 16,000 limited companies. Contrary to the argument by Larson (1977: 10) that a new profession has to create its market, the auditing profession in Sweden for many years instead faced the problem of a very low supply of authorized public accountants.

As can be expected, the SSA members strongly opposed the authorization requirements set up by the Auditing Committee at the Stockholm Chamber of Commerce. Its members did not meet these qualifications, and in order to try to eliminate these entrance barriers they argued that the state instead should be responsible for the appointment of auditors. The climate between the SSA and APA auditors during this period was accordingly rather hostile, culminating in the declaration by the SSA auditors in 1921 that henceforth they would be authorizing auditors of their own. If they had gone through with this decision they would have eliminated the monopoly of the

Central Board of Auditing to decide upon the rules for entrance into the authorized auditing profession. This was a very clever move from the SSA auditors, and it forced the Central Board of Auditing to act. The conflict was settled in 1930, at least for a time, when the Central Board of Auditing in order to protect its domain introduced the approved examiner function and the special auditing examination.

Consolidation of the Profession

External Demands

In January 1932 the accounting firm Price Waterhouse had received instructions from the International Telephone & Telegraph Corporation (ITTC) to examine the accounts of the L. M. Ericsson Telephone Company of Sweden, part of an industrial group owned by the Swede Ivar Kreuger. During preliminary discussions an Ericsson controller disclosed to a manager in Price Waterhouse New York "that about 27.5 million Swedish kroner [*sic!*] listed as 'cash' actually consisted of claims against Kreuger companies" (Jones 1995: 179–182). This was a significant event in the process of the breakdown of the Kreuger consortium (Reinius 1998: 29), and, in turn, it came to be extremely important for the development of the accounting profession in Sweden, since it revealed deficiencies in auditing practices.

The death of Ivar Kreuger in Paris in March 1932 and the collapse of his group created significant problems both for individuals and Swedish banks. As a result the Swedish government appointed a commission, which instructed Price Waterhouse to investigate the entire Kreuger & Toll group. In these investigations, which took seven months to complete, Price Waterhouse came to Stockholm with a team from various continental offices and from London. Criticism was raised against the way the auditors of the Kreuger Company had done their auditing. Step by step the shortcomings of the company's accounting system were unmasked.

> The frauds had survived undetected for so long because of the lax state of company law, which allowed Kreuger to maintain a high level of secrecy around the group's affairs. In January 1933, G. O. May testified to the United States Banking and Currency Subcommittee, observing that "the Kreuger & Toll frauds could not have been concealed if either the audits of the companies had been coordinated under a single control, or the

audits, though not so coordinated, had been carried out in all cases with a proper honesty, efficiency, and independence" (Jones 1995: 180–181).

The investigation also showed that the auditor of the company, Anton Wendler, a public accountant authorized by the Stockholm Chamber of Commerce and a member of APA, was not independent of Ivar Kreuger.

After several years of committee work between 1933 and 1941 a new Companies Act was approved in 1944. In many ways the Act strengthened the position of the authorized public accountants. From then on it became mandatory for an authorized public accountant to be appointed by a chamber of commerce, and the title "authorized public accountant" thus became protected by law. It became compulsory for all listed companies to have an authorized public accountant. The lawmakers pointed out, however, that there was no possibility at the time of enforcing limited companies to have a qualified auditor (authorized public accountant or approved examiner), because there were still too few of these to go round. The content in the financial audit was specified in great detail in this law for the first time. Many of the stipulations in the new act can be traced back to the earlier reactions to the Kreuger Crash. In the proposal of the law-drafting board, the importance of the auditors' independence vis-à-vis their clients was stressed (SOU 1941/9: 456; Wallerstedt 1988: 238; Sjöström 1994: 73 and 91).

Responses in the Field

Regulation. The Crash triggered an intensive debate in Sweden, which engaged people both inside and outside the field. The issue at stake was the organization of the whole institution of auditing, and very soon the various stakeholders were taking measures to secure the system. The legislative authorities suggested stricter rules regarding auditing procedures in companies, and in 1932 the Ministry of Justice issued a memorandum in which they proposed an amendment to the Companies Act. Here it was stipulated for the first time in Sweden that auditors should be "well acquainted with business." At the same time auditors in companies were initiating improvements in their auditing procedures, especially in the case of consolidated accounts, where consolidated balance sheets were now introduced. The Board of the Stock Exchange responded to the demands of the chairman of APA and the Central Board of Auditing, and decided in November 1932 that listed companies should henceforth be recommended to have at least one authorized public accountant. The APA also looked into the possibility of introducing some kind of third liability insurance and tightened up the requirements for entry into the society. From then on an authorized public accountant had to have been in practice for one year before he or she could join the APA. The SSA and APA initiated and agreed upon some changes in the statutes for the Central Board of Auditing. The period of practical experience required for qualifying as an authorized public accountant was extended from three to five years. In addition an upper age limit of fifty-five was introduced for becoming an accountant to prevent people entering the profession as a last resort upon retirement or after failure in other areas. All those who had any kind of interest in the auditing system were thus reacting to what had happened (Wallerstedt 1988: 245, 283; Sjöström 1994: 79–84).

International Cooperation. The Kreuger Crash did not only show the need for changes in regulation, however. It also provided firm evidence of the need to have an auditing system capable of dealing with corporations with worldwide operations. This was even more evident after the Second World War, when several of the Swedish accounting firms started cooperation with international partners. John Wendlers Revisionsbyrå, for instance, started to cooperate with Arthur Young in the beginning of the 1960s, and this certainly added to interest from the bigger accounting firm later to merge with John Wendler. The interest of Arthur Young to establish cooperation with a Swedish accounting firm emanated from Arthur Young having clients such as RCA and Mobil Oil in Stockholm (Sjögren, 2000: 76–77).

P. O. Öhrlings Revisionbyrå and Bohlins Revisionsbyrå established their international contacts at the same time as John Wendler. In the beginning of the 1960s, the CEO of P. O. Öhrlings Revisionsbyrå visited Cooper Brothers & Co. in London and after some years Öhrlings and Cooper Brothers signed a formal contract of cooperation. Bohlins signed its first formal agreement of cooperation with Peat, Marwick, Mitchell & Co. in 1961, although informal cooperation had been going on since the middle of the 1950s. Around 1965, P. O. Öhrlings Revisionsbyrå, for instance, started to implement Cooper Brothers Co. auditing manuals in their offices in Sweden. In this process Öhrlings used a case that was produced by Cooper Brothers. In order to speed up the introduction of international auditing practice the leading men within APA established a group consisting of authorized public accountants from different firms in Sweden. A Swedish case based on the same auditing principles that had been used in the Cooper Brothers' case was produced. According to Jan Johansson, a former authorized public accountant in P. O. Öhrlings Revisionsbyrå, the case used the "modern" auditing methods that had been suggested by Skinner and Andersen (1966) in their very influential book at the time, *Analytical Auditing.* The Swedish auditors had by then "realized that they had to abandon the old auditing philosophy of acting as checking clerks" and from then on they introduced different sampling methods when performing the audits (FAR 75 år: 36–37; Jan Johansson, personal interview, February 20, 2001).

Consulting. The expansion of the audited companies both in terms of scale and scope also drew the auditing companies more and more into providing advice to their clients. From around 1950 the largest of the accounting firms in Sweden thus began to set up separate specialist departments. The first such department in Bohlins Revisionsbyrå AB, for instance, appeared in 1956. It was an organization department, later renamed the Management Consulting Department. The impetus behind this step was the introduction of the charts of accounts that first appeared in the 1940s and that led to great changes in Swedish companies. Auditors were expected to have the necessary competence to solve the problems that arose in companies, but the problems were in fact too complex for them to handle. A need thus arose for people who could specialize in the specific problems involved. In 1968 Bohlins set up a separate corporate finance department (Carlsson 2001; Reinius 1998: 87–96).

The Structure of the Field

The Kreuger Crash and the measures taken after it no doubt strengthened the position of authorized public accountants. However, in 1948, together with the approved examiners, accountants were still only doing the audits for 43 percent of the 4,300 largest limited companies in Sweden, compared to 11 percent in 1930. This was due to the fact that there were only small numbers of both accountants and examiners. Although they had increased considerably in number they could not match the growth in limited companies, which more than doubled in the period 1950–1975 (Sillén 1949; Schön 2000: 375).

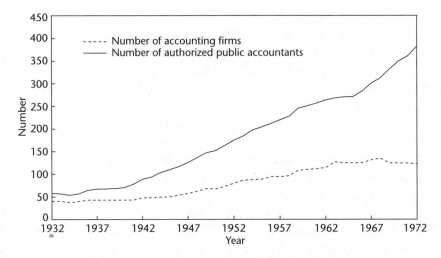

FIGURE 11.1   The development of the number of accounting firms and authorized public accountants in Sweden, 1932–1972

The number of accounting firms in Sweden rose from forty-two in 1932 to 126 in 1972, while the number of authorized public accountants rose during the same period from 59 to 387 (see Figure 11.1). The arithmetical mean thus increased from 1.37 to 3.07 in the period. However, single individuals ran most of the companies: the median size of the accounting firms both in 1932 and 1971 was one authorized public accountant. A large majority of the firms (85 percent) had less than six authorized public accountants. The three largest firms with twenty, twenty-four, and forty-two authorized public accountants, respectively, accounted for 2 percent of the population of firms and 22 percent of the total number of authorized public accountants. These three firms—Öhrlings Revisionsbyrå, Hagström & Bredberg Revisionsbyrå, and Bohlins Revisionsbyrå—represent today the main pillars of the "Big Five" in Sweden, and they had already in 1972 reached their dominant positions as a result of organic development and merger activities.

Discussion

The second phase (1932–1972) can be characterized as a period of internal adjustments for the years up until the 1960s. The situation in the 1930s was turbulent after the Kreuger Crash. The confidence of the public and many other stakeholders in the field had been seriously shaken, and actions were taken in various ways to strengthen the position of the auditing profession. All stakeholders thus took action to tighten up their own rules. The APA auditors and the Central Board of Auditing both tightened their entrance requirements. The structure of the field, however, was much the same as in the 1930s, and only one new professional organization—the Society of Approved Examiners—had been added to the field.

A new Companies Act, approved in 1944, replaced the old Companies Act from 1910. In the new act the title "authorized public accountant" acquired protection in law, and it became compulsory for all listed companies to have an authorized public accountant. At the time the lawmakers stressed, however, that there was no possibility of forcing limited companies to have a qualified auditor. The supply of qualified auditors was still insufficient. The APA auditors in this way achieved a very strong closure mechanism by a state regulation. The Central Board of Auditing gained power, and from now on it became impossible for any other organization to admit new auditors into the profession. The closure mechanisms into the profession were in fact so strong that the population of authorized public accountants, still after nearly sixty years, did not match the demand from the market.

The lawmakers wanted to define what kind of work that an auditor was supposed to perform in limited companies, and the act included detailed instructions as to how an audit should be performed. By this stipulation the state thus (probably with the Kreuger Crash in mind) for the first time tried to define the necessary knowledge base of performing an audit for a limited company.

The structure of the field that had emerged during this period was to be strengthened in the period to follow: lots of small firms, very few medium-sized firms, and even fewer big firms. The three largest firms at the end of this period today represent the main pillars of the "Big Five" in Sweden. And this resembles the international development whereby by 1970 the "Big Eight" constellation began to take shape. The six dominating firms in the United Kingdom in 1971 were in order of size: Peat, Marwich and Mitchell; Price Waterhouse; Deloitte; Coopers Brothers; Thompson, McLinlock; and Turquand, Youngs (Matthews *et al.* 1998: 46–47). The big firms in Sweden had signed a contract of cooperation with some of these accounting firms at the end of the 1960s, and all of them are today, in various ways, connected to the "Big Five." This cooperation with the international accounting firms soon influenced the auditing methods that were used in Sweden.

Internationalization and Diversification

External Demands

National Regulation. In 1973 the system of authorization that had been in operation since 1912 through the chambers of commerce finally came to an end. From then on the state, by way of the National Board of Trade, became the new authorizing and supervisory authority. In this way a long-felt wish on the part of the SSA was fulfilled, and the influence of business interests through the Chamber of Commerce and its Central Board of Auditors ceased. There was intensive discussion of the appropriateness of the title of the "approved examiners," and this was finally changed to "approved accountant." In 1995 the importance of the authorization system was clearly recognized when a special state body—the Supervisory Board of Public Accountants—replaced the National Board of Trade as the authorizing authority (Wallerstedt 1999; Sjöström 1994: 134–136).

A new Companies Act was passed in 1975 and thenceforth companies with at least SEK 1 million in restricted equity were to have a qualified auditor (authorized public accountant or an approved accountant). The most important feature of the new act, however, was that the specific stipulations of the Companies Act of 1944 regarding the auditing process were replaced by the requirement that the annual reports of the companies were to be examined according to Generally Accepted Auditing Standards (GAAS). These standards were to be interpreted according to the recommendations of the profession and to statements issued by the National Board of Trade. The year following the introduction of the Companies Act a new Accounting Act (1976) was introduced, and in it the prominence of the professional societies was again enhanced, this time by the introduction of the General Accepted Accounting Principles (GAAP). In order to support the application of the new rules an accounting standards board was set up the same year. The government appointed the members of this board, among them members of the profession (Wallerstedt 1998: 159–160).

In the Riksdag the question of how to handle economic crimes came to the fore in the 1970s. In a report from the Crime Prevention Council, for instance, a suggestion was made that auditors should be used in the fight against economic crime.[3] Since it was observed in the Riksdag that economic crime was most common in the small limited companies, it was concluded that there was a need to have an audit requirement covering all limited companies. Among other issues that were discussed in the Riksdag was the question of the independence of the auditor. In one motion it was suggested that the county administration should replace companies in appointing auditors.

In 1977 a committee was appointed to investigate the legal proceedings in cases of company insolvency, and the Riksdag later decided that professional secrecy should be eased when possible economic crime was involved. From now on, for instance, an auditor was obliged to disclose relevant information to the next auditor if an audit assignment ceased prematurely, and in the case of crimes against the tax or fee regulations the auditors were obliged to include this in their audit reports (Sjöström 1994: 155–179).

By 1983 the supply of authorized and approved auditors was expected to be sufficient. An important modification was therefore made in the Companies Act implying that at least one auditor in a limited company should be authorized or approved. It soon became evident that there were too many interests to be attended to by the Accounting Standards Board, and another body—the Swedish Financial Accounting Standards Board—was created in 1989 jointly by the government, business, and the APA.

International Regulation. Sweden is a member state of the European Union (EU) since 1995. One of the central aims of the EU is to create a common market with a free flow of the factors of production between the member states, that is, to create a common environment for business throughout Europe. This means that the legal practices of the member states have to be adjusted to the European Statutory Requirements. Directives issued by the EU are the instruments used to achieve harmonization on different issues. The fourth and seventh directives concern the field of financial reporting, and they deal with the annual accounts of individual companies and with consolidated accounts. Each member state has to incorporate the directives into its laws and regulations. In 1995 an Annual Accounts Act was introduced in Sweden, whereby the EU directives were incorporated. A separate law for auditors and auditing was also introduced in 1995 and 1999, respectively. The harmonization of the Swedish accounting and auditing regulations with the EU directives provided the impetus for these acts (Flower, 1999: 14–18; Wallerstedt 1999: 160–161).

Two organizations were set up on the international level in the 1970s: the International Accounting Standards Committee (IASC) and the International Federation of Accountants (IFAC). Their main aim has been to develop and support accounting and auditing standards. The IASC was founded in 1973 as an independent private sector body. Its assignment is to develop accounting standards (IAS) to be used by the international capital market. The intention of the standards is to develop the external reports of the companies in such a way that they will be in the same format irrespective of where they are worked out. An additional central aim for IASC is to accomplish global acceptance for the IAS.

The International Federation of Accountants (IFAC) was founded in 1977. In 2001 it had 153 member bodies (that is, national professional accountancy organizations in 113 countries), representing two million accountants. IFAC strives to develop the profession and harmonize its standards—International Standards on Auditing (ISA)—worldwide. IFAC is closely connected to the International Accounting Standards Committee (IASC) [www.ifac.org/About/, 2001-06-04].

In 2000 the EU announced that it intended to rely on the accounting standards that were developed by IASC as of 2005. Nevertheless IAS have a very strong position among the EU member states. By 2001 the IAS have been nearly completely incorporated into the standards issued by the Swedish Financial Accounting Standards Council (Danielsson and Emore 2001).

Responses in the Field

Responses to Domestic Regulation. The stipulation in the new Companies Act in 1983 about statutory audit in limited companies certainly strengthened the profession. From then on the authorized and approved accountants, who together amounted to 2,600, were supposed to audit 125,000 limited companies in Sweden each year. In the years to follow the accounting firms thus had to recruit a great number of new auditing assistants in order to be able to meet the future demand of audit services (Figure 11.2).

The debate and actions within the profession during this last period, however, were dominated by two issues: the implementation of Generally Accepted Auditing Standards (GAAS) and General Accepted Accounting

Principles (GAAP) and by a debate whether or not it was in accordance with the audit assignment to act as a public authority by delivering information about the clients to official authorities.

According to the Companies Act GAAS and GAAP were to be interpreted according to recommendations of the profession and to statements that were issued by the National Board of Trade, which from now on became the new supervisory authority of the accounting profession. With the introduction of GAAS and GAAP, refinement of the principles thus was left to the profession, which in this way became an important standard-setting body.

Discussions within the APA and the Nordic Association of Authorized Public Accountants led to a decision about GAAS at APA's annual meeting in 1977. This decision contained rules about professional appearance, auditor independence, incompatible business activities, professional confidentiality, publicity and acquisition, and statements of accounts.

The development of GAAP followed about the same procedure as in the case of the development of GAAS. There were professional discussions at a national as well as on a Nordic level. However, the most important standard-setter when it came to GAAP was the Accounting Standards Board, which was created to promote the development of GAAP and to consider how best to apply the new accounting law in practice.

During the end of this period the state, despite fierce protests from the profession, stipulated that auditors should disclose suspicions of crime in company matters to any of the board members and the general manager. Auditors were further required to make a formal report in the audit report if the company had not fulfilled its obligations in tax matters.

Internationalization. On the company level, international cooperation nowadays is organized as a network of competencies used when needed by the other firms in the global networks. In an international assignment it is very important to follow the auditing manuals, since the group accounts have to be performed in the same way throughout the whole group in different parts of the world. For instance, the auditors within the KPMG network involved in the auditing of international companies thus meet on a regular basis at least once a year to discuss common issues about auditing. The auditors also meet on seminars dealing with the industry in which they are specialized. In the late 1990s specialization has been promoted within KPMG in Sweden (for instance in pharmaceuticals, building, information, communication and entertainment, insurance, and automobiles). In London there are around 300 persons working only with information, communication, and entertainment (ICE). Specialist competence in the industry audited is required, but an auditing team also comprises other kinds of specialists, for example, in tax matters, information technology, stock values, and finance. Thus, a lot of people with different competencies are engaged in an auditing project.

Another way to spread the company culture around is through individual mobility between countries. KPMG performs international training of auditors in Brussels, where the use of the KPMG manuals is in focus. "We are completely controlled by our auditing-manuals, which are developed on an international basis" (M. Kimby 1999, interview). In these different ways each auditor will create a network of people within KPMG around the kind of international activities that he or she is engaged in.

Diversification. At the end of the 1980s the consulting activities of the Swedish auditing companies had developed in such a way as to become independent units. In 1991 Andersen Consulting, Ernst & Young Consulting, KPMG Management, and Coopers & Lybrand ranked third, sixth, seventh, and eighth in size among the consultancy firms in the country (*Affärsvärldens Konsultguide* 1992: 8–9). In fact the norm systems that developed inside and outside the profession were built on the assumption that auditors should devote themselves to a certain amount of consultation activity (Fant 1994; Sandström 1980: 404). In the "General Agreements" drawn up for authorized public accountants in 1992 in the Nordic countries, the perception of specialist services was as follows:

> It is economic in terms of skill and effort for professional accountants in public practice to be able to offer other financial and management consultancy services to their clients, since they are already closely familiar with the clients' businesses. Many companies (particularly the smaller ones) would be adversely affected if they were denied the right to obtain other services from their auditors. ("Revisorns oberoende" 1992: 97)

The accounting firms have gradually extended their consulting territory into new areas, and the consulting domain within the big firms has expanded in relation to auditing. In this way the authorized public accountants have changed their jurisdiction and "blurred" their way into the consultancy profession. More than 50 percent of the revenues of the "Big Five" certainly emanates from consulting today. This development has revived the old discussion about conflicts of interest—about the independence of audits carried out in companies that are also consultancy clients.

A variety of forces have been behind the growth of the specialist services in the auditing profession. One is that auditing work has become increasingly complex, as the new areas have come to demand auditing services. Single auditors cannot nowadays possess the competence to solve everything themselves. It is almost always necessary to consult specialists in different areas. The growth of specialist departments can certainly be explained to a certain extent by this internal demand for services. Interviews with auditors in the "Big Three" in Sweden have supported such a conclusion. Another impetus behind this development has been the concentration of industry due to acquisitions and internationalization. The leading industrial firms have been expanding rapidly, acquiring smaller competitors, and merging with their peers. These clients now make new demands upon the auditors, requiring that specialist advice and a network of offices should be available to take care of their growing number of subsidiaries at home and overseas (Jones 1995: 19–20; Peters and Tapper 1998). Yet another explanation of the growth of the specialist services is that the auditing companies have responded to market opportunities. Management consultancy has been stimulated in the auditing profession by the achievements of organizations specializing in this area. At the present time the profession has diversified and spread into most management areas, competing with the big international management firms both nationally and internationally. In Sweden the management consulting departments in the accounting firms rank among the ten largest consultancy firms at least. And the tendency is for such services to expand within the auditing profession.

The Structure of the Field

The number of accounting firms in Sweden rose from 128 in 1973 to 374 in 1999, while at the same time the number of authorized public accountants rose from 396 to 2,002 (Figure 11.2). Around 90 percent of the population of small accounting firms (with one to five authorized public accountants) accounted for 23 percent of the total number of these accountants. Thirteen medium-sized firms (with six to a hundred authorized public accountants) employed 16 percent of the total number of such accountants.

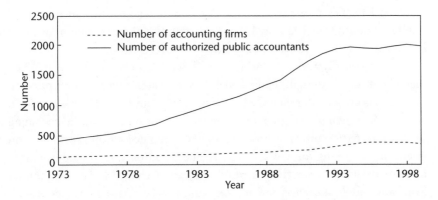

FIGURE 11.2   Development in the number of accounting firms and authorized public accountants in Sweden, 1973–1999

The three largest firms with a total of 1,185 authorized public accountants employed 59 percent of the total number of such accountants. The structure of the population of accounting firms thus displayed many small firms, a few medium-sized firms, and still fewer large firms.

As mentioned above, the three largest accounting firms in Sweden reached dominant positions very early. They have long histories and in fact they have dominated the market since the middle of the twentieth century. All three started in the 1910s or 1920s, and have since defended their positions by way of organic growth, mergers, or both. Öhrlings Pricewater-houseCoopers was founded in 1924 under the name of Öhrlings Revisions-byrå AB. In 1996 it adopted the name of its international partner and became Öhrlings Coopers & Lybrand. When Coopers & Lybrand and Price Water-house merged in 1997 to become PricewaterhouseCoopers, the Swedish firm was renamed Öhrlings PricewaterhouseCoopers. Ernst & Young's history goes back to 1914 when two sisters, Dagmar and Thyra Svensson, acquired authorization. In 1934 Sven Hagström joined the firm, and since the 1970s it has operated under different names, as a result of frequent merger activities: Hagström & Bredberg Revisionsbyrå (from 1971), Hagström, Bredberg & Wendler AB (from 1976), Hagström Revisionsbyrå (from 1978), Hagström & Sillén (from 1984), and Hagström & Olsson (from 1990). In 1991 it finally adopted the name of its international partner Ernst & Young.

Similarly KPMG's ancestor was Lars Ture Bohlin, who became an authorized public accountant in 1923. In 1994 the international partner became a part of the firm's name—KPMG Bohlins (from 1998 KPMG).

Historically the accounting firms have been client-followers. When their clients have internationalized their businesses, the need for international services has grown, and then the big accounting firms have either set up local firms of their own or acquired already operating local firms. At the beginning of this internationalization process, however, the accounting firms had no intention of looking for new customers. The ambition was to establish long-term relationships. But this situation very soon changed. The accounting firms are now looking for new markets and can be classified as a combination of client-followers and market-seekers.

When the customers get bigger they need different kinds of services. It is all but impossible for a small auditing company to deal with a big customer, as a small company cannot supply all the kinds of service that a big client needs and demands. Nowadays, great emphasis is put on the importance of competence in various management areas. The accounting firms have to be as well equipped as their customers. Big investments are very costly for an auditing company, and money can be saved if certain types of investment can be coordinated within one big firm. The accounting firms thus have to follow their clients both in size and geographical presence. Many clients nowadays have an international profile, and they need to be able to rely on a big and well-known auditing company. If a client chooses an international arena for investments, then the accounting firm needs to be there too.

In the later years the major accounting firms in Sweden have joined the big international accounting firms, and this has influenced their internal development when it comes to auditing methods and the culture within the accounting firms. The Big Five in Sweden are members of international networks of auditors using the same auditing methods in order to be able to perform their international auditing assignments. This standardization has become necessary to assist members in the auditing network all over the world.

Discussion

In the third and last phase (1973–1999) positions between the actors in the field changed. The state, by finally taking over responsibility for the authorization procedures, entered as an actor. The National Board of Trade, which was the first state authorizing authority (1973), was replaced in 1995 by the Supervisory Board of Public Accountants, which then became the supervisory and regulatory authority in authorization matters. But even if the state had entered the field as an actor the profession itself had increased in power.

The detailed instructions in the Companies Act of 1944 were replaced by the requirement in the new acts of 1975 and 1976 that the annual reports of the companies were to be examined according to GAAS and GAAP. And these standards were to be interpreted according to the recommendations of the profession. In this way it was recognized that the state did not have the competence to issue stipulations about this field, which by its nature changes and improves over time. The standards were instead jointly created by the government, business, and the APA through the Swedish Financial Accounting Standard Board and recommendations of the profession and statements issued by the National Board of Trade. There were four new acts relating to the auditing profession and they significantly strengthened the importance— and the power—of the profession.

When the supply of qualified auditors finally was supposed to match demand in 1983, the legislation was changed in such a way that every limited company from then on was obliged to appoint one auditor who was either authorized or approved. From this time the qualified auditors have had a monopoly of expertise in providing auditing services to the population of limited companies in Sweden, which in 1999 had reached the number of 264,165.

The domain of the auditing profession has been expanding ever since the 1980s, as new auditing and consulting areas have emerged in great numbers. The "Big Three" accounting firms in Sweden are now part of the international "Big Five." An important impetus behind this development has been the globalization of the big industrial firms, and their need for accounting and consulting services in different areas. In order to achieve a size capable of matching these firms, the accounting firms had to merge in order to acquire the necessary competencies. Another finding is that a first-mover advantage has been present, that is, the firms that are established early are also those that have survived through a strategy of expansion. This trend has been affected by internal growth combined with the selective acquisition of small independent firms, sometimes combined with mergers with other firms of equal size (Hallén and Wallerstedt 2000).

The population of accounting firms today consists of a few very big firms and many small ones. The rarity of the medium-sized firms holds for both Sweden and the United Kingdom. The big firms have adopted certain features of "big business," which means that they have a uniform international corporate style and that they have introduced common auditing procedures and common technical standards throughout their global networks. The big accounting firms no longer look to their professional associations on matters of policy and practice; instead they turn to their own committees and research groups (Jones 1995: 248).

Conclusions

The development of the auditing profession has been part of a worldwide development. The evolution of cross-border links has been going on since the first part of the nineteenth century (Matthews *et al.* 1998). Already in 1893 *The Accountant* announced that the profession had achieved great power and that it had interrelations worldwide. In fact, accountancy was the first profession to operate cross-nationally. According to Macdonald (2000: 53), no other profession today has such a large proportion of clients made up of giant corporations, which require worldwide service.

The "Big Three" in Sweden—Öhrlings PricewaterhouseCoopers, Ernst & Young, and KPMG—are nowadays parts of or partners in these international accounting firms. As shown in this chapter the local Swedish accounting firms initiated cooperation with international partners such as Coopers Brothers & Co. and Peat Marwick, Mitchell & Co. as early as the 1960s. The incentive behind these partnerships was the growing importance of large joint-stock industrial companies with operations all over the world, for which consolidated accounts had to be prepared consistently throughout a whole group. These international partnerships very soon influenced auditing practice within the Swedish firms, which from then on implemented the auditing methods that were used by these international firms.

Consultant activities became a natural part of the auditing assignment when professional auditing emerged in the middle of the nineteenth century. These services today account for more than 50 percent of the activities in the firms. Auditors have performed consultancy work in addition to auditing since the emergence of the accountancy profession in Sweden. These assignments dealt with the kind of management problems that were topical those days; for instance, organization of accounting systems and cost accounting. The number of consulting assignments grew in importance and from around the 1950s the big Swedish accounting firms began to set up separate specialist departments.

Today auditors in the big international accounting firms in Sweden meet on a regular basis with their colleagues within their global networks in order to develop and update their specialist competencies. In an auditing project various competencies are required, and an auditing team thus often consists of different kinds of specialists.

Besides responding to the demand from their clients, the big firms also have moved into the consulting business stimulated by the achievements of organizations specializing in this area. This is a good illustration of the argument by Abbott (1988) that professions must be treated as the ecology of an interacting system, in which the professions in different stages of their development are "blurring" their professional boundaries (McKenna 1995: 53). According to McKenna (1995) this kind of blurring of professional boundaries is both a response to demand and a result of training in more than one profession.

The growing importance of the Big Five can be seen as a strengthening of the professional associations, as most of the officials in these associations are recruited from the Big Five firms. One explanation, of course, is that the smaller accounting firms have difficulties in releasing an auditor for time-consuming assignments in professional associations. Today the big firms are thus actively involved in their own professional associations. It is "not much of an exaggeration to say that in Britain the big firms—the worldwide firms—*are* the Institute, both Scottish and English, and the same is true of other Western industrial societies" (Macdonald 2000: 53). Partly, this strengthening of the importance of the Big Five thus can be seen as a strengthening of the profession.

However, another development has been going on parallel to the growing importance of the Big Five. The development of accounting and auditing services has come to be a matter for organizations such as the European Union and the international professional organizations. Since Sweden became a member of the European Union in 1995 the legal practices have been adjusted to the European Statutory Requirements by the Annual Accounts Act (1995) and the Auditors Act (1999). The objective of the European Union directives is to harmonize company legislation within the European community. The European Union directives, among other things, deal with public annual accounts, accounting principles, group accounts, and the accounting profession.

When the European Union in 2000 announced that it intended to rely on IAS, that is, the accounting standards that were developed by IASC, the importance of the international professional association IASC certainly was enhanced. The IAS have a very strong position among the European Union member states, and by 2001 the IAS have been nearly completely incorporated into the standards issued by the Swedish Financial Accounting Standards Board. Alongside the strengthening of the importance of the Big Five accounting firms both in Sweden and worldwide, the developments thus point to an enhanced power of institutions on a European and global level.

In conclusion, the large international accounting firms have consolidated their positions both in Sweden and internationally, and they have developed toward offering an increasing number of consultant activities. The kind of consultant activities that are offered depends on the kind of management problems that call for advice. New consulting areas today are, for instance, e-business, e-integration, and e-outsourcing. Over the years the accountants have thus moved into and developed competence in most management areas. In this way the Big Five accounting firms, which have spread their operations into every important international industrial firm in the world, have become important carriers of the better known management ideas.

At the same time, as the auditing firms have developed into international groups in a way that can be characterized as a strengthening of the profession, state regulations have also been strengthened and harmonized internationally. What we can see now are strong, international firms met by strong, international regulations.

V   *Conclusions*

12   The Dynamics of Management Knowledge Expansion

Kerstin Sahlin-Andersson and Lars Engwall,
Uppsala University, Sweden

The preceding chapters have portrayed and provided explanations of the dramatic expansion of management knowledge. They have analyzed activity processes that have expanded the supply and flow of such knowledge. In this concluding chapter, we will reflect upon three sets of findings from our analyses: (1) significant characteristics of the expansion, (2) sources of variations of management knowledge, and (3) the impact of management knowledge expansion. These findings are informative in relation to central questions in institutional theory and therefore add to theoretical understandings of the transfer of knowledge, institutional change, and the role of actors in processes of institutionalization and institutional change.

Significant Characteristics of the Expansion

The contributions to this volume have shown that self-sustaining processes are instrumental for the increased diffusion of management ideas. Such self-sustaining processes evolve as carriers expand in scope, scale, and type. Moreover, self-sustaining processes of expansion evolve as the stock of management knowledge expands through processes of creolization.

Self-Sustaining Processes

The literature on management fads and fashions (see, for example, Abrahamson 1996; Abrahamson and Fairchild 1999; Røvik 1996) may give the impression that the boom we see today for management knowledge is something temporary. Others may argue that the supply of management knowledge is reaching such heights that we should expect saturation. Neither of these views appears to be correct. First, the view of management knowledge as a collection of fads or fashions often describes—and criticizes—this knowledge as being only old wine in new bottles. Thus, although we can expect the present fads and fashions to disappear or become outmoded, we may also expect that the basic ideas behind them will come back packaged in a different form. Second, there are reasons to believe that management knowledge has properties quite different from those of goods and services, for which we see saturation. As a matter of fact, the expansion of management knowledge appears to have the character of interrelated self-sustaining processes. In Chapter 3, Ernst and Kieser developed explanations of the expansion of management consultants through a close analysis of interrelations between consultants and their clients. They showed that an increased demand and supply of management consulting services mutually enhanced each other in self-sustaining processes.

Even though relations between consultancies and their clients are far from problem-free, as discussed by Armbrüster and Kipping in Chapter 5, along with the supply of certain types of knowledge there arises a demand for complementary knowledge. The broadcasting of general management knowledge has led to an increased demand for more change-oriented knowledge and situation-specific advice that can be used for organizations in their translation and adoption of general knowledge. This development, however, is not unidirectional. When organizations see the need to react to and assess the services and models they are offered, they demand more general competence in management knowledge.

Hence, self-sustaining processes for the expansion of management knowledge are formed in the elaborated relations between consultants and their clients. However, these relations are also embedded in networks of relations wherein other carriers play significant roles. With the expansion of management consultancies, a growing market emerged for MBA graduates from business schools (see Ruef in Chapter 4). Many MBAs entered management consultancies, and many entered companies requesting the consultancies' services. These MBAs were taught to perceive organizational matters in terms of management and hence became highly receptive to and active in searching for management knowledge. This development suggests that the composition of formal competencies in organizations has a significant impact on the demand and receptivity of various types of knowledge in these organizations. Given the many generations of MBAs and others in leading positions in business having general management education, we can expect a continuous demand for and receptivity to management knowledge. These observations also suggest that the expansion of one type of carrier adds to the expansion of another.

A further aspect of this self-sustaining expansion is the interconnectedness of various traditions and fields of knowledge. In this way, *a creolized body of knowledge* has formed (Thrift 1999); management knowledge builds on many sources, and it is a discipline without a clear core and without clearly defined boundaries. As has been shown to be the case for creole culture (see Hannerz 1996), the field of management knowledge is characterized as vital, innovative, diverse, and pervasively marked by inequality. As management knowledge has expanded, it has not replaced the fields of knowledge on which it draws. Instead, this field remains open to new ideas; as the links with other fields such as engineering, accounting, law, and auditing remain clear, management knowledge appears applicable to these areas. In such ways, management knowledge has come to be applied in diverse functions across companies. The field continues to be inspired by these other areas and to incorporate findings from them. This interchange makes the field vital and innovative.

Expansion in Scope

A significant feature of the expansion of management knowledge is that *the scope of the activity* in which carriers are engaged and the type of knowledge they carry have broadened. A way for carriers to attract resources and attention is to develop new sets of activities, new ideas, new models, and new ways of circulating their ideas. Business advisors have developed not only management consultant services but also their own research units, publications, and educational programs. Universities and business schools not only broadcast knowledge widely through their extended executive education and MBA programs, they also develop specific ties to certain businesses and industries.

When reviewing definitions of management knowledge in Chapter 1, we concluded that management knowledge is not clearly limited to a certain set of problems or activities. Instead, what is claimed to be of relevance for the management of operations tends to acquire the status of management knowledge. So when carriers in the field broaden their activities, they also broaden the field of management knowledge. The actions of the carriers in broadening their scope of activities also result in enhanced competition and further blurring of the borders between those carriers.

Another significant feature of the development of carriers has been that they have broadened *the geographical scope* of their activities. We have been able to witness the internationalization not only of business advisors and management consultants but also of business schools and business publications. Globalization in general, with expanding markets and weakening protective sovereignties of nations and states, facilitates the increased mobilization of people, resources, companies, regulations and, not least, the flow of rationalized management ideas (see Meyer in Chapter 2; also Strange 1996). Direct and close relations between carriers and their clients also add to the geographic broadening of the distribution of management knowledge. Business advisors and management consultants to a large extent follow their clients (see Wallerstedt in Chapter 11). When business companies internationalize their operations, the need for international services grows. The advisory firms then either establish local firms of their own or acquire already established local firms. As schools and publications, in responding to the enhanced competition, develop close relations with individual business firms, they, too, tend to become client followers. They follow their business partners, and as these partners internationalize, the carriers broaden the geographic scope of their activities.

Expansion in Scale

The tendencies of expansion in scope that we have described have been associated with an expansion in scale and a resulting increase of concentration of resources among carriers. In the consultancy field, this concentration has to a large extent happened through mergers and acquisitions. The already large Anglo-American accountancy firms have gradually grown even larger through the acquisitions of local operators all over the world (see Wallerstedt in Chapter 11). In this way, they have created international networks of accountancies, whereby they are able to serve their multinational clients globally. However, these clients have also, as pointed out previously, pushed the consultancies to broaden their services. Thus, as accountants have felt the need to move into consulting on strategy, information technology systems, and legal advice, they have added new units to their operations. In the same way, the traditional consultancies have added new expertise to their companies. More and more resources are in this way gathered into the large consultancies. This tendency also means that the field of management knowledge widens—a development that, in turn, paves the way for further expansion, concentration, and broadening of the services offered by the consultancies. Similar tendencies of concentration can be observed in the media.

In this respect, business schools exhibit different expansionary tendencies from those observed in consultancies and media. So far we have not seen many mergers and acquisitions among business schools. However, like the other types of carriers, they expand in scale through the addition of new student groups, both abroad and at their home base. Internationally, large business schools start programs with counterparts in other countries or even set up their own foreign campuses. As in the airline industry, strategic alliances have become a frequently used method for international expansion of business education (see, for example, Ahrne *et al.* 2000).

For all types of carriers, size has become a significant factor for future success. The fact that a carrier is large provides better visibility, which in turn tends to strengthen the brand name. This is particularly important in the field of management knowledge, since the demand for the products offered by the different carriers is highly dependent on their reputation. The dynamics displayed in such exercises can be expected to lead to a continued concentration among carriers and to an increasing emphasis on brand names—not only the branding of organizations but also of their "management knowledge products." In competition with each other, carriers—business schools, media, consultants, and specific departments for knowledge development within large firms—work to develop the new and improved management knowledge products that are brand named and widely distributed (see also Wedlin 2000). Hence, the expansion of the scale of carriers of management knowledge led to an enhanced packaging and concentration of the production and dissemination of management knowledge. Moreover, with the forming of more or less global organizations and alliances of carriers of management knowledge, channels open up for faster and wider mediation of knowledge. This can be expected to lead to an intensified and faster mediation of knowledge in these networks (see also Thrift 1999).

Expansion of Carriers

The four types of carriers of management knowledge that we explored in some detail in Chapter 1 (management education programs, management consultancies, business media, and multinational firms) all have their roots in the industrialism of the late 1800s. However, several of the contributions in this volume have demonstrated that, over time, other types of organiza- tions have also been highly significant carriers: states, expert groups, and intergovernmental and nongovernmental organizations. For instance, expert groups—more or less connected with nation-states and intergovernmental organizations—were significant carriers of the quality movement. The sig- nificance of such groups became particularly evident after comparative analyses. Tiratsoo, for instance, in Chapter 8 partly explained the lack of suc- cess of the American quality model in the United Kingdom in the 1950s by pointing at the obvious lack of effectiveness characterizing the British expert groups involved in the quality movement at the time. In Japan, however, expert groups were not only facilitating but also actively promoting and car- rying the quality movement. Another example was provided by the efforts of the Ford Foundation after the Second World War to export American man- agement education to Europe (see also Gemelli 1995). The International Standards Organization (ISO) has developed and sold a whole range of stan- dards building on and thus carrying management knowledge (see Walgen- bach and Beck in Chapter 7; also Furusten 2000). Another more recent example concerns the more or less global distribution of new public man- agement reforms (see, for example, Hood 1995; Christensen and Laegreid 2001). Certainly, academic institutions, media, and consultancies were sig- nificant carriers and promoters of new public management. Furthermore, international organizations, primarily the Organization for Economic Coop- eration and Development (OECD), also have become significant carriers of these management ideas (Sahlin-Andersson 2000, 2001). Together these examples show how new types of carriers have been mobilized and formed as a result of the expansion and dissemination of management knowledge. As the group of carriers expands, the body of management knowledge in turn expands and becomes more widely circulated.

    A significant characteristic of the organizations we have mentioned is that to an increasing extent they develop *policy-oriented knowledge* that is shaped as advice. With the expansion of management knowledge, not only consultants and business advisors offer such advice. As universities and inter- national organizations more generally have found themselves being in com- petition with these advisors, they too meet the demand to show results and to be of direct practical value for the field. This pressure has led them increasingly to develop models of similar kind, with an enhanced competition among the various types of carriers as a result.

Further Research

Since carriers are so crucial for the proliferation of management knowledge, further study of them is essential in order to understand more about how and why certain types of knowledge expand and flow. From such studies we could learn how carriers operate, how they go about "picking up" and editing ideas, and how they develop ties and relations with other carriers as well as users of ideas. Once we start picturing the circulation of knowledge as an active process, and those circulating ideas as active agents in the process, we need to learn more about the interests, activities, and developments of the latter. In this volume, we have focused on management consultants and their interaction with other carriers. Further studies could elaborate upon the role of other carriers, not only in their interaction with consultancies but also to what extent they carry management knowledge in other constellations and settings.

Apparently, carriers are most important for setting trends in motion, but once a trend has started to roll a wide variety of organizations jump on the bandwagon. These organizations expand their activities in line with their active roles in the management knowledge fields. Once formed and expanded, they search for activities to maintain their organizations. In this way, self-reinforcing spirals of management knowledge expansion are set in motion. The expansion of management knowledge involves waves of fashion, but the self-sustaining character of this expansion suggests that it is more important to focus on the driving forces that give rise to and link fashion waves with each other.

An important message from the contributions in this volume is that a self-sustaining, inherent dynamic characterizes the expansion of carriers, in particular, and of management knowledge more generally. Hence, important insights into this expansion are to be found as we search for endogenously rather than exogenously developed forces for this expansion. In order to find these endogenously developed forces, we need to combine studies of carriers with studies of how ideas flow. When following the flow of certain ideas it will be possible to see how providers as well as users are formed as a result of the expansion of such knowledge.

Sources of Variations of Management Knowledge

The widely diffused knowledge that is the focus of this volume has been questioned by many authors (for example, Hilmer and Donaldson 1996; Locke 1996; Micklethwait and Wooldridge 1996). Its ideological base has been criticized for being too simple, general, and standardized. This critique assumes that the expansion of management knowledge homogenizes ideas as well as managerial practice. Support for this view of homogenization is found in several studies of the diffusion of management ideas. These studies show that the worldwide flow of management knowledge across continents and sectors has led organizations to become increasingly similar (DiMaggio and Powell 1983, 1991; Meyer and Rowan 1977; Scott and Meyer 1994). The self-sustaining forces behind the expansion of management knowledge (as treated in the previous section) support this view of homogenization still further.

It is consequently easy to find emerging similarities in management knowledge and management practice across countries and societal sectors, but the chapters in this volume also point to the importance of paying attention to local particularities and emerging variations. Four features appear particularly conducive to the appearance of variations: (1) the ambiguity of labels, (2) processes of translation, (3) the significance of context, and (4) political processes.

The Ambiguity of Labels

Røvik's analysis in Chapter 6 of three successful organizational recipes shows that the features of the ideas could partly explain the variation in flows. Important features of ideas that traveled fast and far were that they were well packaged with a label. They were formed as advice that promised to add to the effectiveness as well as the individualism of the receiver. They were general and universal so that they seemed appropriate to apply in many different settings (see also Byrkjeflot in Chapter 10).

Labels often diffuse easily from one setting to another, but this does not necessarily mean that knowledge remains the same as it flows. Studies that have analyzed the flow of certain ideas only by following the appearance of certain labels may have overemphasized homogenization. Models that are placed under the same label attain different local flavors as they are being circulated in different settings. In the transfer of knowledge from one setting to another, this same knowledge is being translated. Even in a globalized world, differences among continents, countries, sectors, and industries do have an impact on how widespread knowledge is translated and used.

Even if labels appear quite precise and stable over time and space, our analyses portray widely disseminated management knowledge as being simultaneously highly plastic, varied, and ambiguous. This feature of the body of knowledge—combining ambiguity and precision—is one explanation for its success. The ambiguity means that ideas seem capable of being applied in many settings. Actors with the most diverse expectations and interests can be attracted by this body of knowledge or can find that it fits their needs and wants (see also Sahlin-Andersson 1992). Røvik in Chapter 6 and Tiratsoo in Chapter 8 both gave examples of how very precise stories about the origin of an idea accompanied widely disseminated ideas. Moreover, they pointed out that such stories were constructed as the ideas became well-known, as is clearly shown, for example, in the case of the quality concept—an idea that has been accompanied by several partly contradictory stories of its origin.

To present a technology, a program, or a concept in terms of best practice is another way in which management knowledge is packaged so that it appears precise, is easy to transport, and is attractive for organizations to adopt. At the same time, this concept of best practice has been demonstrated to be quite ambiguous (see Ernst and Kieser in Chapter 3). Since management knowledge is shaped and reshaped as it flows, it is reasonable to assume that carriers shape and frame best practice. Best practice tends to be formed, not so much in the setting to which it refers, but in the process of circulation.

Processes of Translation

One virtue of putting the carriers at the center of an analysis of the expansion and flow of management knowledge is that this emphasis points to the importance of asking what these carriers diffuse, or, in other words, what it is that is being circulated. When knowledge is transferred from one setting to another, it is translated (Latour 1986). Knowledge is disembedded from its situation and then re-embedded in new contexts (Czarniawska and Joerges 1996). In this way, knowledge transfer is an active process not only of transporting but also of performing knowledge and its translations (see also Sevón 1996). Carriers present models, ideas, and experiences in various ways as they circulate them, most commonly in the form of written or oral texts. Such texts are edited differently depending on the context in which the editing is done and the use that the writer sees for the text. Through the process of editing, an idea may be formulated more clearly and made more explicit, but reformulation may change not only the form of the text but also its focus, content, and meaning. Usually there are both written and implicit rules or conventions that guide this kind of editing. In earlier writings, we have termed these "editing rules" in order to imply that they are derived from the context in which the editing takes place, that they restrict the process of representing and retelling, and that they are only to a limited extent explicit and should therefore be understood as "rules that have been followed" (Sahlin-Andersson 1996, 2001).

Local experiences and reforms tend to be presented to others in terms of existing prototypes or examples and with the use of references, categories, scientific concepts, theoretical frameworks, and widespread classifications that are familiar. These concepts, references, and frameworks form the infrastructure of editing, thereby restricting and directing how the accounts are given. In such a way, widespread and well-known classifications may be used to sort out what is being told as accounts are delivered and transferred (see also Bowker and Star 1999). Concepts, ideologies, examples, and interests are not the same everywhere. Examples and ideologies that dominate one setting, and may be taken for granted in this setting, may be unknown or unpopular in another setting. The infrastructure, and thus the editing rules, differ between situations and contexts. As contexts differ over time and space, processes of translation lead to variation over time and space. Three contexts have assumed importance for the way in which knowledge has been translated as it has been circulated: the context of the receivers, the context of the carriers, and the context of the knowledge flow.

The Significance of Context

We have addressed the prevalence of management knowledge across continents and societal sectors. In part, this expansion was the result of ideas spreading from one source throughout the world. With this expansion, ideas were received variously and hence penetrated sectors and countries differently (see, for example, Tiratsoo in Chapter 8). As shown in Chapters 6 through 8, quality programs were introduced in the United States as well as in Europe and Japan, but these programs were shaped differently. Variations may be accounted for not only by the processes through which they were introduced but also by the fact that the new programs were not introduced in a vacuum. When ideas reached new locations and organizations, they were translated differently; they were mixed with traditions and other models and ideas and edited according to rules and conventions of the local context. In this way, the flow of quality models resulted not only in homogenization but also in variation.

Variations do not only emerge as ideas are received and put into use in a local setting; they also arise from the diversity of sources of knowledge. Byrkjeflot, in Chapter 10, demonstrates that engineering, and its connection with business, has been important for the development of management knowledge both in the United States and in Germany, but in very different ways.

In the United States, engineers developed management. In Germany, management ideas were developed more as a contrast and complement to the very technique-specific ideas of German engineering. The American engineering ideology was universalistic and with a managerial purpose. These ideas could travel more easily than the German management ideas, which were less formalized and more clearly linked to specific industries and authority structures. This does not mean that the German version of management—and its connection with business—was less influential in the local setting. German engineers developed an ideology of technical competence and patriotism and saw themselves as representatives of the whole field of technical education and industry. They were successful in management positions, partly because they did not develop an identity that separated them from other technical workers. Instead, their management was clearly and closely linked to technical skills and technical education. Hence, it seems too narrow to view management knowledge as rooted in the professionalization of U.S. engineers. Europe and other regions each developed their distinct systems of knowledge formation in management, only partly as a response to American influences. The analysis in Chapter 10 points to the importance of institutional, partly nation-specific factors for the development of management knowledge. Designs of the education system, business system, and the role of the state—aspects of society that display considerable variation among countries—have been shown as highly significant to the location, method, and extent of management knowledge development. Moreover, Byrkjeflot points to important differences between countries in terms of the professionalization of certain groups. These differences affect how and to what extent various groups have come to develop and adopt management knowledge.

Another context of relevance for how knowledge develops and is translated is found in the flows of knowledge. The wide diffusion of ideas requires opportunities for mediation. We have described how the formation of worldwide organizations, networks, and alliances open channels for the mediation and flow of knowledge. Furthermore, management knowledge has largely been circulated as integral or additional parts of other ideas, technologies, resources, financial assistance programs, business exchanges, and other media. The diffusion of quality models to England, Japan, and Germany were, to a large extent, packaged together with other resources, restoration programs, regulations, and standards. This kind of diffusion especially holds true for the circulation of knowledge by international organizations, expert groups, and similar carriers mentioned previously. Although their main purpose is not to explore and expand management knowledge, they have been mobilized with the expansion of certain management ideas.

ISO is a standard that is built on management knowledge (Furusten 2000; see also note 1 in Chapter 7 by Walgenbach and Beck). It prescribes that procedures should be organized and checked according to such knowledge. The circulatation and adoption of such standards are often tied to other regulations. ISO standards, for instance, have been widely distributed by standardization organizations, as well as by multinational companies, who demand that their subcontractors apply such standards, and by the European Union, which in its directives refers to these standards (see Walgenbach and Beck in Chapter 7; Mendel 2001).

The American post–World War II support of the restructuring of European economies provides another example of how management knowledge may be circulated as an integral part of other technologies and programs. This financial support program brought American educational programs and managerial principles more generally to Europe. Similar processes are at work today. The World Bank, IMF, OECD, and other organizations pursuing support programs demand that countries and other receivers of support should follow certain (new public) management principles in order to get access to loans and financial support from them. In this way, again, what drives the expansion of management knowledge is not the demand for such knowledge among receiving organizations, but the way in which carriers pick up and distribute this knowledge.

Our examples suggest that the flow of management knowledge—or certain management models—is partly driven by how these processes of circulation fit and are integrated with other circulated ideas and institutional changes. This integration means that the success of ideas may not necessarily be observable in individual patterns of diffusion; instead, such flows must be contextualized in time and space. The research design of studies in the diffusion of ideas needs to be contextualized so as to capture the important couplings between various flows and changes.

Political Processes of Management Knowledge Expansion

Organizations that are similar, or see themselves as similar, tend to imitate each other and interact with each other (see, for example, DiMaggio and Powell 1983). This logic has been repeated and illustrated throughout this volume. However, the picture here appears somewhat diverse and complex. Under some circumstances, distance may facilitate the adoption of new ideas, whereas proximity may augment resistance to adoption. For example, the more distant Japanese were less skeptical than the British with regard to American quality programs (see Tiratsoo in Chapter 8). With proximity, the likelihood is higher that those being exposed to ideas are already familiar with how these ideas have been formed and used in other settings and may be cognizant of whatever mistakes and negative consequences the ideas may have brought about. However, such negative aspects are usually discarded as models are translated and edited over large distances. It appears more difficult to learn about failures and mistakes over large distances, and thus successes are overreported (see also Lerdell and Sahlin-Andersson 1997).

Again, we acknowledge that processes of management knowledge expansion involve activity, struggle, and interests. This observation is interesting in relation to the common critique of neoinstitutional theory as leaving no room for actors. In Chapter 7, Walgenbach and Beck suggest that many studies have overlooked the political elements of the expansion, partly because of methodological and theoretical shortcomings. With the ambition of further analyzing the role of actors and activities in the expansion of and resistance to management knowledge, the authors in this volume have combined institutional theory with theories that place greater emphasis on actors and movements—social movement theory, professionalization theory, and actor network theory. With the aid of these theoretical combinations, we have started to learn about the many different roles that actors play in the processes of expansion. We have pointed to the important roles of carriers as disseminators, translators, editors, mediators, and adopters of management knowledge, but we have also pointed to the importance of actors' resistance to the expansion of certain models. The chapters in this volume point to the importance of learning more about the political elements of the processes of expansion and about reactions and resistance to management knowledge in various settings.

Further Research

In view of our analysis of variations, it is important to be somewhat cautious when generalizing about the expansion of management knowledge from studies of this development in single settings or single locations. Instead, we find it important to develop comparative analyses of various kinds. In addition to comparative empirical studies of the kind reported (see, for example, Chapter 8 by Tiratsoo) and the longitudinal studies of various kinds (see Chapter 4 by Ruef and Chapter 9 by Luo), much is to be learned from a side-by-side comparison of studies from various periods, localities, and aspects of management knowledge. Such studies provide a way to picture single aspects in detail but also to constantly remind us of the limits of this knowledge. Processes look different in other settings and times. Moreover, these diverse but thematically coherent studies provide common ground for making comparative analyses. The contributions in this volume point to the importance of doing further historical and comparative studies. We need to explore further to what extent various popular ideas are related, how local institutions can influence the translation of globally disseminated ideas, and how these local settings in turn may be reshaped by global ideas.

The Impact of Management Knowledge Expansion

Organizational Practice

This volume does not deal directly with organizations receiving and demanding management knowledge. Instead, several of the chapters analyze relations between carriers and receivers of ideas. In this way, they provide some insights into significant but diverse effects on organizations. Earlier research can lead us to draw two opposite conclusions. On the one hand,

widely distributed management ideas seem to have limited impact on organizational practice. Studies have shown that rational myths, even though
widely diffused, remain loosely coupled to organizational operations (Meyer
and Rowan 1977). Widespread ideas give rise to much talk but do not have
much impact on action (Brunsson 1989). Widely spread management models do influence accounting systems, evaluation models, and standards
(Power 1997; Brunsson and Jacobsson 2000), but such accounting and evaluation systems leave great possibilities for organizations to decouple practice
from models. In light of these findings, it is not surprising to find that Tiratsoo's figures on defects (in Chapter 8) partly seem to remain unaffected by
the extended quality programs. Moreover, we have claimed that management
knowledge is extremely plastic, such that almost everything can be incorporated in the stock of management knowledge. In other words, what is said
to be management knowledge may include old, unaffected practices. As
widespread models are incorporated in local organizations, they may be
transformed to the extent that they confirm old practices rather than give
impetus for changing the organization and its operations.

Other findings indicate that the expansion of management knowledge
has fundamental effects on organizational practice. In Chapter 9, Luo
demonstrated that organizations that used large resources in personnel
training clearly turned to more management-oriented approaches. Similarly,
in Chapter 3, Ernst and Kieser discussed how organizations demanded assistance from management consultants, and with the expansion and use of such
knowledge, those organizations demanded further assistance and more management knowledge. In Chapter 5, Armbrüster and Kipping showed how
organizations demanded more management knowledge in order to act upon
the knowledge they had already received, and Ruef in Chapter 4 showed the
tremendous growth in numbers of MBA graduates. Many of these graduates
were hired by management consultancies as well as by companies. In their
daily operations, both these groups exercised perspectives and ideas that they
had learned during their management education. If nothing else, this indicates
that the expansion of management knowledge seems to have a decisive
impact on the allocation of attention and resources. One aspect of the
expansion of management knowledge is that the perceived relevance of and
receptivity to such knowledge has expanded in organizations.

Management knowledge has come to be seen as relevant not only for
managers but also for members of organizations more generally (see Luo in

Chapter 9). Hence, management knowledge has come to penetrate all types of organizations at all levels. The fact that management knowledge grew out of various kinds of expertise of relevance for organizations—engineering, law, auditing, accounting, and other professions—helps show the relevance of the present creolized knowledge to the many different kinds of operations that make up modern enterprise. As this integrated body of knowledge is adopted by organizations, it seems to integrate them. Concepts of management have thus become the modern *lingua franca*. In order to be able to communicate in modern organizations and be able to handle upcoming problems, it is becoming increasingly important to know this language; it has developed into a significant prerequisite in the competition for financial capital, as well as for social capital. This tendency suggests that even though we find that individual management models or techniques are often only loosely coupled to organizational operations, those models carry the potential to redirect the allocation of organizational resources, attention, and operations. In order to explore these more indirect effects of adopting management ideas, it seems important to follow organizations over time and not to limit studies locally within the organization.

The expansion of management knowledge follows the simultaneous dramatic expansion of organizations. First, as more operational settings are seen as organizations, they are also seen as being in need of management (Brunsson and Sahlin-Andersson 2000). Hence, there has been an expansion of potential receivers or targets for management knowledge. This was emphasized by Meyer in Chapter 2 and clearly demonstrated empirically by Luo in Chapter 9 as she followed the development of personnel training. Second, with organizational expansion, whole groups of organizations with a capacity to carry management knowledge have evolved, thereby providing an expanded supply of management knowledge. We have especially focused on the expansion of consulting organizations (see especially Chapters 3–5 and 11).

These explanations can be contrasted with the more functional explanations of the expansion and the claims that management knowledge spreads because it is understood to enhance the performance of organizations. Of course, such a view is widely held, but it is clearly very difficult—and seldom tried—to measure and prove the effectiveness of applying particular management ideas in various settings. The effect of management knowledge on organizational practice is mostly anecdotal (see Chapters 3–6, 8, and 9). Moreover, when more elaborate explanations are sought for outcomes of applying specific management ideas or techniques, explanations of successes or failures tend to be explored more in the way certain techniques are implemented than in the body of knowledge as such. These evaluations tend to lead to a quest for more, rather than less, management knowledge (Olson et al. 1998).

Institutional Change

We have repeatedly referred to the importance of institutional change when analyzing the expansion of management knowledge. The analyses have shown that the expansion of management is facilitated and driven by institutional changes (most clearly shown in Chapter 2 by Meyer and in Chapter 9 by Luo), and that diffused ideas may be institutionalized (see Walgenbach and Beck in Chapter 7). Furthermore, in this chapter we have argued that the expansion of management knowledge may lead to institutional changes by self-sustaining processes. We have portrayed the carriers of management knowledge as most evidently playing an important part in the diffusion and expansion of certain types of knowledge. They facilitate, drive, and thrive on the expansion of management knowledge. Moreover, we have argued that carriers should be looked upon both as mediators of specific ideas and as actors whose activities both influence and are supported by more fundamental institutions in modern society. When the expansion of management knowledge expresses and adds to institutional change, carriers become important actors in that change process.

In the neoinstitutional literature, there has been an ongoing discussion about the role of interests and actors (for example, DiMaggio 1988; DiMaggio and Powell 1991; Greenwood and Hinings 1993; Oliver 1991; Powell 1991; Scott 1995; Scott *et al.* 2000). The concept of *institutional entrepreneur* has been coined and developed to capture the role of actors and activities in institutional change (DiMaggio 1988). Such entrepreneurs are often described as being the leading and central actors in the field. Institutional entrepreneurs have an interest in, and the means to maintain and make use of, dominating institutions or to transform these institutions to better fit their interests. These discussions on the role of interests and actors for institutional change are highly inspired by Bourdieu's (1977) notions of a field as a battlefield: on one side are the dominating actors whose positions and interests are served by the present composition of the field, and on the other side are peripheral actors who seek to reach more central positions where they might change the institutional composition (or, in Bourdieu's terminology, the "doxa") of this field. Our analyses have pointed to the importance of involving more actors in field analyses that aim at exploring and explaining institutional change.

Carriers may not have an explicit interest themselves in changing dominant institutions, but the impact of their activities may implicitly do so. Carriers are mainly driven by interests in expanding their own activities and ensuring their own survival. Hence, the relationship among actors, interests, activities, and institutional change has been portrayed as being, at least in part, much more indirect than what has been suggested by concepts such as *institutional entrepreneur*. This indicates that the institutional entrepreneur is only one type of actor that is important in processes of institutional change. Carriers do seem to play important although different roles in such change processes.

The role of these carriers in processes of institutional change can be analyzed by applying a model developed by Galison (1997) in his studies of microphysics. The field is different, but in terms of the relation between various "layers" of changes, the logic applies to the changes we seek to map out here. Galison reacted to the view of scientific revolutions that implied that theoretical and experimental breakthroughs occurred contemporaneously (Galison 1997: 795–803). He therefore argued that

> [The] shared intuition that there are blocks of unified knowledge that float past each other without linking has been expressed in many places and many ways. As compelling as this antipositivist picture is, recent historical and philosophical work on experimentation suggests that it needs revision. (pp. 796–797)

Based on his historical account, Galison showed that physics and physicists, like other cultures, do not constitute a single, monolithic structure but consist of subcultures—each with its own rhythms of change, standards of demonstration, practices, and inventions. Although scientific developments are often described as paradigmatic shifts marked by great discoveries and new theories, these developments are not necessarily theoretically driven. Rather, parallel processes of experimentation, development of new instruments, and general theoretical developments combine in a more ecological fashion to produce new scientific insights (see Figure 12.1 and Fujimura 1996). Actors working with experimentation, developments of new instruments, and theoretical developments follow their own rhythms, driven by

Instrument [1]	Instrument [2]	Instrument [3]	....

Theory [1]	Theory [2]	Theory [3]	....

Experiment [1]	Experiment [2]	....

FIGURE 12.1   Intercalated periodization. Source: Galison (1997: 799)

their own interests, traditions, and contexts ("subcultures" in Galison's model). This means that shifts in instruments and experiments may parallel continuities in theories, and vice versa. These subcultures are partly autonomous, partly interrelated, and thus the development is characterized by intercalated local continuities.

Galison's model of intercalated periodization suggests that each subculture has its break points. A revolutionary change in theory may thus not lead experimenters to break with their established procedures at the same time. This means that no one subculture is on the top, or is leading the development, but the development could better be portrayed as a layered brick structure, where each subculture has its own layer and follows its own rhythm but is surrounded by and interrelated with the others.

In a similar fashion, in the field of management knowledge, we claim that carriers play an active role in coining, circulating, and applying knowledge in various areas. In this way, they may not only affect local practices but also drive the field of knowledge in certain directions and play a role in more general institutional changes. In the field of management knowledge, which is formed and expanded not so much within research laboratories but rather in the interconnection between various users and carriers of management knowledge, we can still draw parallels to Galison's model. We can make a distinction between those developing instruments for organizational development, accounting, auditing, quality control, and other management devices; those theorizing about these developments; and those experimenting with various forms of management. Carriers of the kinds we have mainly focused on in this volume—management consultants—provide and distribute instruments, concepts, technologies, and more general ideas. Theorists who analyze these developments are mainly found in universities, whereas those who are experimenting with management and management knowledge are found in consultancies, companies, and other organizations.

We have shown through the contributions in this volume that the expanding shape of management knowledge has been formed through the interaction among carriers. We have suggested that management consultants have come to orchestrate the field of management knowledge, and that the role of theorists is rather to reflect and analyze than to drive the development. Galison's model implies that this may be one phase in the development of the field of knowledge. Hence, the relationship between (1) theorists and other carriers and users of management knowledge and (2) the dynamics of knowledge expansion may change over time. The parallels drawn here to studies of the development of natural sciences show that the significant role of carriers in knowledge development and institutionalization is not unique to the field of management knowledge.

Further Research

The evidence provided in this volume suggests that it is important to put studies of management knowledge in a historical perspective, that is, not only to look at management ideas in the present context. It is then particularly important to undertake further studies of the various sources of knowledge. In this way, we will be able to better understand how modern management knowledge has been shaped in a long-term process. As a result, we could become more sophisticated in dealing with such knowledge. Rather than labeling expanded management knowledge as "new wine in old bottles," we will be able to see how historical processes have produced the concepts and methods we have today. We have started an analysis of how various "layers of actors" in the field interact and how they at times lead or follow developments in other "layers." Further studies of interactions among the various groups of actors in fields of management knowledge can add to our understanding of what drives institutional changes. Moreover, from such studies we may learn what paves the way for institutional changes and for the expansion of certain types of knowledge. In undertaking such studies, we should take advantage of the reasoning of Galison (1997) that we referred to in the last part of this chapter. It suggests that further studies and analyses of this field should build upon studies of how other fields of knowledge have developed. These studies of knowledge development can provide us with models and concepts that can be used to shed further light on how carriers and interaction among carriers drive the expansion of management knowledge.

Reference Matter

Notes

Chapter 3

We are grateful to Cornelia Hegele, Martin Seichert, Sandra Spreeman, Peter Walgenbach, and Thomas Weinert, as well as the participants of the 1999 SCANCOR workshop on *Carriers of Management Knowledge* for valuable comments and insights.

1. Notice the term itself: departments dealing with staff matters are now called "human resource departments" instead of "personnel departments." This reflects the increased claims to sophistication and professionalization that the specialists working within this domain are making.

2. Consultants appeal to this expectation when they market their services as integrated or holistic. This is the case in Germany, where hardly a word is so frequently used by consultants as *ganzheitlich* ("holistic").

3. A famous German management guru preaches to his top management clients that chaos is natural in organizations. Instead of trying to get rid of this chaos, management should surf on it (Gerken 1992). This message helps top managers arrive at the pleasant conclusion that their leadership might be more effective than they had thought.

4. In the following analysis, only the term *effectiveness* will be employed, as in the given context it represents the wider concept. It also encompasses the notion of performance quality (see Cameron 1986).

5. This may apply to individual consultants as well as to the consultancy firm itself. In the acquisition phase of a consultancy project, usually consultants with long years of experience are involved in the negotiations with a potential client. The consultants who are finally assigned to the project, however, are often much younger and

less knowledgeable. What may result is a discrepancy between the initially perceived level of expertise, which represents a criterion for the choice of a particular consultant, and the level of expertise received in the consultancy process itself.

6. This represents a possible dilemma for consultants who are interested in achieving a high degree of client satisfaction, which, however, should not be attained at the cost of delivering an inferior solution for the company.

7. In a previous version of this chapter, we only included the first reaction, emphasizing the insecurity of managers. At the SCANCOR workshop (Stanford University, Sept. 1999), however, John Meyer and other participants pointed out that this is likely to be the result of a "Teutonic depressive" bias and that another, more positive ("Californian") type of manager exists. An insightful discussion of managers' insecurity and their relation to consultants is also given by Sturdy (1997b).

8. The commodification of knowledge, which we have discussed before, plays an important role here, as it greatly facilitates the spreading of management practices.

9. Of course, this may not generally apply to all organizations, as it can be assumed that considerable differences exist, as Fincham (1999) points out on the basis of case studies. For example, larger organizations that have highly qualified experts among their members are possibly in a better position to fend off addiction than organizations that are less well equipped with the brain power necessary to develop a strategy for keeping its demand for consultants under control. One can also assume that some organizations change consultancies frequently, whereas others stay with the same consultancies for a long time. There might also be considerable differences between organizations with high budgets for consultants and organizations with low budgets. It would be extremely interesting to analyze these and other related issues empirically.

Chapter 4

This research was supported by the Center for Entrepreneurial Studies at the Stanford Graduate School of Business. I would like to thank Nikolaus Beck, Nils Brunsson, Royston Greenwood, Matthias Kipping, Christopher McKenna, Peter Mendel, John W. Meyer, Francisco Ramirez, and members of the Stanford Comparative/Historical Workshop for their helpful comments on earlier versions of this paper.

1. This simple generalization is complicated by the historical relationship between management consulting and consulting engineers (see Washburn, 1996). The relationship will be examined in greater detail in my review of the history of the management consulting specialty.

2. Such facets of the profession's emergence would be institutionalized in succeeding decades by the adoption of "up-or-out" systems of employment at consulting firms. Based on direct recruitment from graduate business schools and internal promotion, these human resource systems mimicked those of law firms (McKenna 1999).

3. Investment banks continued to provide management consulting services

but were expected to hire outside consultants to certify organizations issuing new securities.

4. Paradoxically, management consultants often need to reformulate their generic solutions so as to appeal to the purportedly unique identity of their clients. Only a few years ago, New York-based Towers-Perrin consulting was publicly embarrassed when its "customized" solutions turned out to be generated by a common cookie-cutter formula (O'Shea and Madigan, 1997: 13–15).

5. A comparison of sample statistics with known population parameters suggests clear undersampling of foreign alumni compared to MBAs maintaining a permanent residence in the United States. Accordingly, cases in which respondents did not maintain a permanent U.S. residence were removed in order to focus the investigation on the American context.

6. An examination of raw frequencies in the sample reveals a ten-fold increase in the number of management consultants from 1965 to 1995. Of course, this statistic fails to account for the more general development of new MBA programs in the United States, which have served as primary feeders for management consulting firms in the post–World War II period.

7. A square root transformation is applied to reduce positive skew in this variable's distribution.

8. These categories are neither mutually exclusive nor exhaustive. Other possible roles include self-employed and unemployed business professionals.

9. Note that the degrees of freedom reported for these models reflect a competing risks formulation, which includes a full set of parameter estimates for entries into nonconsulting careers that are not reported in Table 4.1.

Chapter 5

We are grateful to John Meyer and Alfred Kieser for helpful comments at the 1999 conference of the Scandinavian Consortium for Organizational Research, Stanford, California.

1. Theories of cognitive dissonance (Festinger 1957; Brehm and Cohen 1962) also seem meaningful in this regard.

2. Management gurus and academics also often conduct consulting assignments. The nature of their kind of consulting, however, is different: unlike projects of large consulting firms, they are not concerned with the details of corporate restructuring. Not least due to the guru status of some actors, this form of advice has developed into a special form of management consulting and must be distinguished from the business of the large consulting firms.

3. The sociology of radical change is also concerned with structural conflict, modes of domination, deprivation, and contradiction—issues consultancies are rarely concerned about.

4. For the resistance of middle managers against the introduction of organizational change in a different context, the transfer of Japanese manufacturing organization to the United States, see Florida and Kenney (1991).

5. The divisionalization of organizational structures between the 1960s and the 1980s.

Chapter 6

1. Development dialogue (*medarbeidersamtaler*) is a Scandinavian translation and adaptation of various American performance appraisal systems (for example, appraisal and counseling) to Scandinavian worklife traditions. There have been many attempts in the literature to give a distinct definition to development dialogue (for example, Holt-Larsen and Bang 1993; Wollebæk 1989; Mikkelsen 1996). Most describe it as a periodic (regularly recurring), systematic (planned and well-prepared) personal dialogue between a leader and the employee about various issues concerning the relationship between the employee and the organization. It is emphasized that DD is a formalized system that includes all employees within the organization, thereby distinguishing it from more spontaneous meetings and informal communication between leaders and workers. The aim of introducing development dialogue should be, according to the Scandinavian recipe pioneers, to promote openness and confidence, thus preventing conflicts and enhancing the quality of the work environment.

2. There are a number of publications that survey the actual dissemination of MBO and TQM. For MBO, see Mansell (1977), Schuster and Kindall (1974), Luthans (1976), Philgren and Svenson (1989). For TQM, see Lawler, Mohrman, and Ledford (1992) and Pastor, Meindl, and Hunt (1998). There have only been a few attempts to survey the actual dissemination of development dialogue. An extensive survey carried out in Denmark, however, revealed that a full 84 percent of Danish organizations with more than 200 employees (both public and private) had adopted DD in 1992. There is much evidence that DD is just as widespread in the remaining Scandinavian countries. The consulting firm PriceWaterhouseCoopers surveyed extensively a range of European countries in the early 1990s and found that, of all public and private organizations with more than 200 employees, 70 percent had introduced various performance appraisal systems. In most organizations where such systems had been implemented, personal talks between the leader and the individual worker was an important element (Cederblom 1982).

Chapter 7

We would like to thank Joseph Brüderl, Demet Çetin, Lars Engwall, Berit Ernst, Kerstin Sahlin-Andersson, Anne Tempel, Michael Woywode, and Yong Suk Jang for helpful comments. We are indebted to Lutz Werner for his assistance in collecting and coding the data for the quantitative analysis. Financial support from the Deutsche Forschungsgemeinschaft, SFB 504, at the University of Mannheim, is gratefully acknowledged.

1. ISO 9000 is a series of standards for quality management issued by the International Organization for Standardization.

2. The journal *Qualität und Zuverlässigkeit* (QZ, Quality and Reliability) is the official organ of the German Society for Quality. The public discussion on QM is published primarily in this journal. We contacted a chair for quality science, which confirmed this information. Further, we talked to the editor-in-chief and two members of the editorial board to find out the extent to which the authors and the contents of the journal reflect the development in the discussion on QM in Germany. We were told that the submitted articles were not reviewed by a blind review, and the editors do not have detailed statistics on how many submitted articles were rejected. Some of the articles were submitted on request of the editors, but most of the articles, especially those in the nontechnical area of QM, were submitted on the authors' own behalf. Thus, the statement that we do not analyze an artifact that only reflects the preferences of the editors appears to be reasonable. On the contrary, it seems justified to state that the journal reflects the perception of the development of QM as well as public discussion of QM. Articles about ISO 9000 and TQM, however, have obviously been published in other academic journals. However, as our focus is on the course of resource mobilization, it seems appropriate to choose the publication of the quality-management movement as a source of data in order to test the extent to which its strategies have been successful and the extent to which it could attract authors who were able to bestow the movement and its concepts with legitimacy.

3. Of course the German title of a *professor* is no distinct category of education in itself. However, to achieve this title, one must either obtain a Ph.D. and write a habilitation (scientific monograph; usually more voluminous than a dissertation) or one must obtain a Ph.D. and teach at a Fachhochschule (polytechnic, that is, a minor, basically occupationally oriented university) thereafter. We argue that these two requirements for becoming a German professor can be regarded as qualifications that form a separate category of education.

4. That is for articles that refer to no specific industry written by an engineer with at most a university diploma who works as a practitioner.

Chapter 8

This chapter develops a paper that was presented at the 1999 SCANCOR conference. The author is very grateful for comments that were made to him on that occasion; and later helpful advice from Jim Obelkevich, two anonymous referees, Lars Engwall and Kerstin Sahlin-Andersson.

1. The word *ringi* consists of two parts: *rin*, meaning "submitting a proposal to one's superior and receiving his or her approval," and *gi*, meaning "deliberations and decisions." The *ringi* system was used in Japanese business in order to ensure that decisions were widely discussed and supported. A document outlining choices would be drawn up; passed up the organization, with each tier adding their comments; considered by the top management and amended as necessary; and then returned to the original drafter for implementation.

Chapter 9

1. These are for skill improvement training. For qualifying training, 7.9 percent of the organizations provided formal leadership training, and 12.3 percent of the organizations provided formal training in communication skills.

2. According to the 1997 survey conducted by the Conference Board of 315 corporations, 44 percent of the corporations attempted to measure the value of training, but less than 20 percent measured nontechnical training programs for their ROI (return on investment). It also reports that many leading executives doubt that a vigorous ROI measure of nontechnical training is feasible or useful (Hackett, 1997).

3. The survey listed twenty-one items for employers to choose; for example, employee orientation, sound employee-selection policies and procedures, presentable personnel office and facilities, grievance-handling system, use of attitude and opinion surveys, clearly defined working rules, supervisory training, and employee training. The items were then ranked in frequency of employers' answers. The sound employee selection was ranked higher (second) than supervisory training (fifth) and employee training (tenth) in their frequency of use (Gaudet, 1960).

Chapter 10

I thank Kim Voss, Neil Fligstein, Göran Ahlström, Robert Locke, Peter Lundgreen, and John Meyer for comments, but take the whole responsibility for the content of the chapter.

1. Lundgreen (1990), Lee and Smith (1992), and Meiksins and Smith (1996) have also made comparisons between continental Europe and the United States, however, and Robertson (1981) and Elbaum (1991) have dealt with the United States and Great Britain.

2. *Accreditation* is defined as "the process whereby an organization or agency recognizes a college or university or a program of study as having met certain predetermined qualifications or standards" (Zaret 1967: 177).

3. Struck also argued that the industrial education system was developed at a time when Germany was a country of small shops. The methods of production had not yet become so highly specialized as in the United States (Struck 1930: 91). Robertson

(1981: 56) makes a similar argument in order to account for the difference between Great Britain and the United States.

4. See for instance Hughes (1989: 244–245), Lee and Smith (1992: 11), or Meiksins and Smith (1996: 67).

5. This argument about Dugald Jackson taking the initiative and GE taking a passive role is confirmed by Lecuyer (1995). He also argues that "MIT administrators and faculty groups shaped the school's policies without much industrial interference" (1995: 87).

6. He notes that two schools had abandoned the idea. Among the most prestigious colleges only MIT adopted the model. Evidence at the time indicated that graduates trained under the plan did not "surpass others of equal ability in either responsibility or earning power."

7. "Editorial," *Bulletin of the Society for the Promotion of Engineering Education* (1912), 3: 354; quoted in Noble (1977: 206).

8. Of seventy people at the first meeting of the SPEE in 1893 there were only three practicing engineers and two from abroad, the rest were professors in engineering schools (Zaret 1967: 54); 767 out of 938 members were teachers in 1910. The share of practitioners did increase from 19 percent in 1910 to 25 percent in 1911, but journalists and publishers were also included among practitioners. The distinction between teachers and practitioners was not used in the statistics after 1915, but there is no indication of a dramatic increase in the share of members representing industrial interests after 1911 (*Bulletin of the Society for the Promotion of Engineering Education* 1910: 377, 1918, 1924).

9. The notion of professionals here refers to the elite in the professional association. The professors were the predominant group in this elite until the 1870s, when the industrialists began to take over.

10. When he was hired to do the project, Wickenden was vice president in AT&T and part of the "business camp." Nonetheless, the whole report was based on the philosophy that improvement should come from within the profession (Zaret 1967: 143). The other major report on engineering education between the wars, the Mann report (1918), did not see the lack of comprehensiveness of the American system as a problem. Mann was a physicist, and his academic background may have influenced the conclusions in the report.

11. The new leaders were not clergymen, as the old college presidents had been. McGivern mentions Charles Eliot, a chemist, Gilman, with background in political geography, and Andrew White, a historian (McGivern 1960: 119).

12. For accounts that emphasize professionalization as a strategy to create order in insecure and chaotic environments see Bledstein (1976) and Wiebe (1967).

13. It was necessary to avoid the "old World's class rigidities" and eliminate "prejudices of caste" according to an article by N. Shaler, the dean of the engineering school at Harvard, published in the *Atlantic* in 1893 (Sinclair 1992: 86, 87).

14. A wide range of proprietary schools had been established outside of Prussia at this level from 1890 on, and the Prussian state had also started to fund technical schools at this level. It was these schools that later developed into *Ingenieurschulen* and *Fachchocschulen* (Gispen 1989: 216).

15. See also Harbison and Myers (1959: 129), who argue that German managers do not tend to think of themselves as professional managers but as engineers, lawyers, accountants, and so forth. The top managers resist professionalization in the belief that it may threaten their position of formal authority.

Chapter 11

1. For a few years after 1912 an exception was made to the rule regarding attendance at the Stockholm School of Economics, as the school had only been established in 1909.

2. In presenting the numbers of authorized public accountants in this chapter I refer to accountants that were members of APA. In the years 1934 to 1963 around 70 percent of the authorized accountants were members of APA. In the 1990s around 90 percent of the authorized public accountants were members of the APA.

3. This debate in Sweden can be compared with the situation in the middle of the 1850s and continuing at least until the twentieth century in England, when the primary objective of auditing was the detection of fraud (Matthews et al. 1998: 94–99; Power 1997: 21).

Bibliography

Abbott, Andrew. 1988. *The System of the Professions: An Essay on the Division of Expert Labor*. Chicago: University of Chicago Press.

———. 1991. "The Order of Professionalization: An Empirical Analysis." *Work and Occupations* 18: 355–384.

Abrahamson, Eric. 1991. "Managerial Fads and Fashion: The Diffusion and Rejection of Innovations." *Academy of Management Review* 16: 586–612.

———. 1996. "Technical and Aesetic Fashion." In B. Czarniawska and Guje Sevón, eds., *Translating Organizational Change*, pp. 117–138. Berlin: deGruyter.

Abrahamson, Eric, and Gregory Fairchild. 1997. "Management Fashion: Life-cycles, Triggers, and Collective Learning Processes." Paper presented at the Academy of Management meeting.

———. 1999. "Knowledge Industries and Idea Entrepreneurs." Presented at the Academy of Management meeting, Chicago, Aug. 6–11.

Adler, A. 1929. *The Science of Living*. New York: Greenberg.

Affärsvärldens Konsultguide. 1992–1997. Stockholm: Affärsvärlden förlag AB.

Agresti, A. 1990. *Categorical Data Analysis*. New York: Wiley.

Ahrne, Göran, Nils Brunsson, and Christina Garsten, 2000. "Standardization through Organization." In Nils Brunsson, Bengt Jacobsson, and associates, *A World of Standards*, pp. 151–168. Oxford: Oxford University Press.

Ahlström, Göran. 1982. *Engineers and Industrial Growth*. London: Croom Helm.

Alexander, J.C. 1993. *Soziale Differenzierung und kultureller Wandel. Essays zur neofunktionalistischen Gesellschaftstheorie*. Frankfurt/M.: Campus.

Altenkirch, F. 1972. "20 Jahre ASQ—Rückblick und Ausblick." *Qualität und Zuverlässigkeit* 17: 180–182.

Alvarez, José Luis. 1998. "The Sociological Tradition and the Spread and Institutionalization of Knowledge for Action." In José Luis Alvarez, ed., *The Diffusion and Consumption of Business Knowledge*, 13–57. New York: St. Martin's Press.

Alvarez, José Luis, Carmelo Mazza, and Jordi Mur. 1999. *The Management Publishing Industry in Europe*. CEMP Report No. 5, September 1999.

Alvesson, Mats. 1993. "Organization as Rhetoric: Knowledge-Intensive Firms and the Struggle with Ambiguity." *Journal of Management Studies* 30: 997–1015.

American Management Association. 1954. *Management Education for Itself and Its Employees: Parts 1–3*. New York: American Management Association.

———. 1958. Quality Control in Action. New York: American Management Association.

Anderson, C. A. 1977. "Locus of Control, Coping Behaviors, and Performance in a Stress Setting: A Longitudinal Study." *Journal of Applied Psychology* 62: 446–451.

Anglo-American Council on Productivity. 1953. *Inspection in Industry*. London: British Productivity Council.

Anon. 1956. "Electric Shaver Production." *Mass Production* [no vol.]: 70–77.

Anon. 1962. "Why 'Made in Japan' May Have a New Meaning." *Machinery* 69: [no pp.].

Anon. 1965. "It All Came Out in the Wash." *Focus* 1: 15.

Armbrüster, Thomas, and R. Schmolze. 1999. "Milk Rounds, Case Studies, and the Aftermath. A Critique of the Management Consulting Profession." Presented at the Second International Conference on Management Consultancy Work, London, Feb. 20.

Armenakis, A. A., and H. B. Burdg. 1988. "Consultation Research: Contributions to Practice and Directions for Improvement" *Journal of Management* 14: 339–365.

Armenakis, A. A., K. W. Mossholder, and S. G. Harris. 1990. "Diagnostic Bias in Organizational Consultation." *Omega* 18: 563–572.

Armstrong, Peter. 1984. "Competition between the Organizational Professions and the Evolution of Management Control Strategies." In Kenneth Thompson, ed., *Work, Employment and Unemployment*, pp. 97–120. Philadelphia: Open University Press, Milton Keynes.

Arrow, Kenneth J. 1985. "The Economics of Agency." In J. W. Pratt and R. J. Zeckhauser, eds., *Principals and Agents: The Structure of Business*, pp. 37–51. Boston: Harvard Business School Press.

Ashford, Martin. 1998. *Con Tricks: The World of Management Consultancy and How to Make It Work for You*. London: Simon & Schuster.

Asian Productivity Organisation. 1968. *Achievements in the First Decade of the Productivity Drive in Japan*. Tokyo: Asian Productivity Organisation.

Association of Consulting Management Engineers. 1954–55. *Guide to Professional Practice: Suggestions for Preparing Proposals; Interim Report Practice; Survey Report Practice*. New York: ACME.

Association of Consulting Management Engineers. 1959. *Personal Qualifications of Management Consultants*. New York: ACME.

Association of Consulting Management Engineers. 1964. *Numerical Data on the Present Dimensions, Growth, and Other Trends in Management Consulting in the United States*. New York: ACME.

Astley, G., and R. Zammuto. 1992. "Organization Science, Managers, and Language Games." *Organization Science* 3, no. 4.

Badawy, M. K. 1976. "Applying Management by Objectives to R & D Labs." *Research Management* (Nov.): 35–40.

Bank, J. 1992. *The Essence of Total Quality Management*. New York: Prentice Hall.

Barley, Stephen R. 1992. "The New Crafts." Working paper. Philadelphia: National Center for the Educational Quality of the Workforce, University of Pennsylvania.

Barley, Stephen R., and Gideon Kunda. 1992. "Design and Devotion: Surges of Rational and Normative Ideologies in Managerial Discourse." *Administrative Science Quarterly* 37: 363–399.

Barley, Stephen R., G. W. Meyer, and D. C. Gash. 1988. "Cultures of Culture: Academics, Practitioners and the Pragmatics of Normative Control." *Administrative Science Quarterly* 33: 24–60.

Barnard, Chester. 1938. *The Functions of the Executive*. Cambridge: Harvard University Press.

Barnett, J. 1953. "Inspection and Quality Control in U.S.A." *Engineering Inspection* 17: 47–58.

Barnett, Michael N., and Martha Finnemore. 1999. "The Politics, Power and Pathologies of International Organizations." *International Organization*, 53(4): 699–732.

Barnett, W. P. 1995. "Telephone Companies." In G. R. Carroll and M. T. Hannan, eds., *Organization in Industry*, pp. 277–289. New York: Oxford University Press.

Baron, James N., Frank R. Dobbin, and P. Devereaux Jennings. 1986. "War and Peace: The Evolution of Modern Personnel Administration in U.S. Industry." *American Journal of Sociology*: 92(2): 350–383.

———. 1988. "Mission Control? The Development of Personnel Systems in U.S. Industry." *American Sociological Review* 53: 497–514.

Barron, D. 1995. "Credit Unions." In G. R. Carroll and M. T. Hannan, eds., *Organizations in Industry*, 137–162. New York: Oxford University Press.

Bauman, Zygmund. 1995. "Searching for a Centre that Holds." In M. Featherstone, S. Lash, and R. Robertson, eds., *Global Modernities*, pp. 140–154. London: Sage.

BDU (Bundesverband Deutscher Unternehmensberater). 1996. *Der Markt für Unternehmensberatung—Facts & Figures*. Bonn. BDU.

Beck, Ulrich. 1992. *Risk Society*. London: Sage.

Becker, Gary. 1962. "Investment in Human Capital: A Theoretical Analysis." *Journal of Political Economy* (supplement): 70(pt. 2), 5.

Beer, K. H. 1981. "Performance Appraisal: Dilemmas and Possibilities." *Personnel Review* 16(4): 18–25.

Belbin, R. M. 1970. *Quality Calamities and Their Management Implications*. London: British Institute of Management.

Benders, Jos, and M. Van Bijsterveld. 1997. Leaning on Lean: The Demand Side of Management Fashions. Unpublished manuscript, University of Nijmegen, Nederland.

Benders, Jos, Robert-Jan Van den Berg, and Mark Van Bijsterveld. 1998. "Hitchhiking on a Hype: Dutch Consultants Engineering Re-engineering." *Journal of Organizational Change Management* 11(3): 201–215.

Bentsen, Eva Zeuthen, Finn Borum, Gudbjörg Erlingsdóttir, and Kerstin Sahlin-Andersson, eds. 1999. *Når styringsambitioner møder praksis*. Copenhagen: Copenhagen Business School.

Berger, P. L., B. Berger, and H. Kellner. 1973. *The Homeless Mind. An Approach to Modern Conciousness*. New York: Random House.

Berger, P. L., and T. Luckmann. 1966. *The Social Construction of Reality. A Treatise in the Sosiology of Knowledge*. Harmondsworth, Middlesex, U.K.: Penguin.

Berry, Michel. 1991. "Comment être jeune et consultant?" *Gérer et comprendre* June: 58–64.

Bessant, John, and Howard Rush. 1995. "Building Bridges for Innovation: The Role of Consultants in Technology Transfer." *Research Policy* 24: 97–114.

Birnbaum, Pierre. 1988: *States and Collective Action*. Cambridge: Cambridge University Press.

Bishop, John H. 1997. "What We Know About Employer-Provided Training: A Review of the Literature." *Research in Labor Economics* 16: 19–87.

Biswas, S., and D. Twitchell. 1999. *Management Consulting. A Complete Guide to the Industry*. New York: Wiley.

Blackler, Frank. 1995. "Knowledge, Knowledge Work and Organizations: An Overview and Interpretation." *Organization Studies* 16(6): 1021–1046.

———. 1996. Response to Prichard (1996). *Organization Studies* 17(5): 858–860.

Bledstein, B. J. 1976. *The Culture of Professionalism. The Middle Class and the Development of Higher Education in America.* New York: W. W. Norton.

Bloomfield, Brian P., and A. Best. 1992. "Management Consultants: Systems Development, Power and the Translation of Problems" *Sociological Review* 40: 533–560.

Bloomfield, Brian P., and Ardha Danieli. 1995. "The Role of Management Consultants in the Development of Information Technology: The Indissoluble Nature of Socio-Political and Technical Skills." *Journal of Management Studies* 32(1): 23–46.

Bloomfield, Leonard. 1935. *Language.* London: Allen & Unwin.

Blossfeld, Hans-Peter, and Götz Rohwer. 1995. *Techniques of Event History Modeling: New Approaches to Causal Analysis.* Mahwah, N.J.: Erlbaum.

Boston, Jonathan, J. Martin, J. Pallot, and P. Walsh. 1996. *Public Management: The New Zealand Model.* Oxford University Press: Auckland.

Bourdieu, Pierre. 1977. "The Production of Belief. Contribution to an Economy of Symbolic Goods." *Media, Culture and Society* 2(3): 261–293.

———. 1984. *Distinctions.* Cambridge: Harvard University Press.

Bowker, G. C., and S. L. Star. 1999. *Sorting Things Out. Classification and Its Consequences.* Cambridge: MIT Press.

Boyer, Robert, Elsie Charron, Ulrich Jürgens, and Steven Tolliday, eds. 1998. *Between Imitation and Innovation. The Transfer and Hybridization of Productive Models in the International Automobile Industry.* New York: Oxford University Press.

Braverman, Harry. 1974. *Labor and Monopoly Capital: The Degradation of Work in the Twentieth Century.* New York: Monthly Review Press.

Brehm, Jack W., and Arthur R. Cohen. 1962. *Explorations in Cognitive Dissonance.* New York: Wiley.

British Productivity Council. 1957. *Quality Control.* London: British Productivity Council.

British Productivity Council and National Council for Quality and Reliability. 1967. *Results of Quality and Reliability Year.* London: British Productivity Council and National Council for Quality and Reliability.

Broadberry, S. N., and N.F.R. Crafts. 1998. "The Post-War Settlement: Not Such a Good Bargain After All." *Business History* 40: 73–79.

Brunsson, Nils. 1989. *The Organization of Hypocrisy: Talk, Decisions and Actions in Organizations.* Chichester: Wiley.

———. 2000. "Standardization and Fashion Trends." In Nils Brunsson, Bengt

Jacobsson, and associates. *A World of Standards*, pp. 151–168. Oxford: Oxford University Press.

Brunsson, Nils, and Kerstin Sahlin-Andersson. 2000. "Constructing Organizations. The case of Public Sector Reform." *Organization Studies* 21(4): 721–746.

Brunsson, Nils, Bengt Jacobsson, and associates. 2000. *A World of Standards*. Oxford: Oxford University Press.

Bücken, C. 1949. "Nutzbarmachung der Betriebsstatistik." In H. Opitz, ed., *Wirtschaftliche Fertigung und Forschung*, pp. 121–143. München: Hanser.

Bureau of Labor Statistics. U.S. Department of Labor. 1977. *Occupational Training in Selected Metalworking Industries, 1974: A Report on a Survey of Selected Occupations*. Washington, D.C.: Department of Labor, Bureau of Labor Statistics.

Burrage, Michael. 1993. "From Practice to School-Based Professional Education: Patterns of Conflict and Accommodation in England, France and the United States." In Sheldon Rothblatt and Björn Wittrock, eds., *The European and American University Since 1800*, pp. 142–187. Cambridge University Press.

Burrage, Michael, Konrad Jarausch, and Hannes Siegrist. 1990. "An Actor-Based Framework for the Study of Professions." In Michael Burrage and Rolf Torstendahl, eds., *Professions in Theory and History: Rethinking the Study of the Professions*, pp. 203–225. London: Sage.

Burrell, Gibson, and Gareth Morgan. 1979. *Sociological Paradigms and Organisational Analysis: Elements of the Sociology of Corporate Life*. London: Heinemann.

Butman, John. 1997. *Juran. A Lifetime of Influence*. New York: Wiley.

Byrkjeflot, Haldor. 1998. "Engineers and Management in Germany and the USA—A Discussion of the Origins of Diversity in Management Systems." *Enterprise et Histoire* 19: 47–74.

Byrne, J. A., and G. Williams. 1993. "The Alumni Club to End All Alumni Clubs." *Business Week* Sept. 20: 41.

Byrne, Marjorie. 1957. "Don't Believe This Management Legend." *Manager* 25: 891, 893.

Cailluet, Ludovic. 1995. "Stratégies, structures d'organisation et pratiques de gestion de Pechiney des années 1880 à 1971." Ph.D. dissertation, University of Lyon II, France.

Callan, V. J., D. J. Terry, and R. Schweitzer. 1994. "Coping Resources, Coping Strategies and Adjustment to Organizational Change: Direct Buffering Effects?" *Work and Stress* 8: 372–383.

Calvert, Monte A. 1967. *The Mechanical Engineer in America 1830–1910*. Baltimore: John Hopkins Press.

———. 1972. "The Search for Engineering Unity: The Professionalization of Special Interest." In Jerry Israel, ed., *Building the Organizational Society*, pp. 42–54. New York: Free Press.

Cameron, K. S. 1986. "A Study of Organizational Effectiveness and Its Predictors." *Management Science* 32: 87–112.

Campbell, John L., and Leon Lindberg. 1990. "Property Rights and the Organization of Economic Activity by the State." *American Sociological Review* 55 (Oct.): 634–637.

Canback, S. 1998. "The Logic of Management Consulting (part one)." *Journal of Management Consulting* 10(2): 3–11.

Caplen, Rowland. 1969. "A Short History of the Institution of Engineering Inspection." *Quality Engineer* 33: 5–20.

Caplow, Theodore. 1954. *The Sociology of Work*. Minneapolis: University of Minnesota Press.

Cappelli, Peter, Laurie Bassi, Harry Katz, David Knoke, Paul Osterman, and Michael Useem. 1997. "Chapter 4: Job Training Programs and Practices." *Change at Work*, pp. 122–153. New York: Oxford University Press.

Carlson, Bernhard W. 1988. "Academic Entrepreneurship and Engineering Education: Dugald C. Jackson and the MIT-GE Cooperative Engineering Course, 1907–32." *Technology and Culture*, 29 (July): 536–569.

Carlsson, Leif. 2001. "Framväxten av en intern redovisning i Sverige 1900–1945." Ph.D. dissertation, Dept. of Business Studies, Uppsala University.

Carnevale, Anthony, Leila J. Gainer, and Janice Villet. 1990. *Training in America: The Organization and Strategic Role of Training*. San Francisco: Jossey-Bass.

Carnoy, Martin and Henry Levin. 1985. *Schooling and Work in the Democratic State*. Stanford, Calif.: Stanford University Press.

Caroll, S. J., and H. L. Tosi. 1973. *Management by Objectives. Applications and Research*. New York: Macmillan.

Carroll, Glenn R. 1996. "Long-Term Evolutionary Change in Organizational Populations: Theory, Models and Empirical Findings." Working Paper. International Institute for Applied Systems Analysis, Laxenburg, Austria.

Carroll, Glenn R., and Michael T. Hannan. 1995. "Automobile Manufacturers." In G. R. Carroll, and M. T. Hannan, eds., *Organization in Industry*, pp. 195–214. New York: Oxford University Press.

Carr-Saunders, A. P., and P. A. Wilson. 1933. *The Professions*. Oxford: Oxford University Press.

Caselton, S. 1971. "A History of the Institution—Its Formation and Development." *Production Engineer* 50: 199–209.

Caulkin, S. 1997. "The Great Consultancy Cop-out." *Management Today* (March): 32–36.

Cederblom, D. 1982. "The Performance Appraisal Interview: A Review, Implications, and Suggestions." *Academy of Management Review* 7(2): 219–227.

Chabaud, D., and G. Rot. 1997. "Standardization and Organizational Forms. The Case of a French Car Maker." Presented at the SCANCOR/SCORE seminar on Standardization of Organizational Forms, Arild, Sweden, September.

Chamberlain, Arthur Henry. 1908. *The Condition and Tendencies of Technical Education in Germany.* Syracuse, N.Y.: Bardeen.

Chandler, Alfred. 1977. *The Visible Hand: The Managerial Revolution in American Business.* Cambridge: Harvard University Press.

Chandler, A. D. Jr. 1990. *Scale and Scope. The Dynamics of Industrial Capitalism.* Cambridge, Mass.: Belknap Press.

Chilton, Kenneth. 1984. "Regulation and the Entrepreneurial Environment." In C. Kent, ed., *The Environment for Entrepreneurship*, pp. 91–115. Lexington, Mass.: Lexington Books.

Christensen, Tom, and Per Laegreid, eds. 2001. *New Public Management: The Transformation of Ideas and Practice.* Ashgate: Aldershot.

Clark, Burton R. 1978. "Academic Differentiation in National Systems of Higher Education." *Comparative Education Review* 22: 242–258.

Clark, Timothy. 1995. *Managing Consultants—Consultancy as the Management of Impressions.* Buckingham: Open University Press.

Clark, Timothy, and David Greatbatch. 2001. "Whose Idea Is It Anyway? Collaborative Relationships in the Creation of Management Guru Ideas." In Matthias Kipping and Lars Engwall, eds., *Management Consulting: The Emergence and Dynamics of a Knowledge Industry.* Oxford: Oxford University Press.

Cleaver, P. C. 1963. "The Cost of Unreliability to the Royal Air Force." In *Society of Environmental Engineers Symposium and Exhibition Proceedings*, Part One, 7–12. London: Kenneth Mason.

Coleman, J. S. 1975. "Social Structure and a Theory of Action." In P. M. Blau, ed., *Approaches to the Study of Social Structure*, pp. 76–93. New York: Free Press.

Collins, David. 2000. *Management Fads and Buzzwords.* London: Routledge.

Collins, H. M. 1993. "The Structure of Knowledge." *Social Research* 60(1): 95–116.

Collins, Randall. 1979. *The Credential Society.* New York: Academic Press.

Commons, John R. 1921. "Chapter 2: Faith in People." In John R. Commons, Willis Wisler, et al., eds., *Industrial Government.* New York: Macmillan.

Considine, M., and M. Painter, eds. 1997. *Managerialism. The Great Debate.* Melbourne: Melbourne University Press.

Consultants News. 1999. "Management Consulting Today." http://www.kennedyinfo.com/mc/overview.html.

Contu, Alessia, and Hugh Willmott. 1999. "Learning and Practice: Focussing on

Power Relations." Presented at the Society for Organizational Learning Conference, Cambridge, Mass., Oct. 8–9.

Craig, Robert L. 1987. *Training and Development Handbook: A Guide to Human Resource Development*. 3rd ed. American Society for Training and Development. New York: McGraw Hill.

Crainer, Stuart. 1997. *Corporate Man to Corporate Skunk. The Tom Peters Phenomenon*. Oxford: Capstone.

Crainer, Stuart, and Des Dearlove. 1998. *Gravy Training. Inside the Shadowy World of Business Schools*. Oxford: Capstone.

Crosby, P. B. 1986. *Qualität bringt Gewinn*. Hamburg: McGraw Hill.

Cyert, Richard M., and James G. March. 1963. *A Behavioral Theory of the Firm*. Englewood Cliffs, N.J.: Prentice-Hall.

Czarniawska, Barbara. 1997. *Narrating the Organization. Drama of Institutional Identity*. Chicago: University of Chicago Press.

Czarniawska, Barbara, and Bernward Joerges. 1996. "Travels of Ideas." In Barbara Czarniawska and Guje Sevón, eds., *Translating Organizational Change*, pp. 13–48. Berlin: De Gruyter.

Czarniawska, Barbara, and Guje Sevón, eds., 1996. *Translating Organizational Change*. Berlin: de Gruyter.

Czarniawska-Joerges, Barbara. 1990. "Merchants of Meaning: Management Consulting in the Swedish Public Sector." In Barry A. Turner, ed., *Organizational Symbolism*, pp. 139–150. New York: de Gruyter.

Daeves, K., and A. Beckel. 1948. *Großzahlforschung und Häufigkeitsanalyse—Ein Leitfaden*. Weinheim: Verlag Chemie.

Dahmen, Erik. 1950. *Svensk industriell företagarverksamhet. Kausalanalys av den industriella utvecklingen 1919–1939*, Vols. 1 and 2. Stockholm: IUI.

Danielsson, Magnus, and Precious Emore. 2001. "Internationaliseringen av den svenska redovisningen." Department of Business Studies, Uppsala University (mimeo).

Datsch Abhandlungen und Berichte. 1908–1929. Vols. 1–9. Berlin DATSCH.

David, Robert. 1999. "Industry-Environment Co-Evolution: Environmental Change and the Spread of Management Consulting in the Twentieth Century." Presented at the Academy of Management Meetings, Chicago, Ill.

Dawes, P. L., G. R. Dowling, and P. G. Patterson. 1992. "Criteria Used to Select Management Consultants." *Industrial Marketing Management* 21: 187–193.

Dawson, William H. 1919. *The Evolution of Modern Germany*. London: Unwin.

Deal, Terrence E., and Allan A. Kennedy. 1982. *Corporate Cultures*. Reading, Mass.: Addison-Wesley.

Dean, Joel. 1938. "The Place of Management Counsel in Business." *Harvard Business Review* 16: 451–465.

deCharms, R. 1968. *Personal Causation*. New York: Academic Press.

Dees, Bowden C. 1997. *The Allied Occupation and Japan's Economic Miracle*. Richmond, Surrey: Curzon Press.

Deming, W. E. 1982. *Quality, Productivity and Competitive Position*. Boston: MIT, Center for Advanced Engineering Study.

Department of Prices and Consumer Protection. 1978. *A National Strategy for Quality*. London: Department of Prices and Consumer Protection.

Department of Trade and Industry. 1971. *Report of a Committee on the Means of Authenticating the Quality of Engineering Products and Materials*. London: HMSO.

Deutschmann, C. 1997 "Die Mythenspirale. Eine wissenssoziologische Interpretation industrieller Rationalisierung." *Soziale Welt* 47: 55–70.

Dichtl, M. 1998. *Standardisierung von Beratungsleistungen*. Wiesbaden: Gabler.

DiMaggio, Paul. 1988. "Interests and Agency in Institutional Theory." In L. G. Zucker, ed., *Institutional Patterns and Organizations: Culture and Environment*, pp. 3–21. Cambridge, Mass.: Ballinger.

———. 1991. "Constructing an Organizational Field as a Professional Project: U.S. Art Museums, 1920–1940." In W. Powell and P. DiMaggio, eds., *The New Institutionalism in Organizational Analysis*, pp. 267–292. Chicago: University of Chicago Press.

DiMaggio, Paul, and Walter W. Powell. 1983. "The Iron Cage Revisited: Institutional Isomorphism and Collective Rationality in Organizational Fields." *American Sociological Review* 48: 147–160.

DiMaggio, Paul J., and Walter W. Powell, eds. 1991. *The New Institutionalism in Organizational Analysis*, pp. 1–38. Chicago: University of Chicago Press.

DIN ISO 9001. 1994. *Qualitätsmanagementsysteme—Modell zur Qualitätssicherung/QM-Darlegung in Design/Entwicklung, Produktion, Montage und Wartung*. Deutsches Institut für Normung. Berlin: Beuth

DIN-Mitteilungen. 1996. "Neues aus der DQS." *DIN-Mitteilungen* 75: 871–874.

DiPrete, Thomas. 1993. "Industrial Restructuring and the Mobility Response of American Workers in the 1980s." *American Sociological Review* 58: 74–96.

Djelic, Marie-Laure. 1998. *Exporting the American Model. The Postwar Transformation of European Business*. Oxford: Oxford University Press.

Dobbin, Frank, and John Sutton. 1998. "The Strength of a Weak State: The Rights Revolution and the Rise of Human Resources Management Divisions." *American Journal of Sociology*, 104(2): 441–76.

Dodge, Arthur F. 1942. "Characteristics of Good Clerks." *Personnel Journal*.

Donaldson, L. 1995. *American Anti-Management Theories of Organization— A Critique of Paradigm Proliferation*. Cambridge: Cambridge University Press.

———. 1996. *For Positivist Organization Theory: Providing the Hard Core*. London: Sage.

———. 1999. *Performance-Driven Organizational Change: The Organizational Portfolio*. Thousand Oaks, Calif.: Sage.

Dower, John W. 1999. *Embracing Defeat. Japan in the Wake of World War II*. New York: Norton.

Drucker, Peter F. 1954. *The Practice of Management*. New York: Harper and Row.

———. 1976. "What Results Should You Expect? A Users Guide to MBO." *Public Administration Review*, 36(1): 12–19.

du Gay, P., and G. Salaman. 1992. "The Cult(ure) of the Customer." *Journal of Management Studies* 29: 615–633.

Durkheim, Emile. 1893. *De la division du travail social*. Paris: Ancienne Librairie Germer Baillère.

Eberwein, W., and J. Tholen, J. 1990. *Managermentalität. Industrielle Unternehmensleitung als Beruf und Politik*. Frankfurt am Main: Verlagder Frankfurter Allgemeinen Zeitung.

Eberts, Ray, and Cindelyn Eberts. 1995. *The Myths of Japanese Quality*. Upper Saddle River, N.J.: Prentice Hall.

Economist, November 27, 1999, pp. 15–16.

Economist, August 26, 2000, p. 66.

Economist, September 16, 2000, pp. 72, 77.

Edelman, Lauren, Steven Abraham, and Howard Erlanger. 1992. "Professional Construction of the Legal Environment: The Inflated Threat of Wrongful Discharge Doctrine." *Law and Society Review* 26: 47–83.

Edwards, Johan Richard, ed. 2000. *The History of Accounting: Critical Perspectives on Business and Management*. London: Routledge.

Egeberg, M. 1989. "Mot instrumentelle modeller i statsvitenskapen?" In M. Egeberg, ed., *Institusjonspolitikk og forvaltningsutvikling. Bidrag til en anvendt statsvitenskap*, pp. 15–27. Oslo: Tano.

Eisenhardt, K. 1989. "Agency Theory: An Assessment and Review." *Academy of Management Review* 14: 57–57.

Elbaum, Bernhard. 1991. "The Persistence of Apprenticeship in Britain and Its Decline in the United States." In Howard F. Gospel, ed., *Industrial Training and Technological Innovation*, pp. 194–212. London: Routledge.

Elkjær, B., P. Flensburg, J. Mouritsen, and H. Willmot. 1991. "The Commodification of Expertise: The Case of System Development Consulting." *Accounting Management & Information Technology* 1: 139–156.

Engwall, Lars. 1992. *Mercury Meets Minerva*. Oxford: Pergamon Press.

———. 1999. *The Carriers of Mangement Ideas*. CEMP Report No. 7, Department of Business Studies, Uppsala University.

Engwall, Lars, and Carin Eriksson, 1999. "Advising Corporate Superstars. CEOs and Consultancies in Top Swedish Corporations." Presented at the 15th EGOS colloquium, Warwick University, 4–6 July.

Engwall, Lars, and Elving Gunnarsson, eds. 1994. *Management Studies in an Academic Context*. Uppsala: Acta Universitatis Upsaliensis, Studia Oeconomiae Negotiorum 35.

Engwall, Lars, and Vera Zamagni. 1998. "Introduction." In Lars Engwall and Vera Zamagni, eds., *Management Education in Historical Perspective*, pp. 1–18. Manchester: Manchester University Press.

Erlingsdottir, Gudbjørg. 1999. *Förförande ideer*. Ph.D. Dissertation, University of Lund.

Eurich, Nell P. 1985. *Corporate Classrooms: The Learning Business*. Princeton, N.J.: Carnegie Foundation for the Advancement of Teaching.

European Commission. 1995. "A European Quality Promotion Policy or the European Way Towards Excellence." Working document. Brussels.

———. 1996. "Working Document of the Services of the Commission Concerning a European Quality Promotion Policy for Improving European Competitiveness." SEC (96) 2000, Brussels.

Evan, William M. 1969. "The Engineering Profession: A Cross-Cultural Analysis." In Robert Perucci and Joel E. Gerstl, eds., *The Engineers and the Social System*, pp. 99–137. New York: Wiley.

Evans, Peter B., Dietrich Rueschemeyer, and Theda Scocpol. 1985. *Bringing the State Back In*. New York: Cambridge University Press.

Fant, J.-E. 1994. "Revisorns Roll—en komparativ studie av revisorers, företagsledares och aktieägares attityder till extern revision i Finland och Sverige." Helsingfors: Svenska Handelshögskolan.

FAR 75 år—en rapsodisk skildning av utvecklingen 1923–98. Stockholm: FAR Förlag AB.

Faust, Michael. 1998. "Die Selbstverständlichkeit der Unternehmensberatung." In J. Howald and R. Kopp, eds., *Sozialwissenschaftliche Organisationsberatung. Auf der Suche nach einem spezifischen Beratungsverständnis*, pp. 147–182. Berlin: Edition Sigma.

Fayol, Henry. 1950. *General and Industrial Management*. London: Pitman. First published in 1916.

Feigenbaum, A. 1956. "Total Quality Control." *Harvard Business Review* 34: 93–101.

———. 1983. *Total Quality Control*. 3rd edition. New York: McGraw-Hill.

Feigenbaum, A. V. 1991. *Total Quality Control*. New York: McGraw-Hill.

Fenton, E., and A. M. Pettigrew. 2000. "Theoretical Perspectives on New Forms of Organizing." In A. Pettigrew and E. Fenton, eds., *The Innovating Organization*. London: Sage.

Festinger, Leon. 1957. *A Theory of Cognitive Dissonance*. Stanford: Stanford University Press.

Final Report of the Committee on Consumer Protection. 1961–62 Cmnd.1781. (British Government Parliamentary Paper [P.P.] 1961–62): xii.

Fincham, Robin. 1995. "Business Process Reengineering and the Commodification of Managerial Knowledge." *Journal of Marketing Management* 11: 707–719.

———. 1999. "The Consultant-Client Relationship: Critical Perspectives on the Management of Organizational Change." *Journal of Management Studies* 36: 335–351.

Finnemore, Martha. 1996. *National Interests in International Society*. Ithaca: Cornell University Press.

Fisher, Berenice M. 1967. *Industrial Education, American Ideals and Institutions*. Madison.: University of Wisconsin Press.

Fletcher, C. 1986. "The Effects of Performance Review in Appraisal: Evidence and Implications." *Journal of Management Development* 5(3): 3–12.

Fligstein, Neil. 1987. "The Intraorganizational Power Struggle: Rise of Finance Personnel to Top Leadership in Large Corporations, 1919–1979." *American Sociological Review* 52: 44–58.

———. 1990. *Transformation of Corporate Control*. Cambridge: Harvard University Press.

Fligstein, Neil, and Haldor Byrkjeflot. 1996. "The Logic of Employment Systems." In James Baron, David Grusky, Donald Treiman, eds., *Social Differentiation and Stratification*, pp. 11–37. Boulder, Colo.: Westview Press.

Flipo, J.-P. 1988. "On the intangibility of services." *The Services Industries Journal* 8 (3): 286–299.

Florida, Richard, and Martin Kenney. 1991. "The Transfer of Japanese Industrial Organization to the US." *American Sociological Review* 56: 381–398.

Flower, John. 1999. "Introduction." In Stuart McLeay, ed., *Accounting Regulation in Europe*, pp. 1–23. London: Macmillan.

Fortune. 1944. "Doctors of Management." 30(1) (July): 142–146, 201–213.

Frank, David, John Meyer, and David Miyahara. 1995. "The Individualist Polity and the Centrality of Professionalized Psychology." *American Sociological Review* 60(3): 360–377.

Franzkowski, R., H. Fuhr, and B. Liesch. 1984. "28. EOQC-Konferenz in Brighton." *Qualität und Zuverlässigkeit* 29: 351–352.

Frazis, Harley, Mary Joyce, Michael Horrigan, and Maury Gittleman. 1998. "Results from the 1995 Survey of Employer-Provided Training." *Monthly Labor Review* (June): 3–13.

Fricke, J. G. 1992. "Quality Assurance, Program Evaluation, and Auditing: Different Approaches to Effective Program Management." *Canadian Public Administration*, 34(3): 435–452.

Fridenson, Patrick. 1994. "La circulation internationale des modes manageriales." In J.-P. Bouilloud and B. P. Lecuyer, eds., *L'invention de la gestion. Histoire et pratiques*, pp. 81–89. Paris: L'Harmattan.

Fuhr, H. 1993. "Der Einfluß der Normen der Reihe ISO 9000 auf Qualitätssicherungssysteme bei der Aus- und Weiterbildung." *DIN-Mitteilungen* 72: 327–331.

Fuhr, H., and T. Stumpf 1993. "DGQ-Aus- und -Weiterbildungskonzept." *Qualität und Zuverlässigkeit* 38: 25–30.

Fujimura, Joan H. 1996. *Crafting Science: A Sociohistory of the Quest for the Genetics of Cancer*. Cambridge, Mass.: Harvard University Press.

Furusten, Staffan. 1998. "The Creation of Popular Management Texts." In J. L. Alvarez, ed., *The Diffusion and Consumption of Business Knowledge*, pp. 141–163. London: Macmillan.

———. 1999. *Popular Management Books*. London: Routledge.

———. 2000. "The Knowledge Base of Standards." In N. Brunsson, B. Jacobsson, and associates, *A World of Standards*, pp. 71–84. London: Oxford.

Furusten, Staffan, and David Lerdell. 1998. "Managementiseringen av förvaltningen." In G. Ahrne, ed., *Stater som organisationer*, pp. 99–122. Stockholm: Nerenius & Santérus.

Galaskiewicz, Joseph, and Ronald Burt. 1991. "Interorganizational Contagion in Corporate Philanthropy." *Administrative Science Quarterly* 36: 88–105.

Galison, Peter. 1997. *Image and Logic*. Chicago: Chicago University Press.

Galvin, T., and Ventresca, M. 1999. "Intermediaries and Sources of Strategic Innovation: Categories of Competition and Identity in the U.S. Higher Education Consulting Field Since the 1980s." Presented at the SCANCOR workshop on Carriers of Management Knowledge, Stanford University, Stanford, Calif., Sept. 16–17.

Gamson, W. A. 1987. "Introduction." In M. N. Zald, and J. D. McCarthy, eds., *Social Movements in an Organizational Society—Collected Essays*, pp. 1–7. New Brunswick, N.J.: Transaction Books.

Garmannslund, K. 1994. *Nye Medarbeidersamtaler mot år 2000*. Oslo: Fortuna.

Gaston-Breton, Tristan. 1998. *Histoire d'une grande entreprise familiale: Lesieur (1908–1993)*. Paris: Seuil.

Gaudet, Frederick J. 1960. "Labor Turnover: Calculation and Cost." *AMA Research Study* no. 39. American Management Association: New York.

Gemelli, G. 1995. "American Influence on the European Management Education: The Role of the Ford Foundation." European University Institute Working Paper RSC No. 95-3, Florence.

Gerken, G. 1992. *Manager . . . die Helden des Chaos*. Düsseldorf: Econ.

Gerschenkron, Alexander. 1962. "Economic Backwardness in Historical Perspective." In Burt Hoselitz, ed., *The Progress of Underdeveloped Countries*, pp. 5–30. Chicago: University of Chicago Press.

Gherardi, Silvia. 2000. "Introduction." *Organization* 7(2): 211–223.

Gherardi, Silvia, and Davide Nicolini. 2000. "To Transfer Is to Transform: The Circulation of Safety Knowledge." *Organization*, 7(2): 329–348.

Giddens, Anthony. 1979. *Central Problems in Social Theory: Action, Structure and Contradiction in Social Analysis*. Berkeley: University of California Press.

———. 1984. *The Constitution of Society*. Berkeley: University of California Press.

———. 1990. *The Consequenses of Modernity*. Stanford: Stanford University Press.

———. 1991. *Modernity and Self-Identity: Self and Society in the Late Modern Age*. Cambridge, U.K.: Polity Press.

Girard, R. 1988. "Are Performance Appraisals Passé?" *Personnel Journal* 67(8): 89–90.

Gispen, C.W.R. 1988. "German Engineers and American Social Theory: Historical Perspectives on Professionalization." *Comparative Studies in Society and History* 30(3) (Summer): 550–574.

Gispen, Kees. 1989. *New Profession, Old Order: Engineers and German Society 1815–1914*. Cambridge: Cambridge University Press.

Glückler, Johannes, and Thomas Armbruester. 2001. "Trust and Networked Reputation: The Mechanisms of the Management Consulting Market." Presented at the EGOS colloquium, Lyon, July 2001.

Goodman, R. A. 1999. "Emerging Conundrums in Modern Organizations: Exploring the Postindustrial Subculture of the Third Millennium." In R. A. Goodman, ed., *Modern Organizations and Emerging Conundrums*. New York: Lexington.

Gordy, C. B. 1957. "Japan Manufacturing Plants: Are They Well Managed?" In file headed "USOM General (Sept.–Dec. 1957)," box 15, 1264, National Archives, Washington, D.C.

Gouldner, A. 1954. *Patterns of Industrial Bureaucracy*. Glencoe, Ill.: Free Press.

Grabert, S., G. F. Kamiske, C. Malorny, H. Michael, and H. D. Sander. 1993. "Qualitätsmanagementsysteme nach DIN ISO 9000: Wo liegen die Schwierigkeiten?" *Qualität und Zuverlässigkeit* 38: 269–274.

Grayden, Elizabeth. 2000. "The Diffusion of Management Education: An Examination of the Drivers and Implications of the Growth of Sub-Sectors within the Management Education Industry." Paper in Human Resources and Industrial Education, University of Minnesota.

Grayson, Lawrence. E. 1977. "A Brief History of Engineering Education in the United States." *Engineering Education* 68: 246–264.

———. 1993. *The Making of an Engineer: An Illustrated History of Engineering Education in the United States and Canada*. New York: Wiley.

Green, R.F.D. 1957. "Statistics as an Aid to Quality." *FBI Review* 91: 64–65.

Greene, James H. 1937. *Organized Training in Business*. New York: Harper & Brothers.

Greenwood, R., and C. R. Hinings. 1993. "Understanding Strategic Change: The Contribution of Archetypes." *Academy of Management Journal* 36(5): 1052–1081.

Greenwood, R., C. R. Hinings, and R. Suddaby. 2002. "Theorizing Change: The Role of Professional Associations in the Transformation of Institutionalised Fields." *Academy of Management Journal* 45(1): 23–58.

Greiner, L. E., and R. O. Metzger. 1983. *Consulting to Management*. Englewood Cliffs, N.J.: Prentice Hall.

Guillén, Mauro F. 1994. *Models of Management: Work, Authority, and Organization in a Comparative Perspective*. Chicago: University of Chicago Press.

Guion, R. M. 1975. "Gullibility and the Manager." *Personnel Administrator* (Jan.): 20–23.

Gulick, L., and L. Urwick. 1937. "Papers on the Science of Administration." New York: Institute of Public Administration.

Gummesson, Evert. 1996. *Relasjonsmarkedsføring fra 4P til 30R*. Oslo: Kolle Forlag.

Gundrey, Elizabeth. 1966. *Value for Money*. London: Zenith.

Habbe, Stephen. 1950. *Company Programs of Executive Development*. Studies in Personnel Policy, no. 107. New York: National Industrial Conference Board.

Habermas, Jürgen. 1981. *Theorie des kommunikativen Handelns*. Bd. II: *Zur Kritik der funktionalistischen Vernunft*. Frankfurt/M.: Suhrkamp.

———. 1987. *Toward a Rational Society*. Cambridge, U.K.: Polity Press.

Hackett, Brian. 1997. "The Value of Training in the Era of Intellectual Capital: A Research Report." Report Number: 1199-97-RR. New York: The Conference Board.

Hackman, J. R., and R. Wageman. 1995. "Total Quality Management: Empirical, Conceptual, and Practical Issues." *Administrative Science Quarterly* 40: 309–342.

Hadenius, Stig, and Lennart Weibull. 1972. *Massmedier: en bok om press, radio och TV*. Stockholm: Bonnier.

Hagedorn, Homer J. 1955. "The Management Consultant as Transmitter of Business Techniques." *Explorations in Entrepreneurial History* 7: 164–173.

Hallén, Lars, and Eva Wallerstedt. 2000. "Two Cases in the Internationalization of the Accounting Industry." Presented at the Marcus Wallenberg Symposium on Critical Perspectives on Internationalisation, Department of Business Studies, Uppsala, Sweden, Jan. 10–11.

Hamada, Koichi. 1996. *Consumers, the Legal System and Product Liability Reform: A Comparative Perspective between Japan and the United States*.

Center Discussion Paper, no. 759. New Haven, Conn.: Economic Growth Center, Yale University.

Hamel, Gary H., and C. K. Prahalad. 1994. *Competing for the Future.* Boston: Harvard Business School Press.

Hammer, Michael, and James Champy. 1993. *Reengineering the corporation. A Manifesto for Business Revolution.* London: Brealey.

Handlingar till 18:e svenska Handelskammarmötet. 1930: 5–7, 60–61. Stockholm: K. L. Beckmans boktryckeri.

Hannan, Michael T. 1995. "Labor Unions." In G. R. Carroll, and M. T. Hannan, eds., *Organizations in Industry*, pp. 121–136. New York: Oxford University Press.

Hannan, Michael T., and John Freeman. 1977. "The Population Ecology of Organizations." *American Journal of Sociology* 82: 929–964.

Hanner, Per V. A. 1963. *Public Accountancy in Sweden—A Review.* Stockholm: Emil Kihlström Tryckeri AB.

Hannerz, Ulf. 1996. *Transnational Connections: Culture, People, Places.* London: Routledge.

Hans, R. 1992. "Verantwortung der obersten Leitung." *Qualität und Zuverlässigkeit* 37: 249–251.

Hansen, M. T., N. Nohria, and T. Tierney. 1999. "What's Your Strategy for Managing Knowledge?" *Harvard Business Review*, 77(2) (March–April): 106–116.

Hansen, W. 1994. "DQS-Nachrichten." *Qualität und Zuverlässigkeit* 39: 500.

Harbison, Frederick and Charles Myers. 1959. *Management in the Industrial World.* New York: McGraw-Hill.

Hartmann, Heinz. 1959. *Authority and Organization in German Management.* Princeton, N.J.:Princeton University Press.

———. 1967. "Unternehmertum und Professionalisierung." *Zeitschrift für die gesamte Staatswissenschaft* 123: 515–540.

———. 1972. "Arbeit, Beruf, Profession." In T. Luckmann and W. M. Sprondel, eds., *Berufssoziologie*, pp. 36–52. Köln: Kiepenhauer & Witsch.

Hasek, G. 1997. "The Era of Experts." *Industry Week* 246(10): 60–67.

Haskell, Thomas. L., ed. 1984. *The Authority of Experts: Studies in History and Theory.* Bloomington: Indiana University Press.

Hatton, C. H. 1957. "Observations on the Quality of Japanese Products." In file headed "Observations on the Quality of Japanese Products," box 13, 1266, National Archives, Washington, D.C.

Havelock, Ronald G. 1969. *Planning for Innovation Through Dissemination and Utilization of Knowledge.* Ann Arbor: Institute for Social Research, University of Michigan.

Hedmo, Tina. 2001. "The Europeanisation of Management Education." Presented at the 16th Scandinavian Academy of Management Meeting, Uppsala, August 2001.

Henkoff, Ronald. 1993. "Jobs in America: Winning the New Career Game." *Fortune* (July) 12) 128(1): 46–49.

Herbst, Jurgen. 1982. "Diversification in American Higher Education." In K. H. Jarausch, ed., *The Transformation of Higher Learning 1860–1930. Expansion, Diversification, Social Opening and Professionalization in England, Germany, Russia and the United States.* (Historisch-sozialwissenschaftliche Forschungen bd. 13), 196–218. Stuttgart: Klett-Cotta.

Heverly, M. A. 1991. "Total Quality Management: Institutional Research Applications." Presented at the 14th Annual Conference of the Eastern Evaluation Research Society, May 1991, Princeton, N.J.

Higashi, H. 1969. "Quality Control in Japanese Small-Scale Manufacturers." In *International Conference on Quality Control Proceedings 1969*, pp. 485–487. Tokyo: Japanese Union of Scientists and Engineers.

Hill, Stephen. 1991. "Why Quality Circles Failed But Total Quality Management Might Succeed." *British Journal of Industrial Relations* 29(4): 541–568.

Hilmer, Fred, and Lex Donaldson. 1996. *Management Redeemed. Debunking the Fads that Undermine Corporate Performance.* East Rosewill, NSW: Free Press Australia.

Hinton, Sir Christopher. 1963. "Japan Revisited." *Chartered Mechanical Engineer* (Mar.): 160–161.

Hofstede, Geert. 1980. *Culture's Consequenses.* Beverly Hills: Sage.

Holmes, Alan R., and Edwin Green. 1986. *Midland: 150 Years of Banking Business.* London: Batsford.

Holt-Larsen H., and S. M. Bang. 1993. "Development Dialoguees as an Alternative to Performance Appraisal: A Tool for Strategic Human Resource Development in Europe." In G. R. Ferris and K. M. Rowland, eds., *Research in Personnel and Human Resource Management*, Suppl. 3: 171–188. Greenwich, Conn.: JAI Press.

Hood, Christopher. 1991. "A Public Management for All Seasons?" *Public Administration* 69 (Spring): 3–19.

———. 1995. "The New Public Management in the 1980s: Variations on a Theme." *Accounting, Organization and Society* 20 (2–3): 93–109.

Hopkins, Harry. 1964. *The New Look: A Social History of the Forties and Fifties.* London: Secker and Warburg.

Hopper, K. 1985. "Quality, Japan, and the U.S.: The First Chapter." *Quality Progress* 18: 34–41.

Hopwood, Anthony, Michael Page, and Stuart Turley. 1990. *Understanding Accounting in a Changing Environment.* Hertfordshire: Prentice Hall.

Huczynski, A. A. 1993. *Management Gurus: What Makes Them and How to Become One*. London: Routledge.

Ibsen, H. 1882/1967. *An Enemy of the People*. London: Heinemann.

Imaizumi, M. 1969. "QC Circle Activities in Japan." In *International Conference on Quality Control Proceedings 1969*, Supplement, pp. 21–25. Tokyo: Japanese Union of Scientists and Engineers.

Inspection Engineer. 1956. 20: 3.

Inspection Engineer. 1957. 21: 1.

Inspection Engineer. 1959. 23: 57.

Institution of Mechanical Engineers. 1963. *Proceedings of the Discussion on Quality and Reliability*, pp. 22–25. London: Institution of Mechanical Engineers.

Institution of Production Engineers. 1958. *Quality: Its Creation and Control*. London: Institution of Production Engineers.

Institution of Production Engineers. 1970. *Quality. Its Creation and Control in the Seventies*. London: Institute of Production Engineers.

Ishikawa, Kaoru. 1963a. "Quality Control in Japan (1958–1962)." *Reports of Statistical Application Research*, Union of Japanese Scientists and Engineers 10: 25–136.

———. 1963b. *Quality Emphasis in Japan's Postwar Trade*. Tokyo: Union of Japanese Scientists and Engineers.

———. 1969. "Education and Training of Quality Control in Japanese Industry." In *International Conference on Quality Control Proceedings 1969*, pp. 423–426. Tokyo: Japanese Union of Scientists and Engineers.

Ishiwara, T. 1966. "A Quality-Up Drive in the Watch Industry." *Industrial Quality Control* 22: 126, 134–137.

Ivancevich, J. M. 1972. "A Longitudinal Assessment of Management by Objectives." *Administrative Science Quarterly*, 17(1): 126–138.

———. 1974. "Changes in Performance in a Management by Objective Program" *Administrative Science Quarterly* 19(4): 563–574.

Jackson, Bradley G. 1996. "Re-engineering the Sense of Self: The Manager and the Management Guru." *Journal of Management Studies* 33(5): 571–590.

Jackson, T. 1997 "Survey—Management Consultancy: Growth and Revenues Seem to Be Unstoppable." *Financial Times* (Sept.): 19.

Jacoby, Sanford M. 1985. *Employing Bureaucracy: Managers, Unions, and the Transformation of Work in American Industry, 1900–1945*. New York: Columbia University Press.

Jarausch, Konrad H. 1990. *The Unfree Professions: German Lawyers, Teachers, and Engineers, 1900–1950*. New York: Oxford University Press.

Jepperson, Ronald L. 1991. "Institutions, Institutional Effects, and Institutionalization." In Paul J. DiMaggio and Walter W. Powell, eds., *The New Institutional-*

ism in Organizational Analysis, pp. 143–163. Chicago: University of Chicago Press.

Jones, Edgar. 1995. *True and Fair. A History of Price Waterhouse.* London: Hamish Hamilton.

Jorem, K. 1985. "Medarbeidersamtaler: Et Nyttig Verktøy." In K. Jorem, ed., *Sjefer i Utakt: Når Leder og Organisasjon ikke Går i Takt,* pp. 90–101. Oslo: Bedriftsøkonomens Forlag.

Judge, T. A., C. J. Thoresen, V. Pucik, and Welbourne, T. 1999. "Managerial Coping with Organizational Change: A Dispositional Perspective." *Journal of Applied Psychology* 84(1): 107–122.

Juran, J. M. 1990. *Handbuch der Qualitätsplanung.* Landsberg am Lech: Verlag Moderne Industrie.

Juran, J. R. 1988. *Juran on Planning for Quality.* New York: Free Press.

Kampa, H. 1996. "DGQ aktualisiert ihre Ausbildung." *Qualität und Zuverlässigkeit* 41: 138–140.

Kanter, Rosabeth Moss. 1983. *The Change Masters: Innovation for Productivity in the American Corporation.* New York: Simon & Schuster.

———. 1989. *When Giants Learn to Dance: Mastering the Challenge of Strategy, Management in Careers in the 1990s.* New York: Simon & Schuster.

Katz, H., and J. Keefe. 1993. "Training and Restructuring of Work in Large Unionized Settings." Center for Advanced Human Resource Studies Working Paper 93–19, Cornell University, Ithaca, NY.

Kennedy, C. 1994. *Managing with the Gurus.* London: Random House.

Kennedy Research Group (KRG). 1999. "Management Consulting Today: A Brief Overview." [www.kennedypub.com/mc/overview.html].

Kesner, Idalene F., and Sally Fowler. 1997. "When Consultants and Clients Clash." *Harvard Business Review* (Nov.–Dec.): 22–38.

Kieser, Alfred. 1997. "Myth and Rhetoric in Management Fashion." *Organization* 4(1): 49–74.

———. 1998. "Unternehmensberater—Händler in Problemen, Praktiken und Sinn." In H. Glaser, E. F. Schröder, and A. von Werder, eds., *Organisation im Wandel der Märkte. Erich Frese zum 60. Geburtstag,* pp. 191–225. Wiesbaden: Gabler.

———. 2002. "On Communication Barriers Between Management Science, Consultancies and Business Companies." In T. Clark and R. Fincham, eds., *Critical Consulting,* pp. 206–227. Oxford: Blackwell.

Kieser, Alfred., C. Hegele, and M. Klimmer. 1998. *Kommunikation im organisatorischen Wandel.* Stuttgart: Schäffer-Poeschel.

Kilian, H. J. 1984. "Das Prüfwesen als Teil der Qualitätssicherung im internationalen Maschinenbau." *DIN-Mitteilungen* 64: 74–75.

Kipping, Matthias. 1996. "The U.S. Influence on the Evolution of Management Consultancies in Britain, France, and Germany Since 1945." *Business and Economic History* 25(1): 112–123.

———. 1997. "Consultancies, Institutions and the Diffusion of Taylorism in Britain, Germany and France, 1920s to 1950s." *Business History* 39(4): 67–83.

———. 1999a. "American Management Consulting Companies in Western Europe, 1920 to 1990: Products, Reputation and Relationships." *Business History Review* 73(2): 190–220.

———. 1999b. "Creating Dependency: How Consultancies Market Their Services, 1920s to 1990s." Presented at the Business of Addiction workshop, University of Reading, Berkshire, U.K. (ec. 10–11).

Kipping, Matthias, and Thomas Armbrüster. 1999. "The Consultancy Field in Western Europe." Report to the European Union for the CEMP project, the Creation of European Management Practices, University of Reading, Department of Economics.

Kipping, Matthias, and Celeste Amorim. 1999. *Consultancies as Management Schools.* The University of Reading, Discussion Paper in Economics and Management, Series A, vol. 9, no. 409.

Kipping, Matthias, and Ove Bjarnar, eds. 1998. *The Americanisation of European Business. The Marshall Plan and the Transfer of US Management Models.* London: Routledge.

Kipping, Matthias, and Lars Engwall, eds. 2002. *Management Consulting: The Emergence and Dynamics of a Knowledge Industry.* Oxford: Oxford University Press.

Kirstein, H. 1989. "Deming in Deutschland?" *Qualität und Zuverlässigkeit* 34: 487–491.

Knoke, David, and Arne L. Kalleberg. 1994. "Job Training in U.S. Organizations." *American Sociological Review* 59: 4.

Knorr-Cetina, K. 1994. "Primitive Classification and Postmodernity: Towards a Sociological Notion of Fiction." *Theory, Culture and Society* 11: 1–22.

Kochan, T., and P. Osterman. 1991. *Human Resource Development and Utilization: Is There Too Little in the U.S.* Cambridge: Sloan School of Management, Massachusetts Institute of Technology.

Kocka, Jurgen. 1980. *White Collar Workers in America 1890–1940.* London: Sage.

Kogut, Bruce, and David Parkinson. 1993. "The Diffusion of American Organizing

Principles to Europe." In Bruce Kogut, ed., *Country Competitiveness*, pp. 179–202. Oxford: Oxford University Press.

Konsultguiden. 2002. http://db.afv.se/afv/owa/w3?page=Kg Rankning Bransch&n=Br&v=KG MAN 2002-04-23.

Kotler, P. 1994. *Marketing Management*. Englewood Cliffs, N.J.: Prentice-Hall.

Koyanagi, K. 1952. *Statistical Quality Control in Japanese Industry*. Tokyo: Japanese Union of Scientists and Engineers.

Kranakis, Eda. 1997. *Constructing a Bridge: An Exploration of Engineering Culture*. Cambridge, Mass.: MIT Press.

Kubr, Milan. 1993. *How to Select and Use Consultants: A Client's Guide*. Management Development Series, no. 31. Geneva: International Labour Organisation.

Kusakabe, Hisashi. 1969. "Outline of the Japanese Inspection System of Goods for Export." In *International Conference on Quality Control Proceedings 1969*. Tokyo: Japanese Union of Scientists and Engineers, pp. 719–722.

Landes, David S. 1986. *The Unbound Prometheus, Technological Change and Industrial Development in Western Europe from 1750 to the Present*. Cambridge: Cambridge University Press. First published in 1969.

Landes, W. S. 1955. "Report on Visit to Canon Camera Co. Ltd." In file headed "W. S. Landes Reports," box 14, 1266, National Archives, Washington, D.C.

Larson, Magali S. 1977. *The Rise of Professionalism: A Sociological Analysis*. Berkeley: University of California Press.

Larsson, R., and Bowen, D. E. 1989. "Organization and Customer: Managing Design and Coordination of Services." *Academy of Management Review* 14(2): 213–233.

Lash, Scott. 1989. "Coercion as Ideology—The German Case." In N. Abercrombie, et al., eds., *Dominant Ideologies*, pp. 65–97. London: Routledge.

Latour, Bruno. 1986. "The Powers of Association." In John Law and Kegan Paul, ed., *Power, Action and Belief*, pp. 264–280. London: Routledge.

Lave, Jean, and Etienne Wenger. 1991. *Situated Learning: Legitimate Peripheral Participation*. Cambridge: Cambridge University Press.

Lawler, E. E., S. A. Mohrman, and G. E. Ledford. 1992. *Employee Involvement and Total Quality Management*. San Francisco: Jossey-Bass.

Lawrence, Peter. 1980. *Managers and Management in West Germany*. New York: St. Martin's Press.

———. 1992. "Engineering and Management in West Germany: A Study in Consistency?" In Gloria Lee and Chris Smith, eds., *Engineers and Management—International Comparisons*, pp. 72–99. London: Routledge.

———. 1996. *Management in the USA*. London: Sage.

Lawrence, P. R., and Lorsch, J. W. 1967. *Organization and Environment: Managing Differentiation and Integration.* Boston: Harvard University Press.

Layton, E. T. 1986. *The Revolt of the Engineers.* Baltimore: John Hopkins University Press. First published in 1971.

Lazonick, William. 1991. "Organizational Capabilities in American Industry." In Howard F. Gospel, ed., *Industrial Training and Technological Innovation,* pp. 213–234. London: Routledge.

Lecuyer, C. 1995. "MIT, Progressive Reform, and 'Industrial Service,' 1890–1920." *Historical Studies in the Physical and Biological Sciences,* 0026: 35–88.

Lee, Gloria and Chris Smith. 1992. "Engineers and Management in Comparative Perspectives." In Gloria Lee and Chris Smith, eds., *Engineers and Management—International Comparisons.* London: Routledge.

Legge, K. 1995. *Human Resource Management: Rhetorics and Realities.* London: Macmillian.

Lerdell, David, and Kerstin Sahlin-Andersson. 1997. *Att lära över gränser. En studie av OECDs förvaltningspolitiska samarbete.* Report to the Swedish Public Management Commission, Stockholm, SOU 1997: 33.

Lerner, F. 1988. "Geschichte der Qualitätssicherung." In W. Masing, ed., *Handbuch der Qualitätssicherung,* pp. 19–32. München: Hanser.

Lewin, A. Y., and Minton, J. W. 1986. "Determining Organizational Effectiveness: Another Look, and an Agenda for Research." *Management Science* 32: 514–538.

Levitt, T. 1981. "Marketing Intangible Products and Product Intangibles." *Harvard Business Review* 59 (May–June): 94–102.

Li, Chen-Nan. 1928. "A Summer in the Ford Works." *Personnel Journal,* June.

Lillrank, Paul, 1995. "The Transfer of Management Innovations from Japan." *Organization Studies* 16(6): 971–989.

Lindvall, Jan. 1998. "The Creation of Management Practice: A Literature Review." CEMP Report no. 1, Uppsala University.

Lindvall, Jan, and Cecilia Pahlberg. 1999. "SAP/R3 as Carrier of Management Knowledge." Paper presented at the SCANCOR workshop on Carriers of Management Knowledge, Stanford University, Stanford, Calif., Sept. 16–17.

Littler, Craig R. 1982. *The Development of the Labor Process in Capitalist Societies. A Comparative Study of the Transformation of Work Organization in Britain, Japan and the USA.* London: Heinemann.

Locke, E. A. 1978. "The Ubiquity of the Technique of Goal Setting in Theories of and Approaches to Employee Motivation." *Academy of Management Review* 3(3): 594–601.

Locke, Robert R. 1984. *The End of the Practical Man. Entrepreneurship and*

Higher Education in Germany, France and Great Britain 1880–1940. Greenwich, Conn.: JAI Press.

———. 1989. *Management and Higher Education since 1940. The Influence of America and Japan on West Germany, Great Britain and France*. Cambridge: Cambridge University Press.

———. 1996. *The Collapse of the American Management Mystique*. Oxford: Oxford University Press.

Lockyer, K. G., J. S. Oakland, and C. H. Duprey. 1982. "Quality Control in British Manufacturing Industry: A Study." *Quality Assurance* 8: 39–44.

Loh, L., and N. Venkatraman. 1992. "Diffusion of Information Technology Outsourcing: Influence Sources and the Kodak Effect." *Information Systems Research* 3: 334–358.

Ludwig, Karl-Heinz, and Wolfgang König. 1981. *Technik, Ingenieure, und Gesellschaft: Geschichte des Vereins Deutscher Ingenieure, 1856–1981*. Düsseldorf: VDI-Verlag.

Luhmann, N. 1980. *Gesellschaftsstruktur und Semantik. Studien zur Wissenssoziologie der modernen Gesellschaft*. Frankfurt/M.: Suhrkamp.

———. 1987. *Soziologische Aufklärung 4. Beiträge zur funktionalen Differenzierung der Gesellschaft*. Opladen: Westdeutscher Verlag.

Lundgreen, Peter. 1983. "Differentiation in German Higher Education." *The Transformation of Higher Learning 1860–1930*. Stuttgart: Klett-Cotta.

———. 1990. "Engineering Education in Europe and the USA, 1750–1930: The Rise to Dominance of School Culture and the Engineering Professions." *Annals of Science* 47: 33–75.

———. 1994. "Die Ausbildung von Ingenieuren an Fachsculen und Hochschulen in Deutschland, 1770–1990" In Peter Lundgreen and André Grelon, eds., *Ingenieure in Deutschland 1770–1990*, pp. 13–78. Frankfurt: Campus Verlag.

Lundgreen, Peter, and André Grelon, eds. 1994. *Ingenieure in Deutschland 1770–1990*. Frankfurt: Campus Verlag.

Luthans, F. 1976. "How to Apply MBO." *Public Personnel Management* 5(2): 83–87.

Lynch, Lisa. 1992. "Using Human Resources in Skill Formation: The Role of Training." In Thomas Kachan and Michael Useem, eds., *Transforming Organizations*. New York: Oxford University Press.

Lyttle, J. 1991. "Pandora's Music Box." *Daily Telegraph* 1 (Aug.): 15.

Macdonald, Keith M. 2000. "A Professional Project—The Case of Accountancy." In John R. Edwards, ed., *The History of Accounting* Vol. IV: 36–59. London: Routledge.

MacDuffie, John Paul, and Thomas A. Kochan. 1995. "Do U.S. Firms Invest Less in Human Resources? Training in the World Auto Industry." *Industrial Relations* 34: 147–68.

Machan, Dyan. 1988."Sigmund Freud Meets Henry Ford." *Forbes*, 141(13) (June 13): 120, 122.

Maclagan, P. 1989. "Methodolgy Choice and Consulting Ethics in Management Science." *Omega* 17: 397–407.

Malinowski, B. 1955. *Magic, Science, and Religion.* New York: Anchor.

Malorny, C., and K. Kassebohm. 1994. *Brennpunkt TQM: Rechtliche Anforderungen, Führung und Organisation, Auditierung und Zertifizierung nach DIN ISO 9000ff.* Stuttgart: Schäffer-Poeschel.

Manders, C.R.S. 1964. *Export Inspection Systems for Japan.* London: Department of Scientific and Industrial Research.

Manegold, Karl-Heinz. 1978. "Technology Academised." In Wolfgang Krohn, Edwin Layton, Jr., and Peter Weingart, eds., *The Dynamics of Science and Technology: Social Values, Technical Norms, and Scientific Criteria in the Development of Knowledge*, pp. 137–158. Doordrecht, Holland: Reidel.

Mann, Charles Riborg. 1918. "A Study of Engineering Education." *The Carnegie Foundation for the Advancement of Teaching*, bull. no. 11.

Mann, N. R. 1989. *The Keys to Excellence—The Story of the Deming Philosophy.* Los Angeles: Mercury.

Mansell, R. 1977. "A Comprehensive Bibliography on Management by Objectives." *Exchange Bibliography*, no. 1400. Monticello, Ill.: Council of Planning Librarians.

March, James G. 1991. "Organizational Consultants and Organizational Research." *Journal of Applied Communication Research* 19: 20–31.

———. 1999. "A Learning Perspective on the Network Dynamics of Institutional Integration." In Morten Egeberg and Per Laegreid, eds., *Organizing Political Institutions*, pp. 129–155. Oslo: Scandinavian University Press.

March, James G., and Johan P. Olsen. 1995. *Democratic Governance.* New York: Free Press.

March, James G., and H. A. Simon. 1958. *Organizations.* New York: Wiley.

March, James G., and R. I. Sutton. 1997. "Organizational Performance as a Dependent Variable." *Organization Science* 8(6): 698–706.

Marcusen, Martin. 2000. *Ideas and Elites: The Social Construction of Economic and Monetary Union.* Aalborg, Denmark: Aalborg University Press.

Masing, W. 1978. "Die Entwicklung der Qualitätssicherung seit Ende der zwanziger Jahre." *Qualität und Zuverlässigkeit* 23: 57–59.

———. 1996. "40 Jahre QZ." *Qualität und Zuverlässigkeit* 41: 1090.

Matthews, Derek, Malcolm Anderson, and Edwards John Richard. 1998. *The*

Priesthood of Industry. The Rise of the Professional Accountant in British Management. Oxford: Oxford University Press.

Mayo, Elton. 1945. *The Social Problems of an Industrial Civilization.* Cambridge, Mass.: Harvard University Press.

Mazza, Carmelo. 1998. "The Popularization of Business Knowledge Diffusion. From Academic Knowledge to Popular Culture?" In J. L. Alvarez, ed., *The Diffusion and Consumption of Business Knowledge.* London: Macmillan.

Mazza, Carmelo, and José-Luis Alvarez. 2000. "Haute Couture and Prêt-à-Porter. The Popular Press and the Diffusion of Management Practices." *Organization Studies* 21(3): 567–588.

Mazza, Carmelo, Kerstin Sahlin-Andersson, and Jesper Strandgaard Pedersen. 1998. "MBA: European Constructions of an American Model." SCORE Reports no. 4. Stockholm University.

McCarthy, J. D., and M. N. Zald. 1987. "Resource Mobilization and Social Movements: A Partial Theory." In M. N. Zald, and J. D. McCarthy, eds., *Social Movements in an Organizational Society: Collected Essays,* pp. 15–47. New Brunswick, N.J.: Transaction Books.

McCarthy, J. E. 1994. *Basic Marketing: A Managerial Approach.* Homewood, Ill.: Richard D. Irwin.

McClelland, Charles E. 1980. *State, Society and University in Germany 1700–1914.* Cambridge: Cambridge University Press.

McGivern, James G. 1960. *The First Hundred Years of Engineering Education in the United States (1807–1907).* Spokane, Wash.

McGregor, Douglas. 1960. *The Human Side of Enterprise.* New York: McGraw-Hill.

McKenna, Christopher D. 1995. "The Origins of Modern Management Consulting." *Business and Economic History* 25(1): 51–58.

———. 1997. "The American Challenge: McKinsey & Company's Role in the Transfer of Decentralization to Europe, 1957–1975." *Academy of Management Best Paper Proceedings,* pp. 226–231.

———. 1999. "Selling Corporate Culture: Codifying and Commodifying Professionalism at McKinsey and Company, 1940–1980." Working paper, Department of History, Johns Hopkins University, Baltimore, Md.

McKenzie, R. M., and D. S. Pugh. 1957. "Some Human Aspects of Inspection." *Institution of Production Engineers Journal* 36: 378–387.

Mead, George H. 1934. *Mind, Self and Society.* Chicago: Chicago University Press.

Meiksins, Peter. 1988. "The 'Revolt of the Engineers' reconsidered." *Technology and Culture,* 29(2): 219–246.

Meiksins, Peter, and Chris Smith. 1996. "A Comparative Perspective on the Organization of Technical Work." In Peter F. Meiksins and Chris Smith, eds.,

Engineering Labour: Technical Workers in Comparative Perspective. London: Verso.

Meister, Jeanne C. 1997. *Corporate Universities: Lessons in Building a World-Class Work Force.* McGraw-Hill.

Mendel, Peter J. 2001. "Global Models of Organization: International Management Standards, Reforms, and Movements." Dissertation, Dept. of Sociology, Stanford University, Stanford, Calif.

Meyer, H. H., E. Kay, and J. French. 1965. "Split Roles in Performance Appraisal." *Harvard Business Review* 43: 123–129.

Meyer, John W. 1992. "Conclusion: Institutionalization and the Rationality of Formal Organizational Structure." In John W. Meyer and W. Richard Scott, eds., *Organizational Environments: Ritual and Rationality.* Newberry Park, Calif.: Sage.

———. 1994. "Rationalized Environments." In W. R. Scott and J.W. Meyer, ed., *Institutional Environments and Organizations: Structural Complexity and Individualism,* pp. 28–54, 228–254. London: Sage.

———. 1996. "Otherhood: The Promulgation and Transmission of Ideas in the Modern Organizational Environment." In Barbara Czarniawska and Guje Sévon, eds., *Translating Organizational Change,* pp. 241–252. Berlin—New York: de Gruyter.

———. 1997. "Cultural Conditions of Standardization." Presented at the SCAN-COR/SCORE seminar on Standardization of Organizational Forms, Arild, Sweden, Sept.

Meyer, John W., John Boli, and George M. Thomas. 1987. "Ontology and Rationalization in the Western Account." In G. M. Thomas, J. W. Meyer, F. O. Ramirez, and J. Boli, ed., *Institutional Structure: Constituting State, Society and the Individual,* pp. 12–37. Newbury Park, Calif.: Sage.

Meyer, John, John Boli, George Thomas, and Francisco Ramirez. 1997. "World Society and the Nation-State." *American Journal of Sociology,* 103(1) (July): 144–181.

Meyer, John W., and Ronald L. Jepperson. 2000. "The 'Actors' of Modern Society: The Cultural Construction of Social Agency." *Sociological Theory* 18: 100–120.

Meyer, John W., and Brian Rowan. 1977. "Institutionalized Organizations: Formal Structure as Myth and Ceremony." *American Journal of Sociology* 83: 364–385.

Micklethwait, J., and Woolridge, A. 1996. *The Witch Doctors: What the Management Gurus Are Saying, Why It Matters and How to Make Sense of It.* London: Heineman.

Mikkelsen, A. 1996. *Medarbeidersamtaler og Læring i Organisasjoner*. Oslo: Cappelen Akademiske Forlag.

Millar, Robert. 1963. *The Affluent Sheep*. London: Longmans.

Miller, G. A. 1956. "The Managerial Number Seven, Plus or Minus Two: Some Limits on Our Capacity for Processing Information." *Psychological Review* 63: 81–97.

Miller, Vincent A. 1987. "The History of Training." In Robert L. Craig, ed., *Training & Development Handbook: A Guide to Human Resource Development*. 3rd Edition. New York: McGraw-Hill.

Mills, P. K., and J. H. Morris. 1986. "Clients as 'Partial' Employees of Service Organizations: Role Development in Client Participation." *Academy of Management Review* 11(4): 726–735.

Mitchell, V.-W. 1994. "Problems and Risks in the Purchasing of Consultancy Services." Service Industries Journal 14: 315–339.

Miura, Shin. 1964. "The Progress of Quality Control in Japan." *Symposium on Quality Control. Documents and Proceedings*, pp. 106–153. Tokyo: Asian Productivity Organisation.

Mizuno, S. 1969. "Company-wide Quality Control Activities in Japan." *International Conference on Quality Control Proceedings 1969*, pp. 423–426. Tokyo: Japanese Union of Scientists and Engineers.

Monahan, Susanne C., John Meyer, and W. Richard Scott. 1994. "Employee Training: The Expansion of Organizational Citizenship." In W. Richard Scott and John Meyer, eds., *Institutional Environments and Organizations: Structural Complexity and Individualism*, pp. 255–271. Newbury Park, Calif.: Sage.

Montgomery, John. 1965. *The Fifties*. London: Allen and Unwin.

Moore, Gerald. 1984. *The Politics of Management Consulting*. New York: Praeger.

Morgan, C., and Murgatroyd, S. 1994. *Total Quality Management in the Public Sector*. Celtic Court, Buckingham: Open University Press.

Morrison, S. J. 1981. "A Comparative Quality Assurance Study of British, European, American and Japanese Manufactured Products. The Pilot Study Phase." Unpublished report. University of Hull, U.K.

Motoring Which (October 1968): 144–145.

Müller, Detlef, Fritz Ringer, and Brian Simon. 1987. *The Rise of the Modern Educational System*. Cambridge: Cambridge University Press.

Müller-Rossow, K. 1972. "Über die Stellung der Qualitätssicherung in einem Betrieb." *Qualität und Zuverlässigkeit* 17: 226–228.

National Industrial Conference Board. 1949. *Quality Control. Methods and Company Plans*. New York: National Industrial Conference Board.

National Productivity Council. 1963. *Quality Control in Japan, USA and Britain*. New Delhi: National Productivity Council.

Nettl, J. P. 1968. "The State as a Conceptual Variable." *World Politics* 20(4): 559–592.

Neukom, John. 1975. *McKinsey Memoirs: A Personal Perspective.* (Published privately.)

Nevins, Mark D. 1998. "Teaching to Learn and Learning to Teach: Notes Towards Building a University in a Management Consulting Firm." *Career Development International* 3(5).

New Society, 18 March 1965.

Nichols, T., and H. Beynon. 1977. *Living with Capitalism. Class Relations in the Modern Factory.* London: Routledge & Keegan Paul.

Nietzsche, F. 1912. *Der Wille zur Macht.* Leipzig: Kröner.

Nishibori, Eizaburo. 1969. "My 20 Years' Experience and Conclusion in Introducing QC in Japanese Industry." In *International Conference on Quality Control Proceedings 1969.* Tokyo: Japanese Union of Scientists and Engineers: 849–852.

Nixon, Frank. 1960. "Control of Product Quality" *F.B.I. Review* no. 116: 43–46.

———. 1962. "Management and Quality Costs." *Quality* 6: 22–25.

———. 1963. "Organisation, Man and Reliability." *Quality Engineer* 27: 50–8.

———. 1964a. "Spending to Save. Product Quality and Reliability." *Times Review of Industry and Trade* 2: 18.

———. 1964b. "Quality Reporting, Quality Auditing, and Quality Achievements in European Countries." *Proceedings of the 8th European Conference on Quality Control*, Baden-Baden, pp. 51–63.

———. 1971. *Managing to Achieve Quality and Reliability.* London: McGraw-Hill.

Noble, David F. 1977. *America by Design*, p. 49. New York: Oxford University Press.

Nonaka, Ikujiro. 1994. "A Dynamic Theory of Organizational Knowledge Creation." *Organization Science* 5(1): 14–37.

———. 1995. "The Recent History of Manufacturing for Quality in Japan." In J. M. Juran, ed., *A History of Manufacturing for Quality*, pp. 518–541. Milwaukee, Wisc.: Quality Press.

Nozick, R. (1974). *Anarchy, State, and Utopia.* New York: Basic Books.

Oakland, J. S. 1986. "Research into Quality Control in British Manufacturing Industry." *Business Graduate Journal* 16: 30–34.

Observer, 27 September 1998.

OECD (Organization for Economic Cooperation and Development). 1995. *Governance in Transition. Public Management Reforms in OECD Countries.* Paris: OECD.

Oliver, C. 1991. "Strategic Responses to Institutional Processes." *Academy of Management Review* 16: 145–179.

Olson, Olov, James Guthrie, and Christopher Humphrey, eds. 1998. *Global Warning: Debating International Developments in New Public Financial Management.* Oslo: Cappelen Akademisk Forlag.

Olsten Corporation. 1994. *Skills for Success.* Melville, N.Y.: Olsten Corporation.

Olzak, S. 1992. *Dynamics of Ethnic Competition and Conflict.* Stanford, Calif.: Stanford University Press.

Olzak, S., and E. West. 1991. "Ethnic Conflicts and the Rise and Fall of Ethnic Newspapers." *American Sociological Review* 56: 458–474.

Orlemann, J. 1995. "DIN ISO 9000ff. in der Wirtschaft—eine Untersuchung in der Technologieregion Karlsruhe." IHK-UTB. Karlsruhe: Industrie & Handelskammer.

O'Shea, James, and Charles Madigan. 1997. *Dangerous Company. Management Consultants and the Businesses They Save and Ruin.* New York: Times Books.

Ott, Ellis R. 1953. "Statistical Quality Control." *Ten Years Progress in Management,* pp: 660–663. New York: American Society of Mechanical Engineers.

Parsons, Talcott. 1951. *The Social System.* Westerville, Ohio: Glencoe.

———. 1956. "Suggestions for a Sociological Approach to a Theory of Organizations." *Administrative Science Quarterly* 1: 63–85.

———. 1991. "A Tentative Outline of American Values." In Roland Robertson and Bryan Turner, eds., *Talcott Parsons—Theorist of Modernity.* London: Sage.

Pastor, J. C., J. Meindl, and R. Hunt. 1998. "The Quality Virus: Inter-Organizational Contagion in the Adoption of Total Quality Management." In J. L. Alvarez, ed., *The Diffusion and Consumption of Business Knowledge.* London: Macmillan.

Patterson, P. G. 1995. "Choice Criteria in Final Selection of a Management Consultancy Service." *Journal of Professional Services Marketing* 11 (2): 177–188.

Perrow, Charles. 1986. *Complex Organizations: A Critical Essay.* 3rd ed. Random House: New York.

Personnel Journal. 1928–1996.

Perucci, Robert, and Joel E. Gerstl. 1969. *The Engineers and the Social System.* New York: Wiley.

Peters, Anja, and Susanne Tapper. 1998. "'När två blir en.' En fallstudie av fusioner inom revisionsbranschen." Department of Business Studies, Uppsala University.

Peters, Thomas J., and Robert H. Waterman Jr. 1982. *In Search of Excellence: Lessons from American Best-Run Companies.* New York: Harper & Row.

Petrick, K. 1995. "Das Konzept der Zusammenführung von Qualitätsmanagement und Umweltmanagement." In K. Petrick and R. Eggert, eds., *Umwelt-und*

Qualitätsmanagementsysteme—Eine gemeinsame Herausforderung, pp. 1–52. München: Hanser.

Pfeffer, Jeffrey. 1994. *Competitive Advantage Through People: Unleashing the Power of the Work Force.* Harvard Business School Press: Boston.

Pfeifer, T. 1986. "Forschung und Entwicklung zur methodischen und wirtschaftlichen Verbesserung der Qualitätssicherung." *Qualität und Zuverlässigkeit* 31: 57–58.

Pfeifer, T., J. Heine, D. Köppe, M. Lücker, and G. Orendi. 1991a. "Länderspiegel Qualitätssicherung." *Qualität und Zuverlässigkeit* 36: 135–140.

————. 1991b. "Länderspiegel Qualitätssicherung." *Qualität und Zuverlässigkeit* 36: 201–206.

Philgren, G., and A. Svenson. 1989. *Målstyrning: 90–talets Ledningsform för Offentlig Verksamhet.* Stockholm: Liber.

Pinault, Lewis. 2000. *Consulting Demons. Inside the Unscrupulous World of Global Corporate Consulting.* New York: HarperBusiness.

Political and Economic Planning. 1955. "The British Standards Institution." *Planning* 21: 101–119.

Pollitt, Christoffer. 1990. *Managerialism and the Public Services.* Oxford: Basil Blackwell.

Powell, Walter W. 1991. "Expanding the Scope of Institutional Analysis." In Walter W. Powell and Paul J. DiMaggio, eds., *The New Institutionalism in Organizational Analysis*, pp. 183–203. Chicago: University of Chicago Press.

Powell, Walter W., and Paul J. DiMaggio, eds. 1991. *The New Institutionalism in Organizational Analysis.* Chicago: University of Chicago Press.

Power, Michael. 1994. "The Audit Society." In Anthony G. Hopwood and Peter Miller, eds., *Accounting as Social and Institutional Practice*, pp. 299–316. Cambridge: Cambridge University Press.

Power, Michael. 1997. *The Audit Society: Rituals of Verification.* Oxford: Oxford University Press.

Previts, Gary, and Barbara Merino. 1979. *A History of Accounting in America: An Historical Interpretation of the Cultural Significance of Accounting.* New York: Wiley.

Prichard, Craig. 1996. "A Commentary and Response on Blackler: Knowledge, Knowledge Work and Organizations: An Overview and Interpretation." *Organization Studies* 17(5): 857–860.

Prusak, Laurence, ed. 1997. *Knowledge in Organizations.* Boston: Butterworth-Heinemann.

Public Histoire. 1991. *L'identité d'un groupe. Lafarge-Coppée 1947–1989.* Paris: Lafarge-Coppée.

Pugh, Peter. 1988. *The History of Blue Circle*. Cambridge: Cambridge Business Press.

Quality Control Specialist Study Team. 1958. *Quality Control in Japan*. Tokyo: Japan Productivity Center.

Qualität und Zuverlässigkeit. 1989. "Lehrstuhl Qualitätssicherung an der TU Berlin eingerichtet." *Qualität und Zuverlässigkeit* 34: 64.

———. 1992. "The European Quality Award—Ein Qualitätspreis für Europa." *Qualität und Zuverlässigkeit* 37: 66.

———. 1995. "Gesellschaft für Qualitätswissenschaft gegründet." *Qualität und Zuverlässigkeit* 40: 492.

Rae, John B. 1955. "Engineering Education as Preparation for Management: A Study of MIT Alumni" *Business History Review* 29: 64–74.

Rafts, B. G. 1964. "Quality and Reliability." *Quality Engineer* 28: 81–89.

Ramsay, H. 1996. "Managing Sceptically: A Critique of Organizational Fashion." In S. Clegg and G. Palmer, eds., *The Politics of Management Knowledge*. London: Sage.

Rassam, C., and D. Oates. 1991. *Management Consultancy: The Inside Story*. London: Mercury.

Raube, S. A., and associates. 1947. *Personnel Activities in American Business*. National Industrial Conference Board Studies in Personnel Policy, no. 86. New York: National Industrial Conference Board.

Reger, R., L. Gustafson, S. M. DeMarie, and J. V. Mullane. 1994. "Reframing the Organization: Why Implementing Total Quality Is Easier Said than Done." *Academy of Management Review* 19: 565–584.

Reich, Robert. 1983. *The Next American Frontier*. New York: Times Books.

Reinius, Ulla. 1998. *KPMG Bohlins 75 år*. Stockholm: Informationsförlaget.

Research Institute for Consumer Affairs. 1965. *Car Defects*. London: Research Institute for Consumer Affairs.

Revisorn. 1925. 11: 166–170.

"Revisorns oberoende." 1992. *Revisorn en antologi. Artiklar publicerade 1923–1993*, pp. 92–99. Stockholm: Föreningen Auktoriserade Revisorer.

Reynolds News. 1961. 30 July.

Rheingold, Nathan. 1987. "Graduate School and Doctoral Degree: European Models and American Realities." In Nathan Reingold and Marc Rothenberg, eds., *Scientific Colonialism, a Cross-Cultural Comparison*. Washington, D.C.: Smithsonian.

Richardson, G. C. 1954. "Customers' Inspection of Engineering Products and Its Value to Industry." *Engineering Inspection* 18: 50–51.

Rieble-Auborg, Sabine. 1996. "Institutional Arrangements of Germany's Vocational Eduation System—What Are the Policy Implications for the US?" *International Journal of Comparative Sociology* 37(1–2): 174.

Ringer, Fritz K. 1992. *Fields of Knowledge*. Cambridge: Cambridge University Press.

Robertson, Andrew. 1974. *The Lessons of Failure*. London: Macdonald.

Rogers, Everett M. 1983. *Diffusion of Innovations*. New York: Free Press.

Rogers, K. S. 1999. "Masters of Symbol: My Travels in Thought and Work Life in the Czech Republic." In R. A. Goodman, ed., *Modern Organizations and Emerging Conundrums*. New York: Lexington Books.

Röhrs, Hermann. 1995. *The Classical German Concept of the University and Its Influence on Higher Education in the United States*. Hermann Lang: Europäischer Verlag der Wissenschaften.

Rohwer, Götz. 1999. "Transition Data Analysis (TDA) 6.2." Working Papers. Institut für Empirische und Angewandte Soziologie, University of Bremen, Germany.

Rose, Peter. 1987. *The Changing Structure of American Banking*. New York: Columbia University Press.

Ross, S. A. 1973. "The Economic Theory of Agency: The Principal's Problem." *American Economic Review* 63: 134–139.

Rothstein, William G. 1969. "Engineers and the Functionalist Model of Professions." In Robert Perucci and Joel E. Gerstl, eds., *The Engineers and the Social System*. New York: Wiley.

Rotter, J. B. 1966. "Generalized Expectancies for Internal versus External Control of Reinforcement." *Psychological Monographs* 80(1): 609–639.

Røvik, Kjell Arne. 1992. *Den "Syke" Stat: Myter og Moter i Omstillingsarbeidet*. Oslo: Universitetsforlaget.

———. 1996. "Deinstitutionalization and the Logic of Fashion." In Barbara Czarnaiwska and Guje Sevón, eds., *Translating Organizational Change*, pp. 139–172. Berlin: de Gruyter.

———. 1998. *Moderne organisasjoner. Trender i organisasjonstenkingen ved tusenårsskiftet*. Bergen: Fagbokforlaget.

Røvik, Kjell Arne, I. Almestad, and A. Røkenes. 1995. *Tidsspille eller Forbedring: Innføring av Målstyring og Rutineforbedring ved Sosialkontorene*. no. 95/7. Oslo: Norsk Institutt for By- og Regionforskning.

Rubinson, Richard. 1987. "Class Formation, Politics and Institutions: Schooling in the United States." *American Journal of Sociology* 92: 519–548.

Rudolph, Frederick. 1990. *The American College and University: A History*. New York: Knopf. First published in 1962.

Ruef, Martin. 1999. "Social Psychological Profiles of MBA Alumni." Unpublished Technical Report. Stanford, Calif.: Stanford Graduate School of Business.

Ruef, Martin, and W. Richard Scott. 1998. "A Multidimensional Model of Organizational Legitimacy: Hospital Survival in Changing Institutional Regimes." *Administrative Science Quarterly* 43: 877–904.

Rupert, J. "What on Earth's Going Wrong?" *Independent*, March 14, 1998.

Rüschemeyer, D. 1985. "Spencer und Durkheim über Arbeitsteilung und Differenzierung: Kontinuität oder Bruch?" In N. Luhmann, ed., *Soziale Differenzierung. Zur Geschichte einer Idee*, pp. 163–180. Opladen: Westdeutscher Verlag.

Saatweber, J. 1994. "Inhalt und Zielsetzung von Qualitätsmanagementsystemen gemäß den Normen DIN ISO 9000 bis 9004." In B. Stauss, ed., *Qualitätsmanagement und Zertifizierung. Von DIN ISO 9000 zum Total Quality Management*, pp. 63–91. Wiesbaden: Gabler.

Sahlin-Andersson, Kerstin. 1992. "The Social Construction of Projects." *Scandinavian Housing and Planning Research* 9: 65–78.

———. 1996. "Imitating by Editing Success: The Construction of Organizational Fields." In Barbara Czarniawska and Guje Sevón, eds., Translating Organizational Change, pp. 69–92. Berlin: DeGruyter.

———. 2000. "Arenas as Standardizers." In Nils Brunsson, Bengt Jacobsson, and associates, *A World of Standards*, pp. 100–113. Oxford: Oxford University Press.

———. 2001. "National, International and Transnational Constructions of New Public Management." In Tom Christensen and Per Laegreid, eds., *New Public Management: The Transformation of Ideas and Practice*, pp. 43–72. Ashgate: Aldershot.

Sahlin-Andersson, Kerstin, and Tina Hedmo. 2000. "Från Spridning till Reglering: MBA-modellers utbredning och utveckling i Europa." *Nordiske Organisasjonsstudier* 2(1): 9–33.

Saint-Martin, Denis. 2000. *Building the New Managerialist State: Consultants and the Politics of Bureaucratic Reform in Britain, Canada and France*. Oxford: Oxford University Press.

Sandström, Jan. 1980. "Revisorns lagliga skyldigheter och rättigheter—några synpunkter." *Revisorn en antologi. Artiklar publicerede 1923–1993*, pp. 398–405. Stockholm: Föreningen Auktoriserade Revisorer.

Sarvary, M. 1999. "Knowledge Management and Competition in the Consulting Industry." *California Management Review* 41(2): 95–107.

Sasaki, Satoshi. 1995. "The Emergence of the Productivity Improvement Movement in Postwar Japan and Japanese Productivity Missions Overseas." *Japanese Yearbook on Business History* 12: 39–71.

Sattler, E. 1972. "Gemeinschaftsarbeit in der Deutschen Gesellschaft für Qualität." *Qualität und Zuverlässigkeit* 17: 187–189.

Sauer, M. 1987. "Normung im neuen Konzept der EG-Kommission." *DIN-Mitteilungen* 66: 600–603.

Schleh, E. C. 1953. "Make Your Executive Merit Rating Realistic." *Personnel* 29: 480–484.

———. 1955. *Successful Executive Action.* New Jersey: Englewood Cliffs.

Schofer, Evan. 1999. "Science Associations in the International Sphere, 1875–1990." In J. Boli and G. Thomas, eds., *Constructuring World Culture*, pp. 249–266. Stanford, Calif.: Stanford University Press.

Schön, Lennart. 2000. *En modern svensk ekonomisk historia. Tillväxt och omvandling under två sekel.* Stockholm: SNS Förlag.

Schuster, F. E., and A. F. Kindall. 1974. "Management by Objectives: Where We Stand Today. A Survey of the Fortune 500." *Human Resource Management* 13(1): 8–11.

Scott, W. Richard. 1995. *Institutions and Organizations.* Thousand Oaks, Calif.: Sage.

———. 1998. *Organizations: Rational, Natural, and Open Systems.* 4th ed. Englewood Cliffs, N.J.: Prentice Hall.

Scott, W. Richard, and S. Christensen, eds. 1995. *The Institutional Construction of Organizations.* Thousand Oaks, Calif.: Sage.

Scott, W. Richard, and John Meyer. 1988. "Environmental Linkages and Organizational Complexity: Public and Private Schools." In H. Levin and T. James, eds., *Comparing Public and Private Schools*, pp. 128–153. New York: Falmer Press.

———. 1991. "The Rise of Training Programs in Firms and Agencies: An Institutional Perspective." In Barry M. Staw and L. L. Cummings, eds., *Research in Organization Behavior*, 13: 297–326. Greenwich, Conn.: JAI.

———. 1994. "Developments in Institutional Theory." In W. Richard Scott and John W. Meyer, eds., *Institutional Environments and Organizations: Structural Complexity and Individualism*, pp. 1–8. Thousand Oaks, Calif.: Sage.

Scott, W. Richard, Martin Ruef, Peter J. Mendel, and Carol A. Caronna. 2000. *Institutional Change and Healthcare Organizations: From Professional Dominance to Managed Care.* Chicago: University of Chicago Press.

Selchert, M. 1997. *Organisationsstrukturen und Professionalität. Formen und Funktionen professioneller In-house Dienstleistungen.* Hamburg: Dr. Kovac.

Servan-Schreiber, Jean-Jacques. 1967. *Le défi américain.* Paris: Seuil.

Sevón, Guje. 1996. "Organizational Imitation in Identity Transformation." In Barbara Czarniawska and Guje Sevón, eds., *Translating Organizational Change*, pp. 49–67. Berlin—New York: de Gruyter.

Shapiro, Eileen C., Robert G. Eccles, and Trina L. Soske. 1993. "Consulting: Has the Solution Become Part of the Problem?" *Sloan Management Review* (Summer), 89–95.

Sharma, A. 1997. "Professional as Agent: Knowledge Asymmetry in Agency Exchange." *Academy of Management Review* 22: 758–798.

Shay, Philip. 1966. *Ethics and Professional Conduct in Management Consulting.* New York: ACME.

Shelley, Kristina. 1997. "A Portrait of the M.B.A." *Occupational Outlook Quarterly* 41: 26–33.

Shenhav, Yehouda. 1995. "From Chaos to Systems: The Engineering Foundations of Organization Theory, 1879–1932." *Administrative Science Quarterly* 40: 557–585.

———. 1999. *Manufacturing Rationality: The Engineering Foundations of the Managerial Revolution.* Oxford: Oxford University Press.

Shewhart, W. A. 1931. *Economic Control of Manufactured Products.* New York: Van Nostrand.

Sillén, Oskar. 1949. "Auktoriserade revisorer förr, nu och framdeles." *Affärsekonomi.* 22(6): 319–321, 330–332.

Simmel, G. 1957. "Fashion." *American Journal of Sociology* 62: 541–558.

Sjögren, Göran. 2000. *Från sifferprickare till previsionär. Ernst & Youngs svenska historia.* Karlshamn: Lagerblad.

Sjöström, C. 1994. *Revision och lagreglering—ett historiskt perspektiv.* Linköping Studies in Science and Technology, Thesis No. 417.

Skinner, Ross MacGregor, and Rodney James Anderson. 1966. *Analytical Auditing.* Toronto: Sir Isaac Pitman House.

Sorge, Arndt. 1979. "Engineers in Management: A Study of British, German, and French Traditions." *Journal of General Management,* 5(1): 47–57.

Sorge, Arndt, and Malcolm Warner. 1986. *Comparative Factory Organization.* WZB., Gower.

SOU. 1941. *Lagberedningens förslag till Lag om Aktiebolag mm Motiv, no. 9.* Stockholm. Nordstedt.

Spencer, H. 1876. *The Principles of Sociology,* vol. 1. New York: Appleton.

Starbuck, W. H. 1992. "Learning by Knowlege-Intensive Firms." *Journal of Management Studies* 29: 713–740.

Storp, H. J., J. Bröckelmann, and M. Saal. 1991. "Länderspiegel Qualitätssicherung." *Qualität und Zuverlässigkeit* 36: 73–76.

Stover, Carl, F. 1964. "Observations on the Philosophy of Training." Presented at the Twentieth Annual Conference of the American Society of Training Directors, San Francisco, June.

Strang, David. 1995. "Health Maintenance Organizations." In Glenn R. Carroll and Michael T. Hannan, eds., *Organizations in Industry,* pp. 163–182. New York: Oxford University Press.

Strang, David, and M. W. Macy. 1999. "In Search of Excellence: Fads, Success Stories, and Adaptive Emulations." Presented to the Academy of Management Meeting, Chicago, Aug. 9–11.

Strang, David, and John W. Meyer. 1994. "Institutional Conditions for Diffusion." In W. R. Scott and J. W. Meyer, eds. *Institutional Environments and Organizations: Structural Complexity and Individualism*, pp. 100–112. London: Sage.

Strange, S. 1996. *The Retreat of the State*. Cambridge: Cambridge University Press.

Streeck, Wolfgang. 1989. "Skills and Limits of Neo-Liberalism: The Enterprise of the Future as a Place of Learning." *Work, Employment & Society* 3(1): 89–104.

Struck, F. Theodore. 1930. *Foundations of Industrial Education*. London: Wiley.

Stumpf, T. 1972. "Zwanzig Jahre ASQ-Ausbildung." *Qualität und Zuverlässigkeit* 17: 183–186.

———. 1976. "Planung des Qualitätssicherungssystems." *Qualität und Zuverlässigkeit* 21: 65–67.

Stumpf, T., and P. Franke. 1986. "Das neue DGQ-Ausbildungskonzept für Qualitätssicherungs-Führungspersonal." *Qualität und Zuverlässigkeit* 31: 384–386.

Sturdy, Andrew. 1997a. "The Consultancy Process—An Insecure Business." *Journal of Management Studies* 34 (3): 389–413.

———. 1997b. "The Dialectics of Consultancy." *Critical Perspectives on Accounting* 8: 511–535.

Suchman, Mark. 1994. "On Advice of Counsel: Legal and Financial Firms as Information Intermediaries in the Structuration of Silicon Valley." Unpublished Ph.D. dissertation, Department of Sociology, Stanford University, Stanford, Calif.

Swanson, B. E., and Ramiller, N. C. 1997 "The Organizing Vision in Information Systems Innovation." *Organization Science* 8: 458–474.

Tano, Masahiro. 1969. "Problems of Export Inspection." In *International Conference on Quality Control Proceedings 1969*, pp. 723–726. Tokyo: Japanese Union of Scientists and Engineers.

Taylor, F. W. 1903. *Shop Management*. New York: Harper.

———. 1911. *The Principles of Scientific Management*. New York: Harper.

Taylor, R. L., and Zawacki, R. A., 1978. "Collaborative Goal Setting in Performance Appraisal: A Field Experiment." *Public Personnel Management* 7(3): 162–170.

Thanheiser, Heinz T., and Gareth P. Dyas. 1976. *The Emerging European Enterprise*. Boulder, Colo.: Westview Press.

Thayer, Paul W. 1989. "A Historical Perspective on Training." In Irwin L. Gold-stein and Associates, eds., *Training and Development in Organizations*. San Francisco: Jossey-Bass.

Thomas, G. B. 1964. "The Special Significance of Total Quality Control." *Quality Engineer* 28: 70–77.

Thompson, S. C. 1981. "Will It Hurt Less if I Can Control It? A Complex Answer to a Simple Question." *Psychological Bulletin* 90 (1): 89–101.

Thrift, Nigel. 1997. "The Rise of Soft Capitalism." *Cultural Values* 1: 21–57.

———. 1999. "The Place of Complexity." *Theory, Culture & Society*. 16(3): 31–69.

Tichy, N. M., and S. Sherman. 1995. *Control Your Destiny or Someone Else Will: How Jack Welch Is Making General Electric the World's Most Competitive Corporation*. New York: Doubleday.

Tilly, C. 1978. *From Mobilization to Revolution*. Reading: Addison-Wesley.

———. 1984. "Social Movements and National Politics." In C. Bright and S. Harding, eds., *Statemaking and Social Movements*. Ann Arbor: Earthscan.

Times (London), 4 October 1960.

Times (London), 26 October 1961.Tippett, L.H.C. 1962. "A View of Quality Control in the United Kingdom." *Industrial Quality Control* (Sept.): 15–17.

Tippett, L.H.C. 1962. "A View of Quality Control in the United Kingdom." *Industrial Quality Control* September: 15–17.

Tiratsoo, Nick. 1999. "High Hopes Frustrated: The British Institute of Management as an Agent of Change, 1947–63." In Franco Amatori, Andrea Colli, and Nicola Crepas, eds., *Deindustrialization and Reindustrialization in 20th Century Europe*, pp. 143–154. Milan: Franco Angeli.

———. 2000. "The United States Technical Assistance Programme in Japan, 1955–62." *Business History* 42: 117–136.

Tiratsoo, Nick, and Jim Tomlinson. 1993. *Industrial Efficiency and State Intervention: Labour 1939–51*. London: Routledge, London School of Economics.

———. 1998. *The Conservatives and Industrial Efficiency, 1951–64. Thirteen Wasted Years?* London: Routledge, London School of Economics.

Tofte, B. 1993. *Total Kvalitetsledelse i Barnehagen*. Oslo: Ad Notam, Gyldedal.

Tolbert, Pamela S., and Lynn G. Zucker. 1983. "Institutional Sources of Change in the Formal Structure of Organizations: The Diffusion of Civil Service Reform, 1880–1935." *Administrative Science Quarterly* 30: 22–39.

Tolbert, P. S., and L. G. Zucker. 1996. "The Institutionalization of Institutional Theory." In S. R. Clegg, C. Hardy, and W. R. Nord, eds., *Handbook of Organization Studies*, pp. 175–190. London: Sage.

Tomlinson, Jim, and Nick Tiratsoo. 1998. "'An Old Story, Freshly Told'? A Comment on Broadberry and Crafts' Approach to Britain's Early Post-War Economic Performance." *Business History* 40: 62–72.

Torstendahl, Rolf. 1982: "Engineeers in Industry, 1850–1910: Professional Men and New Bureaucrats. A Comparative Approach." *Science, Technology and Society in the Time of Alfred Nobel*, pp. 253–270. Oxford: Pergamon Press.

———. 1993. "The Transformation of Professional Education in the Nineteenth Century." In Sidney Rothblatt and Björn Wittrock, eds., *The European and American University Since 1800*. Cambridge: Cambridge University Press.

Training. 1981–1989. Minneapolis, MN: Lakewood Publications.

Training and Development Organizations Directory. 1994. Detroit, Mich.: Gale Research.

Trudgill, Peter. 1974. *Sociolinguistics: An Introduction*. Hammondsworth: Penguin.

Tsutsui, W. M. 1996. "W. Edwards Deming and the Origins of Quality Control in Japan." *Journal of Japanese Studies* 22: 295–325.

———. 1998. *Manufacturing Ideology. Scientific Management in Twentieth-Century Japan*. Princeton, N.J.: Princeton University Press.

Tuckman, A. 1995. "Ideology, Quality and TQM." In A. Wilkinson and H. Willmott, eds., *Making Quality Critical—New Perspectives on Organizational Change*, pp. 54–81. London: Routledge.

Tversky, A., and D. Kahneman, 1974. "Judgement Under Uncertainty: Heuristics and Biases." *Science* (Sept.) 105: 11–24.

Useem, Michael. 1996. *Investor Capitalism: How Money Managers Are Changing the Face of Corporate America*. New York: Basic Books.

U.S. Superintendent of Documents. 1940–1997. *United States Code, General Index*. Washington, D.C.: Government Printing Office.

van Rest, E. D. 1953. "Quality Control in the USA." *Applied Statistics* 2: 141–151.

Veblen, Thorstein. 1954. *Imperial Germany and the Industrial Revolution*. New York: Viking Press. First published in 1915.

Walgenbach, P. 1994. *Mittleres Management. Aufgaben—Funktionen—Arbeitsverhalten*. Wiesbaden: Gabler.

———. 1998. "Zwischen Showbusineß und Galeere." *Industrielle Beziehungen* 5: 135–164.

———. 1999. "Institutionalistische Ansätze in der Organisationstheorie." In A. Kieser, ed., *Organisationstheorien*, pp. 319–353. Stuttgart: Kohlhammer.

———. 2000. *Die normgerechte Organisation*. Stuttgart: Schäffer-Poeschel.

Wallerstedt, Eva. 1988. *Oskar Sillén—Professor och Praktiker. Några drag i före-tagsekonomiämnets tidiga utveckling vid Handelshögskolan i Stockholm*. Acta Universitatis Upsaliensis, Studia Oeconomiae Negotiorum 30. Uppsala: Almquist & Wiksell (dissertation).

Wallerstedt, Eva. 1998. "Regulation as a Response to Critical Events: A Century of

Struggle for the Swedish Auditing Profession." In Glen Morgan and Lars Engwall, eds., *Regulation and Organizations, International Perspectives*, pp. 146–
165. London and New York: Routledge.

Washburn, Stewart. 1996. "Challenge and Renewal: A Historical View of the
Profession." *Journal of Management Consulting* 9(2): 47–53.

Watson, Tony J. 1994. "Management 'Flavours of the Month': Their Role in Managers' Lives." *International Journal of Human Resource Management* 5: 893–
909.

Watts, Ross L., and Jerold L. Zimmerman. 1978. "Towards a Positive Theory of
the Determination of Accounting Standards." *The Accounting Review* (Jan.):
112–133.

Weber, Max. 1968. *Economy and Society: An Interpretive Sociology*. New York:
Bedminster. First published in 1924.

Wedlin, Linda. 2000. "Business School Rankings and the Diffusion of Ideas."
Presented at the EGOS conference in Helsinki, July 2000.

Werr, Andreas. 1999. *The Language of Change: The Roles of Methods in the Work
of Management Consultants*. Stockholm: Stockholm School of Economics.

Werr, Andreas, Torbjörn Stjernberg, and Peter Docherty. 1997. "The Functions of
Methods of Change in Management Consulting." *Journal of Organizational
Change Management* 10(4): 288–307.

Westney, D. Eleanor. 1987. *Imitation and Innovation. The Transfer of Western
Organizational Patterns to Meiji Japan*. Cambridge, Mass.: Harvard University
Press.

Westphal James D., Ranjay Gulati, and Stephen M. Shortell. 1997. "Customization
or Conformity: An Institutional and Network Perspective on the Content and
Consequences of TQM Adoption." *Administrative Science Quarterly* 42: 366–
394.

Which? Contraceptives Supplement. 1971. London: Consumers Association.

White, R. W. 1959. "Motivation Reconsidered: The Concept of Competence."
Psychological Review 66: 297–333.

Whittington, Richard, Michael Mayer, and F. Curto. 1999. "Chandlerism in Post-
War Europe: Strategic and Structural Change in France, Germany and the UK,
1950–1993." *Industrial and Corporate Change* 8(3): 519–550.

Wickenden, W. E. 1930. "A Comparative Study of Engineering Education in the
States and in Europe." Report of the Investigation of Engineering Education.
Pittsburgh: SPEE.

Wilensky, Harold. 1964. "The Professionalization of Everyone?" *The American
Journal of Sociology* Vol. 70(2): 137–158.

Williamson, Oliver. 1981. "The Economics of Organization: The Transaction Cost
Approach." *American Journal of Sociology* 87: 548–577.

Wise, George. 1979. "On Test: Postgraduate Training of Engineers at General Electric, 1892–1961." *IEEE Transactions on Education* E-22(4): 171–177.

Wofford, J. C. 1979. "A Goal-Energy-Effort Requirement Model of Work Motivation." *Academy of Management Review* 4(2): 193–201.

Wolinsky, A. 1993. "Competition in a Market for Informed Experts Services, RAND." *Journal of Economics* 24: 380–398.

Wollebæk, K. 1989. *Medarbeidersamtaler.* Oslo: Universitetsforlaget.

Woodward, C. Douglas. 1974. *BSI. The Story of Standards.* London: British Standards Institution.

Wooldridge, A. 1997. "The Advice Business." *The Economist* (Mar.) 22: S 3-S 22.

Wuppermann, M. 1989. *Geschäftsführer in Deutschland.* Frankfurt am Main: Campus.

Wuthnow, Robert. 1996. *Poor Richard's Principle: Recovering the American Dream Through the Moral Dimension of Work, Business, and Money.* Princeton, N.J.: Princeton University Press.

Yoshino, M. Y. 1968. *Japan's Managerial System. Tradition and Innovation.* Cambridge, Mass.: MIT Press.

Zaret, Matthew Elias. 1967. "An Historical Study of the American Society of Engineering Education." Ph.D. dissertation, School of Education of New York University.

Zbaracki, M. J. 1998. "The Rhetoric and Reality of Total Quality Management." *Administrative Science Quarterly* 43.

Zich, Janet. 1996. "Been There, Done That (A Report on the 1996 Stanford Business School Alumni/ae Career Survey)." Stanford, Calif.: Stanford Graduate School of Business.

Zucker, L. G. 1987. "Institutional Theories of Organizations." *Annual Review of Sociology* 13: 443–464.

Zuckerman, A. 1997. *International Standards Desk Reference.* New York: American Management Association.

Index